"This stellar lineup shines a spotlight on intriguing connections between these influential modern theologians. As appropriating their thought becomes increasingly complicated, this set of essays can be a fresh catalyst for engaging their dogmatic contributions."

Daniel J. Treier,
Knoedler Professor of Theology, Wheaton College

"Edwards and Barth are creative thinkers wrestling with Scripture and a common Reformed heritage, asking all the big questions. In so doing, both present a fresh approach to Christian doctrine under the conditions of varied modernities. The contributors to this volume help bring out their distinctive approaches as well as some noteworthy convergences along the way. Anizor and Strobel organize a productive dialogue."

Michael Allen,
John Dyer Trimble Professor of Systematic
Theology, Reformed Theological Seminary

"Students of Reformed theology will learn much from this rich and wide-ranging exploration of the theologies of Jonathan Edwards and Karl Barth. The answers we ourselves give to the question of what it means to undertake Reformed theology today will certainly have both their quality and responsibility heightened by insights won from study of these 'two eclectic and profound minds in conversation.'"

Philip G. Ziegler,
professor of Christian dogmatics, University of Aberdeen

"One way to illuminate the work of great theologians is to compare them with one another. The scholars who contributed to this volume handle this comparison deftly, and the result is a volume that sparkles with insight."

Keith Johnson,
professor of theology, Wheaton College

REFORMED DOGMATICS *in* DIALOGUE

The Theology of Karl Barth and Jonathan Edwards

STUDIES IN HISTORICAL & SYSTEMATIC THEOLOGY

H
S H S S
S + T
T

REFORMED DOGMATICS *in* DIALOGUE

The Theology of Karl Barth and Jonathan Edwards

Edited by **UCHE ANIZOR** & **KYLE C. STROBEL**

STUDIES IN HISTORICAL AND SYSTEMATIC THEOLOGY

LEXHAM ACADEMIC

Reformed Dogmatics in Dialogue: The Theology of Karl Barth and Jonathan Edwards
Studies in Historical and Systematic Theology

Copyright 2022 Uche Anizor and Kyle C. Strobel

Lexham Academic, an imprint of Lexham Press
1313 Commercial St., Bellingham, WA 98225
LexhamPress.com

Unless otherwise noted, Scripture quotations are from ESV® Bible (The Holy Bible, English Standard Version®), copyright © 2001 by Crossway Bibles, a publishing ministry of Good News Publishers. Used by permission. All rights reserved.

Scripture quotations marked (KJV) are from the King James Version. Public Domain.

Print ISBN 9781683596172
Digital ISBN 9781683596189
Library of Congress Control Number 2022933921

Lexham Editorial: Todd Hains, Andrew Sheffield, John Barach, Mandi Newell
Cover Design: Brittany Schrock
Typesetting: Abigail Stocker, Justin Marr

We would like to dedicate this volume to the numerous theologians at Biola University who have helped to create a rich and vibrant context for theological reflection. Thank you for your continued willingness to pore over difficult texts, wrestle through the implications of Christian belief, and bear witness to the calling of a theologian as a theologian for the church.

CONTENTS

—

ACKNOWLEDGMENTS

—

We would like to begin by thanking Biola University, and more specifically Talbot School of Theology, for creating the space and providing the release time (in Uche's case) to wrestle through the great theological minds of the Christian tradition. It is rare to find a place where you can walk out of a class on Aquinas to a reading group on Maximus to a faculty discussion on Pseudo-Dionysius, but those sorts of interactions are not unusual at Biola. More specifically, the Classical Theology program has provided a place to read the great texts of the Christian tradition with eager-minded students and collaborative faculty, and we are both encouraged that this sort of recovery is still taking place within a distinctively *evangelical* context. We hope that this volume encourages this sort of dialogue as we seek to be faithful witnesses to the gospel in this present evil age.

We would like to thank Lexham Press for catching the vision of this volume and all the contributors who were willing to put two difficult thinkers into conversation. We hope that it was a fruitful endeavor personally and that it will bear fruit in the minds of students and scholars alike. A special thanks goes out to Todd Hains at Lexham for working with us on this volume, as well as those individuals who were willing to read material for us. Thanks to Ty Kieser and Scuter Koo, for your willingness to read drafts for Kyle and provide meaningful and insightful feedback; it is a blessing to have seen you both develop as scholars. We would also like to thank Barnabas Kwok for his willingness to carefully edit a draft of this volume. And thanks to Georgio Khachadourian for compiling our many indexes.

All but two of the chapters of this volume were written explicitly for this project, and so we would also like to thank the publisher and journal that allowed us to reproduce edited and adapted versions of two pieces. We thank Blackwell Publishing for allowing us to reproduce Kyle's chapter "Barth and Edwards" from *The Wiley-Blackwell Companion to Karl Barth*, edited by George

Hunsinger and Keith L. Johnson (Hoboken, NJ: Wiley-Blackwell, 2020), 495–506 (in this volume reworked as chapter 1, "God"), as well as *Pro Ecclesia* for allowing us to reproduce portions of Matt Jenson's "'Where the Spirit of the Lord Is, There Is Freedom': Barth on Ecclesial Agency" in *Pro Ecclesia* 24:4 (2015): 517–37 (found here in modified form as chapter 13, "Church").

Finally, we'd like to thank our families for their constant support as we pursue the joyous task of writing about and reading theologians like Edwards and Barth.

ABBREVIATIONS

—

CD   Karl Barth, *Church Dogmatics*, 4 vols. Edited and translated by Geoffrey W. Bromiley. Edinburgh: T&T Clark, 1956–1975.

KD   *Kirchliche Dogmatik*

WJE   *Works of Jonathan Edwards*, 26 vols (New Haven, CT: Yale University Press, 1957–2008)

WJEO   *Works of Jonathan Edwards Online*. Jonathan Edwards Center at Yale University. http://edwards.yale.edu/archive/.

EDWARDS AND BARTH IN CONVERSATION

—

An Introduction

Uche Anizor and Kyle C. Strobel

Trailed by controversy, heralded and revered as giants in Reformed theology, and yet questioned regarding their true commitment to it, Jonathan Edwards and Karl Barth remain two of the most influential theologians of the modern era. A case could be made for Edwards being the greatest English-language— not just American—theologian ever, and for Barth as the greatest German-language theologian to date. A cursory glance at the sheer volume of writings produced by both men is testimony enough of their importance. However, it is the not mere volume of work that makes one great, but the range, quality, depth, sophistication, timeliness, and prophetic insightfulness of that work. On these points, few, if any, surpass these two modern theologians.

Regardless of its importance in weighing the impact of each thinker, the volume of their output is certainly a reason for the breadth of secondary literature. For both thinkers, their corpus has raised questions concerning development and radical shifts and has led to schools of interpretation based on these possible trajectories. The online edition of Edwards's *Works* housed at Yale numbers seventy-three volumes, composed mainly of sermons but covering notebooks, letters, and a variety of other works. Edwards's interests and work cover the whole range of thorny theological issues—*The End of Creation, The Nature of True Virtue, Original Sin, Freedom of the Will, The History of the Work of Redemption,* and *Religious Affections,* to name a few—not to mention his penetrating analyses of the religious awakenings of his day. Not much in Edwards's work was rote or simplistic, narrow or detached; there was a pastoral care and intellectual seriousness to his writings that few of his heirs have been able to replicate. As for Barth, the voluminous *Church Dogmatics* is the clear reference point for the range, depth, and insightfulness of his theology. However, to capture fully his powers as a theologian,

1

one would also be directed to his Romans commentary; his astute analysis of nineteenth-century Protestant theology; his readings of Calvin, Anselm, and the Reformed Confessions; and *Evangelical Theology*, not to mention his countless occasional pieces and shorter studies such as *Nein!*, *Credo*, *Christ and Adam*, and *The Humanity of God*. His "letter of commendation" is the various influential theologians stimulated by serious engagement with his thought: T. F. Torrance, Hans Urs Von Balthasar, Hans Frei, Colin Gunton, and John Webster, to name just a few.

DIVERGENT CONTEXTS

But the better and more pertinent question facing readers of this book is this: why bring *these two* theologians into conversation? At first glance, these two giants could not be more different. Jonathan Edwards was born on October 5, 1703, in the early New England colonies. Karl Barth was born on the continent, in Basel specifically, on May 10, 1886. These were two men inhabiting two quite different times, countries, and cultures. Edwards lived in that early modern period punctuated by the Enlightenment and plied his trade in an environment increasingly saturated by *au courant* British and continental philosophy. Barth's life and career straddled two eras: the waning years of the late modern period and the contemporary period that followed the Second World War. While history would come to see Edwards's day as one of relative peace, Edwards's own home was used as a barracks housing soldiers, protecting his town from Native American raids in a period of fluctuating tension. Almost the entirety of Barth's work was done against the backdrop of war—including some of the bloodiest wars in human history. Although not always directly so, his theology is a political theology. Edwards's theology, similarly, was political, but the similarities are merely formal. Reading along the history of redemption, as he understood it, Edwards's politics saw God's hand protecting and guiding Britain and her colonies against the Papists and her allies.

Not surprisingly, both came from religious households, but of a different cast. Edwards's father, Timothy, was a successful revival preacher and pastor of East Windsor, Connecticut, where he served for over sixty years.[1] A Puritan

---

1. Kenneth P. Minkema, "Edwards, Timothy (father) (1669–1758)," in *The Jonathan Edwards Encyclopedia*, ed. Harry S. Stout, Kenneth P. Minkema, and Adriaan C. Neele (Grand Rapids:

in outlook, he was the strict but loving father of eleven children—ten girls and one boy, Jonathan. He was also, notably, the son-in-law of the influential Solomon Stoddard, minister of Northampton (which would become Jonathan Edwards's own long-term pastorate). Barth's father, Fritz, was chiefly a professor, first at the anti-liberal College of Preachers in Basel and later at the University of Bern, teaching dogmatics and specializing in New Testament studies. He was relatively conservative theologically but also open-minded, able to maintain friendships with two significant Adolfs—Schlatter and Harnack. Fritz had five children—three boys and two girls—among whom Karl was the eldest.[2] The respective vocations of the fathers undoubtedly shaped their sons' visions for ministry and theological work. Edwards speaks glowingly of his father's revival successes: "[S]omething considerable of the same work began afterwards in East Windsor, my honored father's parish, which has in times past been a place favored with mercies of this nature above any on this western side of New England, excepting Northampton; there having been four or five seasons of the pouring out of the Spirit to the general awakening of the people there, since my father's settlement amongst them."[3] Apparently, as his own ministry would bear out, Jonathan was profoundly and decisively shaped by his father's ministry.[4] Similarly, Barth writes of his father as one "who by the quiet seriousness with which he applied himself to Christian things as a scholar and as a teacher was for me, and still is, an ineffaceable and often enough admonitory example."[5] Two theologians walking in the footsteps of their fathers, one a revivalist pastor and preacher; the other, for most of his life, a university theologian.[6]

Eerdmans, 2017), 185–86; George M. Marsden, *Jonathan Edwards: A Life* (New Haven: Yale University Press, 2003), 17–24.

2. Eberhard Busch, *Karl Barth: His Life from Letters and Autobiographical Texts*, trans. John Bowden (Grand Rapids: Eerdmans, 1994), 1–11.

3. *WJE* 4:154.

4. This is the conclusion of George Marsden: "So the father more directly than the grandfather set the footsteps in which Jonathan would try to follow," Marsden, *Jonathan Edwards*, 25. Perhaps contrarily, Perry Miller previously asserted: "Physically and mentally, if the language be permissible, Jonathan Edwards was more a Stoddard than a son of Timothy." *Jonathan Edwards* (reprint; Lincoln: University of Nebraska Press, 2005), 36.

5. Karl Barth and Rudolf Bultmann, *Letters 1922–1966*, ed. Bernd Jaspert, trans. and ed. Geoffrey W. Bromiley (Grand Rapids: Eerdmans, 1981), 157.

6. It is true that Edwards had an early stint as a tutor before he settled in his pastorate and eventually took up the position of university president at the end of his life. But nonetheless, his life and work were dominated by his pastoral concerns, and if his presidency would have had

OVERLAPPING CONCERNS

Returning to our original question: why compare these two theologians? Or, more specifically, what are the similarities that would justify such a comparative study? First, they were both men of their times. While separated by almost two hundred years (Barth, in fact, died more than two hundred years after Edwards's death), they were both modern theologians. Each of them felt compelled to speak to the people and issues of their day and to do so in the contemporary idiom. They engaged modern theological and philosophical trends, deploying philosophical concepts in ad hoc ways to support or elucidate a theological position. One writer remarks of Edwards, "His purpose, contrary to the *philosophe*, was to turn the best thought of his time to the advantage of God."[7] While Edwards confronted "Arminianism," Arianism, and various forms of an Enlightenment rationalism, Barth addressed the line of thinking stretching from Schleiermacher and Hegel to Ritschl and Bultmann. Both theologians were on guard against the liberalizing theology pervading their context, perceiving in them an idolatry of the human and a subtle desire to relativize God.

Related to this, what is striking about both theologians is that in their tenacious desire to answer both perennial and contemporary questions, they did not simply assume the conclusions of the (especially Reformed) tradition, yet they refused to ignore that same tradition (indeed operating from within it).[8] Barth writes:

> It is my private view that the exercise of repristinating a classical theological train of thought, which in the days of medieval and Protestant scholasticism was known as "theology," is probably more instructive than the chaotic business of today's faculties. ... But I also know that this *same* kind of thing can and should not return and that we must think *in* our time *for* our time.[9]

---

a longer tenure, there is no doubt that those concerns would have continued to apply pressure to his thought as a whole.

7. Norman Fiering, *Jonathan Edwards's Moral Thought and Its British Context* (Eugene, OR: Wipf & Stock, 2006), 61.

8. Of course, other similarities between the theologians could have been highlighted: they were both intensively biblical (or exegetically minded) theologians; they saw their work as directed toward the good of the church; they were both creative and constructive theologians; and as a result, they were notably idiosyncratic in some of their theological moves. One of the goals of this volume is to draw out similarities with greater detail and nuance.

9. Barth, "Barth to Harnack: An Answer to Professor Von Harnack's Open Letter," in H. Martin Rumscheidt, *Revelation and Theology: An Analysis of the Barth-Harnack Correspondence of*

Indeed, their complex relationship with the Reformed tradition is potentially the main factor that makes a comparison so intriguing. Edwards can, on the one hand, quote Calvin approvingly (for example, three times in *Religious Affections*) and deem him particularly significant in furthering the important work of the Reformation while, on the other hand, also wanting to preserve his independence from the Genevan.[10] Edwards famously wrote in *Freedom of the Will*, "I should not take it at all amiss, to be called a Calvinist, for distinction's sake: though I utterly disclaim a dependence on Calvin, or believing the doctrines which I hold, because he believed and taught them; and cannot justly be charged with believing in everything just as he taught."[11] This relative independence from Calvin and the tradition is what prompted one of our colleagues to snicker at the idea of Edwards being a reliable guide into Reformed theology.[12] Michael McClymond and Gerald McDermott speak of three ways to be Reformed: (1) originalist: those who desire to go back to the roots (e.g., Calvin); (2) confessionalist: those who desire to root theology in the historic Reformed confessions; and (3) developmentalist: those who hold that the tradition develops over time and the newer proponents are more trustworthy guides than former ones.[13] In this framework, Edwards is clearly in the third camp, mooring this theology to his predecessors and yet believing the Reformed tradition was living and not merely static.

Barth's relationship to the Reformed tradition is perhaps more complex. On the one hand, he expressed *formal* continuity with the tradition in terms of sources and language (from Scripture, confessions, old Reformed writers) as well as the pedagogical organization of his work.[14] On the other hand, he diverged *materially* from the Reformed Orthodox tradition on a number of points, including

---

1923 (Eugene, OR: Wipf & Stock, 2011), 41–42.

10. See *WJE* 9:422.

11. *WJE* 1:131.

12. We do not want to overstate Edwards's independence solely on the basis of his statement or his scant direct references to Calvin. As one scholar notes, it is likely that Calvin's authority on many doctrinal areas was taken for granted in New England and thus absorbed by Edwards. See Peter J. Thuesen, "Editor's Introduction," in *WJE* 26:57.

13. McClymond and McDermott, *Theology of Jonathan Edwards*, 663–64.

14. Carl R. Trueman, "Calvin, Barth, and Reformed Theology: Historical Prolegomena," in *Calvin, Barth, and Reformed Theology*, ed. Neil B. MacDonald and Carl R. Trueman, Paternoster Theological Monographs (Eugene, OR: Wipf & Stock, 2008), 24–25.

- The doctrines of Scripture and revelation

- The doctrine of election

- The importance of the distinction between natural and super-natural revelation

- Covenant theology (as it was handed down through Cocceius)

- The attributes of God

- The over-spiritualization of eschatology[15]

Thus, to answer whether Barth is a Reformed theologian in continuity with the tradition depends on the criteria we employ. He would certainly fit within the "developmentalist" category outlined earlier. Daniel Migliore captures Barth's stance: "Barth's attitude to the old Reformed tradition is deferential yet critical. ... He thinks *with* and *after* but not infrequently also *against* old Reformed orthodoxy."[16] Barth is a theologian whose work was done within the atmosphere of the Reformed faith, even if his conclusions on several loci would feel "strange" and "alien" to those steeped in that tradition.[17]

It is this relation to the Reformed tradition, in which it guides and governs their thinking but does not determine it, that makes a comparison between these specific thinkers interesting. Both are theologizing along the contours of the Reformed confessions and yet feel free to name problems with these constructions. Both recognize the scholastic scaffolding that, having seeped into Reformed thought, takes the focus away from God and puts it elsewhere, and both see this as the great theological error of their contemporaries. Both are concerned to give an account of God in himself who is also God for us, an account in which being *for us* does not take away from the *in himself*. Yet each theologian addresses these issues differently, even as they did so as *Reformed* thinkers. Attending to these similarities and differences proves instructive for contemporary dogmatics that seeks to be faithful to the tradition but is

---

15. See Daniel L. Migliore, "Karl Barth's First Lectures in Dogmatics: *Instruction in the Christian Religion*," in *The Göttingen Dogmatics: Instruction in the Christian Religion*, vol. 1, ed. Hannelotte Reiffen, trans. Geoffrey W. Bromiley (Grand Rapids: Eerdmans, 1991), xxxv–xxxix; Trueman, "Calvin, Barth, and Reformed Theology," 20–24.

16. Migliore, "Karl Barth's First Lectures in Dogmatics," xxxviii–xxxix.

17. Trueman, "Calvin, Barth, and Reformed Theology," 26.

not bound by its judgments. This raises a series of questions that help shape this volume: Why did Barth respond differently to the Reformed orthodoxy than Edwards? Why did they both see a need to re-envision the doctrine of the Trinity? As Christocentric theologians, how did they deploy Christ in their theological systems? Their overlap in terms of tradition, sources, concerns, and approaches, their divergences from each other, and the puzzling fact that Barth never (as far as we can tell) engaged Edwards directly present more than enough reasons to justify a constructive conversation between these theologians.

THE GOAL OF THIS VOLUME

In putting these two eclectic and profound minds in conversation, the goal of this volume is not to provide comprehensive comparisons but to engage representative strands of thought from within various theological loci. Toward this end, the content of this volume follows a relatively traditional format, starting with a series of chapters all moored directly to the doctrine of God (including, within that, aesthetics), moving to questions concerning humanity, sin, atonement, moral theology, church, and eschatology. Along the way, there is a chapter on philosophy, a pressing issue for both thinkers, who readily engaged the philosophical discussions of their day with heavy-handed *theological* concerns. Each topic is impossibly broad, and nearly all of them have book-length expositions for each thinker. Nonetheless, putting these two theologians into conversations on these specific topics, and the narrower emphases within each chapter, is not random or arbitrary. It is precisely in these places where we find such interesting and insightful points of comparison and contrast.

Our hope is that these comparisons and contrasts unveil a dedication to the Reformed tradition that is neither naïve nor blind but is set on articulating the Reformed vision in a new age with new polemics. Watching each thinker navigate these polemics, sometimes turning to surprisingly traditional commonplaces or radicalizing a doctrine in a new way, is as insightful as it is instructive. Like all great theologians, both Edwards and Barth prove fruitful conversation partners even when, maybe especially when, one disagrees with them. To read these thinkers honestly and charitably, one cannot help but recognize a life wielded for the truth of the gospel—to be captivated by Christ and the God who gives himself, in his freedom, to his creatures.

1

GOD

Kyle C. Strobel

Comparing the work of a figure as profound and intricate as Jonathan Edwards (1703–1758), the New England divine, with the work of Karl Barth opens the interpreter to various sorts of temptations. It is tempting to reduce one figure into the other or to use one figure as the plumb line along which to evaluate the other. It is tempting, likewise, either to ignore differences or to exacerbate them—rejecting historical differentiation or overemphasizing it. Keeping these temptations in mind, the goal for this essay is to highlight a *shared impulse* by Edwards and Barth. In particular, this essay focuses on the impulse to ground God's life *pro nobis* back into the eternal life of God, such that the God who is for us in Christ Jesus is a true revelation of God *in se*. From there, the divine attributes will serve as an example of how this impulse forms their unique theological reflections. In articulating a shared *impulse*, it is not necessary that the overall formal structure (or material content) of the impulse is identical. To bring this impulse to the fore, this essay focuses positively on the shared instinct in Barth and Edwards and not the ways they differ. Furthermore, because of space, this is a broad sketch and not a highly nuanced account. It is important not to over-read these positive claims as much as to recognize two great minds in the tradition seeking faithfulness to the revelation of God.

GOD AND CREATION

Early in his discussion of God's revelation, Barth declares, "*God* reveals Himself. He reveals Himself *through Himself*. He reveals *Himself*."[1] "God, the Revealer," Barth adds, "is identical with His act in revelation and also identical

---

1. *CD* I/1, 296.

with its effect."[2] The desire to support the claim that God's self-revelation is a true revelation of himself leads Barth to avoid bifurcation between God *ad intra* and God *ad extra*; the God who is *a se* is the God who has revealed himself in Christ Jesus. "If we are dealing with His revelation," Barth quips, "we are dealing with God Himself and not, as Modalists in all ages have thought, with an entity distinct from Him."[3] In light of this, Barth continues, "In a dogmatics of the Christian Church we cannot speak correctly of God's nature and attributes unless it is presupposed that our reference is to God the Father, the Son, and the Holy Spirit."[4] To develop this theme, it is important to begin with the God of love and freedom.

GOD OF LOVE AND FREEDOM

For both Edwards and Barth, to talk about God is to talk about God in his revelation. In this section, our focus is the important discussion of the "Being of God as the One Who Loves in Freedom," from §28 of *Church Dogmatics*. In the *leitsatz* (or summary paragraph), Barth provides a helpful overview: "God is who He is in the act of His revelation. God seeks and creates fellowship between Himself and us, and therefore He loves us. But He is this loving God without us as Father, Son and Holy Spirit, in the freedom of the Lord, who has His life from Himself."[5] God is who he is without us, and yet, Barth wants to emphasize, "God is who He is in His works. He is the same even in Himself, even before and after and over His works, and without them. They are bound to Him, but He is not bound to them. ... But He is who He is without them. He is not, therefore, who He is only in His works."[6] It is in God's works that he is revealed as the One he is.[7]

Barth, in his criticism of Protestant orthodoxy, nevertheless lauds Polanus on his definition of the essence of God as "*Essentia Dei est ipsa Deitas, qua Deus a se et per se absolute est et existit*" ("The essence of God is his deity, by which God is and exists absolutely from himself and through himself"),[8] a defini-

---

2. *CD* I/1, 296.

3. *CD* I/1, 311.

4. *CD* I/1, 312.

5. *CD* II/1, 257.

6. *CD* II/1, 260.

7. *CD* II/1, 260

8. *CD* II/1, 261, quoting Polanus, *Synt. Theol. Chr.*, 1609, col. 865.

tion Edwards basically follows. But the focus of Barth's criticism concerns the way that Protestant orthodoxy abstracted the Trinity, and therefore the act of revelation, away from a discussion of God's self-revelation in history. The essence of God "is something which we shall encounter either at the place where God deals with us as Lord and Savior, or not at all."[9] Barth wants to hold together the being and act of God without abstracting from the reality of God's triune life as Father, Son, and Spirit. Barth clarifies helpfully, noting, "We are in fact interpreting the being of God when we describe it as God's reality, as 'God's being in act,' namely, in the act of His revelation, in which the being of God declares His reality: not only His reality for us—certainly that—but at the same time His own, inner, proper reality, behind which and above which there is no other."[10]

Discussion of God's being is always, necessarily, discussion of God's act. Barth declares, "We are dealing with the being of God: but with regard to the being of God, the word 'event' or 'act' is *final*, and cannot be surpassed or compromised."[11] In his discussion, Barth affirms the instincts of the tradition. "Thus it was quite right when the older theology described the essence of God as *vita*, and again as *actuositas*, or more simply as *actus*."[12] God is pure act, Barth affirms, and as such supersedes all that we know as activity or event, and his differentiation from all other activity also includes a kind of immanence to it. "But the particularity of His working and therefore His being as God is not exhausted by this dialectical transcendence which, however strictly it may be understood, must always be understood with equal strictness as immanence. On the contrary, without prejudice to and yet without dependence upon His relationship to what is event, act and life outside Him, God is in Himself free event, free act and free life."[13] This life and event, Barth declares, is "the particularity of the being of a person."[14]

Barth articulates God's being as "being in person,"[15] not, with Edwards and much of the tradition, through a psychological analogy but in affirmation that

---

9. *CD* II/1, 261.
10. *CD* II/1, 262.
11. *CD* II/1, 263.
12. *CD* II/1, 263.
13. *CD* II/1, 264.
14. *CD* II/1, 267.
15. *CD* II/1, 268.

the essence of God is what is revealed in God's act as Father, Son, and Spirit
(a focus Edwards shares through his idiosyncratic use of the psychological
analogy).[16] God is *a se* and complete in himself and therefore does not create
for the purpose of finding fulfilment for unfulfilled desire. Rather, "God is He
who, without having to do so, seeks and creates fellowship between Himself
and us. He does not have to do it, because in Himself without us, and therefore without this, He has that which He seeks and creates between Himself
and us."[17] What God is *in se* is the fullness he offers the creature, a fullness
that "implies so to speak an overflow of His essence that He turns to us."[18]
The language of overflow highlights that God is not creating an intermediary
between himself and humankind and that who he is *ad extra* is not somehow
other than who he is *ad intra*. Barth's overview is helpful:

> Therefore what He seeks and creates between Himself and us is in fact
> nothing else but what He wills and completes and therefore is in Himself.
> It therefore follows that as He receives us through His Son into His fel-
> lowship with Himself, this is the one necessity, salvation, and blessing
> for us, than which there is no greater blessing—no greater, because God
> has nothing higher than this to give, namely Himself; because in giving
> us Himself, He has given us every blessing. We recognize and appreci-
> ate this blessing when we describe God's being more specifically in the
> statement that He is the One who loves. That He is God—the Godhead
> of God—consists in the fact that He loves, and it is the expression of His
> loving that He seeks and creates fellowship with us.[19]

God is blessed within himself, and he opens that blessing to his creatures
in the Son; this is a blessedness that is always the blessedness of love.[20] The
love that God's creatures come to know in the Son is the love of a God who
has given *himself* to them. This is an eternal love and is "being taken up
into the fellowship of His eternal love."[21] God is love in freedom, which is

---

16. Barth, of course, would have been allergic to any use of the psychological analogy. See
CD II/1, 337–38.

17. *CD* II/1, 272.

18. *CD* II/1, 273.

19. *CD* II/1, 275.

20. *CD* II/1, 283.

21. *CD* II/1, 280.

to be "determined and moved by oneself" and "unlimited, unrestricted and unconditioned from without."[22] Barth links this freedom of God to the sovereignty, majesty, holiness, and glory of God, aligning it with the *aseitas Dei*.[23] The freedom of God means that "nothing can accrue to Him from Himself which He had not or was not already; because, therefore, His being in its self-realisation or the actuality of His being answers to no external pressure but is only the affirmation of His own plenitude and a self-realisation in freedom."[24] It is *this God*, the God of absolute freedom, who gives himself to his creatures. In his freedom God is present to his creatures by giving himself and uniting the creature to himself, not as a creature does but in a way that does not restrict God's transcendence and immanence. "God is free to be wholly inward to the creature and at the same time as Himself wholly outward: *totus intra et totus extra*."[25]

THE OVERFLOWING FULLNESS OF GOD

In the thought of Jonathan Edwards, we discover a remarkably similar impulse to the one sketched above.[26] Edwards would fully affirm Barth's prodding: "Now that we are asking: What is God? what is His divinity, His distinctive essence as God? we can only ask again: Who is God?"[27] Talk of God is talk of God as Father, Son, and Holy Spirit. God is not an "it" but a subject who is the pure actuality of love. It is *this God* who is eternally for the elect in the person of the Son, and it is *this God* who, in his freedom, is the God of love.[28] In the freedom of his love, God is fullness that overflows to the creature. In Edwards's thought we find a God whose being is being in person and who, as such, is a "knowing, willing, acting I" (to use Barth's language).[29]

---

22. *CD* II/1, 301.

23. *CD* II/1, 302.

24. *CD* II/1, 306.

25. *CD* II/1, 315.

26. Kyle C. Strobel, *Jonathan Edwards's Theology: A Reinterpretation* (T&T Clark, 2013), 21–72.

27. *CD* II/1, 300.

28. I am borrowing Barth's emphasis on freedom here, but it is fitting. As the procession of God's love and, in Edwards's understanding, God's will, God's life is the pure movement of love in freedom that is the full and concrete expression of that freedom as Father, Son, and Holy Spirit.

29. *CD* II/1, 284.

Edwards emphasizes God's blessedness and personhood to articulate an account of God's life as the pure actuality of love. It is *this life* that will overflow to the creature, and as such, it is the life of God that will determine the content of the Christian's existence. As I have argued elsewhere, Edwards's doctrine of God is best categorized as "religious affection in pure act."[30] God is the truly religious One in that God's life is the infinite actuality of love and delight in the knowledge of the Father and Son in the Holy Spirit. There is a sense in which Edwards, with Barth, can say that God is God without the creature in the fullness of his blessedness, and yet, like Barth, Edwards presses hard on this, claiming that "in some sense it can be truly said that God has the more delight and pleasure for the holiness and happiness of his creatures: because God would be less happy, if he was less good, or if he had not the perfection of nature which consists in a propensity of nature to diffuse his own fullness."[31]

The preference for "person" language to talk about the being of God is similar for both thinkers, but so is Barth's worry about overemphasizing person language concerning the divine hypostases.[32] Edwards develops this differently, arguing that the hypostases of the divine essence are features of the one person of God that are three "persons" only insofar as they interpenetrate each other (i.e., as they exist in perichoretic union). In this sense, Barth's knowing, willing, and acting I is the Father whose knowing and willing, as perichoretically united in pure act, are known as persons through the life and ministry of the Son and Spirit in the economy. The economic activity of God is undivided, in this sense, because the activity and identity of God are undivided *in se*. In narrating the processions of the divine essence, Edwards explains the procession of the Spirit by claiming, "There proceeds a most pure act, and an infinitely holy and sweet energy arises between the Father and Son: for their love and joy is mutual, in mutually loving and delighting in each other," going on to claim that this "is the eternal and most perfect and essential act of the divine nature, wherein the Godhead acts to an infinite degree and in the most perfect manner

---

30. Oliver D. Crisp and Kyle C. Strobel, *Jonathan Edwards: An Introduction to His Thought* (Eerdmans, 2018), 39–66.

31. *WJE* 8:447.

32. See *CD* I/1, 351–68 for Barth's explanation of personal language and his use of the terms Father, Son, and Spirit.

possible. The Deity becomes all act; the divine essence itself flows out and is as it were breathed forth in love and joy."[33] God is *a se* and is free in the fullness of his life. It is not in spite of this fullness but because of it that God can overflow to the creature.

Like Barth, Edwards affirms that God is God without the creature but also names the reality that the God known in revelation is eternally inclined to the creature in his own fullness. Edwards affirms the traditional Reformed line that God creates for his own glory, affirming that who God is *ad extra* is an extension of who he is *ad intra* and that God's *ad extra* movement is grounded in eternity and in God's self-regard. In this sense, Edwards states,

> This propensity in God to diffuse himself may be considered as a propensity to have himself diffused, or to his own glory existing in its emanation. A respect to himself, or an infinite propensity to, and delight in his own glory, is that which causes him to incline to its being abundantly diffused, and to delight in the emanation of it. ... *God looks on the communication of himself, and the emanation of the infinite glory and good that are in himself to belong to the fullness and completeness of himself*, as though he were not in his most complete and glorious state without it.[34]

As with Barth's use of "overflow," Edwards turns to God's diffusing himself and emanating himself in creation as a way to link God's life *ad intra* with his *ad extra* mission for us. It is with respect to himself that God diffuses his glory to the creature, and this diffusion is nothing other than God's self in Christ Jesus and the Spirit. Furthermore, in God's eternal act of election in the Son, God stands in a relation to the creature (the church specifically) *as though he were incomplete without her*. "In election, believers were from all eternity given to Jesus Christ."[35] Likewise, "we must suppose that Christ, in some respect, is first in this affair, and some way or other the ground of our being chosen, and God's election of him some way or other including and inferring the election of particular saints."[36] This is not Barth's view of election,

---

33. *WJE* 21:121.
34. *WJE* 8:439, my emphasis.
35. *WJE* 17:282.
36. *WJE* 18:178.

of course, but the grounding of the creature's election in Christ's election is at least a shared part of the overall Reformed impulse being highlighted.

In grounding God's "pronobeity" in Christ Jesus in eternity, Edwards locates all of creation and its ends in God's redeeming and reconciling activity by mooring it to who he is within himself, such that the God revealed in Christ Jesus is the only God there is. Edwards highlights this impulse in two key texts. First, focusing on the connection of God's life *ad intra* with his *ad extra* overflow, Edwards states, "This twofold way of the Deity's flowing forth *ad extra* answers to the twofold way of the Deity's proceeding *ad intra*, in the proceeding and generation of the Son and the proceeding and breathing forth of the Holy Spirit; *and indeed is only a kind of second proceeding of the same persons.*"[37] Second, grounding the act of creation in God's life, Edwards claims that it was God's

> last end, that there might be a glorious and abundant emanation of his infinite fullness of good *ad extra*, or without himself, and the disposition to communicate himself or diffuse his own *fullness*, which we must conceive of as being originally in God as a perfection of his nature, was what moved him to create the world.[38]

God has a disposition to communicate himself, which Edwards glosses as God willing to diffuse his own fullness. This, he claims, is *originally* in God as a perfection of his nature. It is this perfection that moves God to create the world. While the language is cumbersome, Edwards is arguing that the act of God's life, his pure actuality of knowing and willing in love, is the grounding of his *ad extra* overflow in creation and ultimately redemption. The God revealed in creation is a "second proceeding" of the Son and Spirit in their mission to redeem, and redemption is offering the life of God to the creature as a participation in God's life of knowing and loving (i.e., religious affection). The goal of religious affection for the creature is nothing else than a finite participation in the pure actuality of God's affectionate self-knowing—the Father gazing upon the Son and the Son gazing upon the Father in the love of the Spirit. The theological mooring for this knowledge is the beatific vision, which is the goal of all creaturely existence. In Edwards's words,

---

37. *WJE* 20:466, my emphasis.
38. *WJE* 8:433–34.

The saints shall enjoy God as partaking with Christ of his enjoyment of God, for they are united to him and are glorified and made happy in the enjoyment of God as his members. … They being in Christ shall partake of the love of God the Father to Christ, and as the Son knows the Father *so they shall partake with him in his sight of God*, as being as it were parts of him as he is in the bosom of the Father.[39]

As Barth claimed, what God creates between himself and creatures he is already in himself. The goal of the elect creature is fellowship with God: sharing in God's love in the Son by the Spirit. In his utter fullness, God is for his creature as the creator who is not bound by a contrastive notion of transcendence and immanence. Edwards argues that "God's acting for himself, or making himself his last end, and his acting for their sake, are not to be set in opposition; or to be considered as the opposite parts of a disjunction: they are rather to be considered as coinciding one with the other, and implied one in the other."[40] In being for himself in the freedom and fullness of his love, God is for his own (i.e., the elect) in Christ Jesus.

GOD'S SELF-REVELATION AND THE DIVINE ATTRIBUTES

It proves helpful, briefly, to address how Edwards constructs his notion of God's self-revelation and, in particular, the divine attributes in light of Barth's own development. Barth's emphasis on God being known in his revelation as God himself, and not something distinct from him, is an instinct he shares with Edwards, and Edwards shares Barth's desire to reconstitute the divine attributes (but does so in a very different way). It is helpful to briefly sketch Barth's inclination before turning to Edwards's own idiosyncratic development.

Early in Barth's discussion of the divine perfections, he states, "Since God is Father, Son and Holy Ghost, i.e., loves in freedom, every perfection exists essentially in Him."[41] God's perfect life of abundance is a life of one-

---

39. Jonathan Edwards, "Excerpt from 'The Portion of the Righteous,'" in *Jonathan Edwards: Spiritual Writings*, eds. Kyle C. Strobel, Adriaan C. Neele, and Kenneth P. Minkema, Classics of Western Spirituality (Paulist Press, 2019), 173, my emphasis.

40. *WJE* 8:440–41.

41. *CD* II/1, 323.

ness and multiplicity; the "*One* is He who loves in freedom," and the "*many* are His perfections—the perfections of His life."[42] In terms of the perfections, Barth claims, "[e]ach of these is perfect in itself and in combination with all the others. For whether it is a form of love in which God is free, or a form of freedom in which God loves, it is nothing else but God Himself, His one, simple, distinctive being."[43] To know God entails knowing his perfections, but to know his perfections, Barth argues, one must know them within the knowledge of God, in the knowledge of his loving in freedom.[44] At the heart of Barth's proposal is his claim that the perfections exist in God essentially, such that he will say, "He not only has it [i.e., what is "perfect"] as others might have it. He has it as His own exclusively. And not only so, but He *is* it, so that it has its essential being in Him."[45]

We pause here because Barth is setting up the divine attributes such that it is impossible to talk about God generically—outside of his revelation—as if God were simply the sum total of creaturely attributes expanded to their highest possibility. Barth refuses a doctrine of God in which God's perfections could be excised and analyzed away from God's triune life.[46] The "special task" of the doctrine of the divine attributes, Barth proposes, is to recognize that God "exists in these perfections, and these perfections again exist in Him and only in Him as the One who, both in His revelation and in eternity, is the same."[47]

Starting with the Lord, and, more specifically, the Lord of *glory*, Barth seeks an account of the perfections that makes certain that "God is actually and unreservedly as we encounter Him in His revelation."[48] This means that the multiplicity perceived in God's revelation is not in the revelation alone but is true of God *in se*.[49] But Barth is also worried about any account of the divine perfections focused so fully on "a collection of mighty potencies" that

---

42. *CD* II/1, 323, my emphasis.

43. *CD* II/1, 322.

44. *CD* II/1, 322.

45. *CD* II/1, 323.

46. Barth names Stoicism and Neo-Platonism foreign impulses to generalize a doctrine of God that functions apart from the Trinity. This makes simplicity an "all-controlling principle" and turns the discussion of God's attributes into an analysis of "pure being." *CD* II/1, 329.

47. *CD* II/1, 324.

48. *CD* II/1, 325.

49. *CD* II/1, 332. Barth positively quotes Augustine, who spoke of God's *multiplex simplicitas*. *CD* II/1, 329.

in the midst of this cacophony of attributes the Lord becomes lost. In the face of this deluge, the creature is so overwhelmed by the multivalent nature of revelation that no harmony can be found. The Lord to whom the perfections belong is lost behind them.[50] But this is not the biblical picture, according to Barth. Rather, "according to Scripture, all the glory of God is concentrated, gathered up and unified in God Himself as the Lord of glory." The perfections are never to overtake focus on God but should lead to contemplation of God himself. In part, therefore, Barth's exposition is to give a positive account of the divine perfections as naming something of God essentially, as those perfections "of His own being as He who loves in freedom."[51]

Throughout Barth's discussion of the divine perfections, he is seeking to correct the tradition. More importantly, for our purposes, Barth is working closely with the Reformed High Orthodox and is seeking to follow their general inclination while rejecting several key features of their account that he believes leads them away from the God of Scripture.[52] Edwards is doing the same thing. Barth's dialectic, in part, is a response to the High Orthodox bifurcation between the incommunicable attributes and the communicable attributes. Barth is troubled by the notion that theologians should begin with God's being in general, only afterward turning to his triune nature. In discussing this faulty ordering, Barth notes, "The order undoubtedly implies that it is a question first of what the being of God is properly in itself, and only then of what it is improperly in its relationship *ad extra*."[53] Dialectic is the form that theology must take, for Barth, to avoid speaking of God as disparate parts, bifurcating God, or having an incoherent account of God who is one way in revelation and another in himself.

This brief sketch reveals Barth's driving inclination, and it reveals two key features that Edwards anticipates. First, Edwards reconstructs his discussion such that the only way to talk about the "attributes" of God is to talk about the Son and the Spirit.[54] Second, the single attribute of God, what is named by

---

50. *CD* II/1, 325.

51. *CD* II/1, 332.

52. I follow Reeling Brouwer in his focus on Barth's thorough use of the High Orthodox. See his *Karl Barth and Post-Reformation Orthodoxy* (Burlington, VT: Ashgate, 2015).

53. *CD* II/1, 349.

54. In his explanation of Barth's "actualism," Justin Stratis names its negative feature as a rejection of "a supposedly free-standing divine 'essence' which may be consulted independently as a canon by which to interpret God's acts." Justin Stratis, "Speculating about Divinity? God's

God's simplicity, is the divine glory or, more precisely, the pure actuality of God's religious affection. In Edwards, we do not find the distinction between the incommunicable attributes and the communicable attributes of God doing significant dogmatic work because God is addressed only in relation to personhood and revelation, and what is true of God *in se* is communicable to the creature through Christ as the very purpose of salvation.[55] It may be true that God is omnipresent, but Edwards finds that relatively uninteresting (and extrinsic, and therefore not a constitutive feature of God's life *in se*). What is profound is that God is the fullness of love binding together God's life in the Father and Son by the Holy Spirit.

In the development of his doctrine of the Trinity, Edwards sketches a doctrine of the divine attributes by making the distinction between real and relative attributes in God, claiming, "There are but these three distinct real things in God; whatsoever else can be mentioned in God are nothing but mere modes or relations of existence. There are his attributes of infinity, eternity and immutability: they are mere modes of existence."[56] Whatever is "real" in God names a divine person, and whatever is relative is an extrinsic attribute of God (or, put differently, these "attributes" give language to the mode of existence of the "real attributes").[57] In other words, proper talk about God is talking about the divine persons and not generic talk of God as "being." Rather than reading the full breadth of revealed attributes back into God's life, Edwards, with Barth, focuses the attributes on the personal nature of God as a description of *who* God is and how that life refracts in a creaturely modality.[58] Specifically, the goal of Edwards's discussion is to moor

---

Immanent Life and Actualistic Ontology," *International Journal of Systematic Theology* 12:1 (2010): 21. The rejection of the divine essence serving as a "canon" to interpret God's acts is, likewise, a helpful way to consider Edwards's impulse.

55. See Strobel, *Jonathan Edwards's Theology: A Reinterpretation*, 370–98.

56. *WJE* 21:131. Edwards does run the discussion of the attributes in a slightly different direction when he makes the distinction between the moral and natural attributes of God. See *WJE* 2:256. Space does not allow engagement with this issue, other than to say that "moral" and "natural" are a way to articulate the divine attributes and revelation, such that knowing God requires the Spirit's work of illumination.

57. For more on this, see Kyle C. Strobel, "The Nature of God and the Trinity," in *The Oxford Handbook of Jonathan Edwards*, ed. Douglas A. Sweeney and Jan Stievermann (Oxford: Oxford University Press, 2021), 131–32.

58. One particularly odd turn in Edwards's account is when he posits four "unexercised attributes" in God that are extrinsic, but "fitting," for God to exercise in creation. The attributes Edwards names are power, wisdom, righteousness, and goodness. See *WJE* 8:428–29. Barth would

the divine attributes to personhood such that an articulation of the divine attributes is always and only an articulation of *who* God is. This preferences God's life of love in himself and attends fully to his knowing and willing as Father, Son, and Spirit. Furthermore, all attributes predicated on God's personhood are grounded in the processions and are therefore simply aspects of God's knowing or willing. For instance, Edwards claims, "There are the attributes of goodness, mercy and grace, but these are but the overflowings of God's infinite love."[59] This differs from Barth, who denies that grace is God's love in relation to creatures, because he wants to say that the form of "grace exists in God Himself and is actual as God is in point of fact hidden from us and incomprehensible to us."[60] Edwards would affirm this incomprehensibility, of course, but what is hidden and incomprehensible is not that God is somehow gracious *in se* (Edwards would have understood this as a category fallacy) but that he is the fullness of love, and in that fullness of love, he is for us in Christ Jesus.

Rather than turning to *pure* dialectic to ground God's revelation as a true revelation of God in himself, Edwards turns to beauty as refracted in a creaturely mode through the presence of the divine persons of Son and Spirit. The focus is on the immediate reality of God's self in Son and Spirit and therefore of the truth of God in history (bearing in mind that God's "real" attributes are both communicable and communicated in the economy). But the nature of God's life *in se* must refract in creaturely forms because in his descent into the flesh, the divine attributes take on new modes of existence (even as they are grounded in God's life in eternity as a mode of his love). Edwards's exposition of this takes on the texture of a dialectic, a dialectic ultimately resolved in the person of the Son through the Spirit's work to unite the created and uncreated, using the typology of Christ as the Lion and the Lamb to address the "diverse excellencies" in Christ. Because each nature has "diverse" excellencies, their union in Christ by the Spirit creates a scenario in which opposing virtues and attributes must be dialectically united through that union (e.g., that Christ is of infinite highness and infinite condescension). Edwards claims,

---

be critical of this, as well as Edwards's intrinsic/extrinsic distinction, and is so concerning related issues in the High Orthodox. See *CD* II/1, 349.

59. *WJE* 21:131.
60. *CD* II/1, 357.

In the person of Christ do meet together, infinite glory, and the lowest humility. Infinite glory, and the virtue of humility, meet in no other person but Christ. They meet in no created person; for no created person has infinite glory: and they meet in no other divine person but Christ. For though the divine nature be infinitely abhorrent to pride, yet humility is not properly predicable of God the Father, and the Holy Ghost, that exist only in the divine nature; because it is a proper excellency only of a created nature. ... But in Jesus Christ, who is both God and man, these two diverse excellencies, are sweetly united.[61]

Edwards claims that the "human excellencies" of Christ are "communications and reflections of the divine"[62] such that Christ was not revealing something untrue of God, but the divine was "accommodated to our apprehensions."[63] Unlike Barth, Edwards does not read into the life of God attributes like humility or grace but recognizes these as appropriate refractions of the life of God through a creaturely modality that reveals the truth about who God is. The person of Christ brings the full reality of the life of God with him in the economy such that he is the locus of all creaturely knowledge of God in the Spirit. Christ is the center of Edwards's doctrine of revelation because in Christ, humankind comes to see God face to face.

CONCLUSION

In both Edwards and Barth, there is an impulse to reject bifurcation (although I do not use the qualifier "any" here) between God in se and God pro nobis. While both affirm divine aseity, there is also a predisposition to press hard on God's inclination to overflow. Barth notes that God "had no need of a creation. He might well have been satisfied with the inner glory of His threefold being, His freedom, and His love," only to add that God "is not satisfied, but that His inner glory overflows and becomes outward."[64] Both Edwards and Barth note this overflow and ground it in the divine glory, and both seem to incline God

---

61. *WJE* 19:568.

62. *WJE* 19:590.

63. Jonathan Edwards, "Jesus Christ Is the Shining Forth of the Father's Glory," in *The Glory and Honor of God*, vol 2 of *The Previously Unpublished Sermons of Jonathan Edwards*, ed. Michael D. McMullen (Nashville: Broadman & Holman, 2004), 233.

64. *CD* II/2, 121.

toward creation from within this satisfaction in himself. Building on this impulse and the desire to affirm that God himself is revealed in revelation, both Barth and Edwards radicalize the divine attribute discussion. Whereas Barth turns to the dialectic of love and freedom to ground his development, Edwards focuses on personhood, turning to God's descent in the incarnation to ground the refraction of the divine nature in a human modality, resolving this dialectic in the person of the Son by the work of the Spirit (developed through Edwards's Spirit-Christology).

Both Edwards and Barth are driven by the inclination that God "seeks and creates fellowship with us" by receiving "us through His Son into His fellowship with Himself."[65] To know and love God, one must participate in God's self-knowing and be loved from within his love (John 17:26). At the heart of this impulse is the idea that it really is God who confronts the Christian in revelation and salvation, and the grace of God is God's self-giving love overflowing to catch the creature up into himself. For both thinkers, glory becomes the sphere in which the economy is understood, in which God's life, overflow, and creaturely participation are grounded. In Barth's words, which Edwards would heartily affirm, "God's glory is God Himself in the truth and capacity and act in which He makes Himself known as God."[66] For both, there is something like a threefold movement of glory; "glory" names the truth of God in himself, God in his *ad extra* overflow, and the creature being caught up in that overflow.[67] Edwards claims,

> In the creature's knowing, esteeming, loving, rejoicing in, and prais-
> ing God, the glory of God is both exhibited and acknowledged; his
> fullness is received and returned. Here is both an *emanation* and
> *remanation*. The refulgence shines upon and into the creature, and
> is reflected back to the luminary. The beams of glory come from God,
> and are something of God, and are refunded back again to their orig-
> inal. So that the whole is *of* God, and *in* God, and *to* God; and God is
> the beginning, middle and end in this affair.[68]

---

65. CD II/1, 275.

66. CD II/1, 641.

67. JinHyok Kim, *The Spirit of God and the Christian Life: Reconstructing Karl Barth's Pneumatology* (Minneapolis: Fortress Press, 2014), 202–7.

68. WJE 8:531.

The locus of this glory is Christ, known in the incarnation and illuminated by the Spirit, which Barth rightly emphasizes when he states, "But the beginning, centre and goal of these works of the divine glory is God's Son Jesus Christ."[69] Edwards would affirm this emphasis and does so when he names Christ as the "end of all God's works *ad extra*."[70] Edwards would, furthermore, agree with the movement of glory in Barth's thought when he makes comments like, "God stands in need of nothing else. He has full satisfaction in Himself. ... Yet He satisfies Himself by showing and manifesting and communicating Himself as the One who He is."[71] God's glory is God's life *in se*, God's life overflowing, and as Barth notes, "God's glory is also the answer awakened and evoked by God Himself of the worship offered Him by His creation to the extent that in its utter creatureliness this is the echo of God's voice."[72] In this light, it is worthwhile quoting Edwards again: "*God looks on* the communication of himself, and the emanation of the infinite glory and good that are in himself to belong to the fullness and completeness of himself, *as though he were not in his most complete and glorious state without it.*"[73] By looking upon himself as incomplete without the creature, God includes creaturely response within his self-glorification such that being for himself and being for us are united in Christ.

While there are many formal and material differences between Edwards's and Barth's theologies, this impulse is an important point of overlap. Both, it would seem, articulate an account of God's aseity not as a negative judgment but as a positive affirmation of the fullness of God's life and self-giving. John Webster narrates this impulse well:

> In Christian dogmatics, such a materially rich notion of aseity cannot be articulated apart from the doctrine of the Trinity, for Trinitarian teaching offers a conceptual paraphrase of the life of God, both in his inner depth and in his gracious turn to that which is not God. It is as Father, Son and Spirit that God is of himself, utterly free and full, in the self-originate and perfect movement of his life; grounded

---

69. *CD* II/1, 667.

70. *WJE* 18:178.

71. *CD* II/1, 667.

72. *CD* II/1, 667–68.

73. *WJE* 8:439–40, my emphasis.

in himself, he gives himself, the self-existent Lord of grace. God *a se* is the perfection of paternity, filiation and spiration in which he is indissolubly from, for and in himself, and out of which he bestows himself as the Lord, savior and partner of his creature.[74]

What funds the impulse to hold tightly together God *in se* with God *pro nobis* is a notion of aseity that focuses on God's life of abundance, seen through an emphasis on the divine freedom, fullness, and blessedness. Webster avers, "Aseity is *life*: God's life *from* and therefore *in* himself." Furthermore, "In speaking of God's aseity we have in mind both the 'immanent' and the 'economic' dimensions of the divine life."[75] A positive doctrine of aseity that focuses on God's fullness is not focused on securing God in himself *apart from* the economy, however much the immanent must have logical precedence to the economic.[76] For both thinkers, there is a worry that God is established first *in se* without a proper articulation of his self-revelation in creation and redemption, and in both, "glory" is utilized to hold together the fullness of his life "in himself" and "for us." The key difference, it would seem, at risk of oversimplification, is that Barth's Christocentric distinctive and Edwards's Trinitarian focus set each thinker on a different trajectory. But at the heart of their projects is a shared focus on who God is for us in Christ to the glory of God.

---

74. John Webster, *God and the Works of God*, vol. 1 of *God without Measure: Working Papers in Christian Theology* (London: T&T Clark, 2016), 18–19.

75. Webster, *God and the Works of God*, 19.

76. Webster, again: "There is a certain priority to the first statement ('God is from himself'): the 'immanent' or absolute dimension of God's self-existence stands at the head of everything else that must be said. ... Nevertheless, the priority of the immanent would be badly misperceived if it were not related to the necessary further statement: 'from himself God gives himself'. Without this second statement, the first would risk abstraction from God's relative acts," *God and the Works of God*, 19. It is this worry about abstraction that seems to drive both Barth and Edwards's constructions.

2

SCRIPTURE

Doug Sweeney and Kevin Vanhooozer

What does eighteenth-century Northampton have to do with twentieth-century Basel? Admittedly, not much: they are separated by thousands of miles, hundreds of years, and different languages. Yet each was arguably home to the leading pastor-theologian of his day. Furthermore, both men read the Bible theologically as the Word of God for the people of God, and each therefore had to contend with modern challenges to such reading and to the doctrine of Scripture. Each was both child and critic of the Enlightenment after his own fashion. As concerns theological orientation, both Edwards and Barth located themselves within the Reformed tradition, yet both also felt free to reframe certain doctrines in light of current external challenges and, at least in Barth's case, certain internal shortcomings. Finally, each set his respective doctrine of Scripture in the broader economy of triune self-communication and paid special attention to the indispensable role of the Holy Spirit, though they parsed this role differently.

JONATHAN EDWARDS

Barth would write directly and dogmatically about the nature and purpose of the Bible, living as he did in an age when older views of these matters were contested and often rejected by scholars. But Edwards lived and worked in a Reformed civilization, where traditional Protestant views of these and other related doctrines were enforced by law. He took a conservative Reformed view of the Bible largely for granted, mostly improvising on it as he wrote on other themes. He was unique in the degree to which he emphasized the unity of the canon of the Bible—or at least the Protestant canon—and the Spirit's role in helping people hear, understand, believe, and cherish the "divine things" that sanctified its pages. This uniqueness owed a great deal to the naturalizing tendencies of those within his mental world who criticized older Christian doctrines of the Bible, mainly Spinozists, deists, Arians, and left-leaning Trinitarians gaining ground in Protestant Europe in the age of the Enlightenment. It also owed a thing or two to the so-called "Great Awakening," in which demand was high for doctrinal and pneumatic biblical preaching aimed at anxious, sensitive souls. But again, in the main, Edwards's view of sacred Scripture was conservative, on purpose, and dependent on the writings of Reformed antecedents.[1]

Edwards held what can seem today an especially high view of the Bible's inspiration, quite common though it was among the Christians in his world. He taught that God "indited" the Scriptures through the Bible's human authors and thus "dictated" to ministers the things they are to preach.[2] He rarely verged on a *passive* view of Scriptural dictation, as if God had dropped the Bible from the blue on golden plates. But neither did he focus on the personal contributions of the Bible's human authors to the degree that most late-modern biblical scholars would. He taught that God chose his penmen, gave them ears to hear God speaking and "extraordinary gifts" for relaying his Word to others, and revealed in and through them "an infallible rule of faith and works and manners to the church," a "sure rule which if we follow we cannot err."[3]

As one would assume given his lofty view of biblical inspiration, Edwards sided with thinkers like Calvin who said that Scripture is self-authenticated (αὐτόπιστον), full of inherent proof of its divine source and power. As he puts the matter briefly in *Religious Affections* (1746), "The gospel of the blessed God don't go abroad a begging for its evidence, so much as some think; it has its highest and most proper evidence in itself."[4] Edwards attributed the

---

1. We deal with Edwards's view of Scripture at greater length in Douglas A. Sweeney, *Edwards the Exegete: Biblical Interpretation and Anglo-Protestant Culture on the Edge of the Enlightenment* (New York: Oxford University Press, 2016), and Douglas A. Sweeney, *Jonathan Edwards and the Ministry of the Word: A Model of Faith and Thought* (Downers Grove, IL: IVP Academic, 2009), from which some of the following is adapted.

2. See *WJE*, 2:457; 4:228, 380, 481; 15:231, 518; 17:180; 18:236; 19:307; 24:513; Edwards, sermon on Luke 10:38-42 (July 1754), Box 7, F. 560, L. 6v., Beinecke Rare Book and Manuscript Library, Yale University (hereafter Beinecke); and Edwards, sermon on 1 Corinthians 2:11-13 (May 7, 1740, at the "ordination of Mr. Billing"), Box 10, F. 719, L. 3v., Beinecke.

3. *WJE* 9:365 and 14:265-66.

4. See the final paragraph of the "Preface" to *The Bay Psalm Book: A Facsimile Reprint of the First Edition of 1640* (Chicago: University of Chicago Press, 1956), unpaginated; and Edwards,

faith of true believers in the Word to what he called "intrinsic signatures of divinity" within it. "They see that excellency and ... image of God in the Word," he attests, "that constrains the mind to assent to it and embrace it as true and divine." Or, morphing sensory metaphors, the Lord's people "hear God speak" amid the pages of the Bible. They recognize God's voice. To them, "he speaks like a God. His speech is ... excellent, holy, wise, awful and gracious," Edwards claims. He compares this recognition of the voice of God in Scripture to the glimpse that Peter got of Jesus' glory in the Gospels on the Mount of Transfiguration. "Peter, when he saw this, his mind was strongly carried to believe, and he was sure that Christ was a divine and holy person without sitting down to reason about it; he was convinced and assured at once irresistibly, and was as it were intuitively certain." Likewise, saints sense the presence and glory of God within the Word. It is a "lamp" that shines a heavenly light of glory round about them. Or, as Jeremiah prophesied so many years ago (Jer 23:29), it is a "fire" and a "hammer" that "dissolves the Rocky Hearts of the chil[dren] of men."[5]

In keeping with tradition, Edwards touted both "external" and "internal" proofs of the Bible's credibility. "God is not wont to speak to men," he told his flock, without providing us "sufficient means to know" that he is speaking. "He has given the world great evidence that [Scripture] ... is his word. [Both] external [and] internal" evidence abounds. There are "all the kinds of evidence" for Scripture, he avers, "it is possible a revelation should have: there are all kinds of internal evidences from the majesty, holiness, sublimity, harmony, etc.; and there are all kinds of external evidences, prophecy and miracles" confirmed outside the canon. Nevertheless, he deemed the Bible's inner testimony best for most people. Scripture is for all, he taught, and laity have little time to trudge through the evidence that lies beyond its bounds. Most are simply "not capable of any certain or effectual conviction of the

Religious Affections, WJE 2:307. For more on this theme from Calvin and other Reformed luminaries, see especially Calvin's *Institutes* (1559), 1.7, and Henk van den Belt, *The Authority of Scripture in Reformed Theology: Truth and Trust*, Studies in Reformed Theology (Leiden: Brill, 2008). Similar statements may be found in ancient writers such as Justin, Clement of Alexandria, and Origen. See Justin Martyr, *Dialogue with Trypho*, 7.2; Clement of Alexandria, *Stromata*, 2.2, 7.16; and Origen, *Contra Celsus*, 1.2.

5. Edwards, "Profitable Hearers of the Word," WJE 14:251–52; Edwards, Miscellany 410, WJE 13:470–71; Edwards, "Types of the Messiah," WJE 11:253; and Edwards, sermon on Jeremiah 23:29 (April 1749), Box 5, F. 361, L. 1r., Beinecke.

divine authority of the Scriptures, by such arguments as learned men make use of," he advises. Common people need the Spirit's help discerning the Word of God—and this is part of what God grants to those who turn to him in faith. "The child of God doth ... see and feel the truth of divine things," he says. The saints "can feel such a power and kind of omnipotency in Christianity, and taste such a sweetness, and see such wisdom, such an excellent harmony in the gospel, as carry their own light with them, and powerfully do enforce and conquer the assent and necessitates their minds to receive it as proceeding from God, and as the certain truth."[6]

Edwards taught that sacred Scripture is essential to our flourishing, even in public life. He accentuated the need for both reason and revelation, for knowing both "what reason and Scripture declare" on relevant matters. He thought the "doctrines of Christianity" themselves "most rational, exceeding congruous to ... natural reason."[7] Moreover, he affirmed the Catholic dictum that to understand the world and its relationship to God, we need the "book of nature" and the "book of Scripture." However, he prioritized the Bible over other sources of knowledge. As he argues in *Distinguishing Marks of a Work of the Spirit of God* (1741), "All that is visible to the eye is unintelligible and vain, without the Word of God to instruct and guide the mind." And as he preached in a sermon on this theme a few years earlier,

> We make a distinction between the things that we know by reason, and things we know by revelation. But alas we scarce know what we say: we know not what we should have known ... had it not been for revelation. ... Many of the principles of morality and religion that we have always been brought up in the knowledge of, appear so rational that we are ready to think we could have found 'em out by our own natural reason. ... [But] all the learning, yea, all the common civility that there is in the world, seems to be either directly or indirectly from revelation, whether men are sensible of it or no. ... Everything that is good and useful in this fallen world, is from supernatural help.[8]

---

6. Edwards, "Yield to God's Word, or Be Broken by His Hand," *WJE* 25:211; Edwards, Miscellany 382, *WJE* 13:451; Edwards, *Religious Affections*, *WJE* 2:304–306; and Edwards, "A Spiritual Understanding of Divine Things Denied to the Unregenerate," *WJE* 14:78.

7. Edwards, "True Nobleness of Mind," *WJE* 14:231–32.

8. Edwards, *The Distinguishing Marks of a Work of the Spirit of God*, *WJE* 4:240; and Edwards, "Light in a Dark World, a Dark Heart," *WJE* 19:720.

This became a central theme in his response to English deists. In opposition to their call for a religion of nature and reason, Edwards insisted on the need for supernatural revelation—even for the maintenance of a healthy civic virtue. We have seen that he believed that God has spoken in the Bible. It is "unreasonable," in fact, he said, "to suppose that ... there should be a God, an intelligent voluntary being, that has so much concern with [us], and with whom we have infinitely more concern than with any other being, and yet that he should never speak." Further, if God has really divulged himself in writing in the Bible, we should honor holy Scripture as "the fountain whence all knowledge in divinity must be derived."[9] We should also grant it pride of place in secular conversation on the world and our place within it—topics treated by the deists and other non-traditional thinkers under "natural religion." Edwards argues in his "Miscellanies" in 1728, "Were it not for divine revelation, I am persuaded that there is no one doctrine of that which we call natural religion [but] would, notwithstanding all philosophy and learning, forever be involved in darkness, doubts, endless disputes and dreadful confusion." He repeats this conviction in his notes on the "Importance of Doctrines & of Mysteries in Religion." Many moderns "deceive themselves thro' the Ambiguity or Equivocal use of the word REASON," he writes. "They argue as tho we must make our Reason the highest Rule to Judge of all things[,] even the doctrines of Revelation." But "this way of Rejecting every thing but what we can first see for agreeable to our Reason Tends by degrees to bring every Thing relating not only to revealed Religion but even natural Religion into doubt[,] to make all appear with Dim Evidence like a shadow or the Ideas of a Dream till they are all neglected as worthy of no Regard." He also preached about this notion to the people of Northampton in a sermon later printed on the history of redemption. Our reason tells us much about the work of God in the world, he said, but "nothing else ... informs us what [the] scheme and design of God in his works is but only the holy Scriptures."[10]

Supernatural revelation and the spiritual light it offers were, for Edwards, essential for clarifying the nature of reality. It was not that the world could not be known without the Bible or that Scripture was a textbook in history

---

9. Edwards, Miscellany 544, *WJE* 18:89–90; and "Sermon 525, Hebrews 5:12" in *WJEO* 54:46.
10. Edwards, Miscellany 350, *WJE* 13:421.

or natural science. Rather, for Edwards, Word and Spirit shone a light on worldly wisdom, rendering knowledge more real, sure, and even beautiful than before. In a remarkable notebook entry dating from 1729, he depicts this so vividly that we quote him here at length:

> A mind not spiritually enlightened [by means of the Bible and God's Spirit] beholds spiritual things faintly, like fainting, fading shadows that make no lively impression on his mind, like a man that beholds the trees and things abroad in the night: the ideas ben't strong and lively, and [are] very faint; and therefore he has but a little notion of the beauty of the face of the earth. But when the light comes to shine upon them, then the ideas appear with strength and distinctness; and he has that sense of the beauty of the trees and fields given him in a moment, which he would not have obtained by going about amongst them in the dark in a long time. A man that sets himself to reason without divine light is like a man that goes into the dark into a garden full of the most beautiful plants, and most artfully ordered, and compares things together by going from one thing to another, to feel of them and to measure the distances; but he that sees by divine light is like a man that views the garden when the sun shines upon it. There is … a light cast upon the ideas of spiritual things in the mind of the believer, which makes them appear clear and real, which before were but faint, obscure representations.[11]

Edwards said as much in churches dozens of times throughout his life, heralding special revelation and the clarity it yields as a brilliant, heavenly light that illuminates for saints a world more vivid, polydimensional, and brimming with vitality than anything they had ever known before. He told his people that revelation works "in the hearts of those" who "truly entertain it" like "a light that shines in a dark place." The "spiritual understanding" it provides, furthermore, is "like a gleam of light that breaks in upon the soul through a gloomy darkness. Of all the similitudes," in fact, employed in Scripture "to describe to us this spiritual understanding, light is that which doth most fully represent it and is oftenest used."[12]

---

11. Edwards, Miscellany 408, WJE 13:469–70.

12. Edwards, "Light in a Dark World, a Dark Heart," WJE 19:724; and Edwards, "A Spiritual Understanding of Divine Things Denied to the Unregenerate," WJE 14:77.

Edwards drafted scores of pages on this "supernatural light," as well as its role in the production of a "spiritual understanding," stating that spiritual light from Scripture constitutes a greater blessing "than any other privilege that ever God bestowed." Readers who receive this light and keep it "bring forth Christ" in their hearts; Christ is truly "formed in them"; they are bonded through the Word with the living Word of God; and this union is "more blessed" than "to have Christ" within one's "arms, or at the breast, as the virgin Mary had." Spiritual knowledge even grants what Edwards spoke of in a sermon as "an earnest" or "the dawnings" of the beatific vision. It enables the people of God to share in the very life of God (2 Pet 1:4). For the assistance in the souls of those who have this special blessing "is not only from the Spirit, but it also partakes of the nature of that Spirit."[13]

The best posture for disciples who would understand the Bible, argues Edwards, is "to sit at Jesus' feet." That is to say, they should "go to him whose Word it is and beg of him to teach," for "he has reserved to himself this work of enlightening the mind with spiritual knowledge, and there is no other can do it; there is none teaches like God." With Mary of Bethany in the gospels, the sister of Lazarus and Martha—who took "a pound of ointment of spikenard, very costly, and anointed the feet of Jesus, and wiped his feet with her hair" (John 12:3, KJV)—they should be careful not to distract themselves with "[trouble] about many things." Rather, as Jesus said to Martha, only "one thing is needful: and Mary hath chosen that good part" (Luke 10:41-42, KJV), for she had clung to Christ and hung on his every word. Similarly, we should cling to every word that comes from the mouth of God, for "the word of God is the great means of our eternal good. ... 'tis the most necessary means, and without which our souls must famish." It is like "MILK," Edwards muses, flowing "from the breasts of the church." It is like "rain" for which God's people have "a great and earnest thirsting."[14]

Those who avoid this humble posture never really understand the true spirit of the Bible. Unconverted, proud people miss the Spirit's main points. As Edwards cautions in a talk on Jeremiah 8:8 ("the pen of the scribes is in

---

13. Edwards, sermon on Luke 11:27-28, Box 14, F. 1065, L. 1v., L. 6v.-7r., Beinecke; Edwards, "The Pure in Heart Blessed," *WJE* 17:65-66; and Edwards, "Treatise on Grace," *WJE* 21:178-80.

14. Edwards, sermon on Luke 10:38-42, L. 3r.; Edwards, "Profitable Hearers of the Word," *WJE* 14:266; Edwards, "Heeding the Word, and Losing It," *WJE* 19:47; Edwards, "Images of Divine Things," *WJE* 11:93; and Edwards, sermon on Heb. 6:7, Box 11, F. 820, L. 17r., Beinecke.

vain"), "The Bible is all in vain to Them That continue in sin." Or, as he says when treating passages like 1 Corinthians 2 and the parable of the sower, "There is a spiritual understanding of divine things, which all natural and unregenerate men are destitute of."

> Natural men and hypocrites may boast of an extensive understanding, and may have natural abilities in a much greater strength than a godly man, and may abound in acquired knowledge, and may be able to reason with great strength about the holy Scriptures and the doctrines of religion; but yet he [sic] does not, nor can he, understand the Word of God. ... Ungodly men are so far from understanding the Word of God, that those things that are the main things of revelation, the principal things of the gospel and what are the very quintessence and end of all, are what they have no notion at all of and which the godly only apprehend; as particularly, such things as these: the glory of God, the excellency and fullness of Jesus Christ, the nature of holiness, the reason and foundation of duty. These things are the very main things of the Scripture. They are the greatest doctrines of God's Word, and they are the very end of revelation and its life and soul; and yet they are such as natural men have no idea or apprehension of.

Edwards grants that God lavishes "common grace" and "illuminations" on the unconverted scholar. But God gave the Holy Spirit to the godly reader of Scripture and thus tendered her a cognitive advantage. A regenerate person "sees things in a new appearance, in quite another view, than ever he saw before: ... he sees the wonderfulness of God's designs and a harmony in all his ways, a harmony, excellency and wondrousness in his Word: he sees these things by an eye of faith, and by a new light that was never before let into his mind." Further, "spiritual knowledge" grows by the "practice of virtue and holiness," a practice not pursued by those too proud to serve the Lord. "For we cannot have the idea [of anything in the mind, whether physical or spiritual] without the adapted disposition of mind, and the more suitable the disposition the more clear and intense the idea; but the more we practice, the more is the disposition increased."[15]

---

15. Edwards, sermon on Jeremiah 8:8 (December 1749), Box 5, F. 353, L. 1r., Beinecke; Edwards, "A Spiritual Understanding of Divine Things Denied to the Unregenerate," *WJE* 14:72, 79; Edwards,

Others had said as much before, though not always with the same psychological apparatus. Such epistemological claims date from the age of the ancient church and had been echoed in Edwards's favorite early modern Protestant sources. Even the Westminster divines confessed "the inward illumination of the Spirit of God to be necessary for the saving understanding of such things as are revealed in the Word."[16] But after the rise of higher criticism, especially after Spinoza's opposition to the notion that the Spirit gives believers needed help interpreting Scripture, Edwards felt a burden to proclaim this doctrine boldly, and he did so with greater specificity than most. "The believer" has "such a sight and such a knowledge of things that, ever since [conversion], he [has become] another man," Edwards preached. "The knowledge that he has is so substantial, so inward, and so affecting, that it has quite transformed the soul and ... changed his ... innermost principles." Twenty years later, he repeated this assertion in his opus on the *Affections*: "A spiritual taste of soul, mightily helps the soul, in its reasonings on the Word of God, and in judging of the true meaning of its rules; as it removes the prejudices of a depraved appetite, and naturally leads the thoughts in the right channel, casts a light on the Word of God, and causes the true meaning, most naturally to come to mind."[17]

Edwards gleaned from Locke's *Essay Concerning Human Understanding* (seventh ed., 1716) to explain this cognitive change—or at least he made use of idealist understandings of the way we come to know things and combined them with the language of sensationalist psychology. (He was neither a strict empiricist nor a thoroughgoing rationalist, and though he read the *Essay*, he did not usually cite it when developing this theme.) As he argues in the *Affections*, "The passing of a right judgment on things, depends on an having a right apprehension or idea of things" in the mind; and, regrettably, unconverted sinners lack a "sense" of divine things. He expands on this notion in his "Miscellanies" notebooks: "Sinners must be destitute even of the ideas of many spiritual and heavenly things and of divine excellencies, because they don't experience them. It's impossible for them so much as to have the

"Profitable Hearers of the Word," *WJE* 14:248–49; Edwards, "Treatise on Grace," *WJE* 21:180 (on "common grace" and "common illuminations"); and Edwards, Miscellany 123, *WJE* 13:287.

16. The Westminster Confession of Faith, 1.6.

17. Edwards, "A Spiritual Understanding of Divine Things Denied to the Unregenerate," *WJE* 14:81; and Edwards, *Religious Affections*, *WJE* 2:285.

idea of faith, trust in God, holy resignation, divine love, Christian charity; because their mind is not possessed of those things." Edwards believed that this is "why the things of the gospel seem ... so tasteless and insipid to the natural man. They are a parcel of words to which they in their own minds have no correspondent ideas; 'tis like a strange language or a dead letter, that is, sounds and letters without any signification." And he preached about this doctrine using Locke's famed description of direct and reflex knowledge:

> There is a direct knowledge, and there is a reflex knowledge. The direct knowledge is the knowledge the Christian hath of divine things, without himself, of the truth and excellency of the things of the gospel. The reflex knowledge is that which he obtains by reflecting and look-ing inward upon his own heart, and seeing the operations and actings of that, and the workings of the Spirit of God therein. By this reflec-tion, the Christian obtains to know what regeneration is; and what are those actings of the Spirit of God which are so frequently spoken of in Scripture; and the whole applicatory part of religion, which is one half of divinity, and which every natural man is ignorant of.

Word and Spirit leave no mark upon the unconverted mind. The "natural man" may attain extensive knowledge of the Bible—its ancient Near Eastern backgrounds, its writers and their languages—but not the spiritual data it describes.[18]

Even the saints, though, must work to understand the Bible rightly. Their regenerate disposition rarely obviates the need for careful study of the canon. "We must be much in reading the Scriptures," Edwards urged his people often, "if we would get spiritual ... knowledge." We "must be pretty well versed in the Scripture[s], before [we] can see their scope and drift, their connection, har-mony and agreement," he explained. "A notional knowledge of divine things, must go before a spiritual." For intimacy with God comes from time spent in reading the Bible, meditation, and prayer, not just superficial spiritual trysts or rapturous affairs. As Edwards liked to say to businesspeople in his parish, God "gives us the gold" in providing us with Scripture but bequeaths it "in a

---

18. Edwards, *Religious Affections*, WJE 2:296–97; Edwards, Miscellany 239, WJE 13:354–55; Edwards, Miscellany 123, WJE 13:286–87; and Edwards, "A Spiritual Understanding of Divine Things Denied to the Unregenerate," WJE 14:80.

mine that we might dig for it and get it in a way of our own industry." This deepens our desire for it and draws us near to him. If biblical treasure were "thrown plentifully before every man's face, and everyone could have it without any labor or industry, it would not be prized as it now is."[19]

KARL BARTH

Like Edwards, Barth was a pastor of a Reformed church. His theology developed as a response to the dual challenge of proclaiming the Word of God despite the various challenges of "modernity." However, whereas Edwards had to confront eighteenth-century deists and other critics, Barth's opponents were nineteenth- and early twentieth-century theological liberals (and fundamentalists). Bruce McCormack suggests that we best view Barth's theology as an attempt to understand "what it means to be orthodox *under the conditions of modernity*."[20] Our aim here is to respond to a related question: what does it mean to be *Reformed* under the conditions of modernity? In particular, if John Webster's assessment is correct that "Classical Reformed theology spoke of Scripture as the cognitive principle of theology," did Barth intend to preserve Scripture as the cognitive principle of theology "after modernity"?[21]

REVELATION AND THE WORD OF GOD

One of the things that makes theology "modern" is an acute consciousness of human limitations, especially the awareness that all human thinking is conditioned by one's place and time.[22] Yet precisely for this reason, another mark of modern theology is an anthropocentric focus, best represented by Schleiermacher, who argues that the task of theology is to understand faith as the feeling of absolute dependence. Barth's theology is a reaction to

---

19. Edwards, "A Spiritual Understanding of Divine Things Denied to the Unregenerate," *WJE* 14:94–95; and Edwards, "Profitable Hearers of the Word," *WJE* 14:265, 246–47.

20. Bruce L. McCormack, *Studies in the Theology of Karl Barth: Orthodox and Modern* (Grand Rapids: Baker Academic, 2008), 17.

21. Cf. Richard A. Muller, *Holy Scripture: The Cognitive Foundation of Theology*, vol. 2 in *Post-Reformation Reformed Dogmatics: The Rise and Development of Reformed Orthodoxy, ca. 1520 to ca. 1725*, 2nd ed. (Grand Rapids: Baker Academic, 2003).

22. Cf. Bruce L. McCormack: "it was the rise of 'historical consciousness' … that was most basic to the emergence of what we tend to think of as 'modern' theology." *Studies in the Theology of Karl Barth*, 10–11. See also McCormack, "Introduction: On 'Modernity' as a Theological Concept," in *Mapping Modern Theology: A Thematic and Historical Introduction*, ed. Bruce L. McCormack and Kelly Kapic (Grand Rapids: Baker Academic, 2012), 1–19.

nineteenth-century theological liberalism, specifically, the precarious tendency to conflate divine revelation with human religious experience.

The obligation to preach eventually led Barth to sharply distinguish the
words of human beings from the Word of God. In a 1916 church address, "The
Strange New World within the Bible," Barth argues that the Bible is primarily not the expression of human religious experience or reflection on divine
revelation, "the world of God": "It is not the right human thoughts about
God which form the content of the Bible, but the right divine thoughts about
men. The Bible tells us not ... how we find the way to him, but how he has
sought and found the way to us."[23] Barth here works a theocentric correction on anthropocentric theological liberalism: his early dialectical phrase
is marked by his emphasis on the contradiction between God and humanity,
God's Word and human words.

Barth burst onto the German-speaking theological scene in 1919 with
his *Romans* commentary, in which he discovered anew the decisive contrast
between divine and human righteousness.[24] The cross of Christ contradicts
every human effort either to make oneself right with God or to speak truly of
God. God does not simply put the crowning touch on human efforts; rather,
God demolishes them. What guides Barth in his comments on Romans is his
conviction that there is an "infinite qualitative distinction" between time and
eternity, humanity and God. God stands over against the world, and this is
Paul's predominant note: a heavenly righteousness has appeared that stands
in judgment over all human righteousness. Similarly, Barth saw that a heavenly knowledge stands in judgment over all human knowledge, especially
human knowledge of God. God is God, utterly beyond us—unless and until
he makes himself known. Yet even when God does make himself known,
he remains God, which means that humans cannot know him the way they
know other objects.

Barth is nothing if not a theologian of the Word of God. All knowledge of
God must begin with God's self-revelation, with God's decision to speak by
his Word. The possessive matters: it is *God's* Word, not a human possession.
Barth takes his cue from John 1 in identifying the Word that was with God
with the Son, the Word who was God and who became flesh. Indeed, this may

---

23. Barth, *The Word of God and the Word of Man* (Gloucester, MA: Peter Smith, 1978), 43.

24. Barth produced an extensively revised second edition in 1922.

be Barth's signature move: to identify the Word of God with God the Son, an active speaking subject. God's Word is his personal address, that is, a divine address that comes to human beings in the person of Jesus Christ. Jesus is the one Word of God, *in* history but not *of* it. This raises the obvious question, "What is the relationship of the Bible to the Word of God?"

REVELATION AND HOLY SCRIPTURE

Epistemology is first philosophy for many moderns. Barth, too, is modern to the extent that he was preoccupied with theological epistemology, in particular, the problem of how to speak of God given Kant's stipulation that our concepts apply only to things we experience in space and time. This was Barth's battle on the Western front of modernity, as it were. When he served as university lecturer at first Göttingen and then Münster, he had to lecture both on books of the Bible and on Reformed theology. This second front—premodern Scripture and tradition—allowed him to explore the texts of the New Testament, the works of Calvin and Zwingli, and the Heidelberg Catechism and other Reformed confessions. This happy coincidence meant that Barth began to use properly dogmatic (i.e., Reformed) and not simply dialectical (i.e., modern) concepts in his engagements with Scripture.[25]

Of special interest in the context of comparing him with Edwards is Barth's recovery (and revamping) of the "Scripture principle." In his 1923 lectures, "The Theology of the Reformed Confessions," Barth sets out two propositions: "The church recognizes the rule of its proclamation solely in the Word of God and finds the Word of God solely in Holy Scripture"; "The specific content of the Reformed confession lies in its relation to the Word of God spoken in the Scriptures."[26] The first proposition brings Barth closer

---

25. John Webster notes that Barth's retrieval of the Reformed tradition was "perhaps the ... crucial phase of his development." Webster, *Barth's Earlier Theology* (Edinburgh: T&T Clark, 2005). However, Ryan Glomsrud contends that Barth's recovery of the Reformed tradition "was intertwined with the inheritance of nineteenth-century conceptions of that tradition." "Karl Barth as Historical Theologian: The Recovery of Reformed Theology in Barth's Early Dogmatics," in *Engaging with Barth: Contemporary Evangelical Critiques*, ed. David Gibson and Daniel Strange (Leicester; London: Inter-Varsity Press, 2008), 86. For a contrasting view, see Rinse H. Reeling Brouwer, *Karl Barth and Post-Reformation Orthodoxy* (London: Routledge, 2016). The extent of Barth's knowledge and appropriation of primary Reformed sources remains a disputed point. What is indisputable is that at many points, Barth felt both obliged and free to rethink classical Reformed theology, sometimes in radical ways (e.g., election).

26. Barth, *The Theology of the Reformed Confessions* (Louisville: Westminster John Knox, 2002), 41, 44.

to the Reformers, but the way in which he interprets the second proposition distances him.

What is striking, and should not be missed, is that when Barth departs from the classic Reformed tradition, he does so not out of deference to modernity—theological liberalism and historical criticism—but for properly theological reasons pertaining to the freedom and sovereignty of God, which are traditional Reformed themes. Equally striking is how Barth's distinctive understandings of these quintessential Reformed doctrines also distinguish him from his Reformed forbearers. Divine sovereignty means divine freedom, yet the way Barth understands God's freedom may owe something to his preoccupation with modern epistemology and the question of whether God is an "object" of knowledge and human religious experience. Barth insists that God and God's Word are too free to be captured by anything creaturely, especially Schleiermacher's feeling of absolute dependence. God is always and everywhere free either to reveal or not reveal himself to anyone. Barth, like Edwards, is happy to describe God's revelation in terms of his self-communication, yet Barth is adamant that God remains the active subject of his revelation. Unlike human discourse, which can be textually inscribed, God's revelation *cannot* be preserved in writing. John Webster notes that Barth is "very far indeed from deploying the Scripture principle in such a way that the Bible as *text* becomes the *principium* of Christianity."[27] God's Word means God's *speaking*, and this divine address is as much event as it is content: "The word of God cannot be separated from the God who speaks it and indeed from the act or event of his speaking."[28] Revelation for Barth is personal, not propositional. The Bible is God's Word *when* and *where* and *to whom* God chooses to reveal himself through it. This event-like aspect of divine revelation contrasts with the classic Reformed understanding, in which God's Word (written) is his (covenantal, personal) bond.

Barth's understanding of revelation is intimately related to his understanding of the triune God: God the Father (the Revealer) reveals himself in his Son (the Revelation) through his Spirit (the Revealedness). And this leads to the second reason Barth distances himself from the classic Reformed

27. John Webster, *Barth's Early Theology*, 48.

28. Mark D. Thompson, "Witness to the Word: On Barth's Doctrine of Scripture," in Gibson and Strange, *Engaging with Barth*, 177.

view, namely, to hold Christ preeminent in all things—even the doctrine of revelation. As early as the 1924 *Göttingen Dogmatics*, and continuing in his magnum opus, *Church Dogmatics*, Barth speaks of the threefold form of the Word of God. The Son is the Word of God in its eternal, purest form, that is, God in his self-revelation. Barth agrees with the Reformed insistence on Scripture as the norm for faith and life. Scripture is a form of the Word of God because, very simply, it presents Christ, or rather, it is the medium in and through which God freely chooses to reveal himself. Strictly speaking, then, Scripture *becomes* the Word of God when God graciously decides to speak through it.[29] The third form of the Word of God is preaching, namely, the form the written Word takes when it is proclaimed and used by God to address the church.

WHAT SCRIPTURE IS: THE WORD'S WITNESS

Barth treats the doctrine of Holy Scripture in the second part of volume 1 of CD, "The Doctrine of the Word of God," and what he says there is materially the same as what he says thirty years later in his 1962 lectures in the United States published as *Evangelical Theology*. The primary Word of God is for Barth God's active self-presentation in the person and history of Jesus Christ. What the prophets and apostles have written in the Bible stands to the Word of God as the primary human *witness* to divine revelation.[30]

"Witness" preserves the singular status of Jesus Christ as *the* Word of God, yet it also ties the words of the prophets and apostles to Christ and has the advantage of being a biblical concept (cf. John 5:39). The prophets and apostles were commissioned witnesses called by the Word of God to render a particular service. At the same time, the notion of witness creates a conceptual gap between the Bible and revelation: "A witness is not absolutely identical with that to which it witnesses."[31] Barth nevertheless accords the prophets and apostles an authority that surpasses that of later theologians: "Even the

---

29. Bruce McCormack argues that Scripture has its very being in this becoming. That is, when Scripture becomes the Word of God, it becomes what God has determined it to be. "The Being of Holy Scripture Is in Becoming: Karl Barth in Conversation with American Evangelical Criticism," in *Evangelicals & Scripture: Tradition, Authority, and Hermeneutics*, ed. Vincent Bacote, Laura C. Miguélez, and Dennis L. Ockholm (Downers Grove, IL: InterVarsity Press, 2004), 55–75.

30. Barth, *Evangelical Theology: An Introduction* (Grand Rapids: Eerdmans, 1963), 26; CD I/2, 462.

31. *CD* I/2, 463.

smallest, strangest, simplest, or obscurest among the biblical witnesses has
an incomparable advantage over even the most pious, scholarly, and saga-
cious latter-day theologian. From his special point of view and in his special
fashion, the witness has thought, spoken, and written about the revelatory
Word and act in direct confrontation with it. All subsequent theology, as well
as the whole community that comes after the event, will never find itself in
the same immediate confrontation."[32] Still, the witness is always and only a
servant to the substance of his testimony, never the master.

If, for Barth, the Bible is merely human witness to revelation, how does
this represent any improvement on the theological liberals he criticized,
for whom the Bible is simply an expression of religious piety? If the Bible is
witness to the Word, what exactly is it? More pointedly, does Barth view the
discourse of Scripture as human or divine, or both?[33] To raise such questions is to bring into focus Barth's relationship to the classic Reformed doctrine of biblical inspiration. Barth's position on this matter is not entirely
straightforward.[34]

Barth is willing neither to identify the biblical witness with divine revelation nor to separate them: "we are tied to these texts."[35] The tie in question
is an *indirect* identity between the Bible and God's Word. God remains the
free and sovereign subject of his revelation; he does not will to reveal himself
to just anyone who reads the Bible. On the contrary, if and when the Bible
witnesses to revelation, thereby becoming a *form* of the Word, it is the result
of a miraculous event of God's grace. "Witness" is an apt term insofar as witnessing is (1) a form of answering speech, accountable to something prior to
and outside of the speaker ("That ... which we have heard, which we have
seen with our eyes ... concerning the word of life," 1 John 1:1), and (2) a mode
of identifying with or participating in the subject matter. Witnessing is the
event whereby God "co-opts" the human words and uses them as a means of

---

32. Barth, *Evangelical Theology*, 32.

33. For a book-length exploration of this issue, see Alfred H. Yuen, *Barth's Theological Ontology of Scripture* (Eugene, OR: Pickwick, 2014).

34. "Barth's bifurcation of the Bible as both a human text that *is* the Word of God and a human text that *becomes* the Word is God is certainly a puzzling aspect of his treatment of Scripture." David Gibson, "The Answering Speech of Men: Karl Barth on Holy Scripture," in *The Enduring Authority of the Christian Scriptures*, ed. D. A. Carson (Grand Rapids: Eerdmans, 2016), 270.

35. *CD* I/2, 492.

his self-revelation. God's Word is therefore God's act; revealing is something only God does, not human words in and of themselves.

To say "Scripture is the Word of God" is, for Barth, not simply a statement about the Bible's content. It is rather a statement about God's willingness to use Scripture to reveal himself through its human author-witnesses. Strictly speaking, says Barth, we should not say, "The Bible *is* the Word of God," but rather, "The Bible *was* and *will be* the Word of God"—when God freely condescends to make the hearing or reading of Scripture the occasion of his self-revelation: "It is round this event that the whole doctrine of Holy Scripture circles."[36] It is here that we most clearly see Barth's "correction" of the classic Reformed doctrine of Scripture.[37]

Edwards taught that God "indited" the Scriptures (i.e., composed, dictated them) through their human authors and thus stands in the Reformed tradition that affirms the verbal inspiration of the biblical text. For Edwards and the Reformed tradition, God's speaking was primarily a past act. For Barth, however, God is the free and active subject of his revelation, and it follows that God's revealing activity does not cease with the composition of the Scriptures. Barth is unwilling to say that the Word of God is simply "there," inscribed on the pages of the biblical text, because the Word of God—namely, God in his free and sovereign act of self-revelation—is never a fixed natural property of anything creaturely. God does not "perform" (i.e., communicate himself) at the reader's command, nor can interpreters read off God's revelation from the human witness: "God's Word is never 'available' for anyone."[38] Biblical inspiration does not mean the divinization of creaturely reality. To think that God's Word is a fixed property of the biblical text was "the naturalistic error of the doctrine of inspiration of the late seventeenth century."[39] The error of post-Reformation Reformed theologians, as Barth understands the matter, was to associate inspiration with a quality of the (fixed) letter of Scripture rather than its (dynamic) event of hearing/reading.

---

36. CD I/2, 503.

37. Barth prefers to speak of being not as substance but as actuality (i.e., more dynamically). McCormack suggests that this is the real issue between evangelicals and Barth, namely, the latter's insistence that revelation is an event of self-disclosure rather than propositional content. See McCormack, "The Being of Holy Scripture," 55–75.

38. Barth, "The Authority and Significance of the Bible: Twelve Theses," in *God Here and Now* (London: Routledge, 2003), 66.

39. Barth, *God Here and Now*, 66.

Barth consistently regards the Bible as a creaturely entity (i.e., human words), never a "divinized" entity. This is why he can allow for errors. Barth not only refers to the authors' "capacity for errors"[40] but says they were "actually guilty of error in their spoken and written word."[41] And yet when God freely uses this fallible human testimony to point readers to the living Christ, the Bible witnesses to revelation and becomes what it is, a form of the Word of God. For Barth, that the Bible witnesses successfully despite its human errors, thereby coming into its own as "witness," depends entirely on God's grace, not the Bible's textual nature.[42]

This is where Barth departs from his post-Reformation Reformed forbears, whom he thinks lost the sovereignty of the Word of God in a slide from supernaturalism into secularism:

> The statement that the Bible is the Word of God was now transformed ... from a statement about the free grace of God into a statement about the nature of the Bible as exposed to human inquiry brought under human control. The Bible as the Word of God surreptitiously became a part of natural knowledge of God, i.e., of that knowledge of God which man can have without the free grace of God, by his own power, and with direct insight and assurance."[43]

Barth therefore has properly theological reasons for denying the verbal inspiredness of the Bible, which he derides as "false doctrine": "The Bible was not grounded upon itself apart from the mystery of Christ and the Holy Ghost. It became a 'paper pope.' "[44] However, David Gibson expresses the worry this raises for traditional Reformed theologians: "While Barth affirms that the human word of the prophets and apostles is the Word of God, nowhere does he intimate that their written words are the *words* of God."[45]

---

40. *CD* I/2, 508.

41. *CD* I/2, 529–30.

42. McCormack describes the Bible's being-in-becoming a true witness in terms not of inerrancy but "dynamic infallibilism." "The Being of Holy Scripture," 73–74. For a critique of McCormack's notion, see Gibson, "The Answering Speech of Men," 282–85.

43. *CD* I/2, 522–23.

44. *CD* I/2, 525.

45. Gibson, "Answering Speech of Men," 287.

INSPIRATION AND ILLUMINATION; WORD AND SPIRIT

Barth views both the nature and interpretation of the Bible as elements in the economy of grace. The Spirit must be at work in both the authors and the readers if Scripture is to become the Word of God that witnesses to Jesus Christ. God's free agency (i.e., lordship) over Scripture does not come to an end with either its composition or its canonization, for Barth insists on the necessity of the Spirit's miraculous work in the *reading* of Scripture as well as its *writing*. For just as the authors of the Bible were fallible, requiring the Spirit's assistance, so are the readers, and so do they.

While Barth is thoroughly Reformed in emphasizing the unity of Word and Spirit, he is his own Reformed man in insisting that inspiration is something that happens to readers of Scripture (in the present) and not only to its authors (in the past). The Reformed Scripture principle confessed the text, what has been written, as "inspired" (θεόπνευστος—2 Tim 3:16). For Barth, however, inspiration describes "the relation between the Holy Spirit and the Bible in such a way that ... this unity is a free act of the grace of God."[46] The Spirit is active in both Scripture's composition and its reception. The Bible does not *actually* witness unless the Spirit actively inspired authors and readers alike: "We must view inspiration as a single, timeless—or rather, contemporary—act of God ... in *both* the biblical authors *and* ourselves."[47] More traditional Reformed critics here accuse Barth of conflating inspiration and illumination (or collapsing illumination into revelation) for his own dogmatic purposes (i.e., preserving the sovereign freedom of God's revelation).[48]

Yet the first and foremost of these dogmatic purposes is exegesis: Scripture is the foremost witness to Jesus Christ, the Word of God, and Barth clearly affirms the superiority of the Bible's authority as God-used human testimony to the gospel. The church's freedom is a freedom "under the Word"—the freedom to hear, understand, and obey Scripture. Indeed, the whole task of Christian dogmatics consists of determining whether and

46. *CD* I/2, 514.

47. Barth, *The Göttingen Dogmatics: Instruction in the Christian Religion*, vol. 1, ed. Hannelotte Reiffen, trans. Geoffrey W. Bromiley (Grand Rapids: Eerdmans, 1991), 225 (emphasis original).

48. See Thompson, "Barth's Doctrine of Scripture,"189; Gibson, "The Answering Speech of Men," 279-82. See also John D. Morrison, "Barth, Barthians, and Evangelicals: Reassessing the Question of the Relation of Holy Scripture and the Word of God," *Trinity Journal* 25 (2004): 187-213, and Kevin Vanhoozer, "A Person of the Book? Barth on Biblical Authority and Interpretation," in *Karl Barth and Evangelical Theology: Convergences and Divergences*, ed. Sung Wook Chung (Grand Rapids: Baker Academic, 2006), 26-59.

to what extent church proclamation and church doctrine agree with the revelation attested in Scripture.[49] This is why Barth's last word to the German church as he went into exile for confronting Hitler was, "Exegesis, exegesis, and yet more exegesis!"[50]

CONCLUSION: EDWARDS, BARTH, AND THE FORMAL PRINCIPLE OF REFORMED THEOLOGY

Edwards and Barth disagreed about the doctrine of inspiration and the nature of the sacred page. Edwards taught that the Bible is the Word of God and thus contains revelation; Barth taught that the Bible is a witness to revelation. But despite their well-known differences on the character of the canon, they shared the formal principle of Protestant theology. What does it mean to be orthodox, Protestant, and Reformed under the conditions of modernity? It means, first, to read the Bible as the Word of God to us, the point of departure on our quest for reliable knowledge of God, and the only norm that norms the faith and practice of the church. It also means, secondarily, a willingness to revisit and re-contextualize its teachings in relation to new developments—the Great Awakening, the Enlightenment, higher criticism, historicism—using the Scripture principle under the guidance of the Spirit to improve our dogmatics and, even more importantly, advance the hearing and doing of the Word of God today. In our late-modern, non- and post-Christian secular world, Reformed Christians still need to do the same.

---

49. *CD* I/1, 283.

50. Cited in Eberhard Busch, *Karl Barth: His Life from Letters and Autobiographical Texts,* trans. John Bowden (Grand Rapids: Eerdmans, 1975), 259.

3
—

ELECTION

Christina N. Larsen

The inimitable Robert Jenson once quipped, somewhat famously, that his beloved Jonathan Edwards "anticipates at most key points the justly praised 'christological' doctrine of election developed by Karl Barth."[1] It is no secret that Edwards, in addition to Barth, provided much inspiration for Jenson's own service to the modern church, and for that, regardless of the popularity of his interpretations of "America's theologian," many might be grateful. However, rather than assess the extent to which Edwards anticipates Barth's Christological moves within his doctrine of election, what follows will examine how Edwards's celebration of God's freedom for the blessing of creatures in Christ's election anticipates Barth's own concern with this freedom to the effect that they comparably push the boundaries established by their Reformed orthodox forebears. Briefly, this chapter contends that, despite the manifold differences in their accounts, Edwards and Barth similarly evince a radical correspondence between the freedom of God in the loving of the blessed divine fellowship *in se* and this freedom directed toward his blessing of creatures in Christ's election, which considerably chastens suggestions that God might not have chosen to pour forth in such blessing. Consequently, even as both theologians work out their understandings of Christ's election in light of Reformed orthodox developments, they depart from the tradition inasmuch as they do not find God's freedom of indifference a central element of his freedom in this pouring forth.[2] So, their respective

---

1. Robert W. Jenson, *America's Theologian: A Recommendation of Jonathan Edwards* (New York: Oxford University Press, 1988), 106.

2. On Edwards's and Barth's complicated relationships with Reformed orthodoxy, see especially Phillip Hussey, Christina N. Larsen, and Kyle C. Strobel, eds., *Jonathan Edwards and*

inclinations to celebrate the freedom of God *pro nobis* in Christ's election bring Edwards and Barth together in a way that significantly sets them apart from their predecessors.

EDWARDS

The basic contours of Christ's election in Edwards's writings are hardly unique among the Reformed. However, Edwards's elucidation in Miscellany 1245 of what it does and does not mean "to be chosen *in Christ*" in Ephesians 1:4 is striking in its understanding of how Christ is "the ground of our being chosen" and, particularly when read with Edwards's grounding of God's freedom to move *ad extra* in End of Creation, proves fruitful for the following comparison with Barth.[3]

Appealing to Thomas Goodwin's reading of Ephesians 1:4, Edwards opens Miscellany 1245 with a brief retort against Arminian notions that individuals' election is grounded in either their future faith in Christ or Christ's future salvation of them, and then he contends that it is equally false to suggest that, in this verse, being "in Christ" refers to the temporal working out of their election. Instead, "Christ purchased our salvation, but not our election" because "God first loved us and then gave his Son for us," and individuals are chosen in Christ from eternity such that their location "in Christ" is in "some way the ground of our being chosen from eternity to be holy and happy, as it is the ground of being blessed with spiritual blessings in time."[4] He then

---

Reformed Dogmatics (Bellingham, WA: Lexham, forthcoming) and Rinse H. Reeling Brouwer, *Karl Barth and Post-Reformation Orthodoxy* (Burlington, VT: Ashgate, 2015). For broader discussion on the theme of divine freedom in its various ramifications among the Reformed orthodox, see especially Richard A. Muller, *The Divine Essence and Attributes*, vol. 3 in *Post-Reformation Reformed Dogmatics: The Rise and Development of Reformed Orthodoxy, ca. 1520 to ca. 1725* (Grand Rapids: Baker Academic, 2003), 443–75, 524–40; and *Divine Will and Human Choice: Freedom, Contingency, and Necessity in Early Modern Reformed Thought* (Grand Rapids: Baker Academic, 2017), 19–79, 211–324.

3. Edwards, "1245. See [No.] 769, at the end of that number. ELECTION," in WJE 23:177–81 (177, Edwards's emphasis). While Edwards's notes pertaining to election are too extensive to list here, Miscellany 1245 and the earlier Miscellany 769 offer his key insights into the election of Christ; see Edwards, "769. CHRIST is often spoken of in Scripture as being by way of eminency THE ELECT," WJE 18:414–18. That Thomas Goodwin, Francis Turretin, and Petrus van Mastricht were on Edwards's mind as he developed his doctrine of election is undoubted. However, true to his style, Edwards does not often mention the Reformed orthodox in his writings on election but tends to incorporate their insights without citation. See Edwards, "292. SUPRALAPSARIANS." WJE 13:383–84 (384).

4. WJE 23:177.

makes a final comment on the verse in view of his reading of Goodwin, clarifying that not only are individuals "elected with Christ … at the same time," but, when they are elected in Christ, "Christ, in some respect, is first in this affair, and some way or other the ground of our being chosen, and God's election of him some way or other including and inferring the election of particular saints."[5] Yet this brief, initial appreciation of the total dependence of creaturely blessing upon Christ's election functions largely as a segue for four "observations" that together clarify how this dependence is grounded ultimately in the Father's eternal loving of the Son.

First, citing Colossians 1:15–19 and Ephesians 3:11: "All things that God ever decreed he decreed for the sake of his beloved. And all was decreed to be brought to pass by his Son. He being the end of all God's work *ad extra*, therefore the accomplishment of all was committed to him." Second: "That which more especially was God's end in his eternal purpose of creating the world, and of the sum of his purposes with respect to creatures, was to procure a spouse, or a mystical body, for his Son," and so creatures' election "might be called an election in Christ" because they are elect to be his body and bride. Third, citing Ephesians 1:4, 9–10: "As God determined in his eternal decrees to create a world, to communicate himself, and his Son might have an object for the object of his infinite grace and love, so God determined that this object should be one." And fourth: "God, in thus determining to communicate his peculiar love and goodness to many individual creatures, as all united into one body of his Son, he chose the race of mankind to be that species of creatures out of which he would take a number to constitute one created, dear child and one body of his Son."[6]

The four observations together parse the dependence of creaturely blessing on the election of Christ. However, Edwards broadens the discussion at the start, establishing the dependence of Christ's election upon the Father's eternal loving of the Son within the divine life. More than a supremely

---

5. *WJE* 23:178. Edwards's suggestion that Christ is the grounds of creatures' election is in no way connected to an interest in hypothetical universalism, though one finds such an interest in New Divinity developments of his legacy; see S. Mark Hamilton, "Jonathan Edwards on the Election of Christ," *Neue Zeitschrift für Systematische Theologie und Religionsphilosophie* 58, no. 4 (2016): 525–48, and the literature cited therein. For analysis of Goodwin's arguments on these points, see Joel R. Beeke and Mark Jones, "Thomas Goodwin's Christological Supralapsarianism," in *A Puritan Theology: Doctrine for Life* (Grand Rapids: Reformation Heritage Books, 2012), 149–59.

6. *WJE* 23:178–80.

fitting way to bring about the aforementioned purposes of spiritual blessing, Christ's election is first and foremost toward the end of blessing the Son with a spouse to be the object of his grace and love because it is the Son who is the eternally beloved of the Father and so the beloved end of all God's works. And so, vitally, Edwards grounds Christ's preeminence in election in his identity as the eternal object of the Father's love. Of course, this refocusing of the discussion around the blessing of the eternally beloved Son significantly orients the remaining observations' cumulative vision of the precise way in which Christ's election grounds the election and, thus, the blessing of those elect in him. *In nuce*, it is fundamentally because creatures are elect toward the end of the Father's blessing his beloved Son with a spouse that the elect Christ is himself the grounds of creatures' election as his supremely blessed body and bride.[7] Hence, it is finally because the Father's love of the Son stands at the end of his electing purposes that Edwards finds that the election of Jesus Christ grounds creatures' election and its ensuing blessings.

Although the language of freedom is absent from the Miscellany, it is clear that Edwards aims to clarify the depths of God's freedom in its immunity from the accidents of history in the blessing of Christ and those elect in him against Arminian claims that he finds to diminish such freedom. He does so by grounding the free election of both Christ and those elect in him in the freedom of the Father's loving of the Son within the blessed divine fellowship *in se*, it being this loving alone from and for which he moves as that which is enacted *ad extra* in the blessing of Christ and his bride. So it is ultimately in the context of affirming God's freedom for extending the Father's loving of the Son outside the fullness of the divine life that Edwards affirms the fittingness of God's end of blessing creatures with holiness and happiness in Christ: whereas God is not outwardly compelled to bless creatures in this way, from the freedom of the Father's loving of the Son within the blessed divine life, he freely elects to bless the Son with a bride so that the Son might be blessed in his blessing of her (a blessing that Edwards elsewhere proposes is patterned after the Son's own blessing by the Father[8]). The Son's blessing of creatures is irreducibly bound up in his free election for the

---

7. The grounding of creatures' election in Christ along these lines is ramified even further elsewhere; see note 17 below.

8. See, for instance, Edwards, "104. End of the Creation," *WJE* 13:273.

Father's blessing of him and further illuminates his preeminence in election as himself the very expression of the blessedness of their loving fellowship.

There is no suggestion that Edwards retracted the crucial grounding of Christ's election in the Father's eternal loving of the Son as outlined in the Miscellany. Yet in his *End of Creation* dissertation, Edwards significantly contextualizes his grounding of the freedom of Christ's election in the Miscellany in an effort to clarify the grounds of God's freedom to move *ad extra*, and this, in turn, significantly draws out the Miscellany's readiness for comparison with Barth.[9]

Edwards argues in the dissertation as a whole that God's glory is the supreme end of creation, God's blessing of creatures in redemption history ultimately serving his *ad extra* communication of his glorious fullness of good. Of course, lest God appear wanting in his *ad extra* movement, Edwards focuses on the freedom of this movement in its total independence from creation in its truly immanent ends. At base, God's pouring forth of his glorious fullness of good is a movement of *ad extra* glorification that follows only from his internal fullness of good rather than from a lack or threat of any kind. For his freedom for glorification is grounded in his divine delight in this glorious good *in se* inasmuch as it is "the same disposition that inclines him to delight in his glory" that "causes him to delight in the exhibitions, expressions and communications of it."[10] It is because "there is an infinite fullness of all possible good in God," and "this fullness is capable of communication or emanation *ad extra*," that it "seems a thing amiable and valuable in itself" that God might cause his glorious fullness of good to "flow forth, that this infinite fountain of good should send forth abundant streams, that this infinite fountain of light should, diffusing its excellent fullness, pour forth light all around."[11] So, just as God is utterly free in his infinite delight in his glorious good *in se*, he is free to delight in the communication of this glorious good abroad and, fittingly, does so. As a diffusion of this delight-inducing fullness, this theocentric movement does not foreclose the blessing of creatures. Rather,

---

9. As both Edwards's Miscellany 1245 and his dissertation *Concerning the End for which God Created the World* (hereafter, *End of Creation*) are the fruit of parallel lines of thought developed over the course of several years, there is good reason not to see the slightly later dissertation as supplanting the Miscellany's Christological moves.

10. *End of Creation*, WJE 8:452.

11. *WJE* 8:432–33.

similar to the way Edwards presents it in Miscellany, God's *ad extra* movement for himself guarantees it inasmuch as his glorification fittingly takes the form of communicating this good to creatures, in what is no less than bringing them to share in his blessed delight in his glorious good alongside him.[12]

Within this basic framework, Edwards tirelessly explores the depths of God's freedom in his movement toward creatures. And his famous deployment of delight and emanation language in this exploration importantly underscores. God's freedom to delight in creatures as themselves subjects of his good without undermining the total freedom of his delight in his glorious good apart from its creaturely effects.[13] However, in his grounding of the freedom of the divine delight in *ad extra* glorification in a divine "disposition" specifically following from God's internal delight in his "infinite fullness of all possible good,"[14] Edwards evinces the conviction that a true understanding of the freedom of the divine delight *in se* is threatened in attempts to conceive of the possibility that God might not have chosen to pour forth of his goodness *ad extra* and, consequently, bless creatures in this way.[15]

Consider how, in response to objections that divine sufficiency, independence, and immutability preclude God's making his own delight an end in his movement *ad extra*, Edwards insists that they do not by affirming the total freedom of this delight from the accidents of history and grounding it in the perfection of the divine life:

> God's joy is dependent on nothing besides his own act, which he exerts with an absolute and independent power. And yet, in some sense it can be truly said that God has the more delight and pleasure for the holiness and happiness of his creatures: because God would be less happy, if he was less good, or if he had not that perfection of nature which consists in a propensity of nature to diffuse of his own fullness. And he would be less happy, if it were possible for him to be hindered in

---

12. See *WJE* 8:428–444, 526–36.

13. For discussion of this and its relevance to Edwards's theology at large, see especially Kyle C. Strobel, *Jonathan Edwards's Theology: A Reinterpretation* (London: Bloomsbury T&T Clark, 2013).

14. *WJE* 8:432.

15. While the following is sympathetic to Strobel's critique of influential interpretations of Edwards's appeal to disposition at this juncture (*Jonathan Edwards's Theology*, 78–94), it is less confident that Edwards toes a relatively standard Reformed line on God's freedom in this affair.

the exercise of his goodness and his other perfections in their proper effects. But he has complete happiness, because he has these perfections, and can't be hindered in exercising and displaying them in their proper effects. And this surely is not thus, because he is dependent; but because he is independent on any other that should hinder him.[16]

Here, Edwards is clear that if God did not move *ad extra* from his delight in his glorious fullness of good, it would also be true that he is not the supremely free and happy God that he no doubt is, because his glorious good would be in some sense less than it is. On Edwards's reckoning, it is because of God's internal delight in his glorious fullness of good that his *ad extra* glorification, which fittingly blesses creatures, is free as both gloriously fitting and delightfully required. While evoking a sense of inevitability, Edwards's defense of God's delight in his movement *ad extra* is hardly a celebration of a divine self-realization. Rather, it is fundamentally a celebration of the extraordinary radiance of the abounding glory of God.

In *End of Creation*, Edwards arguably provides the basis for why it is that the Father's delight in his glorious fullness of good in the Son inevitably leads to his free loving of his Son by blessing him with a bride, it being ultimately in his blessing of creatures in the Son's own pouring forth of this glorious good that he blesses the Son and those elect in him along the lines mentioned in Miscellany 1245. So, in the dissertation, Edwards does not dissolve but details the depths of his grounding of the freedom of Christ's election, and its attendant blessing of creatures, in the loving of the blessed divine fellowship.[17] However, in doing so, he significantly contextualizes his grounding

---

16. *WJE* 8:447. While not explicit in the above quotation, Edwards's gloss on the communicative character of the divine goodness here and throughout the dissertation remains focused on its propensity for *ad extra* communication.

17. There is not space here to elucidate Edwards's complex appreciation of the relationships between the blessed fellowship of the Father and the Son in the Spirit and the divine delight in *ad extra* glorification that follows from God's blessedness in his glorious fullness of good; the relationships between these, the divine decision for *ad extra* glorification, and the logically subsequent decrees in the eternal covenant of redemption; and why the movement of divine glorification blesses the Son by blessing him with a bride, and fittingly does so by means of the Son's carrying out of the work of redemption. On these, see Christina N. Larsen, *The Glory of the Blessed Son: An Approach to the Christology of Jonathan Edwards* (London: Bloomsbury T&T Clark, forthcoming). See also Phillip Hussey, "Jesus Christ as the 'Sum of God's Decrees': Christological Supralapsarianism in the Theology of Jonathan Edwards," *Jonathan Edwards Studies* 6, no. 2 (2016): 107–19, and the literature cited therein.

of this freedom in the Miscellany. For, among other things, it clarifies that to conceive of God in the freedom of his glorious delight, entirely unbound by the accidents of history, one must conceive of him as the "infinite fountain of light" who, in the freedom of his delightful fullness of loving the Son, inevitably elects Christ. And thus, because of the Father's eternal loving of the Son, God will for eternity delight himself in his free loving of the Son in an inevitable movement of *ad extra* glorification by blessing him with a bride in a blessing of creatures with the very fullness of good in which he is eternally blessed *in se*.[18] The following will show that it is when set within this context that an anticipation of Barth in Edwards's understanding of the freedom of Christ's election is particularly clear. But first, a brief look at Barth's discussion on his own terms.

BARTH

Although space allows for merely a selective gloss of Barth's magisterial treatment of Christ's election, broad-stroke attention to his major moves in *CD* II/2 §33 taken with their development in *CD* IV/1 §59 evinces notable similarities between Edwards's and Barth's conceptions of God's freedom for creatures in this election (regardless of whatever adjustments a comparison between Edwards's and Barth's developments elsewhere might require).

After introducing the doctrine of election in §32 at the start of *CD* II/2, Barth begins to develop his radical reworking of the doctrine over the course of §33.[19] Barth opens §33 by reminding his readers that, as the Word of God in whom "God has joined himself to man," Jesus Christ is the one in whom "God reveals Himself" and discloses the truth of all things.[20] However, after orienting his readers thus, Barth quickly moves to elucidate his provocative claim in §32 that knowing election in Jesus Christ requires abandoning traditional views of double predestination, given that they obscure Christ's revelation that election is in its entirety "the whole of the Gospel, the Gospel *in*

---

18. *WJE* 8:433.

19. For analysis of this reworking in light of Barth's earlier revisions in his *Römerbrief* and the *Göttingen Dogmatics*, see Matthias Gockel, *Barth and Schleiermacher on the Doctrine of Election: A Systematic-Theological Comparison* (Oxford: Oxford University Press, 2006), 104–97. On Pierre Maury's doctrine of election and its influence on Barth's reworking, see Simon Hattrell, ed., *Election, Barth, and the French Connection: How Pierre Maury Gave a "Decisive Impetus" to Karl Barth's Doctrine of Election* (Eugene, OR: Wipf & Stock, 2016).

20. *CD* II/2, 94.

nuce."[21] A deep-seated conviction that the blessing of humanity is irreducible to the election of Christ remains inseparable from Barth's noetic concerns throughout the paragraph.

Bolstered by meditation on the Johannine Prologue, Barth argues that Jesus Christ is himself "the election of God before which and without which and beside which God cannot make any other choices," for "He is the beginning of God before which there is no other beginning apart from that of God within Himself." Election is truly *good news* because Christ "is the free grace of God as not content simply to remain identical with the inward and eternal being of God, but operating *ad extra* in the ways and works of God." And election is *only* good news because, as known in him, "Free grace is the only basis and meaning of all God's ways and works *ad extra*."[22]

More, while to know the electing God is to be led to "the sphere of His free will and pleasure," to know God in Jesus Christ alone requires fleeing from simply asserting the fact of divine sovereignty and toward clarifying its reality in Jesus Christ. On Barth's reckoning, the tradition's detachment from the gospel lies largely in a conception of free electing that "is absolutely unconditioned, or is conditioned only by the Subject in and for itself as such"—a *decretum absolutum* that cannot reveal who God truly is.[23] Rather, the Prologue's alignment of election and God's Word in Jesus Christ dispels any temptation to celebrate God's freedom thusly, given that, in this alignment, the Evangelist witnesses to a freedom "included in the choice by which God (obviously first) decides for Himself."[24] When eyes are turned toward Jesus Christ as the particular reality of this freedom, he reveals the freedom of election as God's gracious self-determination to be Jesus Christ in his covenantal blessing of humanity.

Concerns of an incipient *decretum absolutum* linger on as Barth further clarifies—again from John and in declared opposition to the tradition—that it is only as both the subject and object of election that Jesus Christ reveals God in the fullness of his gracious freedom.[25] And Barth's concern

---

21. *CD* II/2, 13–14. For Barth's initial evangelical reorientation of the doctrine in §32, see 3–18.

22. *CD* II/2, 94–95.

23. *CD* II/2, 100.

24. *CD* II/2, 101.

25. On the revelation of this gracious freedom in Jesus Christ as electing God and elected man, see *CD* II/2, 103–27, and on its implications for interpreting the double character of Barth's

for the freedom of Christ's election reaches something of a zenith in his astonishing historicization of election wherein Jesus Christ is this subject and object as himself the decree in the fullness of his history from eternity.

For Barth, Jesus Christ is the eternal decree of the God who truly reveals himself in the history of his self-giving affirmation of covenantal partnership with humanity.[26] Of course, it is not simply the reality of God's revelation in the decree but the depths of the particular freedom therein revealed that animates much of his concern. Barth contends that Jesus Christ reveals the freedom of the God who, in electing the union of God and man in Jesus Christ, is free both as the one who lovingly "pledges and commits Himself to be the God of man" apart from human coercion of any kind and as the one who completes this election as the elected man who "can and actually does elect God, thus attesting and activating himself as elected man."[27] In this, Christ reveals the freedom of God as the freedom of the one who freely lives in love in his gracious affirmation of human freedom in the covenant, entirely free from threats of synergism or collapse into world-process. And he reveals that election is the "decree of the living God" and not the decree of a God whose freedom is self-imprisoned by a past decision or arbitrary *decretum*. The God revealed in "the living person of Jesus Christ" is free in his faithful blessing of a free humanity with a living freedom and is altogether impervious to the accidents of history.[28]

By *CD* IV/1, Barth develops the implications of this historicization considerably. Space precludes engagement with debates surrounding the intent, extent, and merits of his mature "bit of 'Hegeling'" at this point and beyond, yet a cursory turn to his insistence in §59 that when one looks to God's free blessing of humanity in Christ, one must confess the freedom of God's movement *pro nobis* in light of its grounds in the Son's eternal obedience helpfully

---

supralapsarianism, see 161–75.

26. Barth here explores the astounding revelation of this as his gracious "election to suffering" (CD II/2, 120) that reveals the grace that stands at the beginning of the totality of God's work in the freedom of "the Lamb slain from the foundation of the world" (123) as well as the shocking depths of this good news in the obedience of the suffering Christ *pro nobis*, "which is the actualisation of the overflowing of the inner glory of God" (125–26); see 120–27.

27. CD II/2, 177.

28. CD II/2, 180. See also 180–88.

intensifies the comparison with Edwards, whatever one might make of Barth's developments elsewhere.[29]

In defense of Christ's deity, following a critique of kenoticisms that frustrate attempts to profess that God "is God in His unity with the creature," Barth insists in §59 that the Son's humiliation is bafflingly "natural" to the Godhead because it is no less than a "continuation" of the Son's eternal obedience to the Father.[30] Jesus Christ is truly God and truly reveals God, and when one knows him "in the form of a servant," one sees "the other and inner side of the mystery of the divine nature of Christ and therefore of the nature of the one true God" and must confess "that He Himself is also able and free to render obedience."[31] In Barth's estimation, a rejection of the Son's eternal obedience is a refusal to behold the revelation of the mystery of the God who is free for the world as the one who has freely come into the world to save it, and such subordinationism and modalism must be duly condemned in their refusal to see the work of very God in Christ's humiliation and rejected "as errors in which we cannot do justice to the mystery of the deity of Christ."[32]

Barth confesses the Son's eternal obedience to the Father in order to confess that in the Son's blessing of humanity, "He is not untrue to Himself but genuinely true to Himself, to the freedom which is that of His love."[33] Christ's

---

29. Eberhard Busch, *Karl Barth: His Life from Letters and Autobiographical Texts*, trans. John Bowden (Philadelphia: Fortress, 1976), 387. Admitting Barth's dialectical resistance to tidy summary, the following contends that Barth's discussion of the Son's eternal obedience in §59 is concerned, among other things, to establish the antecedent grounds of God's freedom for the creature in Christ's election that follows from the fullness of God's blessed fellowship apart from the creature. While the brevity of this comparative project does not permit engagement with the English and German literature relevant to recent debate on the relationship between election and the Trinity in Barth's thought, the antecedent grounds of God's freedom for the creature has been conceived of variously (see, for instance, George Hunsinger, *Reading Barth with Charity: A Hermeneutical Proposal* [Grand Rapids: Baker Academic, 2015], 88–113; and Tyler R. Wittman, *God and Creation in the Theology of Thomas Aquinas and Karl Barth* [Cambridge: Cambridge University Press, 2019], 129–250) and in tension with particular interpretations of Barth's "actualism" (see especially Bruce McCormack, "Grace and Being: The Role of God's Gracious Election in Karl Barth's Theological Ontology," in *The Cambridge Companion to Karl Barth*, ed. John Webster [Cambridge: Cambridge University Press, 2000], 92–110). Nonetheless, even those less inclined to appreciate in Barth a concern for the antecedent grounds of God's freedom for the creature might appreciate in Edwards and Barth something of a shared impulse to know God's freedom in election *in concreto*, albeit in very different ways.

30. *CD* IV/1, 183, 192, 203.

31. *CD* IV/1, 193.

32. *CD* IV/1, 197. See also 196–97 and 199–200.

33. *CD* IV/1, 193.

humiliating acts "are marked off by their characterisation as an act of obedience from the accidental events of nature or destiny" because of the total
freedom of the Son's movement *pro nobis* from that which is not God.[34] Only
the freedom of the divine life grounds the freedom of this life in the world,
and "He is in and for the world what He is in and for Himself."[35] Fully aware
that the mystery of divine humiliation "offends" beloved caricatures of God's
freedom, Barth nonetheless proclaims this mystery lest he blasphemously
conceive of the relationship between the Father and the Son as in some sense
dependent on something beyond itself.[36] God's "free grace" is "originally in
Himself," so here "we are in fact dealing with an overflowing, not with a filling up of the perfection of God which needs no filling" and therefore must
confess the glory of its source within the fellowship of the blessed divine life.[37]

In sum, for Barth, "Election is that which takes place at the very center
of the divine self-revelation," and so he distances himself from traditional
conceptions of the doctrine in their supposed failures to proclaim who God
is in the fullness of his loving freedom as so clearly manifest in the history
of Jesus Christ.[38] While talk of God's freedom and love is not absent from
such accounts, Barth finds that they do not speak in truth because they do
not recognize that it is "the light of this election" that reveals them and that,
in this election, "the whole of the Gospel is light" and is directed toward the
blessing of humanity.[39] Barth's cries against a *decretum absolutum* are part
and parcel of his sustained lament that true sight of God's freedom is often
missed because it is sought elsewhere than in God's movement of blessing
humanity in the election of Jesus Christ. Instead, proclamation of *this* God's
loving freedom is what is required. And Jesus Christ reveals the freedom of
God in his reconciliation of God and humanity without compromise to the
freedom of either, totally free from internal or external impediment as he
moves from the freedom of the loving fellowship of the Father and Son in the
fullness of its obedient shape alone. It is only when one knows the freedom
of Christ's election in the fullness of such historical particularity, rather than

34. *CD* IV/1, 194.
35. *CD* IV/1, 204.
36. *CD* IV/1, 192.
37. *CD* IV/1, 201.
38. *CD* II/2, 59.
39. *CD* II/2, 14.

in the abstract, that one properly knows the eternal freedom from whence the good news of God's free blessing of creatures so naturally follows.

EDWARDS AND BARTH PUSHING
BOUNDARIES FROM WITHIN

As indicated above, both Edwards and Barth exhibit a sustained concern to underscore the freedom of God's movement *pro nobis* in Christ's election from the accidents of history in order to establish the proper grounds of God's blessing of creatures. Responsibly comparing their respective approaches is complicated because they address distinct theological frustrations, and it would not seem fair to say that Edwards anticipates Barth's most precious moves given their clear divergence at crucial points. Yet despite the substantive differences between the two, their shared affirmation of a radical correspondence between the freedom of God in the fullness of his blessed fellowship *in se* and this freedom in his movement *pro nobis* is notable, especially because in their affirmations they similarly push the boundaries set by their Reformed orthodox forebears.

First, consider how in their descriptions of the freedom that grounds God's freedom *pro nobis* in Christ's election, both Edwards and Barth attend to the *pro nobis* manifestation of this freedom. Although such an approach is hardly original, Edwards and Barth share a notable drive to know God's freedom in this way so that, by reflecting on his freedom in the fullness of its particularity *in se* in view of its *pro nobis* expression, they might clarify how it is that God's free blessing of creatures follows from the freedom of the blessed divine fellowship alone.

In Miscellany 1245, Edwards addresses God's freedom in consideration of what it means to be chosen in Christ, establishing God's absolute freedom from creation in his choosing of his elect. To this end, Edwards no less than Barth grounds the freedom of Christ's election in the freedom of the Father's eternal loving of the Son within the blessed divine fellowship, as it is this that guarantees that the fundamental aim of his choosing is not the blessing of creatures but the loving of the Son. Of course, in order to do so, Edwards describes the internal freedom that grounds God's free electing of Christ in view of the shape of its *pro nobis* enactment. Here Edwards confesses that it is the internal freedom of the Father's loving of the Son that grounds God's freedom for creatures in Christ's election, given that it is finally the

Father's external loving of the Son, in his appropriate blessing of him with a bride, that is achieved in this movement. Edwards appeals to Ephesians and Colossians to argue that it is the Father's freedom to love the Son in this *ad extra* mode that grounds his freedom for creatures instead of the other way around. Yet he does so with a sense that it is only by clarifying the internal ground of God's freedom in view of the particular economic contours decreed by God that one might know that God's freedom *in se* is the sole ground of Christ's free election and its attendant blessing of creatures, rather than allow a sense that the freedom of God's movement *pro nobis* in Christ is in any way conditioned by the accidents of history. In *End of Creation*, Edwards similarly confesses God's total freedom from such accidents in his *ad extra* movement by confessing God's freedom for *ad extra* glorification in terms of God's delight in his glorious fullness of good *in se*, with the recognition that it is ultimately this same delight that is expressed in his glorification.[40]

While undoubtedly distinct in focus, Barth's approach as outlined in §33 and developed in his discussion of the Son's obedience in §59 shares remarkable similarities. In nearly constant celebration of the total freedom of the divine life from all that is not God, Barth's discussion of Christ's election confesses this freedom in its movement for creatures in Jesus Christ as the one in whom God's freedom is known in its decidedly particular shape. Carefully vindicating God of any suggestion that his freedom *pro nobis* is in some sense dependent upon the accidents of history, Barth's historicized approach looks to the free blessing of creatures in Jesus Christ and, from the astounding revelation of its humiliating contours, confesses its grounds in the freedom of the Son's eternal obedience within the blessed divine fellowship. The freedom revealed in the humiliation of Jesus Christ *pro nobis* is grounded not merely in the fullness of God's eternal free loving in a general sense but in this free loving according to its obedient contours, given that God's freedom *pro nobis* follows solely from the blessedness of the divine life *in se* and not in part from a "capricious choice of lowliness."[41] To "accept the humiliation and lowliness and supremely the obedience of Christ as the dominating moment in our conception of God" and thus declare the internal grounds of his humiliation,

---

40. For discussion of how these points connect with Edwards's conception of ultimate ends in *End of Creation*, see Larsen, *Glory of the Blessed Son*.

41. *CD* IV/1, 193.

Barth confesses God's freedom *in se* according to the fullness of its particularity *pro nobis* wherein such obedience is revealed.[42]

For both Edwards and Barth, confession of the internal freedom that grounds God's movement *pro nobis* in Christ's election must be configured in view of the particular *pro nobis* manifestation of this freedom, as if configuring it otherwise would fail to establish that God's blessing of creatures follows only from the free loving of the blessed divine fellowship. Indeed, this focus on God's freedom is not a mere affirmation of divine sovereignty—though affirm this it does—but an affirmation that to speak of the freedom of God is to speak of the blessing of creatures because of the fullness of the divine loving in which this freedom internally consists and so naturally commits itself abroad to creatures. Their respective celebrations of God's freedom for this blessing are, in this, fundamentally celebrations of the revelation of the loving fellowship in which God is supremely blessed and free to bless creatures by bringing them to share in his blessed enjoyment of himself. And one might further appreciate that this is so that, for both, in the light of this revelation, to know God's freedom is not to speculate about hypotheticals but to be blessed by the free loving of the Father, Son, and Holy Spirit that, in no other than an "emanation" or "overflowing" of this free loving, frees creatures to share in the blessedness of this fellowship.

Of course, in the particular way that they do so, both Edwards and Barth effectively suggest that the freedom of God's movement *pro nobis* in Christ's election follows from a radical correspondence between this movement and the reality of his freedom *in se*, such that they press against the Reformed orthodox impulse to affirm God's freedom of indifference in his free willing of creatures, minimizing the notion that God might have not willed to move *ad extra* or have willed to move *ad extra* in some other way. As stressed by Francis Turretin, a key figure in the development of this view within the tradition, it is integral to God's freedom in this affair that "he wills all things as that he could not will them," this being moreover "the greatest proof of his perfection who, as an independent being, needs nothing out of himself."[43]

---

42. *CD* IV/1, 199.

43. Francis Turretin, *Institutes of Elenctic Theology*, trans. George Musgrave Giger, ed. James T. Dennison, Jr., vol. 1 (Phillipsburg, NJ: P&R, 1992), 219 (3.14.5, 7); see also 3.14.3. The standard view affirmed that for both God and humans, a free choice involves a "root indifference" in the will *in actu primo* characterized by freedom of contrariety (and thus freedom of contradiction)

Edwards and Barth eagerly retain hallmarks of the tradition's reflections on God's freedom for creatures: they appeal to the notion of God's willed decree in order to profess the gratuity of God's movement *pro nobis* with the conviction that God's blessedness does not depend on the creature in any way, and their protracted explications of God's total freedom from the accidents of history convey God's freedom of spontaneity such that no external compulsion or constraint bears upon his movement *pro nobis* in Christ. However, insofar as both establish the latter by particularizing God's freedom *in se* with a tone stressing the total fittingness of his movement *pro nobis* in Christ's election, to the degree that this move is the *most* natural movement God might make because of its radical correspondance to the freedom of God in his blessed fellowship *in se*, they at the very least significantly complicate traditional appeals to God's freedom in his *pro nobis* turn.

In Miscellany 1245, Edwards focuses on the supreme fittingness of God's free movement *pro nobis* in Christ's election, wherein, given its correspondence to the eternal divine loving, it was God's good pleasure to express the Father's eternal loving of the Son *ad extra* in his blessing of the Son with "an object for the object of his infinite grace and love."[44] Yet, when this Miscellany is interpreted in the context of *End of Creation*, it is abundantly clear that the suggestion that God might not have willed that the divine loving be enacted in this blessing of Christ and, in turn, creatures, is absurd because in this loving "there is an infinite fullness of all possible good in God."[45] Here, Edwards only explores the possibility that God might not have willed to glorify himself as he has done in order to showcase the poverty of such a statement when one is talking about the freedom of God's exuberant delight in his glorious fullness of good. Rather, "his infinite love to himself and delight in himself will naturally cause him to value and delight in these things."[46] So God's freedom

---

that is overcome by deliberation—though, of course, this does not involve temporal sequence in the case of God. Richard A. Muller, "Jonathan Edwards and the Absence of Free Choice: A Parting of Ways in the Reformed Tradition," *Jonathan Edwards Studies* 1, no. 1 (2011): 3–22 (20). See also note 46 below.

44. *WJE* 23:179.

45. *WJE* 8:432.

46. *WJE* 8:436. For appraisal of Edwards's abandonment of God's freedom of indifference, see Oliver D. Crisp, *Jonathan Edwards on God and Creation* (Oxford: Oxford University Press, 2012), 57–76; and see Philip John Fisk, *Jonathan Edwards's Turn from the Classic-Reformed Tradition of Freedom of the Will* (Göttingen: Vandenhoeck & Ruprecht, 2016) for extensive analysis of Edwards's broader departures from Reformed conceptions of the freedom of the will, including

to delight in his glorious fullness *pro nobis* radically corresponds to his freedom to delight in it *in se* such that it would be a disservice to the blessedness
of the Father's eternal loving of the Son to suggest that God might not have
willed that the divine loving pour forth in this way.

Although Barth affirms in asides that God "does what He does, but without any claim arising that He must do it, or that He must do it in this or that
way," his continual move to know God's freedom *pro nobis* in Jesus Christ follows Edwards's broad impulse and resists considering such hypotheticals.[47]
Barth's suggestions that God might not have acted as he in fact has done
cannot be detached from Barth's perpetual fear that speculation along these
lines inevitably raises suspicion that God is ultimately hidden behind Jesus
Christ. And so, while offering a genuine safeguard in Barth's dialectic, they
nonetheless function alongside an unease about affirming the viability of
God's freedom for these counterfactuals and a confidence that proclaiming
the reality of God's freedom for creatures in Christ is the more important
guard against notions that God is in need of the creature or in any way compelled from within or without. Further, though admittedly cryptic,[48] when

---

his "argument for moral necessity as a freedom of perfection" (351) wherein "the further a
moral agent is removed from indifference, the freer he or she is" (416). One might note that
Paul Helm has challenged Richard Muller's contention that Edwards significantly departs from
the Reformed orthodox when he does not find the will's indifference *in actu primo* integral to
free choice. Helm argues that Edwards sets forth a "compatibilism" that is not the same as but
more akin to the "compatibilism" one finds among the Reformed orthodox. For their current
debate on these points as well as discussion of how Reformed approaches to indifference differ
from Jesuit views, see, most recently, Paul Helm, "Francis Turretin and Jonathan Edwards on
Compatibilism," *Journal of Reformed Theology* 12, no. 4 (2018): 335–55; Richard A. Muller, "Neither
Libertarian nor Compatibilist," *Journal of Reformed Theology* 13, no. 3-4 (2019): 267–86; and the
literature cited therein.

47. *CD* II/2, 11. Wittman suggests that Barth appears "to affirm something like the *libertas
indifferentiae*," but as he "complicates the traditional function … It is more accurate in this regard
to interpret Barth as retaining a thin account of the *libertas contrarietatis* and *contradictionis*." Still,
Wittman appreciates that several find Barth's "hypothetical counterfactual" pronouncements
to be formal rather than material (*God and Creation*, 239 n. 120 and n. 121).

48. Questions of Bromiley's use of "subordination" in the English translation aside, in Barth's
elucidation of this obedience as an intra-trinitarian *prius* and *posterius*, he vigorously attempts
to recast assumptions that such an ordering necessarily "includes a gradation, a degradation
and an inferiority in God." However, insofar as he insists that the "One who obeys in humility"
contrasts with the "majesty" of the "One who rules and commands," it is difficult to escape the
sense that Barth espouses more than an account of divine *taxis* (*CD* IV/1, 202, Barth's stressing
of the oneness of the divine being notwithstanding). See Paul D. Molnar, *Faith, Freedom and the
Spirit: The Economic Trinity in Barth, Torrance and Contemporary Theology* (Downers Grove, IL:
IVP Academic, 2015), 331–40. Of course, Barth's protracted clarifications to acquit himself of
subordinationism or of condoning a reading of the economic Trinity back into the immanent

Barth in §59 moves to hail Christ's humiliation as the "logical final continuation" of the Son's eternal obedience in an effort to stay accusations of divine caprice, Barth is all but strained to the breaking point.[49] His confident reasoning from the humiliation of Jesus Christ to the Son's eternal obedience belies a conviction in a radical correspondence between God's freedom *in se* and *pro nobis* that cannot imagine that God might not have moved to freely bless creatures as he has done because of the very contours of the loving fellowship in which he eternally dwells.

The above are effectively observations of inflection in the case of Barth. However, timbre cannot be ignored when deployed so overtly to forestall perceived theological disaster—Barth's dread of the nominalist threat to the church's confession that God is who he is in Jesus Christ is hardly peripheral. Clearly, for both Edwards and Barth, it is from the free loving of the blessed divine fellowship alone that God freely moves to bless creatures in Christ's election. And confession of God's freedom that presses toward the inevitability of this free blessing better acknowledges the nature of its loving gratuity—and the reconciling effect of its revelation—than does confession of the possibility that God might not have willed such blessing.

While Edwards's and Barth's meditations on the freedom of Christ's election have no shortage of additional parallels that might be pursued elsewhere (such as their eccentric lapsarian accounts, innovative theodicies, and tendencies to be read in both historicizing and eternalizing extremes), one should not collapse their views in appreciation of convictions they share. Beyond the issue of the divergent polemical and exegetical matters that center their respective approaches, Edwards remains committed to the very view of double predestination that Barth rejects, celebrating the freedom of God's good pleasure in the election of individuals so that the gratuity of God's glorious grace might illuminate the praises of the redeemed.[50] Edwards's move suffers no qualms about the veracity of the good news revealed in an understanding of election that is not an unequivocal "yes" to humanity in

---

Trinity make it difficult to escape the sense that even he is not entirely satisfied with his move at this point.

49. *CD* IV/1, 203. Admitting the possibility of translating "logical final continuation" otherwise (see Paul D. Molnar, *Divine Freedom and the Doctrine of the Immanent Trinity*, 2nd ed. [London: Bloomsbury T&T Clark, 2017], 544), this point on practice nonetheless stands.

50. See *WJE* 23:180 and 18:417.

Christ (and the worry that God's freedom would be imprisoned by a decree not in the form of a history is never a concern). However, Barth finds that a double predestination in the election of Christ is what guarantees that this glorious grace is truly good news from the one who is not "incomprehensible darkness" but "incomprehensible light."[51] Even the overarching tones of each project do not sound perfectly harmonious: whereas both find God's freedom for the creature in Christ to follow in some sense from his freedom for himself within the blessed divine fellowship, Barth would hardly be impressed with Edwards's stress on creaturely blessing as a consequential—albeit irreducible—end in God's *ad extra* designs, while Edwards, surely, would worry that Barth does not sufficiently stress that the eternally beloved Son must be the beloved end of all of God's works.

Yet differences aside, both are confident that God is revealed in Christ's election as the one who in his free loving blesses creatures in a free pouring forth of this loving, such that, in the fullness of his blessed fellowship, God is light as the light of the world that blesses creatures with the illuminating communication of himself.[52] It is with this truly shared conviction that both Edwards and Barth resist key means by which their tradition affirms the unapproachability of this light and its freedom for immeasurable radiance within its blessed fellowship. However, it is here that they likewise supply ample resource for discussion—perhaps such as one finds in Jenson—of the blessed God who in the depths of his loving freedom is the unchanging Father of lights and in Christ generously gives himself to be known. Still, the best of this discussion will recognize that Edwards and Barth, even as they push traditional boundaries, do so in an expression of their predecessors' hope to proclaim the astounding freedom of God's love.[53]

---

51. *CD* II/2, 146. For discussion of Edwards's and Barth's differences on the contentious topic of reprobation, see Stephen R. Holmes, *God of Grace and God of Glory* (Edinburgh: T&T Clark, 2000), 199–272, and Oliver D. Crisp, "Karl Barth and Jonathan Edwards on Reprobation (and Hell)," in *Engaging with Barth: Contemporary Evangelical Critiques*, ed. David Gibson and Daniel Strange (New York: T&T Clark, 2008), 300–22.

52. One might note that both Edwards and Barth appear to be influenced by Mastricht in their particular conceptions of the glory of God, including its radiant communication to creatures. On the theme of divine light "after Barth"—which in some key respects also applies after Edwards—with a nod to Mastricht's influential account, see Ivor J. Davidson, "Divine Light: Some Reflections after Barth," in *Trinitarian Theology After Barth*, ed. Myk Habets and Phillip Tolliday (Eugene: Pickwick, 2011), 48–69.

53. I am grateful to Ivor Davidson and Steven Duby for their comments on this chapter.

4

—

CHRIST

Darren Sumner

There is vanishing evidence that Karl Barth—so versed in the post-Reformation scholastic tradition and in European theology of the nineteenth and twentieth centuries—ever had direct encounter with the work of Jonathan Edwards.[1] While both were nourished by the Reformed tradition, they labored in different centuries and on different continents, Edwards driven by preaching and the daily requirements of congregational ministry and Barth by the lecture cycle and the tangible needs of the German and Swiss churches before and after the Second World War. Edwards was a leader in American Pietism and the Great Awakenings, but Barth was famously critical of pietism (though he maintained an affection for Christoph Blumhardt). When we compare their theologies on a rather seminal topic—the doctrine of the person of Jesus Christ—on the surface we find just what we would expect: common affirmations of the ancient creeds, rejection of Christological heresies, and accounts of the incarnation of the Son of God done in a broadly Reformed mode.

However, there is between Edwards and Barth a set of commonalities owed less to Reformed orthodoxy and more to the intellectual freedoms exercised by both men. In both cases, their Christologies evince a desire to think with but also beyond the classical formulations of the Reformed scholastics. Both draw freely on the Reformed tradition, philosophy, and a sometimes *ad*

---

1. Edwards was of some interest to the German Pietists, who had translated certain works already in the eighteenth century—including publishing the *Faithful Narrative* by Johann Steinmetz in 1738. See Jan Stievermann, "Faithful Translations: New Discoveries on the German Pietist Reception of Jonathan Edwards," *Church History* 83, no. 2 (2014): 324–66. Barth's English was never strong.

hoc biblical interpretation without feeling bound and determined by specific articles of the Reformed confessions. Only Scripture, in its bearing witness to the free work of God in Jesus Christ, was to bind the consciences of theologian and preacher alike.

This essay will focus primarily on these areas where Barth and Edwards moved freely and at times at an oblique angle from the traditional doctrine and as a result coincidentally found themselves in similar territory with one another.[2] The common rhetoric within their Christologies is remarkable, since Barth neither read Edwards nor shared many of his more significant influences. Moreover, while Edwards took his departure from a philosophical idealism, Barth's project is critically realistic.[3] Thus, where they arrived at similar conclusions regarding the person and work of Jesus Christ, they came there by different routes.

It should be said that Christology permeates both bodies of work—not surprising, given the distributed nature of Christological teaching within Christian doctrine as well as its priority within Reformed thought. Without any claim of comprehensiveness, I will focus primarily on Edwards's 1734 sermon "The Excellency of Christ" and Barth's mature Christology as presented in volume IV of *Church Dogmatics*.[4] Also crucial to Edwards's (sometimes experimental) views are *A History of the Work of Redemption* (1739)[5] and

---

2. In so doing, I will presume the basic orthodoxy of both Edwards and Barth, each of whom in his own way affirmed the conciliar judgments of Nicaea, Constantinople, Ephesus, and Chalcedon. Space does not permit a full exposition of either theologian's Christology. For that, on Barth see Paul D. Jones, *The Humility of Christ* (London: T&T Clark, 2008) and Darren O. Sumner, *Karl Barth and the Incarnation* (London: T&T Clark, 2014). For monograph-length treatments of Edwards's Christology, see the unpublished dissertations of Michael David Bush, *Jesus Christ in the Theology of Jonathan Edwards* (Princeton Theological Seminary, 2003) and Joseph Crawford Williamson, *The Excellency of Christ: A Study in the Christology of Jonathan Edwards* (Harvard, 1968).

3. Amy Plantinga Pauw, *"The Supreme Harmony of All": The Trinitarian Theology of Jonathan Edwards* (Grand Rapids: Eerdmans, 2002), 52–53; Bruce L. McCormack, *Karl Barth's Critically Realistic Dialectical Theology* (Oxford: Clarendon, 1995).

4. Edwards, *Sermons and Discourses, 1734-1738*, WJE 19:560–94.

5. WJE 9. This work took the form of a series of sermons preached over the spring and summer of 1739. Edwards intended to return to the material and produce a fully developed theological treatise under this title but was prevented from doing so by his new duties as head of the college in Princeton (soon followed by his untimely death). The sermons survived as a sort of rough draft of Edwards's grand ambition, and a decade and a half later, they were published by his friend John Erskine, a Scottish clergyman, under the title Edwards had intended to use for the treatise (Edinburgh, 1774). Erskine also edited the sermons into the form of a continuous treatise, altering the divisions and subdivisions of the work to suit.

The "Miscellanies."[6] Both Edwards and Barth tend to contemplate Christ's person not *in abstracto* but particularly as it pertains to his redemptive work, so that statements about his divine and human natures, his two states of humility and glory, and his unity with the triune God typically serve the theologians' exegetical descriptions of Christ's activity in the world. My thesis is that despite their relative differences, both represent the best of Reformed theology.

THE "EXCELLENCIES" OF CHRIST

Perhaps Jonathan Edwards's richest reflections on Christ's person are in the 1734 sermon. Christ's "excellencies" are his personal attributes, which he receives from either his divine nature or his human nature, or in some cases which are created by the union of those two natures in him. For example, Robert Jenson suggests, Christ's dominion is earned for his divine nature by virtue of his human suffering, while his obedience "is a human manifestation of the trinitarian being-begotten."[7] In these cases both natures are implicated, as for Edwards these sorts of attributes make sense only in the context of the incarnation.

In this sermon, Edwards creatively interprets Revelation 5:5–6—in which Jesus is described as both the "Lamb of God" and the "Lion of Judah"—within the broad context of the ancient doctrine of the communication of attributes (*communicatio idiomatum*). From the ancient church and through the Reformation period, this doctrine insists on speaking of Jesus as enjoying both divine and human attributes at one and the same time. In its earliest interpretations of the New Testament, the church regarded this as a necessary consequence of what would become the two-natures doctrine. Jesus is both God and human, not one and then the other. If his divinity is not set aside at his incarnation, and if the Son's humanity is full and complete, then he must possess all of the qualities that are proper to both of those natures. (This is still true even where the attributes appear to be in conflict, which was the subject of much debate—rising to particular prominence in Cyril

---

6. *WJE* 13, 18, 20, and 23. Of particular importance to the doctrine of Christ's person are Miscellanies 454, 487, 709, 727, 738, and 1219. On the incarnation, life, and work of Christ, also see especially Sermons 13–19.

7. Robert W. Jenson, *America's Theologian: A Recommendation of Jonathan Edwards* (Oxford: Oxford University Press, 1988), 117.

of Alexandria's dispute with Nestorius in the fifth century.) Those qualities are "communicated" without diminishment to his person, which is the locus of the union.

Edwards (and Barth after him) affirms the traditional doctrine such as it is.[8] But in the pulpit, he is more interested in reasoning through the extremities of divine highness and creaturely lowness than he is in "attributes" as we might delineate them more mundanely (e.g., human finitude, passibility, a capacity for hunger and fatigue, etc.). What matters is not what Christ is like, metaphysically described, but rather how the dynamic contrast of these attributes (the "conjunction of excellencies") displays the glory of God in the work of redemption.

Edwards's plan for the sermon then is to explore the implicit contrast of the triumphant "Lion of Judah" and the slain "Lamb of God" by means of seven pairs of attributes in Christ. Like the Lion and the Lamb, the divine and the human, the transcendent and the immanent, these attributes seem at first glance to stand in opposition to one another: Christ's glory and humility, majesty and meekness, and so on. Must not one of these give way to the other? For Edwards, the interplay between them instead displays the real miracle of the gospel. "Christ appeared at the same time, and in the same act, as both a lion and a lamb," both the meek victim who is slain by his enemies and the triumphant one conquering and destroying his real enemy, Satan. "And in nothing has Christ appeared so much as a lion, in glorious strength destroying his enemies, as when he was brought as a lamb to the slaughter: in his greatest weakness, he was most strong; and when he suffered most from his enemies, he brought the greatest confusion on his enemies."[9]

Thus, the interesting thing about the incarnation is not simply the miraculous proximity of Jesus' divinity to his humanity. It is not only the possibility that these two hold together, in the words of Chalcedon, without division or separation and without confusion or change. The "excellency" of the incarnation of God the Son is that his power and glory are displayed precisely *in and through* weakness and humility rather than in spite of these. This provides Edwards with his rhetorical strategy for the sermon. The seven pairs of Christ's "excellencies" are, in brief:

8. *WJE* 23:153–54.
9. *WJE* 19:580–81.

Glory and *humility*. Though God is not prideful, "humility is not properly predicable of God the Father, and the Holy Ghost."[10] Humility is a radical "comparative lowness and littleness before God," and it belongs to a
created nature. Thus, while God possesses all divine glory, Edwards says, it
is uniquely in the incarnation of Jesus Christ that this glory is miraculously
conjoined with humility.[11]

Majesty and *meekness*. The dispositions of the lion and of the lamb also
meet only in Christ. Edwards calls meekness "a calmness and quietness of
spirit arising from humility,"[12] and so, like humility, it is a creaturely virtue.

Reverence toward and *equality with God*. In his time on earth, Jesus maintained the most reverential posture toward God the Father, which includes
his prayers. And yet at the same time, during this sojourn, Jesus himself
remained fully divine—equal to the Father to whom he showed reverence.
It is not a contradiction but yet another expression of his humility that Jesus
did not consider his equality with God as something to be exploited (Phil 2:6).
And it is not merely the adoration of a creature, but "it was a thing infinitely
honorable to God, that a person of infinite dignity was not ashamed to call
him his God, and to adore and obey him as such."[13] Again, what is special
here is not that a human showed reverence to God but that one who is himself worthy of worship instead worships God in humility.

Worthiness of good and *patience in the face of evil*. Edwards turns to the real
conflict of the sermon when he writes of Jesus' perfect innocence, undeserv-
ing of suffering or punishment but wholly worthy of infinite love and esteem
from God and from other men and women. It is remarkable to Edwards not
only that Christ suffered what he did not deserve but that in a deeper dimension he unified that unjust suffering with his own great worth. It is one thing
for the innocent to suffer for the unrighteous but something much more
profound for the *righteous* God of glory to be the one who suffers in this way
(1 Pet 3:18). And it is greater still that Jesus was perfectly patient in enduring

---

10. *WJE* 19:568.

11. This will have further implications for Christian ethics. On Christ's humility as a moral
model for humanity, see Elizabeth Agnew Cochran, "Creaturely Virtues in Jonathan Edwards:
The Significance of Christology for the Moral Life," in *Journal of the Society of Christian Ethics*
27, no. 2 (2007): 73–95.

12. *WJE* 19:568.

13. *WJE* 18:142.

this ignominy, "the greatest sufferings that ever were endured in this world!"[14] Such a conjunction of innocence, worthiness, and patience is again utterly unique in Jesus.[15]

A *spirit of obedience* and *dominion over heaven and earth*. Jesus is lord of all first by right, as he is God, and second by delegation from the Father as his vicegerent. And yet he showed "the greatest spirit of obedience to the commands and law of God that ever was in the universe."[16] Such perfect obedience—not only in act but in reverent devotion—is to be found nowhere else in all of creation, not among the angels, and certainly not among human beings. In obeying God, he not only displays his glory in humility but wins for us our justification by both his obedience and his endurance of punishment.[17]

Absolute sovereignty and *perfect resignation*. God's decrees are equally Christ's own decrees, and all of God's works are his works. And yet when he drew near to the hour of suffering and was sorrowful even unto death (Matt 26:38), Jesus "was absolutely and perfectly resigned."[18] He did not assert his sovereignty, either over those wicked men who were inflicting suffering on him or over his own creaturely flesh, that it might suffer a little less as it bore the lashes. In his mortal agony, he did not cease to bear the peace of God and indeed to *reign over* his situation—thus entering into it freely.

Self-sufficiency and an entire *trust and reliance on God*. Christ's self-sufficiency arises from his identity as God, who has no dependency on creation but on whom all things are dependent.[19] And yet he placed his own trust entirely in God's deliverance (Matt 27:43) and committed himself to the Father's will. In entering into our nature and embracing the vulnerability of suffering and death, the one who depends on nothing else made himself to be radically dependent on the providence of God the Father.

---

14. *WJE* 19:570.

15. Such sufferings would have overcome any mere creature, Edwards says elsewhere, but Christ's divinity supported his humanity and "kept him from sinking, and his courage from utterly failing." *WJE* 18:353.

16. *WJE* 19:570.

17. See also Miscellanies 161 (*WJE* 13:319) and 261 (*WJE* 13:368).

18. *WJE* 19:571.

19. Edwards here makes an explicit affirmation of the ancient doctrine of the Son's eternal generation from the Father (*WJE* 19:571–72). This generation he says was "natural and necessary" and not arbitrary or based on the Father's willing.

This conjunction of diverse attributes marvelously appeared through the whole course of Jesus' life, Edwards concludes—in his conception in the womb of a poor virgin and the manner of his birth, in the form of his public ministry ("he had no place to lay his head") and the relationships he maintained, in his miracle working and casting out demons, and finally in his suffering and sacrifice for sinners.[20] The fact that such contrasting qualities somehow held together in Christ is, again, wholly unique: "There do meet in the person of Christ, such really diverse excellencies, which otherwise would have been thought utterly incompatible in the same subject; such as are conjoined in no other person whatever, either divine, human, or angelical; and such as neither men nor angels would ever have imagined could have met together in the same person, had it not been seen in the person of Christ."[21]

This miraculous conjunction is still manifested now, in Jesus' exalted state in heaven, because his human nature endures and has not been cast aside. This, Edwards says, is why in John's eschatological vision Jesus still appears as a lamb (Rev 14:1), yet is compared to a lion.[22] And the conjunction of excellencies will be manifested in Christ's final judgment at the end of redemption history: when the Lion of the tribe of Judah is seated on his throne, Edwards proclaims, all will flee and hide "from the face and wrath of the Lamb."[23]

COMMON ACTUALIZATION

Karl Barth's treatment of Christ's divine and human attributes is noticeably similar at points, particularly in the desire to read the contrast between Christ's "excellencies" in subversively oppositional ways. For Barth too, the coincidence of finitude and infinitude in Jesus is cause for worshiping God in awe and for a theology that is playfully paradoxical rather than a metaphysical puzzle in need of a rational solution.[24]

---

20. WJE 19:573–81. Edwards elaborates on how these attributes are made evident in the life of Christ in seven ways (WJE 19:576–81). As he moves through each one, he weaves them together: each virtue demonstrated by Christ in his suffering is further proof of those previously identified—his holiness compounding his honor, his honor his obedience, his obedience his love, etc.

21. WJE 19:567.

22. WJE 19:581.

23. WJE 19:582. Edwards appears to be interpolating lamb imagery into the judgment scene of Revelation 20:11–15—though not without reason (cf. Rev. 22:1–3).

24. In this regard, Barth's and Edwards's posture toward the doctrine of incarnation is classically Reformed. By contrast, it was the Lutheran theological tradition that tended to approach the union of natures as a dilemma for Christology's logical coherence. Christ cannot be fully human

Already in *CD* II, Barth had adopted the strategy of pairing together the traditional attributes of God in unexpected and provocative ways, utilizing contrast and counterintuition to describe the God of the Bible. God's character as *gracious* is seen in the light of his radical *holiness*, for example. God's *mercy* toward sinners is illuminated by God's affirmation of himself as *righteous*: "As He is merciful, He is righteous. He is merciful as He really makes demands and correspondingly punishes and rewards."[25] And God's *omnipotence* is understood not flatly, as naked power to do anything, but rather as God's unwavering fidelity to himself, to be the God he will be—the attribute of divine *constancy*.

Thus, Edwards's strategy of illuminating divine and human attributes by means of their proximity to one another (rather than each in contradistinction to the other) will also be at home in Barth's thought. This is seen when Barth treats the two-natures doctrine most extensively in *CD* IV/2. But it also appears first on a grander scale when one looks at the table of contents for Volume IV (the doctrine of reconciliation, which occupied Barth for most of his final two decades on earth).[26] In turning to the person and work of Christ, he establishes from the outset his conviction that Jesus cannot be known apart from the union of the divine and human in his person. That is, the theologian should not treat his divine life and qualities first, and in abstraction, and only then turn to the incarnation and the whole career of his humanity. He cannot be apprehended only as the Logos *asarkos*, whose humanity is reducible to a mere instrument (perhaps out of the theologian's misplaced sense of reverence), any more than he can be only another figure from antiquity whose life and meaning are open to the historian's critical reconstruction. The division between the "Jesus of history" and the "Christ of faith" is untenable; neither can produce Jesus as he really is. Who is Jesus

---

in all his experiences unless his divine power (including omnipotence, omniscience, etc.) was somehow isolated or qualified—for example, so that Jesus' expression of his ignorance (Mark 13:32) may be a true, human ignorance and not a mere figure of speech. Thus, it is primarily the Lutheran theologians who have proposed kenotic Christologies of various forms in order to find a suitable explanation for those apparent tensions that Edwards, Barth, and many other Reformed theologians more readily embraced.

25. *CD* II/1, 383.

26. *CD* IV/1 appeared in German in 1953, and Volume IV/2, in 1955. The final part-volume to be issued before Barth's retirement was IV/3, in 1959. A fourth and final piece of this lengthy treatment of the doctrine of reconciliation was incomplete at Barth's death in 1968, and Volume V was never begun.

as God, as one of the Trinity? He is the Lord as *Servant*, the obedient Son of God who goes into the far country, the Judge who is judged in our place.[27] And who is he *as human*, the child born in Bethlehem? He is none but the Servant as *Lord*, the royal Son of Man who returns home in triumph.[28]

Barth will thus recast the classical discussion of Christ's two natures in more active terms, in which divinity and humanity are mutually implicated in all that the theologian says about Jesus Christ as the *event* of God's being *pro nobis*. Rather than two "natures" as metaphysical abstractions (i.e., a list of attributes) or as concrete particulars (the human body and soul taken up by God the Son), Barth prefers to speak of Christ's divine and human *essences* (*Wesen*, here understood in dynamic rather than substantialist ways). This is because the New Testament attests to Jesus' existence and reality and not to natures as such. Therefore, "the doctrine of the two natures cannot try to stand on its own feet or to be true of itself" since neither of the two natures "exists and is actual as such."[29] The purpose of such an apparatus as that formulated by the early church is merely to offer commentary on John 1:14: "the Word became flesh and dwelt among us."

In Barth's hands, the doctrine of the incarnation now becomes less a grammar of hypostatic union between two *somethings* and instead the narration of an event, "an actuality," the history of the encounter between God and humankind that has its climax and its fulfillment in Jesus.[30] His existence is represented as "His being in His act." In the formulations of Christology, this is nothing other than a meditation on the *communicatio operationum*—the co-operation of God and human essence in Jesus.

Thus, Barth has actualized the classic Christological categories of person, nature, union, and the communication of attributes. Christ's being is an event, a *being in act*. And therefore, a careful examination of the coincidence of divine and human activity in Jesus Christ will itself achieve what the ancient church set out to accomplish by means of those carefully delineated, but inevitably metaphysical, categories.[31] The attributes of divine existence and those of human existence are still important, but more important still

---

27. *CD* IV/1 §59.
28. *CD* IV/2 §64.
29. *CD* IV/2, 66.
30. *CD* IV/2, 105.
31. *CD* IV/2, 105–6.

for Barth are the dialectical contrasts between them—as they are really lived out in Jesus' history.

And here is where he begins to sound like the preacher from New England. Edwards had used such contrasts to make a rhetorical point about the sovereign mystery of God's work in Jesus. For Barth they are, beyond this mystery, the very sum and substance of Christology. God is at work *in and as a human person*, who is meek and vulnerable not in spite of his divine attributes but *as God himself*. The Son does not set aside his glory to enter into the state of humility, but just the opposite: it is a display of his glory that he can do this and be this.[32] The miracle of the cross is not that God suffers *as man* (as Cyril of Alexandria had it[33]) but that the man who suffers *is God* in fullness, who does not see and deal with human suffering from afar but who steps into it and in the event of that encounter draws that suffering into the life of God in order to extinguish it.

Barth is therefore thinking of the conjunction of divine and human attributes in ways that are rhetorically similar to Edwards but based on different commitments. Because Christ's being is in his act, Barth will focus on the communion of divine and human operations (*operationum*) rather than the communication of natural attributes (*idiomatum*). Here Jesus' divine essence is actualized in and through its communion with the human, and the human essence in and through its communion with the divine. This is not merely a conjunction of properties but a real and mutual participation of each essence in the other—actualized in all that Jesus says and does. The two essences may be regarded neither in isolation from one another nor without regard for Jesus' lived history. Therefore, Barth calls the lived reality of divinity and humanity in Jesus a "common actualisation."[34] As in Edwards's

---

32. "To explain in the light of each other the deity and humanity of Jesus Christ on the one hand and His humiliation and exaltation on the other means that in Jesus Christ God—we do not say casts off His Godhead but (as the One who loves in His sovereign freedom) activates and proves it by the fact that He gives Himself to the limitation and suffering of the human creature, that He, the Lord, becomes a servant, that as distinct from all false gods He humbles Himself." *CD* IV/1, 134.

33. This is carefully nuanced in Thomas G. Weinandy, *Does God Suffer?* (Notre Dame: University of Notre Dame, 2000). But Barth critiques the commonplace identification of Christ's humiliation with his humanity as a tautology (*CD* IV/1, 134). The significant thing about his humility, the effective and redemptive thing, is that Jesus did this without ceasing to be God in the fullness of his own divine glory.

34. *CD* IV/2, 73. See also Sumner, *Karl Barth and the Incarnation*, 135–40.

pairs of attributes, whatever Jesus does as the Son of God, he does "in the strictest relationship" with his human essence; and whatever he does as the Son of Man, he does strictly in coordination with his divine essence. The relation between them is the key; therefore, in no case does he act in one without the other.

> The divine expresses and reveals itself wholly in the sphere of the human, and the human serves and attests the divine. It is not merely that the goal is the same. The movement to it is also the same. It is determined by two different factors. But it is along the same road.[35]

And so, in its final form, Barth's revision of the two-natures doctrine looks quite similar to Edwards's great sermon. In Jesus Christ is the perfect and *sui generis* coincidence of divine glory and mortal humility, lordship and obedience, self-sufficiency and voluntary self-resignation. Key to both writers is the great insight that Christ is known not as one and then the other but as one in and through the other. It is not remarkable that God is sovereign or that a human is dependent, that the Son of God walks on water and the Son of Man bleeds under the lash. What is astonishing, both for Edwards and Barth, is that eternity is predicated of a man, and death is predicated of God.

THE SPIRIT AND THE LOGOS

Edwards's Christology is, on the whole, the more traditional of the two. So too does he hew more closely than Barth to the post-Reformation scholastics, whom Barth found frequent cause to criticize. For example, Edwards embraces the vision of a divine *pactum*, a heavenly conference between the Father and the Son in which the two entered into a compact for the work of redemption.[36] But Barth will not permit what he regards as implying multiple agencies in God, such that God's purpose for redemption may be seen as anything other than the triune God's one, eternal determination for creatures. The picture of a *pactum* achieved between two divine subjects in the heavenly realm is mythology.[37]

---

35. *CD* IV/2, 115.

36. *WJE* 9:118. Also see the language of "that eternal transaction" between the Father and the Son in Miscellany 702 (*WJE* 18:297).

37. *CD* IV/1, 63–66.

We will not be surprised, then, that Edwards and Barth also diverge with respect to the relation between the doctrines of Trinity and incarnation. At issue here is the question of just how the union of divine and human essences is effected in Jesus. How does God bring this about? Both men hold the incarnation to be a Trinitarian act. By the power of God the Father and through the agency of the Holy Spirit, the Son is united to humanity in the womb of Mary (Luke 1:35).[38] For Barth, the emphasis is on the freedom of God in election manifested in the Father's act of sending and the Son's obedience in being sent (again, as a twofold execution of the *one* divine will). The Holy Spirit of course plays a critical role in Mary's conception, and subsequently, he fills and directs Jesus.[39]

But Edwards, in keeping with his Puritan roots, gives the Holy Spirit a much greater role in Christology: not only does the Spirit create the union of divinity and humanity, but He also continues to function as the bond between the two natures in Christ throughout Jesus' life. The Spirit himself is the very "principle of assumption" since it is fitting that the same person who created Christ's humanity in Mary's womb should also act "as the principle or union between the manhood of Christ and the person of the Son."[40] The Spirit therefore is sent not merely to be "an external efficient cause, but as an internal *vinculum* between Christ's natures. More precisely, the Spirit of the Son makes that which was *ad extra* by nature *ad intra* by grace."[41] It is the Spirit who makes this created human nature *really to be* the humanity of the Son.

Edwards's is thus an instance of Spirit Christology. Jesus ends up dependent on the Holy Spirit in a way that is not true of Barth's theology. This is because, for Edwards, the Spirit operates as the bond of union between the Son and the Father. Looking forward, so too the believer's own union with

---

38. *CD* I/2, 486.

39. It would not be right to say that the Holy Spirit plays only a minor role in the incarnation, as Barth states that Jesus Christ owes his very *existence* to the Spirit. He derives "His existence as soul and body" from the movement of God in the Spirit's working. *CD* III/2, 334; cf. I/2, 196–202.

40. *WJE* 18:334–35.

41. Seng-Kong Tan, "Trinitarian Action in the Incarnation," in *Jonathan Edwards as Contemporary: Essays in Honor of Sang Hyun Lee*, ed. Don Schweitzer (New York: Peter Lang Publishing, 2010), 135. On this point, see also Robert W. Caldwell, *Communion in the Spirit: The Holy Spirit as the Bond of Union in the Theology of Jonathan Edwards* (Exeter: Paternoster, 2006), 74–97; and Brandon Withrow, *Becoming Divine: Jonathan Edwards's Incarnational Spirituality Within the Christian Tradition* (Wipf and Stock, 2011), 12–34, which includes consideration of Edwards's reliance upon the Spirit-Christology of John Owen.

Christ is effected by the Spirit of Christ, who dwells in her.[42] If the Son's humanity is really to be ontically his own, it is fitting that the Holy Spirit is likewise the enduring bond between the Son and his assumed nature. And so the incarnation derives from, and reflects, the holy Trinity.

This much would suffice as an argument for the ongoing role of the Holy Spirit in Christology. But Edwards has a second and more extensive reason for the Spirit to play such a prominent role here. Indeed, the Spirit *must* be the bond that holds together the Son and his human nature because Christ's humanity stood in need of sanctification. And it is the Holy Spirit who is the Sanctifier, "the very divine holiness."[43] Edwards's Trinitarianism is on full display here. The incarnation is itself the act of sanctification, accomplished by the Father through the Holy Spirit, terminating finally on the Son. The purifying of the human nature and its assumption by the Logos are not two successive steps; rather, on Edwards's account, the union is accomplished "by his being sanctified," by the activity of the Spirit on his humanity:

> He was conceived by the Holy Ghost. He received his first being in this world by the Spirit of holiness. And thus the Father sanctified him when he sent him into the world, and sanctified him in sending him into the world; incarnated him by sanctification. By sending the Spirit, assuming his flesh into being and into the person of the divine Logos, at the same time and by the same act, the Father sent him into the world, or incarnated him by an act of sanctification.[44]

This incarnation by sanctification not only prepared Christ's humanity for union with the Son but also designated him for his offices of priest, prophet, and king. Edwards associates sanctification with Jesus Christ's anointing as Messiah. Thus, the Spirit's role cannot cease after Mary's conception.

---

42. *WJE* 13:528. This is the topic of Miscellany 487. W. Ross Hastings suggests that this union of the saints with Christ by the Holy Spirit is in fact the controlling idea, which provides Edwards with a pattern for the Spirit's uniting of Christ's natures. Both unions, however, draw on the pattern of the Spirit's work in the immanent Trinity. See Hastings, "'Honouring the Spirit': Analysis and Evaluation of Jonathan Edwards' Pneumatological Doctrine of the Incarnation," *International Journal of Systematic Theology* 7, no. 3 (2005): 283–84. Hastings is right to point out that Barth, by contrast, will permit no such analogy.

43. *WJE* 18:333.

44. *WJE* 18:333.

It is by this same Spirit that Christ also did everything he did on earth, including teaching, casting out devils, performing miracles, and offering himself up in sacrifice.[45]

On Barth's view, the third person of the Trinity is God's mode of being that exists in and for fellowship with creatures, revealing God's self to the creature and even dwelling in her personally.[46] It is the Holy Spirit who creates possibility where humanity alone has only impossibility—as, for example, in the capacity of flesh to bear the Word of God. The Holy Spirit makes the incarnation to be a possibility (it is not "of the will of the flesh nor of the will of man, but of God," John 1:13) and an actuality: "the Word became flesh and dwelt among us, and we have seen his glory, glory as of the only Son from the Father, full of grace and truth" (John 1:14). And because this incarnation will be the incarnation of the very Word of God, it is the Holy Spirit who has made human nature itself to be the bearer of revelation, of the actuality of divine presence, and who by his power has made us to be the recipients of it.[47]

With regard to the activity of God on Christ's human nature, it is Barth who may be judged closer to the common Reformed position. While there are references among the Reformed to the Holy Spirit sanctifying the human nature, Barth follows them in working out the character and quality of Christ's humanity more fully by means of the *communicatio gratiarum*. The assumed nature is fashioned not simply as a precondition of the union but also by the effects of that union through its being united with the divine nature and its overflowing abundance of grace.[48] Gifts such as impeccability are habitual graces given to the human nature, say the scholastics.[49] And though he does not take up the language of habitual grace, Barth too focuses on this gifting of the human essence by the Logos: the "grace of His origin" does not alter Christ's humanity as such but exalts that essence to harmony with the divine will and service to the grace of God so that his

---

45. *WJE* 13:531. See also Miscellany 766 (*WJE* 18:412).

46. *CD* I/2, 198.

47. *CD* I/1, 199.

48. The "grace of His origin," *CD* IV/2, 91ff.

49. Heinrich Heppe, *Reformed Dogmatics*, ed. Ernst Bizer, trans. G. T. Thomson (London: George Allen & Unwin, 1950), 434–39. On the Spirit's work of sanctifying the human nature, see 424–26.

human freedom may now be exercised in obedience to God—as true human freedom.[50] This is how he is "sanctified," in the sense of his transcending Adam's sin and its just fate. The quality of being sanctified serves not as a metaphysical presupposition for a union of natures but an actuality into which Jesus lives.

While the Holy Spirit is always working in full harmony with the Father and the Son, beyond Jesus' conception and his baptism in the Jordan, Barth rarely appropriates many specific activities to the Third Person within the sphere of Christology (apart from what Scripture itself plainly states[51]). Within the inner life of God, the Holy Spirit could be said to act upon the Son's humanity to unite it fully to the triune God: the Son's human essence is "set at the side of the Father, brought into perfect fellowship with Him, filled and directed by the Holy Spirit, and in full harmony with the divine essence common to Father, Son, and Holy Spirit."[52] And certainly, Jesus was "sustained by the Father and filled by the Spirit" throughout his life.[53] But Barth does not follow Edwards and other Spirit Christologies in crediting the Spirit uniquely as the source of Jesus' miracle working, nor his resurrection, as a somewhat heavy-handed reading of Jesus being "full of the Holy Spirit" (Luke 4:1) or beginning his public ministry "in the power of the Spirit" (Luke 4:14).

Thus, while the Holy Spirit does not play as prominent a role in Barth's account of the hypostatic union, nor of Jesus' ongoing ministry, the Spirit's role is crucial indeed as the one who accomplishes, fills, and directs Christ's humanity as the locus of God's work of revelation and reconciliation. It is by virtue of the Spirit's work that the Son's humanity, though it is not divinized, indeed may be called the "humanity of God" and that we too have a guarantee that we participate in God's activity.[54]

---

50. *CD* IV/2, 91–92.

51. For a partial catalog, see the excursus in *CD* III/2, 332–35.

52. *CD* IV/2, 72.

53. *CD* IV/2, 95.

54. *CD* I/2, 199. Barth is happy to reverse the typical pattern of Spirit Christology, however: by virtue of his divine origin, Jesus himself "is fully and completely participant ... in the presence and effective working of the Holy Spirit." *CD* IV/2, 94. As he participates in the work of the Spirit, then, the Son is reciprocally "enlightened and impelled inwardly by the comfort and power and direction of the Holy Spirit."

DIALECTICAL CHRISTOLOGY: FROM
NORTHAMPTON TO BASEL

While it is beyond the scope of this essay, there is more to say in comparing the methodologies of Edwards and Barth and the Christological shape of the theologies that they produced. Both are instructed by their Christological convictions in significant ways.[55] But I suspect this is for different reasons, perhaps even reasons that are opposed to one another. Edwards excelled in finding "types" in the natural world and throughout the history of redemption, with Jesus himself as the "antitype," so that the world comes to find its true meaning and purpose strictly in Jesus as the culmination of God's redemptive activity. One example illustrates Edwards's common practice:

> The silkworm is a remarkable type of Christ, which, when it dies, yields us that of which we make such glorious clothing. Christ became a worm for our sakes, and by his death finished that righteousness with which believers are clothed, and thereby procured that we should be clothed with robes of glory.[56]

This use of typology (in the natural world and in the history of ancient Israel as well) is not simply a rhetorical device in the hands of a gifted preacher. The silkworm as a type is not merely an analogy, a simile providing a visible lesson of a spiritual truth. Rather, for Edwards, the types to be discovered in nature and in history are themselves divine realities of a sort: they were placed by God in creation deliberately to lead the mind to that larger scope of the history of God's work of redemption.

This love of typology led Edwards to a high estimation of the natural world and of our ability to find the God of nature there (though only by way of *indication*, the type pointing to the antitype, and not through the

---

55. Michael David Bush says that the key difference between them is that what might be called "Christocentrism" for Edwards is not a deliberately methodological procedure. See Bush, *Jesus Christ in the Theology of Jonathan Edwards*, 13. Christ's role is without equal and unsubstitutable, but if Edwards has anything approaching a theological method, it is likely *theocentric*. Its orientation is around the God of creation from whom all things come and to whom all things finally return.

56. *WJE* 11:59. Edwards also eagerly found types of Christ and his work throughout the Old Testament, an exegetical habit common to the Puritans (here see John F. Wilson, *WJE* 9:59). For more broad comments on Christ as the center of all of God's purpose and work for creation, see for example Miscellany 702 (*WJE* 18:283–309), especially 296–98.

divine immanence of transcendental spiritualism).[57] The relation of type to antitype is akin to the relation of prophecy to its fulfillment. Therefore, in the full manifestation of the light of Christ, the shadow has dropped away. Types identified in nature therefore have the salutary value of indication, of pointing to the genuine article. And in John F. Wilson's estimation, "in his Redemption Discourse he so transformed conventional typological assumptions that the discourse became as much a celebration of the God of nature as a hymn to the Lord of history."[58]

Barth's skepticism about the efficacy of nature and the creature's natural capacity or theological intuition has, by contrast, become the stuff of modern legend. It was to this question that he famously titled his critical response to Emil Brunner, simply, "No!"[59] For Barth had seen the deleterious consequences of natural theology in the long nineteenth century, which culminated in 1914 not merely in the politics of world war but in a theological advocacy for violent conquest—efforts on the part of his teachers, that is, to sanctify Kaiser Wilhelm II's war declaration, as though the German state bore the standard of the Kingdom of God. This was the real-life consequence of a theology that is based on nature and natural capacity rather than on divine grace, God's radical interruption of human posturing.

That is the root and stem of what would become Barth's own Christocentric project. Thus, while Edwards turns to creation out of a confidence that he will find reliable patterns of Jesus Christ there, Barth rules out nature as a competing source for the knowledge of God. Divine revelation is to be found not in nature or in history, and even less so in the human's ingenuity to interpret these, but in Jesus Christ alone. For Edwards, nature points to Jesus. But for Barth, human beings have only proved their lack of credibility in being the interpreters of nature. They have not found indications of God's redemptive work in Jesus Christ there but instead have peered down the well and seen only their own reflections.[60]

---

57. This "made his thought hospitable to a naturalism akin to Emerson's," according to Wilson. *WJE* 9:47–48.

58. *WJE* 9:50.

59. In English, Barth's response is available in Emil Brunner and Karl Barth, *Natural Theology*, trans. Peter Fraenkel (Eugene, OR: Wipf & Stock, 2002).

60. Between Barth and Edwards, both historically but I think also theologically, lies Schleiermacher. Had Barth encountered Edwards's theology, it is plausible that he may have recognized there a similar division of attention between Christ *as he is* and Christ *as he is in us*

It is all the more remarkable, therefore, that the rhetoric of Christology for Edwards and Barth ends up so strikingly similar. This is because both really do engage the work of theology in a mode that is deliberately centered on the person and work of Jesus—Edwards because he believes that the whole world *points to Christ* and Barth because he knows that *the world by itself* can do no such thing. There is duality and movement in both of these. For Edwards, theology begins with the inner life of God and moves toward creatures, finding that it needs a Mediator to get there. For Barth, theology begins with God's encounter with creatures and from that place of encounter goes on to speak of who this God is and who God has made us to be.

Thus, it is not a stretch to suggest that Edwards and Barth share a *dialectical* impulse when it comes to the person and work of Jesus Christ. This refers to a theology done in the midst of unresolved tensions in theology—between humanity and divinity, law and gospel, nature and grace, hiddenness and revelation, etc. Dialectical theology is content to reflect on these without insisting on a resolution of their tension because the theologian is convinced that she "cannot speak of theology's subject matter ... with a single word, in a non-dialectical way."[61] Theology then is rightly provoked, left unsettled, by the Word of God. Whether in Barth's academic theology or Edwards's preaching, this is apparent in their attempts to articulate the fully subversive qualities of the gospel: the God who is high became low without ceasing to be high—and the one who became weak conquered sin and death *in his weakness* and not in spite of it. The apposition of divine and human attributes indicates not only the union of Christ's natures but also the distance to which God is willing to go in the work of redemption, the distance between Christ's "infinite highness" and his "infinite condescension."[62]

---

by the Spirit—the second "center" of Schleiermacher's theology, which, Barth believed, mistook anthropology for pneumatology and finally swallowed up Schleiermacher's desire to be Christocentric. See Barth, *Protestant Theology in the Nineteenth Century*, trans. Brian Cozens and John Bowden (Grand Rapids: Eerdmans, 2002), 411–59.

61. Christophe Chalamet, *Dialectical Theologians: Wilhelm Herrmann, Karl Barth and Rudolf Bultmann* (Zürich: Theologischer Verlag Zürich, 2005), 11. Dialecticism need not regard the two poles as paradoxical; however, it is vital that the dialectical theologian not seek to harmonize or to mediate between them. This is because theology's method is to be dictated by its subject, which is a God who is wholly other and who therefore cannot be comprehended without remainder in tidy theological formulas.

62. *WJE* 19:565.

Barth's dialectical theology is critically realistic: from his teacher Wilhelm Herrmann he learned the skill of careful opposition, by which the theologian attends to thesis and antithesis, Yes and No, without imposing her own synthetic order between them. As an exercise of mortal humility, this is meant to give space for God to speak, even where God's unveiling yet remains veiled. God's truth is therefore mediated, never immediate in its accessibility to the human. One consequence of this is that Barth's Christology is insistently particularist, finding its bearings within the lived history of Jesus Christ as witnessed in holy Scripture before moving to more general theological constructions.[63] Barth's dialectical theology therefore ends up subversive on two fronts: he opposes both the generalizing and speculative approach of the medievals and the overly confident interpolations of the humanists. God is to be found, and therefore known, only in the particular history where God has given himself.

But Edwards's thought is idealist, operating according to the principles of Platonic rationalism. The world reflects imperfectly the sphere of heaven; it is created by God and directed toward God yet stands in need of redemption and guidance (Edwards is still a good Calvinist). Rather than the bourgeois Neo-Kantianism of Europe, Edwards's influences were the more mystical Puritans of British America. The result is a theology that is typological, oriented toward the perfect and the ideal (both in heaven and on earth), moving from the inner life of the Trinity, through the agency of the Holy Spirit, to the newly empowered life of the virtuous Christian. Creation is positively littered with the "images and shadows" of divine things.[64] Jesus is the perfect human who displays the virtues of forbearance, reverence, and obedience in the most perfect of ways (not exploiting his own due glory). In all these ways he is unique in creation, and as the Redeemer, his pattern of virtue is ours to follow.[65] Therefore, Christian existence is the pursuit of religious affection—the ideal that Christ has modeled. Union with Christ is no mere pious sentimentalism but the surface plane of the mirror where the ectype finally touches the archetype.

---

63. George Hunsinger, *How to Read Karl Barth: The Shape of His Theology* (Oxford: Oxford University Press, 1991), 32–35.

64. *WJE* 11.

65. *WJE* 2:123–24.

Thus, it is an ironic symmetry that Barth and Edwards describe the person and work of Christ in such similar ways. For Barth, the dialectical push and pull of Christ's divine and human existence reflects both the grace and the tension of God's self-disclosure in creaturely flesh. The medium certainly cannot accommodate such a thing naturally; and yet by grace God makes it to be so. Edwards reaches essentially the same gospel confession, only by a different route: the condescension of Christ is an "infinite condescension,"[66] and his humility belongs to him not by nature but by the Son's own gracious, willing self-giving. The real mystery of the gospel, therefore, and its power for public proclamation, is in neither his highness nor his lowness alone but in the contrast of the two.

But if Barth learned dialectical reasoning as something suited to a theology exercised with wisdom, Edwards's dialecticism is *ad hoc* and not deliberate. Apart from his playful contrast of Christ's excellencies, any dialectical tensions present in his Christology seem to result more from an absence of systematic consistency. Whereas for Barth, dialecticism was intended to make sense of the mystery of Jesus Christ, for Edwards, it emerges only after the fact as a consequence of other commitments.

This is an only somewhat more generous appraisal of the coherence of Edwards's Christology than that offered by Amy Plantinga Pauw. Certainly, her evaluation is correct: Edwards's theology is full of unresolved tensions, so that "his success in deriving a coherent Christology from his practical trinitarianism must be judged at best partial."[67] Edwards evinces alternately both Alexandrian and Antiochene impulses and renders a set of questions that are not entirely resolved. This is likely because he never attempted the precision of a theological treatise on this doctrine.

This points to a final, somber comparison between Jonathan Edwards and Karl Barth: both men left their work incomplete at their deaths. Barth's Christology was of course more or less finished (though it would have continued to play a decisive role in the unwritten volume V of *CD*, on the doctrine of redemption). But Edwards's formal statement on Christ's person remained unwritten. Before moving to Princeton, he wrote a letter in 1757

---

66. *WJE* 19:565–67.

67. Pauw, *"The Supreme Harmony of All": Jonathan Edwards and the Trinity* (Ph.D. dissertation, Yale University, 1990), 205. See also Caldwell, *Communion in the Spirit*, 74–97.

to the trustees of the College of New Jersey in which he expressed his long desire to write *A History of the Work of Redemption*. Here he planned to revise and extend his now twenty-year-old sermon series into a systematic theology oriented around the full scope of divine work in the world, "the *summum* and *ultimum* of all the divine operations and decrees."[68] The incarnation and the earthly career of Jesus was the briefest period in this divine history, but for Edwards it was the pivot around which the whole work of divine redemption turns.

We might venture to say by way of conclusion, then, that Edwards and Barth agreed that all of theology—from the exposition of the entirety of Scripture, to the formal exercises of theological contemplation, to preaching and ministry to God's people, to the church's missionary activity—is rightly Trinitarian and Christological. Jesus is not merely the messenger or chief actor in the gospel story but is himself its sum and content.

---

68. "To the Trustees of the College of New Jersey" (Oct. 19, 1757), *WJE* 16:728.

5
—

HOLY SPIRIT

Seng Kong Tan

Although Karl Barth and Jonathan Edwards lived two centuries apart on two different continents, they shared a common Augustinian heritage—with its alleged weaknesses—received through the Reformed tradition. Critics of a pneumatological deficit in Barth have diagnosed the source of this ill as either an overly robust Christocentrism or an anemic Augustinian personalism of the Spirit.[1] Similar complaints about Edwards's pneumatology have been advanced, in particular, to his version of the psychological analogy of the Trinity.[2]

In what follows, we will briefly examine how Edwards and Barth thought of the divine personhood of the Holy Spirit. Next, we will look at their pneumatologies construed in psychological and relational terms. A substantial portion of this essay will then focus on each theologian's particular rendering of the mutual love analogy in relation to humility and hierarchy in God and Christ. We will conclude this dialogue between Barth and Edwards by investigating the dynamism in their pneumatological Christologies. The goal

---

1. Philip J. Rosato, *The Spirit as Lord: The Pneumatology of Karl Barth* (London: T&T Clark, 1981). For McCormack, the Spirit is made redundant in Christ's history because Barth ascribed agency to the Logos rather than the "human Jesus." See Bruce L. McCormack, "The Spirit of the Lord Is upon Me: Pneumatological Christology with and beyond Barth," in *The Spirit Is Moving: New Pathways in Pneumatology : Studies Presented to Professor Cornelis van Der Kooi on the Occasion of His Retirement*, ed. Gijsbert van den Brink, Studies in Reformed Theology, vol. 38 (Leiden: Brill, 2019), 124–37. Barth has basically a functional binity, according to Robert W. Jenson, "You Wonder Where the Spirit Went," *Pro Ecclesia* 2, no. 3 (1993): 296–304. The charge of depersonalizing the Spirit is also raised by John Thompson, *The Holy Spirit in the Theology of Karl Barth* (Eugene, OR: Wipf & Stock, 1991).

2. Amy Plantinga Pauw, *"The Supreme Harmony of All": The Trinitarian Theology of Jonathan Edwards* (Grand Rapids: Eerdmans, 2002), 43–50, 160–61.

of this chapter is to draw out variations of an Augustinian pneumatological motif, namely, the Holy Spirit as love, and identify areas of convergence in their theologies.

PERSONHOOD OF THE SPIRIT: DEFICIENT OR RETICENT?

If Barth and Edwards are to be faulted for their restraint vis-à-vis the Spirit's personhood, it must be acknowledged that this pneumatological reticence is part of the received biblical and theological tradition. On the first point, Spirit language in the biblical material is primarily performative speech.[3] "In the New Testament sphere," Barth notes, "there is no one who finds any difficulty in the invisibility of the Spirit."[4] Moreover, as Edwards reminds us, Holy Scripture says nothing about the Spirit being loved, though there is much written on the mutual love between Father and Son and their love toward the saints.[5] Clearly, this pneumatological reserve inherited via the Augustinian tradition is a faithful appropriation of Scripture.

With regard to the charge that the Holy Spirit is reduced to a sub-personal relation of love between two divine persons, it bears noting that a presupposition behind this critique is a generic notion of divine personhood. Here, the Spirit's person is weighted against that of the Father or Son—where there are visible human analogies—and found wanting. In other words, an incipient anthropomorphism, which identifies agency with visibility, drives this analysis. In this respect, Barth's reminder that even the Christian aesthetic tradition has refused depictions of "the Holy Ghost in human form" is apropos—a thrust not inconsistent with the biblical witness.[6] A hidden, mysterious agent who works in the background enabling mutual love, like a matchmaker, is surely not less personal or active than the lover and the beloved.[7]

---

3. Travis E. Ables, *Incarnational Realism: Trinity and the Spirit in Augustine and Barth*, T&T Clark Studies in Systematic Theology 21 (London: Bloomsbury T&T Clark, 2013), 36.

4. *CD* IV/2, 320.

5. Edwards, "Treatise on Grace," *WJE* 21:186.

6. "Thus, even if the Father and the Son might be called 'person' (in the modern sense of the term), the Holy Spirit could not possibly be regarded as the third 'person.'" *CD* I/1, 469–70.

7. Barth writes that "even in all His invisibility and inconceivability the Holy Spirit is not for us merely the great Unknown, that it is not the case that we simply do not have Him, but that we know His power and efficacy." *CD* IV/2, 340.

Having dealt with the allegation of pneumatological reductionism, it should be noted that Edwards and Barth insist on the Spirit's unmitigated personhood by conceptualizing the hypostases as eternal repetitions of the deity.[8] "God is," Barth writes, "the one God in threefold repetition."[9] Similarly, Edwards asserts that the "threefold repetition" of "Holy" in Revelation refers to "the three persons in the Trinity."[10] As conceptually equivalent to the *homoousion*, the *trisagion* does more than simply deny tritheism and subordinationism. If each hypostasis is a repetition of a personal divine essence, then the Spirit cannot be any less personal than Father and Son.

That is why when it comes to nomenclature, Edwards is confident that "person" is an eminently suitable designation for Father, Son, and Spirit.[11] Barth, on the other hand, refuses the term in favor of "way or mode of being" (*Seinsweise*) and consistently refers to the Holy Spirit as "a third mode of being of the one divine Subject or Lord."[12] Despite this difference, Barth and Edwards share the view of God as a psychological being, that is to say, a subject who has volition and intellect.[13] With that definition, Barth contends that "personality" designates the one God and cannot be applied to the three modes of being.[14] In comparison, Edwards illustrates this with the psychological model of the Trinity.[15]

---

8. "*repetitio aeternitatis in aeternitate.*" *CD* I/1, 350.

9. *CD* I/1, 350.

10. Edwards, "Blank Bible," note on Revelation 4:8, *WJE* 24:1213. Elsewhere, with reference to the Son, "the whole Deity and glory of the Father, is as it [were] repeated or duplicated." Miscellany 1062, *WJE* 20:430.

11. "Treatise on Grace," *WJE* 21:181; see also "Discourse on the Trinity," *WJE* 21:133.

12. Citing Quenstedt, Barth affirmed the German equivalent of the patristic phrase for the divine person: "'Mode (or way) of being' (*Seinsweise*) is the literal translation of the concept τρόπος ὑπάρξεως or *modus entitativus*." *CD* I/1, 359; *CD* I/1, 469. See also Bruce L. McCormack, "'The Lord and Giver of Life: A 'Barthian' Defense of the Filioque," in *Rethinking Trinitarian Theology: Disputed Questions and Contemporary Issues in Trinitarian Theology*, ed. Giulio Maspero and Robert Józef Wozniak (London: T&T Clark, 2012), 230–53.

13. Edwards, "Discourse on the Trinity," *WJE* 21:133. "The one 'personality' of God, the one active and speaking divine Ego, is Father, Son and Holy Spirit," who is a self-existent individual with "self-consciousness, cognition, volition, activity, effects, revelation and name." *CD* IV/1, 205.

14. *CD* I/1, 350.

15. Since "person" is an entity with "understanding and will," Edwards applies this across divine and creaturely spheres, with the caveat that "the difference is only in the perfection of degree and manner." *WJE* 21:113. Here, he rules out any univocity of being by positing an ontological gap or difference of manner between creature and Creator, viz., a unity of being and doing in God. In human beings, by contrast, "the habit or principle differs from the act"

PERSON AS PSYCHOLOGICAL:
SPIRIT AS WILL-IN-ACT

Edwards's definition of person together with his psychological description of the Trinity as Mind, Idea, and Love clearly accords full personal agency to the Father. With this modalist-leaning analogy, the Word as intellect-in-action and Spirit as will-in-action would seem to be reduced to two divine powers.[16] Yet Edwards sees no contradiction in simultaneously using generic and personal psychological denominators for the divine persons, for instance, where the Holy Spirit is referred to as both the "holiness of God itself in the abstract" and "the personal love of God."[17] In the main, Edwards characterizes the Holy Spirit as will-in-act, love, and other volitional expressions.[18]

To avoid the hypostatization of every single divine perfection, Edwards qualifies an axiom of divine simplicity—"that everything that is in God is God."[19] Except for the "real attributes" of "understanding and love," namely, the Son and Spirit, none are directly identical to God.[20] All the other moral attributes are folded into either the divine understanding or love, and the rest classified as modal attributes, for instance, infinity, eternity, immutability, and omnipresence.[21] This, however, seems to introduce composition into God, to which an appeal to a *perichoresis* of persons/attributes is made to protect the divine unity.[22] In sum, Edwards stands in continuity with the

---

and is never transcended in glory even as they become more verb-like as God is. Edwards, 528. Sermon on Rom. 8: 29–30, WJE 54.

16. "The Son is the Deity generated by God's understanding, or having an idea of himself, and subsisting in that idea." Edwards, "Discourse on the Trinity," WJE 21:131.

17. 288. Sermon on Cant. 1:3(b) (Jun. 1733), WJE 48; "Treatise on Grace," WJE 21:183. Similarly, the Son could be called the "wisdom of God in the abstract" as well as "the personal wisdom of God." See "Treatise on Grace," WJE 21:187, 183. Here, he follows in the tradition of Augustine, Thomas Aquinas, and the minor Reformed tradition.

18. Other cognate terms include disposition: Edwards, "Discourse on the Trinity," WJE 21:122; will and act: Miscellany 143 (133), WJE 13:298, Miscellany 94, WJE 13:260; beauty: WJE 2:274, Miscellany 293, WJE 13:384; joy and happiness: "Discourse on the Trinity," WJE 21:135; virtue: "True Virtue," WJE 8:557. Ad extra, the Holy Spirit is grace and gift to redeemed creation. See WJE 2:236 and "A Humble Attempt," WJE 5:341, 348.

19. Edwards, "Discourse on the Trinity," WJE 21:131; Miscellany 94, WJE 13:262.

20. Edwards, "Discourse on the Trinity," WJE 21:132. Here, Edwards is affirming the basic insight of the psychological analogy: that truth corresponds to reality and that truth necessarily involves love. Neil Ormerod, "The Psychological Analogy for the Trinity: At Odds with Modernity," *Pacifica: Australasian Theological Studies* 14, no. 3 (2001): 281–94.

21. Edwards, "Discourse on the Trinity," WJE 21:131–32.

22. WJE 21:133. See Kyle C. Strobel, *Jonathan Edwards's Theology: A Reinterpretation*, T&T Clark Studies in Systematic Theology 19 (London; New York: Bloomsbury T&T Clark, 2013), 14, 61–63.

Thomistic tradition in characterizing Word and Love as proper personal names for the Son and Spirit.[23] But by distributing and collapsing God's moral attributes into the divine persons, Edwards injects a novel element into this line of thought.[24]

Contrary to Edwards, Barth was not enamored, to put it mildly, with psychological analogies of God.[25] In *Church Dogmatics*, having made a list of the vestiges of the Trinity (*vestigia trinitatis*), including Augustine's psychological analogies, he rejects this tradition, fearing that it may supplant revelation as a "second root of the doctrine of the Trinity."[26] For him, the "biblical revelation of the Trinity" is the only legitimate foundation of Trinitarian doctrine, which is fundamentally anchored in the confession of Jesus' Lordship.[27]

While Barth overruled the *vestigia* tradition and the overt use of the psychological analogies, it would be inaccurate to conclude that he eschewed psychological characterizations of the divine modes of being altogether. Guided by God's self-revelation and proceeding from the *analogia fidei*, Barth not infrequently depicts the Son as "the eternal Word of the Father who speaks from all eternity" rather than in idealist terms. Yet, on those rare occasions when he designates the Son as "the eternal thought of the Father who thinks from all eternity," and when he describes the Holy Spirit as *caritas*, surely a tacit psychologism it at work.[28]

Those, however, are occasional statements in Barth, and when he does refer to the Spirit as love, it is premised on a reciprocity of love and not a

---

23. Gilles Emery, *The Trinitarian Theology of St Thomas Aquinas*, trans. Francesca Aran Murphy (Oxford: Oxford University Press, 2007), 187, 231.

24. For an evaluation of this, see Oliver D. Crisp, "Jonathan Edwards on Divine Simplicity," *Religious Studies* 39, no. 1 (2003): 23–41.

25. The only *vestigium trinitatis* that Barth gave credence to, following Luther, was the threefold nature of the Word as revelation, Scriptures, and preaching (*CD* I/1, 347). This was a re-contextualization of Luther's "*Grammatica, Dialectica and Rhetorica*" as "the theological encyclopedia ... of exegetical, dogmatic and practical theology."

26. *CD* I/1, 335. Summarizing Bavinck's typology of nature, culture, history, and religion, Barth ends with the Augustinian analogy of the human soul, tracing its reception through the medieval and Reformation theologians right down to Adolf Schlatter.

27. *CD* I/1, 334.

28. *CD* I/1, 436. Here, Barth cites Thomas's description of the Son as the intelligible emanation in God. Strictly speaking, an analogy of the Word points not so much to a trace of the Trinity in the creature, but rather a trace of the created realities in the Trinity. Hence, *vestigia creaturae in trinitate*, rather than *vestigia trinitatis in creatura*. *CD* I/1, 341.

psychology of *self*-love. Where Edwards and Barth stand at different ends of the spectrum with respect to the psychological analogy, they make quite liberal use of the mutual love analogy in their pneumatologies—a theme we will consider next.[29]

THE SPIRIT AS A PROCESSION AND FELLOWSHIP OF MUTUAL LOVE

Already in Barth's earlier conception of God as Revealer, Revelation, and Revealedness, we see a dynamic reinterpretation of Augustine's mutual love model in epistemological terms.[30] "The Holy Spirit," Barth explains, "is the *love* which is the essence of the relation between these two modes of being of God."[31] For him, though the Spirit is the "bond of peace" and "fellowship, the act of communion, of the Father and Son," he insists that the Spirit must not be reduced to "a mere attribute or relation of the Father and the Son."[32] That is because, like the Father and Son, the Spirit is the same divine Subject, Lord, Creator, and Redeemer who is a proper divine agent.[33] Barth's conviction that the Spirit is the personal divine agent of communion is evidenced in his analyses of the procession of the Spirit and *perichoresis*.

In the first case, since the divine essence is the one personal Subject thrice-repeated eternally, the Holy Spirit cannot proceed from either the Father and the Son or their common essence, as if their being and modes of

29. George Hunsinger, "The Mediator of Communion: Karl Barth's Doctrine of the Holy Spirit," in *The Cambridge Companion to Karl Barth*, ed. John Webster (New York; Cambridge; Cambridge University Press, 2000), 177–94. It might be argued that Barth's openness to a future "third article theology" would also take the notion of the Spirit as the "vinculum pacis inter Patrem et Filium" as its primary model. See Barth, *Concluding Scientific Postscript on Schleiermacher*, in *The Theology of Schleiermacher: Lectures at Göttingen, Winter Semester of 1923/24* (Grand Rapids: Eerdmans, 1982), 278.

30. Barth himself draws parallels between Augustine's psychological analogy and "Hegel's 'in itself' of the subjective spirit as thesis, 'for itself' of the objective spirit as antithesis, and 'in and for itself' of the absolute spirit as synthesis." *CD* I/1, 338. On Hegel's influence in the early Barth, see Dale M. Schlitt, *German Idealism's Trinitarian Legacy* (Albany: State University of New York Press, 2016),123.

31. *CD* I/1, 480, my emphasis.

32. *CD* I/1, 470, 483, 487; *CD* I/2, 241.

33. *CD* I/1, 467, 472, 462. See also Frank D. Macchia, "The Spirit of God and the Spirit of Life: An Evangelical Response to Karl Barth's Pneumatology," in *Karl Barth and Evangelical Theology: Convergences and Divergences*, ed. Wook Chung Sung (Grand Rapids: Baker Academic, 2006), 149–71, and Hunsinger, "Mediator of Communion,"180.

being were separable realities.[34] Rather, "the one Godness of the Father and Son is, or the Father and the Son in their one Godness are, the origin of the Spirit."[35] Barth, therefore, rejects a linear procession of the Spirit through the Son as a particularly Eastern interpretation of the *dia tou huiou*, as this would annul the Spirit's *"mediating position,"* which in turn would eviscerate the *"mutual connection"* between Father and Son.[36] Simply put, this does not allow a mutual love construal of the Trinity.

Nonetheless, Barth was willing to accept an interpretation of the *dia tou huiou/per filium*, which affirms that the Son is no mere instrumental cause but an equal Spirator with the Father.[37] Consequently, as "the common factor" of the other two modes of being, the Spirit's procession is not "twofold, but rather [has] a common origin ... from the Father and the Son."[38] Barth denies not only a double procession of the Spirit but also a primal *perichoresis* that entails "a circle of mutual origins" since this would destroy the classical *taxis* of origination.[39]

According to Barth, it is only in the Spirit's procession that the Trinitarian *perichoresis* obtains; therefore, *perichoresis* must be logically posterior to the divine processions. This *perichoresis* is not a unity of *homoousion* but rather the fellowship of Father and Son in their Spirit "because God's fatherhood and sonship as such must be related to one another in this active mutual orientation and interpenetration"—the latter phrase describing the immanent operation of the Holy Spirit.[40] It appears that, for Barth, *perichoresis* is nothing else but the Trinity modeled after the analogy of mutual love.

Although Edwards frequently depicts the Spirit as the divine will-in-operation or love, he also thinks of the Spirit as mutual love.[41] Divine love as descriptive of the Spirit is not to be construed as self-reflexive but rather

34. *CD* I/2, 239, 247; *CD* II/2, 115. See David Guretzki, *Karl Barth on the Filioque* (Farnham, Surrey, UK: Ashgate, 2009), 185.

35. *CD* I/1, 487. See McCormack, "Lord and Giver of Life," 234.

36. *CD* I/1, 482–83 (italics original).

37. *CD* I/1, 484.

38. *CD* I/1, 469, 486.

39. *CD* I/1, 485.

40. *CD* I/1, 487.

41. Steven M. Studebaker, *Jonathan Edwards' Social Augustinian Trinitarianism in Historical and Contemporary Perspectives*, Gorgias Studies in Philosophy and Theology 2 (Piscataway, NJ: Gorgias Press, 2008), and Robert W. Caldwell, *Communion in the Spirit: The Holy Spirit as the*

relational: "God's love to himself, that is, to his Son, I suppose to be the Holy Spirit."[42] Yet this procession of the Spirit does not terminate in the Son. Edwards sees no contradiction between the procession of the Spirit *filioque* and *per filium* for "though the Holy Ghost proceeds both from the Father and the Son, yet he proceeds from the Father mediately by the Son."[43]

Furthermore, "the Son of God is not only the infinite object of love, but he is also an infinite subject" who "infinitely loves the Father."[44] In other words, echoing Augustine, Edwards believes that the Holy Spirit proceeds from and exists as the eternal bond of love between the Father and Son—the *vinculum caritatis* or *amoris*.[45] Accordingly, "that infinite delight there is between the Father and the Son" is none other than their Spirit, and just so, "their love is mutual."[46] In fact, Edwards comments that the silence in Scripture regarding the Holy Spirit, particularly in the Apostle Paul's benedictions, is only apparent "because the Holy Ghost is himself the love and grace of God the Father and the Lord Jesus Christ."[47]

SPIRIT OF HUMILITY AND OBEDIENCE

Up to this point, we have seen how our two theologians from Northampton and Basel hewed the Augustinian line where the Holy Spirit is regarded as the principle of communion (*koinonia*) between Father and Son. Each theologian, of course, has his own unique way of specifying the procession of the Holy Spirit as mutual love in God. As a specific case application, I will now look at

---

Bond of Union in the Theology of Jonathan Edwards, Studies in Evangelical History and Thought (Milton Keynes: Paternoster, 2006).

42. Edwards, Miscellany 151 (141), WJE 13:302. See also Edwards, "Blank Bible," note on Daniel 9:25, WJE 24:767; Miscellany 225, WJE 13:346. Early on, Edwards argued philosophically for the existence of plurality in God: Happiness is greater when love is not self-directed but mutual. See Edwards's entry on "Excellency" in WJE 6:337, which he developed theologically in Miscellany 117, WJE 13: 283–84. Elsewhere, see Edwards, *Ramsay's Principles*, vol. 1, 74–85, as cited in Miscellany 1253, WJE 23: 187.

43. Edwards, "Discourse on the Trinity," WJE 21:181.

44. Edwards, "Sermon Fifteen: Heaven is a World of Love," WJE 8:373.

45. Steven M. Studebaker and Robert W. Caldwell, *The Trinitarian Theology of Jonathan Edwards: Text, Context, and Application* (Farnham, Surrey, UK: Ashgate, 2012), 72.

46. Miscellany 1047, WJE 20:389. Here, Edwards cites passages from John Owen's *Pneumatologia: Or, a discourse concerning the Holy Spirit* ... (London: Nathaniel Ponder, 1674); Edwards, "Discourse on the Trinity," WJE 21:121. Edwards uses the term "bond of love" in Miscellany 781, WJE 18:451.

47. Edwards, "Treatise on Grace," WJE 21:186.

the ways Barth and Edwards deal with the motifs of humility and hierarchy in God and, to this end, how they modified the Augustinian analogy against the threat of subordinationism. Let us begin with Barth.

SPIRIT AS SUBLIMATOR OF *PRIUS-POSTERIUS* DIALECTIC

When Barth contends that the divine and human essences in Christ stand in a relationship of "the higher and the lower" in an "ordered totality," one finds no objection against such a Chalcedonian position.[48] But with his further assertion that "there is in God Himself an above and a below, a *prius* and a *posterius*," in which the Father and Son are related not only as "First and a Second" but also as "One who rules and commands in majesty and One who obeys in humility," traditional Thomist and Barth scholars have leveled the charge of subordinationism.[49]

Any effort at justifying Barth's claim that the Son obeys as God must be considered together with his other controversial assertion that "the humility of Christ is not simply an attitude of the man Jesus of Nazareth" but also "grounded in the being of God."[50] While he ascribes these properties to the deity, a critical distinction must be appreciated and examined: humility as a common perfection of the one God and obedience as a personal property of the Son.[51]

In the incarnation, the paternal humility or "mercy of the Father in which He too is not merely exalted *but lowly* with His Son" was revealed.[52] Consequently, humility as an essential perfection undercuts the subordinationism thesis since each divine mode of being—the one majestic

---

48. CD III/2, 332.

49. CD IV/1, 200–1; CD IV/1, 202. See, for example, Thomas Joseph White, "The Obedience of the Son," in *The Incarnate Lord: A Thomistic Study in Christology*, Thomistic Ressourcement Series, vol. 5 (Washington, DC: Catholic University of America Press, 2015), 277–307, and Paul D. Molnar, "The Obedience of the Son in the Theology of Karl Barth and of Thomas F. Torrance," in *Faith, Freedom, and the Spirit: The Economic Trinity in Barth, Torrance and Contemporary Theology* (Downers Grove, IL: IVP Academic, 2015), 313–54.

50. He continues, "If what the man Jesus does is God's own work, this aspect of the self-emptying and self-humbling of Jesus Christ as an act of obedience cannot be alien to God." CD IV/1, 193.

51. *Contra* McCormack's contention that "Barth has added to the personal properties of the second person of the Trinity the elements of *humility and* obedience" (emphasis mine). See Bruce L. McCormack, "The Doctrine of the Trinity after Barth: An Attempt to Reconstruct Barth's Doctrine in the Light of His Later Christology," in *Trinitarian Theology after Barth*, ed. Myk Habets and Phillip Tolliday, Princeton Theological Monographs 148 (Cambridge: James Clarke, 2012), 111.

52. CD IV/2, 357, my emphasis.

Lord—possesses the same capacity for downward movement. If the Father is as humble as the Son, the Son's majesty is not any less glorious in his life, death, resurrection, and ascension.[53] In fact, the Son's downward mobility is "grounded in the mercy of the Father," just as the exaltation of Jesus, the royal man, is rooted in the Father's majesty.[54] Inasmuch as Father and Son do not contradict each other in their distinction, humility and majesty as divine attributes cannot be set against one another.

Barth regards these divine perfections as non-competitive because humility, as a secondary perfection, is comprehended by majesty, an absolute perfection.[55] The divine majesty as absolute is not susceptible to a further movement of perfection in God, though God can choose to take on humility.[56] Accordingly, in the divine immanent internal operation (*opus internum ad intra*), God's ability to act in a majestic, "exalted," or "absolute way" does not preclude God acting in a humble, "lowly," or "relative" manner in the divine transitive, internal work (*opus internum ad extra*).[57] In the incarnation, humility is revealed as a divine perfection not alien to God's life precisely because it is the "strange form of the divine majesty"—a "high humility."[58]

With that said, how then are the notions of *prius* and *posterius* as well as command and obedience related to majesty and humility? For Barth, God's being is a single eternal act in two modes: self-constitution and self-determination. In the first mode of the divine processions, God self-constitutes in three modes of being as the one absolute God. In scriptural and

---

53. "They saw in the Resurrected His royal power of command as proceeding from His death." CD IV/2, 291. Specifically "reflected in the exaltation of the man Jesus is the majesty of the Son in which He too ... is not just lowly but also exalted with the Father." CD IV/2, 357.

54. CD IV/2, 357.

55. In §31, Barth treats the perfections of the divine freedom, majesty, and sovereignty under the divine simplicity. CD II/1, 445, 463, 489, 525, 608.

56. "In His Godhead ... He did not stand in need of exaltation, nor was He capable of it." CD IV/1, 135.

57. CD IV/1, 187. Absolutely, in an infinite, active, transcendent, impassible manner, as well as relatively, in a passive, immanent, passible, immanent, and human manner. Traditionally classified as first-order absolute and second-order relative attributes, Barth refers to the election as "a spontaneous *opus internum ad extra* of the trinitarian God." CD II/2, 25. See Richard A. Muller, *The Divine Essence and Attributes, vol. 3 in Post-Reformation Reformed Dogmatics: The Rise and Development of Reformed Orthodoxy, ca. 1520 to ca. 1725*, 4 vols. (Grand Rapids: Baker Academic, 2003), 218–19.

58. CD IV/1, 178, 159. "He is in our lowliness what He is in His majesty (and what He can be also in our lowliness because His majesty is also lowliness)." CD IV/1, 204.

traditional language, the Father "eternally begets ... the eternally begotten" Son in divine majesty and freedom.[59] Barth's originality was to eternalize and personalize command and obedience as the prerogatives of Father and Son, respectively—"One who is obeyed and Another who obeys."[60]

In the second mode of the divine missions, the triune God, in an eternal act of self-determination, "shows and affirms and activates and reveals" the divine humility in creation and redemption.[61] In the incarnation, the divine majesty is revealed primarily in the Father's command and rule, while humility is activated in the Son's obedience (though the divine majesty is also revealed in the Son's exaltation). This self-activation represents, as it were, a concentration of the divine humility as the Son fulfills the divine obedience through the addition of a human mode of obedience.

This distinction of self-constitution and self-determination comes out clearly in §64, where Barth expounds the exaltation of Jesus under the "Direction of the Son." It is from the eternal generation "in His mode of being as the Son, as the eternally Begotten of the Father" and the Spirit's procession where the Son is "first loved by [the Father] and then loving Him in return" that the divine modes of being are eternally ordered. Following this eternal *taxis* of subsistence "as the One who is in order secondary and therefore obedient to Him," Barth concludes that the Son "is the one God in His humility. It is to him, therefore, to God in this mode of being, that *the act of humility of the incarnation corresponds.*"[62]

In other words, in eternal election, the Father and the Son self-appropriate majesty and humility, respectively, to be activated and revealed in the incarnation.[63] Majesty and humility correspond to the "height and depth,

---

59. *CD* IV/1, 209.

60. He speaks of eternal generation in the German idealist nomenclature of "the self-positing ... self-posited God." *CD* IV/1, 201. Specifically, Fichte's language of the self-positing Ego mediated through Marburg neo-Kantianism. See D. Paul La Montagne, *Barth and Rationality: Critical Realism in Theology* (Eugene, OR: Wipf & Stock, 2012), 85–86.

61. *CD* IV/1, 209. As Barth phrases it elsewhere, "God *chooses* condescension. He *chooses* humiliation, lowliness and obedience." *CD* IV/1, 199, my emphasis. Barth alludes to this distinction in reference to the incarnation, in which Jesus Christ "*shows* Himself to be the Son of God" in humility, obedience, and divine subordination, but which "does *not* mean that He *becomes* the Son of God thereby." *CD* IV/1, 208, my emphasis.

62. *CD* IV/2, 44–45. The obedience of the Son involves a secondary, derivative relation to the Father: "Obedience implies an above and a below, a *prius* and a *posterius*." *CD* IV/1, 196.

63. Reminiscent of Edwards's move, Barth also appropriated the divine perfections of holiness, mercy, and love to Father, Son, and Spirit respectively (*CD* I/1, 382).

superiority and subordination, command and willingness, authority and obedience, in God Himself"—as manifestations of the distinct modes of fatherly command and filial obedience.[64] It is in this sense that humility can be said to be proper to God as the second mode of the divine being.[65] There is, then, an appropriateness in the Son's humiliation in the incarnation that corresponds to His eternal character as the obedient Son. And that is why "in His humiliation He acted and revealed Himself as the true Son of the true Father."[66]

Having examined the outworking of this dialectic of *prius* and *posterius* in God, we can now analyze the pneumatological dimension, in which the Spirit acts as the principle of distinction and sublimation (*Aufhebung*). With respect to the first, it is because the Spirit proceeds from the Father *and* the Son that the Spirit is "the eternal reality of their separateness ... of their distinctness."[67] In the economy of salvation, the Spirit reveals the Father as the One who commands and the Son as Another who obeys precisely as the Spirit of command and obedience. On the one hand, "the Holy Spirit is Himself ... the commanding of the living God," and on the other hand, the Son fulfilled the divine will because of "the Spirit of this act of obedience, the Spirit of obedience itself."[68]

More than just being the divine principle of distinction, the Holy Spirit is also the principle of sublimation, bringing about a unity-in-distinction beyond creaturely categories.[69] "The work of the Holy Spirit," Barth writes,

---

64. *CD* IV/2, 351.

65. "The humility in which He dwells and acts in Jesus Christ is ... proper to Him. ... in the most inward depth of His Godhead." *CD* IV/1, 193. Similarly: "In itself and as such, then, humility is not alien to the nature of the true God, but supremely proper to Him in His mode of being as the Son." *CD* IV/2, 42.

66. *CD* IV/2, 358,

67. *CD* III/1, 56. As Barth puts this succinctly elsewhere, "The Father is not the Father and the Son is not the Son without a mutual affirmation and love in the Holy Spirit." *CD* IV/1, 209. See Bruce McCormack's analysis of Barth's dialecticism as a theme running throughout his theology, although this comes with a Christological concentration in his later work. Bruce L. McCormack, *Karl Barth's Critically Realistic Dialectical Theology: Its Genesis and Development, 1909-1936* (Oxford: Clarendon, 1995).

68. *CD* IV/2, 373; *CD* II/2, 106. The Christian's participation in the obedience of Christ is likewise possible only by the Spirit. *CD* III/3, 257-58.

69. We are following Garrett Green's translation of *Aufhebung* as "sublimation" (though not in the Freudian sense) and not "sublation" in the Hegelian sense. See "Translator's Preface," in Karl Barth, *On Religion: The Revelation of God as the Sublimation of Religion*, trans. Garrett Green (London: T&T Clark, 2006).

"is to bring and to hold together that which is different."[70] This act of making sublime includes both a negation and transcending union—a simultaneous act of abolition and radical lifting.

In the negative dimension of sublimation, the Holy Spirit annuls our creaturely ideas of distinction and unity in God.[71] That is why this antithesis of command and obedience in the divine being is disanalogous to a superior-inferior relation in two human beings.[72] Barth is adamant that true Christian obedience in Christ is a free, filial obedience and not a slavish, blind obedience—a revelation gifted by the Spirit.[73] Because divine subordination and superordination are united and equal and possess their own dignity in ways unlike created realities, this Trinitarian notion of *prius-posterius* should instead correct our understanding of human relations (as, for example, between husband and wife).[74] Barth rejects subordinationism because it entails confusing the analogical trajectory and, therefore, the character of human and divine subjectivities.[75]

Sublimation as negation also involves the rejection of a solipsistic notion of the divine unity fueled by an implicit subordinationism. Barth contends that being *prius* is not ontologically superior to being *posterius* since descent or "the direction downwards ... has its own dignity."[76] There is no reason, then, to equate subordination to a kind of privation or inferiority of being. Put differently, the divine will in its modality of obedience is equal to the modality of divine command. God is no static monad, for the

---

70. *CD* IV/3, 761. As David Guretzki points out, the Spirit acts as a principle of sublimation insofar as "the Father and the Son are eternally ... maintained and upheld (*Aufhebung*) in their distinct modes of being." Barth's active pneumatology, he argues, contrary to criticism, tends "toward a superordination of the Spirit to the Father and the Son." See Guretzki, *Karl Barth on the Filioque*, 161.

71. "All that Jesus does is, therefore, suffused and irradiated by the way in which He does it. ... And this obedience of Jesus is the clear reflection of the unity of the Father and the Son by the bond of the Spirit in the being of the eternal God Himself, who is the fulness of all freedom." *CD* II/2, 605.

72. For example, Guy Mansini cites the Benedictine abbot-monk relationship in his chapter "Can Humility and Obedience Be Trinitarian Realities?" in *Thomas Aquinas and Karl Barth: An Unofficial Catholic-Protestant Dialogue*, ed. Bruce L. McCormack (Grand Rapids: Eerdmans, 2013), 73–78.

73. *CD* IV/1, 761.

74. *CD* IV/1, 202. See Paul D. Molnar, "The Obedience of the Son in the Theology of Karl Barth and of Thomas F. Torrance," *Scottish Journal of Theology* 67, no. 1 (2014): 50–69.

75. *CD* I/1, 381–82.

76. *CD* IV/1, 202.

Father and Son, while distinct, exist as a living, dynamic unity by virtue of their Spirit.[77] Barth explains,

> He is the one and the other without any cleft or differentiation but in perfect unity and equality because in the same perfect unity and equality He is also a Third, the One who affirms the one and equal Godhead through and by and in the two modes of being, the One who makes possible and maintains His fellowship with Himself as the one and the other.[78]

Besides the apophatic dimension, there are at least three positive aspects to the Spirit's act of sublimation: modal-relational, etiological, and passion-action unities, which we shall investigate in turn.

First, there is a relational unity-in-distinction rooted in the divine modes of being. Just as the divine modes of being are the one God in distinct "self-repetition," so the distinction-in-unity of command and obedience may be seen as the repetitions of the divine will.[79] In the incarnation, there is a *twofold but single will of God* rooted in God's eternal being, which is revealed in the "antithesis of exaltation and abasement" of Jesus Christ.[80] While command and obedience confront each other in antithesis and not "in neutrality" since they flow from the "real differentiation" of the Father and Son, nonetheless, "there is no contradiction, no gaping chasm, between them."[81]

That is because the Father-Son relation is undergirded by a more foundational—and Trinitarian—unity of their eternal being and activity. For it is only the "fellowship and love in the activity of the Holy Spirit as the third divine mode of being of the same kind" that brings about "the ceaseless unity of the One who disposes and the One who complies, the actual oneness and agreement of that which they will and do."[82] The will of God is, therefore, not command or obedience seen in isolation or opposition

---

77. *CD* IV/1, 202.
78. *CD* IV/1, 202–3.
79. *CD* IV/1, 205.
80. *CD* IV/2, 351.
81. *CD* IV/2, 351.
82. *CD* IV/1, 209–10.

but rather a singular Spirit-unified movement of command-and-obedience.[83] This is because they are not only united in the electing love of God for humanity but "first in the eternal love in which the Father loves the Son and the Son the Father," that is, in the Holy Spirit.[84] While the will of God is singular, the Father and Son express it distinctly and in correspondence to their I-and-Thou distinction and unity in their Spirit.[85]

Second, from this fundamental modal-relational unity arises an etiological unity of origin and consequence, in which God's determination in election is rendered indivisible from its fulfilment in history.[86] From the eternal beginnings, it "is in the Holy Spirit that the commission of the Father and the obedience of the Son ... obviously coincide in the decree."[87] Continuing into its outworking *ad extra*, this twofold act of command and obedience have "the same purpose ... the same goal ... as the decisive work of divine love," namely, God's self-giving to the world.[88] Consequently, in the history of Jesus Christ, it is the same Spirit who brings about "the self-evident fulfilment of that determination of a son to his father, the actual rendering of a perfect obedience."[89] There is no disjunction between God's immanent and transitive (or transeunt) work because the Spirit binds together cause and effect, *arche* and *telos*.

In the fulfilment of God's purposes, the Spirit not only enabled Christ's punctiliar acts of obedience but also united them into a life history marked

---

83. This reality is revealed and attested by the same Spirit to the church: "He is the Holy Spirit, the Spirit of truth, because He reveals the life of the man Jesus as the life of the Son with the Father and the Father with the Son; because He discloses the antithesis [of command and obedience] which dominates this life in its necessity as the antithesis which is first in God because it is first opened up, but also overcome and closed again, in the will of God." *CD* IV/1, 352.

84. *CD* IV/2, 352. As God *loves* in freedom, God's essential love (*diligere*) is the ground of God's free, electing love for humanity (*eligere*), and as God loves in *freedom*, God's communion *ad intra* is not closed but self-communicative. *CD* IV/2, 43, 766–68.

85. Darren O. Sumner, "Obedience and Subordination in Karl Barth's Trinitarian Theology," in *Advancing Trinitarian Theology: Explorations in Constructive Dogmatics*, ed. Oliver D. Crisp and Fred Sanders (Grand Rapids: Zondervan, 2014), 141.

86. *CD* IV/1, 209. In both one divine being and will, "He is the same in consequence (and obedience) as the Son as is the Father in origin."

87. *CD* III/1, 56.

88. *CD* IV/2, 351. Elsewhere, Barth cites Bonaventure's appropriation of principle, execution, and goal to the Father, Son, and Spirit respectively. *CD* I/1, 373.

89. *CD* IV/1, 207.

by an ethical-spiritual constancy, in both his divine and human modalities.[90] That is why Jesus' narrative was marked by the divine "steadfastness of grace" in the resurrection and a "steadfastness of obedience" in his prayer life, both of which were held together by the Holy Spirit, who is "the unity of this steadfastness."[91] Since the Spirit enables the movements of humility and majesty in Jesus Christ, it is the same Spirit who directs our attention to the exaltation and humiliation of Jesus Christ.[92]

Last, there is a unity of receptivity and activity. Divine obedience orientated *ad extra* is not only just a passive but also an active implementation or actualization of the divine will.[93] This finds its antecedent in the unified will of God as the originating love of the Father and responsive love of the Son.[94]

> For—as we had first to show—it is in His mode of being as the Son, as the eternally Begotten of the Father, and to that extent, although of the same essence, first loved by Him and then loving Him in return, as the One who is in order secondary and therefore obedient to Him, that He is the one God in His humility.[95]

The obedience of Jesus Christ is, therefore, not merely founded on the Son's "natural" relation to the Father—His eternal generation—since this is purely a receptive relation of being.[96] In addition to this is the procession of the Spirit, in which the Son actively responds to the Father in filial love.

---

90. *CD* II/2, 125–26. See JinHyok Kim, *The Spirit of God and the Christian Life: Reconstructing Karl Barth's Pneumatology* (Minneapolis: Fortress, 2014).

91. *CD* II/2, 126.

92. *CD* IV/2, 348.

93. *CD* IV/1, 195.

94. And as its consequent, there is the objective Word of command going forth, which is received subjectively in human obedience enabled by the Spirit. *CD* I/2, 248.

95. *CD* IV/2, 44.

96. The obedience of the eternal Son in the economy of salvation is the proper mode whereby he enacts the undivided work of the Trinity 'for us and our salvation'. This thesis now enjoys rather wide acceptance among contemporary theologians. In many instances, adopting this viewpoint has resulted in significant revisions of traditional trinitarian metaphysics. The purpose of the present article is to demonstrate that adopting Barth's thesis does not require such revision and that this thesis can and should be appropriated within the orbit of traditional trinitarian theology. We will endeavor to establish our claim by considering the relationship between the Son's eternal generation and his economic obedience, and by addressing three major objections that might be raised against our claim. The personal property of the Son cannot be an unqualified "receptivity" in which not only does he stand in a receptive relation to the Father,

Furthermore, Christ in His humanity fulfilled both the passive and active righteousness by not only "accepting responsibility" for our sins but also "[doing] right" in our place.[97] Not only is this power to be "active and passive" the result of a humanity grounded, constituted, and maintained by the Spirit, but filial obedience is possible, as we have noted, only by the Spirit of Christ.[98]

To sum up this section, Barth has creatively restated Augustine's mutual-love analogy of the Trinity, in which the Spirit is the Sublimator of the dialectic of the Superior and the Subordinate.[99] On this account of the relational nexus within the Trinity, analogy would be a misnomer since the sublimation of command and obedience transcend all creaturely categories.

SPIRIT AS INFLUENCER OF FOUNTAIN AND OBJECT

It might surprise some that Edwards, like his Swiss counterpart, affirms that the condition for the possibility of the incarnation is found in the divine being.[100] His understanding of the seemingly oppositional divine perfections is also not that far removed from Barth's. According to the former, the divine majesty and condescension, though "in our manner of conceiving, are very diverse from one another," are mutually enhancing perfections that "sweetly kiss and embrace each other."[101] In the incarnation and

---

but also, the divine essence of the Son is receptive to his human nature. See Bruce McCormack, "Divine Impassibility or Simply Divine Constancy? Implications of Karl Barth's Later Christology for Debates over Impassibility," in *Divine Impassibility and the Mystery of Human Suffering*, ed. James Keating and Thomas Joseph White (Grand Rapids: Eerdmans, 2009), 178. See also White, *The Incarnate Lord*, 297.

97. *CD* IV/1, 236–37.

98. *CD* III/2, 429; *CD* II/2, 106.

99. A dialectic of "an above and a below [*ein Oben und ein Unten*], a *prius* and a *posterius*, a superiority and a subordination [*einer Vorordnung und Nachordnung*] in God." *CD* IV/1, 196; *CD* IV/1, 214.

100. "How is it that God became man?" (*Quo iure Deus homo*) being the presuppositional question to Anselm's "Why did God become man?" (*Cur Deus homo*). See *CD* IV/1, 184.

101. Edwards, "The Excellency of Christ," *WJE* 19:565; 288. Sermon on Cant. 1:3 [b], in *WJE* 48. Unlike a real difference between human and divine excellencies, the "difference there is between these [divine perfections] is chiefly relative." *WJE* 19:565.

atonement, these perfections were manifested as the "glory of Christ that shone forth in the stable and upon the cross."[102]

Additionally, with Barth, he regards divine condescension as the ground of God's relation to creatures. In a sense, the difference between our two theologians is nominal since Edwards's definition of humility precluded its application to the divine being.[103] While he deems humility as "a proper excellency only of a created nature," nonetheless, this exclusively human virtue finds its greatest resonance in the "infinite condescension in the divine nature."[104] Edwards, thus, grounds Jesus' creaturely humility in condescension—a common divine perfection.[105] The Son *qua* God condescended to become incarnate and *qua* man is humble and meek.[106] It is in Christ, the God-man, where both properties are found since "humility is the nearest and most proper conformity to the condescension of God that can be in a creature."[107]

Unlike Barth, however, Edwards does not speak of command and obedience in relation to Father and Son *ad intra*. Nonetheless, the incarnate Son's filial (and not legal) obedience and subjection to his Father in history mirrors and corresponds to the Son's eternal love to the Father.[108] Yet Edwards does use superiority and subordination language with regard to the divine relations *ad intra*.[109] Since this undoubtedly goes beyond the conventional

---

102. Edwards, 118. Sermon on Cant. 8:1, in *WJE* 44.

103. Humility is "a comparative lowness and littleness before God, or the great distance between God and the subject of this virtue." Edwards, "No. 5 Sermon Fourteen," *WJE* 9:295–96.

104. Edwards, "The Excellency of Christ," *WJE* 19:568; 406. Sermon on Rev. 5:5–6 (Aug 1736), in *WJE* 51.

105. Similarly, the Father, "an infinitely condescending God," by sending His Son and the Spirit shows "wonderful condescension" in indwelling an imperfect church so as to sanctify, illuminate, and comfort her. Edwards, "Charity and Its Fruits," sermon 3, *WJE* 8:247; "The Threefold Work of the Holy Ghost," *WJE* 14:436.

106. In the person of Christ are conjoined, an exceeding spirit of obedience, with supreme dominion over heaven and earth. Edwards, "The Excellency of Christ," *WJE* 19:570. See also "Christ's Sacrifice an Inducement to His Ministers," *WJE* 25:671; 288. Sermon on Cant. 1:3 [b], in *WJE* 48.

107. Edwards, "Charity and Its Fruits," sermon 3, *WJE* 8:247.

108. "But it don't follow hence that Christ, merely because he had human nature, was the proper subject of God's commanding and legislative authority." Edwards, Miscellany 454, *WJE* 13:499.

109. Elsewhere, instead of "superiority," Edwards prefers to use the terms "dependence" and "priority of subsistence." Miscellany 1062, *WJE* 20:430.

boundaries of the divine counsels and the *opus ad extra*, how can Edwards remain immune to the charge of subordinationism?[110]

He does so by maintaining that the divine persons each possess a personal property that renders them both equal and superior to each other. Such a personal characteristic does not undermine their identity "in essence"; on the contrary, it enhances their equality, just as "each has his peculiar honor in the society or family."[111] In a fairly mature manuscript fragment, Edwards elaborates on these superior personal properties:

> In one respect the Father has the superiority: he is the fountain of Deity, and he begets the beloved Son. In another respect the Son has the superiority, as he is the great and first object of divine love. The beloved has as it were the superiority over the lover, and reigns over him. In another respect the Holy Ghost, that is, divine love, has the superiority, as that is the principle that as it were reigns over the Godhead and governs his heart, and wholly influences both the Father and the Son in all they do.[112]

Endorsing the traditional notion of the *taxis* of subsistence, the Father is said to occupy a superior position in the Trinity as the *principium* of the other divine persons.[113] In addition, Edwards suggests a priority of the object in which the Father is dependent on the Son as the eternal beloved.[114] Finally, there is a volitional hierarchy in which the Spirit, as the divine-will-in-act, entirely influences the eternal operations of Father and Son.[115]

Evidently, Edwards is repeating the Augustinian insight that the Spirit is the communion or "principle" of mutual love between Father and Son.

---

110. For examples of Edwards's language of "command," "servant," "subject," and "obedience," see "On the Equality of the Persons of the Trinity," *WJE* 21:147, and Miscellany 1062, *WJE* 20:434, 438, 441.

111. Edwards, "Discourse on the Trinity," *WJE* 21:135. Here, Edwards uses the psychological analogy to characterize the hierarchs: Author, Wisdom, and Excellency.

112. Edwards, "On the Equality," *WJE* 21:147. The editor dates this fragment from early 1740s to no later than 1742. Sang Hyun Lee, *WJE* 21:145.

113. Edwards, Miscellany 1062, *WJE* 20:430.

114. In this passage, it is unclear how the Son has superiority over the Spirit. But we could infer from other places that the Spirit depends on the Son as a mediating object of the Spirit's procession, or an indwelt object in which the Father finds happiness. See also Edwards, "On the Equality," *WJE* 21:146; Miscellany 1253, *WJE* 23:184–85.

115. Edwards refers to the Spirit's "influence" or "influences," whether common or gracious, about seven hundred times in his writings.

But beyond that, he is also inferring that the Spirit actively determines the personal character and superiority of both Father and Son. Since being and operation are identical in God, the Spirit in influencing their immanent action could be said to constitute who the Father and the Son are. As the fountain of deity, the Father's dignity is ennobled by the Spirit's conjunct procession, which ensures the eternal generation of the *beloved* Son. To be precise, the Son is begotten not only as God's self-knowledge but also in love. Furthermore, Edwards roots his pneumatological Christology in the Trinity *ad intra*, whereby the reception of the Spirit by the Son establishes His superiority as the ultimate object of love.[116] As Edwards describes elsewhere, the Son is the *eternal* Messiah or Christ because he is "anointed with the Holy Spirit without measure, strictly speaking, or with the infinite love of the Father toward him."[117]

In Edwards's hands, Augustine's analogy of Lover-Beloved-Love has been reconfigured into a Trinity of hierarchs: fountain-object-influencer. We may call this a kind of hierarchical egalitarianism, pictured as a rotating equilateral triangle of Lover, Beloved, and Matchmaker. Not unlike Barth's portrayal of the Trinity as Superordinate-Subordinate-Sublimator (*prius-posterius-aufhebung*), Edwards's Trinitarian analogy has become fully trilateral, not merely bilateral.

While Edwards maintains the traditional classification of humility and obedience under the economy of the incarnation, he is as insistent as Barth that the divine missions must correspond to the divine processions.[118] More specifically, the human subordination and obedience of the *Logos ensarkos* reflects the *Logos asarkos*'s eternal response of filial love to the Father.[119] We hear echoes of Barth's §64 in the following observations by Edwards:

---

116. Edwards hints elsewhere that "the Son hath this honor that the Father hath not" as a *mediating* object through which the Spirit proceeds and, therefore, by which the Father finds enjoyment and happiness. *WJE* 21:143.

117. Edwards, Miscellany 225, *WJE* 13:346; see also "Blank Bible," note on Dan. 9: 25, *WJE* 24:767.

118. "This twofold way of the Deity's flowing forth *ad extra* answers to the twofold way of the Deity's proceeding *ad intra*, in the proceeding and generation of the Son and the proceeding and breathing forth of the Holy Spirit." Edwards, Miscellany 1082, *WJE* 20: 466).

119. A natural obedience as Son (of Man) follows from the incarnation but not obedience to God as moral governor, which was by covenant of redemption. "But it don't follow hence that Christ, merely because he had human nature, was the proper subject of God's commanding and legislative authority." Edwards, Miscellany 454, *WJE* 13:499.

Indeed, it would have been fitting and excellent in [Jesus Christ], that his will and his actions should be conformed to the Father's will and be subject to him, as it is in itself fit and excellent that the Logos itself should love the Father, and that the Father should love the Son.[120]

In the incarnation, what the Spirit does as divine Influencer is to enable Jesus Christ to obey the Father in filial and legal ways as both a human Son and a man under the law.[121] In this, Barth and Edwards saw a central role played by the Spirit in Christ's humiliation and suffering; where they diverged from each other was on the issue of divine passibility, and on this point, Edwards would remain within the classical fold.[122] Nonetheless, they both perceived a divine dynamism within God's being, one that moved God to condescend as Trinity and the Son to become incarnate.[123]

SPIRIT OF CHRIST: *REGIRATIO* AND CONTRAPUNTAL VECTORS

We have observed an event-based leitmotif in Barth's and Edwards's understanding of the divine condescension, which is ultimately sourced in the divine processions. A quick scan through their terminology on the divine being would show that Barth frequently deploys terms like "event," "movement," "action," "operation," and "activity," while Edwards insists that God is "essentially active."[124] When it comes to human ontology, instead of substances,

---

120. Edwards, Miscellany 454, *WJE* 13:499.

121. Edwards preached the indwelling Spirit in believers as the "a gracious almighty *influencer*, whereby Christ guides and governs the inclinations and actions of the heart ... [causing] a willing obedience to his rules and laws." "The Threefold Work of the Holy Ghost," *WJE* 14:422, my emphasis.

122. Bruce McCormack, "Divine Impassibility or Simply Divine Constancy?: Implications of Karl Barth's Later Christology for Debates over Impassibility," in Keating and White, *Divine Impassibility and the Mystery of Human Suffering*, 183–84.

123. For Barth, only "the personal God has a heart," and therefore, divine love and grace "have their true seat and origin in the movement of the heart of God." *CD* II/1, 370. For Edwards, the end of creation is "that the eternal Son of God ... open and pour forth all that immense fountain of condescension, love and grace that was in his heart" to the church. "The Church's Marriage to Her Sons, And to Her God," *WJE* 25:187.

124. *CD* II/1, 271; *CD* III/2, 356; *CD* IV/1, 7. Within God's life, movement is neither random nor metaphorical but has a trajectory in relation to eternity. *CD* II/1, 593. Edwards, Miscellany 1253, *WJE* 23:184, citing Andrew Michael Ramsay, *The Philosophical Principles of Natural and Revealed Religion* (Glasgow, 1748–49), 1: 78–85.

the latter saw divine events, and the former, histories.[125] We see these two dynamic threads converge in their pneumatological Christologies.

For Edwards, the Holy Spirit is the personal, substantial operation of love in God, or "the Deity in act ... the divine nature as subsisting in pure act and perfect energy."[126] Nowhere more evident is his understanding of the Spirit's eternal procession that includes a circling-back or *regiratio*—the movement of the Father's Love toward the Son, who returns this Love to the Father.[127] Clearly, he does not consider person and action in mutually exclusive terms but views the divine persons as subsistent relations—in particular, the Holy Spirit, who may be denominated "the *operator*" as well as "all act, and nothing but act."[128]

It is the Spirit's role, therefore, to cause all kinds of spiritual unions through this act of procession and return, whether in the Trinity *ad intra*, or *ad extra* in the incarnation, union with Christ (*unio mystica*), and the communion of saints (*communio sanctorum*).[129] In the incarnation, the human nature is hypostatically united to the Father's eternal object of love and as such, participates in the Logos's vision and love of the Father.[130] In this incarnational union, Jesus enters into that eternal circle of I-Thou relationality, that is, the procession and return between the Father and Son in their Spirit.

Since the Holy Spirit *ad intra* is "the end of the other two, the good that they enjoy, the end of all procession," divine love is not only the church's subjective good, it is this very same Spirit who returns the redeemed creation to God—the source and end of all things.[131] Here, then, is a relation of des-

---

125. Marc Cortez, "The Human Person as Communicative Event: Jonathan Edwards on the Mind/Body Relationship," in *The Ashgate Research Companion to Theological Anthropology*, ed. Joshua Ryan Farris and Charles Taliaferro (Farnham, Surrey, UK: Ashgate, 2015), 139–50. Edwin Chr. van Driel, "Karl Barth on the Eternal Existence of Jesus Christ," *Scottish Journal of Theology* 60, no. 1 (2007): 45–61.

126. Edwards, "Discourse on the Trinity," *WJE* 21:121–22. See also "Sermon Fifteen: Heaven is a World of Love," *WJE* 8:373; Miscellany 94, *WJE* 13:260–61. Early on, Barth used a similar phrase: "the pure act of the Spirit." Barth, *The Göttingen Dogmatics: Instruction in the Christian Religion*, vol. 1, ed. Hannelotte Reiffen, trans. Geoffrey W. Bromiley (Grand Rapids: Eerdmans, 1991), 127.

127. In the Trinity *ad intra*, God the Father "must have an object [the beloved Son] on which it exerts itself ... into which it flows, and that flows back to it again." Ramsay, *Principles*, 1:74–85, as quoted in Edwards, Miscellany 1253, *WJE* 23:187.

128. *WJE* 2:202; Miscellany 94, *WJE* 13:260.

129. Edwards, Miscellany 184, *WJE* 13:330.

130. By "the Spirit of the Logos ... the man Jesus hath the spirit and temper of the only begotten Son of God" and, just so, regards "the Father as being his own Father in the manner that he is the Father of the Logos." Edwards, Miscellany 487, *WJE* 13:530; Miscellany 487, *WJE* 13:529.

131. *WJE* 21:146; "On the Equality," *WJE* 21:146. God is "the infinite, inexhaustible, fountain whence all things come at first ... and whither they all shall come at last: for of him and to him

tination, in which the Spirit causes the end of all God's being and operation *ad intra* and *ad extra*.[132] The end of creation is, therefore, the "emanation and remanation" of the Spirit to and from the church, a "constant flowing and reflowing of heavenly and divine love" from Christ's to the saint's heart.[133] For Edwards, while the christological motif of descent and ascent is not absent, it remains a minor key compared with the pneumatological motif of procession and return.[134]

Where the dynamic motif in Edwards is primarily pneumatological, Barth actualizes the Chalcedonian Christology by reconceptualizing Jesus Christ as an event or "an *operatio* between God and man."[135] What the tradition regards as two successive states (*status duplex*) in the work of Jesus Christ—a humiliation (*exinanitio*) followed by an exaltation (*exaltatio*)—Barth reconstructs into "a history" of two simultaneous but distinct trajectories in Jesus Christ.[136] The actualization of this twofold contrapuntal movement takes place in Jesus' pilgrimage into the far country and his homecoming to the Father on our behalf.[137]

On the one hand, as the high-priestly Son of God, Christ exercises "obedience in humility" in his "divine downward movement" toward human beings.[138] On the other hand, as royal Son of Man, Christ is exalted in the "upward movement" so that humanity may participate in the eternal life of

---

are all things, and he is the Alpha and Omega, the beginning and the end." "Images of Divine Things," no. 77, *WJE* 11:79.

132. "He is the end of the other two in their acting *ad intra*, and also in his acting *ad extra*." *WJE* 21:146. Much as Augustine implied, Edwards thinks of the Father as constituted by generation of the Son and spiration of the Spirit. Lewis Ayres, "*Sempiterne Spiritus Donum*: Augustine's Pneumatology and the Metaphysics of Spirit," in *Orthodox Readings of Augustine*, ed. George E. Demacopoulos and Aristotle Papanikolaou (Crestwood, NY: St. Vladimir's Seminary Press, 2008), 146.

133. Edwards, "End for Which God Created the World," *WJE* 8:531; Sarah Pierrepont Edwards, "The Narrative of Sarah Pierrepont Edwards," *WJE* 41.

134. In the incarnation, the Son "came down from heaven and was made flesh and dwelt amongst us. ... Christ since his resurrection is gone into heaven and ... ascended into heaven in our nature." Edwards, 381. Sermon on Gen. 28:12, *WJE* 51. Elsewhere, see Edwards, Miscellany 772, *WJE* 18:422; "Like Rain Upon Mown Grass," *WJE* 22:303; and 381. Sermon on Gen. 28:12, in *WJE* 51.

135. *CD* IV/2, 105. Jesus Christ is God's decree or "eternal movement" toward humankind. *CD* II/2, 91–92.

136. *CD* IV/2, 109–10.

137. From God's eternal life that is both "in unbroken rest and movement," the Son enters the condition of humankind who is alone, a pilgrim in this world, not at peace with himself because he is not at home with God. See *CD* IV/2, 317; *Göttingen Dogmatics*, 73.

138. *CD* IV/1, 635.

God.[139] This descent and ascent are simultaneously united in the prophetic work of the God-man, who "is already exalted in His humiliation and humiliated in His exaltation."[140] This act of reconciliation in the history of Jesus Christ, consisting of "parallel but opposing fulfilment of two great movements, the one from above downwards and the other from below upwards," finds its correspondence in the unity of *prius* and *posterius* by the Spirit within God, as we have previously shown.[141]

To this point, it might appear that the *regiratio* dynamic characterizes Edwards's pneumatology in contrast to the contrapuntal thematic in Barth's Christology.[142] Yet in Barth's view, the journey of the Son into the far country and his homecoming can also be considered "the going out of God only as it aims at the coming in of man; the coming in of man only as the reach and outworking of the going out of God."[143] Furthermore, given that the Holy Spirit is "the basis … of the antithesis which is to be found in [Christ's history], and its overcoming," to wit, "of the humiliation of the Exalted, the Son of God, and … of the exaltation of the Humiliated, the Son of Man," is it not the case that the Spirit also funds both Christ's journey into the far country and our homecoming in Christ?[144]

Having observed that the contrapuntal ascent-descent movement in Jesus Christ is grounded in the eternal *prius-posterius* relation within God in Barth's theology, it is therefore not inappropriate to infer a simultaneous outgoing-incoming dynamic as an extrapolation of the eternal circular

---

139. *CD* IV/2, 317. The Son can only be (and was) exalted as human, but not as God. *CD* IV/1, 135.

140. *CD* IV/2, 110; *CD* IV/1, 133. See Andrew Burgess, *The Ascension in Karl Barth*, Barth Studies (London: Routledge, 2004), 32.

141. *CD* IV/3, 4. This *prius* and *posterius* characterize God's constancy and divine immutability as an eternal, living activity far removed from an abstract immobility. *CD* II/1, 493.

142. A line of investigation beyond the scope of this essay is the classification of majesty and condescension under the rubric of divine glory or beauty. For Barth, beauty is included under the divine perfection of glory (*CD* II/1, 657-66) and is primarily christological; see especially "The Glory of the Mediator," *CD* IV/3, 3-367. For Edwards, it is pneumatological: "Holiness, which is as it were the beauty and sweetness of the divine nature, is as much the proper nature of the Holy Spirit." *WJE* 2:201.

143. *CD* IV/2, 21.

144. *CD* IV/2, 348. Since the external work of the Trinity is undivided, the Word and Spirit have the same "power" and "work," and it follows that Jesus Christ's "outgoing and incoming into this world" in the incarnation is inseparable from the Spirit's "outgoing and self-communicative" work of reconciliation and revelation. *CD* I/1, 150; *CD* I/2, 241; *CD* IV/3, 386, 10. See also *CD* II/1, 412-13.

vector of the Spirit's procession and return.[145] That is, like Edwards, Barth sees the Holy Spirit as the principle of *regiratio ad intra* and *ad extra*—that "eternal love in which God is the one God outwards as well as inwards, the divine principle of creation, reconciliation and redemption."[146] Additionally, is there not textual justification to regard the Spirit-anointed Son's self-sacrifice in history as corresponding to that eternal self-donation of Father and Son in their Spirit?[147] "In this triunity of His essence," Barth muses, "God is eternal love in the self-giving of the Father to the Son and the Son to the Father which is accomplished in the fact that He is ... also the Holy Spirit."[148]

In short, the convergence of the pneumatological procession-return dynamic with the Christological ascent-descent motif represents a continuation and development of an Augustinian soteriological theme—and indeed a Christian one—running through Aquinas to Calvin.[149] To be sure, historians will need to weigh the Platonic (if any) against the biblical elements in their constructions.[150] But it is clear once again how the writings of these two Reformed pastor-theologians from the eighteenth and twentieth centuries are indebted to the fourth-century Doctor of Grace.

CONCLUSION

If we disassociate the notions of visibility from divine agency, the reticence of the Spirit we observe in Augustinian pneumatologies may well be interpreted as the introverted dimension of divine personhood—a kind of humility of the Spirit. Insofar as Barth and Edwards understood the personal as Subject or Mind with volition, their pneumatologies could be deemed

---

145. This ascent-descent vocabulary is not limited to Jesus Christ since the Spirit's mission is not without the Son's: "Jesus is the beloved Son of God, and as such He is from the very outset and throughout His existence the spiritual man, i.e., the true and exalted and royal man who lives by the descent of the Spirit of God and is therefore wholly filled and directed by Him." *CD* IV/2, 324.

146. *CD* IV/2, 43, 766–68.

147. Although Barth does not appropriate to the Spirit the property of perfect action or pure act, he is aware of Adolf Schlatter's observation of the *imago Dei* within Augustinian categories, in which volition is identified with the capacity for action. *CD* I/1, 338.

148. *CD* IV/2, 757.

149. Julie Canlis, *Calvin's Ladder: A Spiritual Theology of Ascent and Ascension* (Grand Rapids: Eerdmans, 2010), especially 96, 114–16, 126. Paul Rorem, "'Procession and Return' in Thomas Aquinas and His Predecessors," *Princeton Seminary Bulletin* 13, no. 2 (1992): 147–63.

150. And adjudicate between Adolf von Harnack's thesis of the Hellenization of Christianity and Jaroslav Pelikan's counter-thesis of a Christianization of Hellenism.

psychological, even though Barth had grave concerns about an *analogia entis* not conditioned by the human being's justification and, therefore, her renewed creatureliness in Christ.[151]

Extending the Augustinian insight that love is psychological, such affection is also dynamic, since it is both the *will-in-act* and *will-in-act*.[152] From this perspective, Barth's locutions of the Spirit as the power of the Son and the Father, as well as Edwards's references to the Spirit as the holiness, love, and grace of Christ and the Father, take on a different light.[153] On the premise of divine simplicity, the Holy Spirit is not only being-in-act but being-as-act since agency and agent are identical.[154]

In another sense, we could consider the mutual love analogy psychological where it includes *modes-of-will-in-act*.[155] If command and obedience or paternal love and filial love are two modes of the one will of God in their Spirit, any tritheism analogous to human hierarchies is ruled out of court. For Barth, the Spirit is the eternal sublimator who negates contradictions and brings about a transcending unity-in-distinction between the superordinate Father and the subordinate Son. Edwards envisioned a circle of hierarchs in God, with the Holy Spirit as the divine influencer that characterizes the personal properties and superiority of Father and Son, who are the eternal fountain and object of love, respectively.

In walking along this Augustinian path with Barth and Edwards, we may conclude that there exists in the divine life the primal call of love from the Father, to which the Son's eternal response is "I do."[156] Upon this ontological foundation—of the fullness of love received and returned—the Father

---

151. Keith L. Johnson, *Karl Barth and the Analogia Entis*, T&T Clark Studies in Systematic Theology 6 (London: T&T Clark, 2010).

152. As Augustine asked rhetorically about the Holy Spirit, "What else after all is charity but the will?" See Augustine, *Trin.* 15.20.38, as cited in Khaled Anatolios, *Retrieving Nicaea: The Development and Meaning of Trinitarian Doctrine* (Grand Rapids: Baker Academic, 2011), 278n87.

153. Or, in McCormack's more agential language, the Holy Spirit is "the effective agent of all that is done by the Father and Son in the relation to the world." McCormack, "Lord and Giver of Life," 251.

154. Like Edwards (see n. 15 *infra*), Barth believed that only God is properly being-in-act, or "the event of God's act ... His conscious decision ... divine Spirit. ... No other being exists absolutely in its act." *CD* II/2, 271.

155. "All God's willing is primarily a determination of the love of the Father and the Son in the fellowship of the Holy Ghost." *CD* II/2, 169.

156. Edwards, "Heaven is a World of Love," *WJE* 8:373. See *CD* I/1, 470.

bids the Son to love the world. In answering "I will," the obedient Son enters into a journey into the far country as the Prodigal, bringing along many in his homecoming to the Father.[157] For Edwards and Barth, this command and obedience of love is both possible and actual by the sublime influence of the eternal Matchmaker—the Spirit of Father and Son.[158] It is upon this deep foundation that Jesus' double love commandment issues forth as the Christian vocation to spirituality, ethics, and missions.[159]

---

157. Hence, the Christological basis of the parable of the prodigal son are the words "my son" and "thy brother." CD IV/2, 24.

158. Edwards proposes a Trinitarian interpretation of the eschatological wedding feast: "'Tis with respect to this her marriage supper, that she, from the motion of the Spirit of the Lamb in her, says, 'Come.' So that you are invited on all hands; all conspire to call you. God the Father invites you: this is the King that has made a marriage for his Son; and he sends forth his servants, the ministers of the gospel, to invite the guests. And the Son himself invites you." "Ruth's Resolution," WJE 19:319.

159. Commenting on Revelation 22:17, Edwards observes that the church's invitation to the world to join "the marriage supper," like "the call of Christ the bridegroom ... is the voice of the Spirit in her." "Ruth's Resolution," WJE 19:319. See also WJE 2:237–38, 249, 284; 8:133.

6

—

CREATION

Uche Anizor

Arguably the most important question with respect to the reality of creation is "why?". Why is there something rather than nothing? And this "why" comes from two directions, so to speak. From one direction, there is the question of motive: what motivated God to create something? What were his reasons, his grounds, to create? From the other direction, there is the question of purpose: to what end did God create an other alongside himself? What were his goals in creating? While not easily separable, these questions are distinct. In his exposition of God's perfection as the one who loves, Barth asks and answers these two "why" questions. "God's loving," he writes, "is an end in itself." He expands:

> All the purposes that are willed and achieved in Him are contained and explained in this end. … Certainly in loving us God wills His own glory and our salvation. But He does not love us because He wills this. He wills it for the sake of His love. God loves in realising these purposes. But God loves because He loves; because this act is His being, His essence and His nature.[1]

God's love is the motivating force and root cause of all things, including creation. Not much is controversial there, I think, given that God's actions have their basis in his nature (as Barth rightly captures). However, the opening claim—that God's love is an end in itself and that he wills his glory because of his love—is more intriguing, especially when we apply it to creation. One of the most well-known and important treatments of this question comes from

---

1. *CD* II/1, 279.

Jonathan Edwards in his treatise *The End for Which God Created the World* (or *End of Creation*), in which he concludes that God's end in creating was and is God's "glory." Are Edwards and Barth saying different things or saying the same thing differently? The aim of this short essay is to answer that very question. We begin with an examination of Edwards's treatment before exploring Barth's statement in the third volume of *Church Dogmatics*. From there we will try to relate their respective theologies of God's glory, election, and divine revelation to the question at hand.

THE END OF CREATION IN EDWARDS

Edwards begins *End of Creation* with an explanation of terms, with the aim of clarifying what he means when he speaks of God's end in creating the world. For our purposes, an "ultimate end" is "that which the agent seeks in what he does for its own sake." It is what the agent "loves, values and takes pleasure in on its own account, and not merely as a means of a further end."[2] By contrast, a subordinate end is something an agent seeks as a means to some other end and not for its own sake. Now, someone may have two different ultimate ends but only one chief end. That is, two things may be sought for their own sake, yet one may be more valued than the other. Moreover, ultimate ends may be categorized as "original" and "consequential." Original ultimate ends are those that are sought independent of all conditions, while consequent ultimate ends are those dependent on certain conditions being met.[3] Thus, what we are concerned with is God's ultimate *original* end in creating the world. Edwards concludes the introduction by leaving the possibility open that there could be multiple original ultimate ends of creation—an important consideration as Edwards's argument unfolds.[4]

ARGUMENTS FROM REASON

Edwards breaks his discourse into two large "chapters." The first deals with rational arguments, and the second, with scriptural arguments for what God's end in creation must be. He begins his arguments from reason by laying out some general observations, which may be summed up as follows. First,

---

2. *WJE* 8:405.

3. *WJE* 8:408–12.

4. *WJE* 8:413–15.

whatever God's end in creation might be, it cannot be the filling of some lack in himself. This defies the very definitions of God (as self-sufficient Creator) as well as creation (as that which *receives* its existence). Second, whatever is good and valuable *in itself* is worthy to be valued by God in itself and on its own account. Something valuable in itself is worthy of being sought as an ultimate end in God's actions. Now, for it to be an end of his actions, it must actually be attainable by his actions. For example, his existence is unattainable by his actions; therefore, it cannot be an end of his actions. Third, that thing that is most valuable in itself prior to creation and can be attained by the act of creation, this is the ultimate and highest end of God in creating. Fourth, since God is the most valuable being, he must be capable of being his own end in creating the world. The esteem we give someone must be in proportion to their value.[5] For Edwards, a significant part of moral rectitude consists in attributing the amount of honor proportionate to the excellency of being. To not do so is wrong or unfitting. God must, therefore, have supreme regard to himself as the greatest Being. This regard to himself is displayed in what he does. Fifth, if facts show that in creating the world God valued something in itself originally, absolutely, and not for some other end, then this must be his ultimate end in creation. Finally, whatever comes about as a result of creation that is valuable in itself and absolutely, this, we may infer, is an ultimate end of God's creating the world.[6] In this section, Edwards is laying the groundwork for the claim that it is only fitting for God to have supreme regard for himself in his work of creating and that this is what we will see in the biblical arguments to follow.

The next question Edwards seeks to answer is "what things that result from the creation of the world are originally valuable in themselves?" He answers the question by making several arguments. He notes, first, that it is "fitting" that God's attributes be put on display in the work of creation. Had he not created, there would be no opportunity to express the attributes of power, wisdom, justice, etc. They would have laid dormant, so to speak.[7] Put indelicately, these attributes exist to be exercised. Next, he argues that

---

5. This is what some writers call "the principle of proportionate regard." See Michael J. McClymond and Gerald R. McDermott, *The Theology of Jonathan Edwards* (New York: Oxford University Press, 2011), 210–11.

6. *WJE* 8:420–27.

7. *WJE* 8:428–29.

if it is fitting that God's perfections be expressed, then it must be desirable that they be known and delighted in by beings other than himself.[8] In other words, God's delight is in creating others who will delight in him eternally and increasingly. Finally, if God's fullness is excellent in itself, then he should desire the "multiplication" and "repetition" of it ad extra. In fact, it is God's "disposition" to overflow and communicate his fullness outside of himself, and this is what moved him to create.[9] In other words, God's original ultimate end in creation was to communicate or emanate the fullness of his perfections.[10]

How can God desiring these things be consistent with God making himself his ultimate end? God's delighting in the display of his perfections, and in their being known, loved, and delighted in, is God making himself his end.[11] Moreover, God's self-communication results not only in his glory being known and loved but also in creatures conforming to it by participating in it. His knowledge overflows to their knowledge, his holiness to their holiness, his happiness to their happiness. This "multiplication" of God's glory is, in a sense, the expression of his perfections in their most complete state.[12] And in God desiring this multiplication, he shows highest regard to himself.

Edwards closes his arguments from reason (i.e., chapter I) by addressing objections, which can reasonably be summarized as follows: it is not becoming (i.e., it is needy, selfish, ignoble, and not beneficent) of God to make himself his end in creating the world.[13] Edwards's response to the charge of non-beneficence captures well his response to all the objections and the sum of his rational arguments: "God in seeking their glory and happiness, seeks himself: and in seeking himself, i.e. himself diffused and expressed (which he delights in, as he delights in his own beauty and fullness), he seeks their

---

8. WJE 8:431–32.

9. WJE 8:432–33. Oliver Crisp lays out four ways scholars interpret disposition language. I am in agreement with the position held by Strobel. See Oliver D. Crisp and Kyle C. Strobel, *Jonathan Edwards: An Introduction to His Thought* (Grand Rapids: Eerdmans, 2018), 92–103.

10. Strictly speaking, however, what moved God to create cannot be a desire to communicate himself to *a creature* but a disposition to communicate himself *in general*, without a view to the creature *per se*. WJE 8:435.

11. WJE 8:437–38.

12. Edwards is trying to express as strongly as possibly God's disposition to emanate his fullness: "So God looks on the communication of himself … as though he were not in his most complete and glorious state without it." WJE 8:439. This statement must be counterbalanced by the many statements that refer to God's own sufficiency.

13. WJE 8:445–58.

glory and happiness."[14] God's glory expressed, delighted in, and conformed to is his ultimate end, while having the wellbeing of the creature also as his end. One "implies" the other because, as Edwards puts it, "God is their good."[15]

ARGUMENTS FROM SCRIPTURE

Scripture is the surest guide to a knowledge of God's ends. Thus, Edwards begins the second part of his dissertation by pointing to the many Scriptures that speak of God as the "first and last" or "beginning and the end" (e.g., Isa 44:6; 48:12; Rev 1:8, 17; 21:6; 22:13). These terms refer to God as the source and end of all things (the "first efficient cause" and "last final cause"). This reading is confirmed by passages that speak of all things coming *from* God and existing *for* God (e.g., Rom 11:36; Col 1:16; Heb 2:10).[16] Though the matter is clearly established by these passages of Scripture, Edwards will proceed in the following chapters to show the pervasiveness of this teaching throughout the Bible.

In the next section, Edwards lays out twelve hermeneutical principles (or "positions") to guide our reading of Scripture in relation to God's end in creation. Two of these positions can be said to underlie the remaining ten. Position 1, restating thoughts from his introduction, maintains that whatever Scripture points to as the ultimate end of God's works of providence in general may be supposed to be his ultimate end in creation.[17] Position 4 states that God's ultimate end in the intelligent and moral world is his last end in the work of creation in general, since "the moral part is the end of all the rest of the creation."[18] Ultimately, what is God's end in creation is his end in providence in the moral world.

Edwards spends the following section amassing Scripture texts that illustrate that the ultimate end of all the goodness of the moral world is to glorify God and, thus, that God's glory (i.e., God himself) is the ultimate end of creation. For example, according to Isaiah 43:6–7 and Ephesians 1:5–6, God predestines and forms a redeemed people (i.e., the good part of the moral world) for his glory. Even the great work of redemption wrought by Christ

---

14. *WJE* 8:459.
15. *WJE* 8:459.
16. *WJE* 8:467.
17. *WJE* 8:469.
18. *WJE* 8:470.

(Phil 2:6–11; Eph 1:3–14) is for God's glory.[19] What may be said about God's glory may equally be said about the notions of God's "name," "praise," and his desire to make his perfections known.[20] In other words, God himself is his end in all his works.

As the treatise nears its climax, Edwards returns to a key issue addressed in the first chapter, namely, whether God had the good of the creature as an ultimate end in creation. Edwards's response is a resounding yes, and he offers ten arguments from Scripture to show that the "communication of good" to humanity was God's ultimate end in creation. In claiming this, Edwards is precluding the notion that God showing love to creatures is toward some other goal (thus making it a subordinate end). For example, he draws attention to the work of Christ (e.g., John 3:16; Eph 2:4; 1 John 4:9–10) and how it was motivated by love of humanity, plain and simple. He argues that if God sent Christ to redeem us for some other goal than our good, then that goal is the thing God truly loved.[21]

After a penultimate section in which he defines the all-important phrase "the glory of God,"[22] Edwards draws together the various rational and biblical strands of his argument to demonstrate one basic thesis, the sum of all he has been saying: God's ultimate end in the creation of the world was not many things, but rather one—God's glory. God's internal glory consists in his infinite knowledge, infinite holiness, and infinite happiness.[23] It follows that the communication of God's fullness consists in the same—knowledge given, received, and returned as knowledge of God, love of God, and joy in God. It is then fairly straightforward to see how God's regard for his glory and his regard for the creature are not in competition but rather represent a singular end in God creating the world. God's ultimate regard for the creature is seen only when we understand that the creature's happiness is bound up in its reflecting of God's glory. Edwards concludes, "God's respect to the creature's good, and his respect to himself, is not a divided respect; but both

---

19. *WJE* 8:475–92.

20. *WJE* 8:493–502.

21. "For if our good be not at all regarded ultimately, but only subordinately, then our interest is, in itself considered, nothing in God's regard or love." *WJE* 8:505.

22. Since defining the "glory of God" will receive separate treatment later on, I have chosen not to summarize Edwards's description here.

23. He uses John 1:14 as evidence that the glory of God consists of grace (holiness and happiness) and truth (knowledge). See *WJE* 8:529–30.

are united in one, as the happiness of the creature aimed at is happiness in union with himself. The creature is no further happy with this happiness which God makes his ultimate end than he becomes one with God."[24] As our union with God grows, so our happiness in him grows—into eternity. Thus, the glory of God—his fullness "emanated" and "remanated"—is the *one* ultimate end of creation.

CREATION AND COVENANT IN BARTH

While one can find statements throughout Barth's *Dogmatics* that speak of God's designs in creating the world, some of his clearest direct statements are found in *CD* III/1. A good starting point for our discussion is a statement made early in the volume regarding God as Creator:

> God is the One who, although wholly self-sufficient in His possession of all perfections, and absolutely glorious and blessed in His inner life, did not as such will to be alone, and has not actually remained alone, but in accordance with His own will, and under no other inward constraint than that of the freedom of His love, has, in an act of the overflowing of His inward glory, posited as such a reality which is distinct from Himself.[25]

What drives a self-sufficient, blessed, and glorious God to create in the first place? Nothing other than the sovereign love of God. Creation is the overflow of God's inward glory. Creation is a gift, which is another way of saying that it flows from the grace of God. Its starting point "is the good-pleasure of the free omnipotence of the divine love."[26]

The world God creates has humanity at its center. But why is this so? Barth's answer: "The reason why God created this world of heaven and earth ... is that God's eternal Son and Logos did not will to be an angel or animal but a man, and that this and this alone was the content of the eternal divine election of grace."[27] The eternal decree is that Word would become flesh, and therefore, God has chosen humanity as the special object of his love and the

---

24. *WJE* 8:533. See also *WJE* 13:199–200.
25. *CD* III/1, 15.
26. *CD* III/1, 15.
27. *CD* III/1, 18.

center of his work of creation. Jesus Christ is not just the Creator and creature, but he is also the key to understanding creation—its beginnings, meaning, and goal—as grace.[28] He is the "key to the secret of creation."[29] God decreed creation so that there could be a people in Christ on whom God could shower kindness and mercy, so that ultimately God would be glorified for his love on display in Christ. All this talk of Christ as the center of our understanding of creation points to the heart of Barth's treatment of the "end" of creation, which can be summed up in a twofold thesis. First, creation is the "external basis" of the covenant, and second, covenant is the "internal basis" of creation. Let us examine these interrelated statements.

CREATION AS THE EXTERNAL BASIS OF THE COVENANT

God did not create out of caprice, out of compulsion, or out of need. He could have existed without a creature. Creation in no way is a limitation of his own glory. Rather, God chooses to bring a world into existence because "He has loved it from eternity, because He wills to demonstrate His love for it, and because He wills, not to limit His glory by its existence and being, but to reveal and manifest it in His own co-existence with it."[30] If God's glory is in some sense the goal of creation, it is not diminished by the existence of creatures but rather put on display by their existence. God is glorified in the free manifestation of his love in the creation of a creaturely counterpart whom he has destined as a recipient of this love. In other words, according to Barth, creation and "covenant"—God's desire to be with humanity—go hand in hand. How are they related? Our focus here is on creation as the "external basis of the covenant." What does Barth mean by this? He writes:

> Covenant is the goal of creation and creation the way to the covenant. … Creation is the external—and only the external—basis of the covenant. It can be said that it makes it technically possible; that it prepares and establishes the sphere in which the institution and history of the covenant take place; that it makes possible the subject which is

---

28. Jesus's role in creation is at least these: (1) He is God the Creator. (2) As the Son, he is an analogy of creation. (3) As elected man, he is loved by God eternally and is the ground and motivation for creation. CD III/155–56.

29. CD III/1, 27. Barth approvingly cites Irenaeus, Cocceius, Witsius, and Wichelhaus as theologians who rightly captured the truth that creation exists for Christ. CD III/1, 55.

30. CD III/1, 95.

to be God's partner in this history, in short the nature which the grace of God is to adopt and to which it is to turn in this history. As the love of God could not be satisfied with the eternal covenant as such; as it willed to execute it and give it form outside the divine sphere, it made itself this external ground of the covenant.[31]

The eternal covenant of grace, founded in the inner Trinitarian choice to love humanity in Christ, is the main storyline. Creation exists to make that storyline possible. What does Barth mean by "covenant" or "covenant of grace"? First, the covenant is an eternal act of the triune God in which he determines to be in a covenantal relationship with the humanity that has yet to be created and, as Bruce McCormack puts it, "to be God in no other way."[32] Second, the covenant of grace is also a history of God's gracious dealings with humanity, culminating in the work of reconciliation accomplished by Christ.[33] Thus, "covenant" has a pre-history and a history, so to speak: it is God's self-determination to be God with us in Christ, and it is the historical outworking of that eternal plan. Barth speaks of creation as a "theatre of the covenant." It is "radically incapable" of serving any other purpose than God's covenant.[34]

Barth advances this point by showing that the whole creation account of Genesis 1:1–2:4a prefigures the covenant and points to it as the secret energy behind the creation.[35] For example, the creation of the firmament (Gen 1:6–8) points to God's protection of humanity from the chaotic waters; it points to the creation of a sphere in which humanity may live at peace with its Creator. The sun and moon (Gen 1:14–19) mark out days in which humanity can act consciously and responsibly in history as God's covenant partner. Even the creation of beasts (Gen 1:24–25) that will eventually be brought low and slain

---

31. CD III/1, 97.

32. Bruce McCormack, "Grace and Being: The Role of God's Gracious Election in Karl Barth's Theological Ontology," in The Cambridge Companion to Karl Barth, ed. John Webster (Cambridge: Cambridge University Press, 2000), 98.

33. "The fellowship which originally existed between God and man, which was then disturbed and jeopardised, the purpose of which is now fulfilled in Jesus Christ and in the work of reconciliation, we describe as the covenant." CD IV/1, 22. See also John Webster, Barth, 2nd ed. (London: Continuum, 2004), 118–19.

34. CD III/1, 99. This is reminiscent of Calvin's view of creation as a theater of God's glory, displaying his wisdom and power in all his works; see, e.g., Calvin, Institutes, 1.5.8. Barth sees creation as primarily displaying the glory of God's covenantal love.

35. CD III/1, 98–219.

ultimately signifies Jesus Christ, and thus the covenant of grace. Thus, when creation is described as "very good" (Gen 1:31), this simply means that it was adapted for the very purpose God had in view for it, namely, that it would be the external basis of his eternal covenant of grace. Creation—as the external sphere for the enactment of God's covenant—reveals the glory of God, that is, the glory of God as the one who loves in freedom.

COVENANT AS THE INTERNAL BASIS OF CREATION

When speaking of covenant as the "internal basis" of creation, we are deal-ing with the same problem but from a different angle. By describing the covenant of grace as the basis for creation, we simply mean that it is the goal of creation and that which makes creation necessary and possible; it is that which gives creation shape, direction, and meaning. "If creation was the formal presupposition of the covenant, the latter was the mate-rial presupposition of the former. If creation takes precedence historically, the covenant does so in substance."[36] Creation is a sign of the covenant and a sacrament: it points to and mediates its substance (i.e., the covenant). Creation is by definition that external act of God that reveals the hidden glory of God's covenantal love.

While Genesis 1 shows creation as preparing for the covenant, Genesis 2 begins to focus on the history of the covenant that gives meaning to creation. Beginning in verse 4, the chapter takes us to the very meaning of creation: God with humanity, the beginning of the history of the covenant. From its vantage point, we understand creation in light of redemption and humanity in light of the covenant founded on and enacted by Christ. For example, in the beginning of the narrative, the Creator is spoken of as Yahweh Elohim, the covenantal name of God.[37] Thus, the reader is immediately confronted with the truth that creation exists as something founded by the Lord of the cove-nant of grace. The ensuing narrative shows this theme in various other ways.[38] Genesis 2 shines a light on Genesis 1 by showing in a variety of ways that the substance and main subject matter of creation is the covenant founded in eternity and enacted in the history to follow.

---

36. *CD* III/1, 232.

37. *CD* III/1, 234.

38. *CD* III/1, 238–96.

To sum up, creation is the result of God's desire to not keep his glory or "overflowing plenitude" to himself as Father, Son, and Spirit but rather to manifest and magnify that glory in something distinct from himself. To be a creature means to be destined to partake in the overflowing fullness of God's life and love, to be "affirmed, elected and accepted by God."[39] Creation exists for the purpose of providing a sphere in which God can demonstrate his covenant love to humanity in Jesus Christ. Creation's end is covenant.

DIFFERING ENDS? PROVISIONAL CONCLUSIONS

Our query thus far points to some significant overlap in Edwards's and Barth's answers to the question of God's end in creation. Both deny any lack or necessity in God driving him to create. Rather, God creates out of his freedom, goodness, love, and desire to demonstrate that love to a creaturely counterpart. One of God's ultimate ends in creation, according to Edwards, is to have humanity participate in his own knowledge, love, and joy—that is, to partake of the kind of life God has in himself as Father, Son, and Holy Spirit. For Barth, the language of covenant is perhaps more prominent. Yet both point to the same thing: God creates in order to enter a relationship or union with humanity. In other words, God creates for love and not as a means to something else. In both theologians, moreover, God also creates to manifest his glory. Very similar accounts, indeed. However, three questions arise regarding their respective treatments. First, do they mean the same thing by the "glory" of God? How might this shape their account of God's ends? Second, how does their doctrine of predestination contribute to their accounts of creation? Finally, how do their commitments regarding divine revelation alter the way they frame the issue? Let us begin with "glory."

WHAT IS "GLORY"?

Much could be said of both theologians' treatments of "glory" since it pervades their writings. But perhaps a way to see whether they have differing visions of "glory" is to observe how they interact with a common source. Both Edwards's and Barth's accounts of glory are influenced by the work of Reformed orthodox theologian Petrus van Mastricht; Barth is explicit about

---

39. CD III/1, 364.

this, Edwards is not.[40] Thus, we will look at how Mastricht treats "glory" and try to decipher the modifications both theologians make to it.

Mastricht writes that there are four "ingredients" of God's glory (i.e., what God's glory means): (1) it is the infinite eminence of his essence and attributes; (2) it is the brightness of this eminence; (3) it is the recognition of that infinite eminence, first within God himself and then shared with creatures through revelation; and (4) it is the celebration and manifestation of this internal excellency (i.e., its being made public and being extolled)—otherwise known as the "glorification" of God. This manifestation and celebration happen primarily in his church as they praise him for the glory of his mercy, wisdom, love, holiness, and justice and rest on his power and goodness.[41]

EMANATION AND REMANATION

Edwards follows Mastricht quite closely, concluding from a study of Greek and Hebrew terms that "glory" means four things. First, it refers to the internal or inherent excellency or worth of a thing. Second, it refers to the emanating or communicating of that internal glory. As this is applied to God, it refers to the communicating and spreading of "God's fullness." Third, "glory" implies the knowledge of God's inherent worth or majesty. In other words, for God to glorify himself means that he makes known his majesty and excellency and perfections. Finally, and related, glory often implies or is summed up by praise. Scripture often uses "glory" and "praise" as synonyms (e.g., Ps 50:23; Isa 42:8). To give glory to God, or to praise him, is to have "the high esteem and love of the heart, exalting thoughts of God, and complacence in his excellence and perfection."[42] To sum up: the glory of God, as it pertains to God's end in creation, is "the emanation and true external expression of God's internal glory and fullness ... Or in other words, God's internal glory

---

40. Stephen Holmes points out that detailed descriptions of what is meant by "the glory of God" were not common among Reformed orthodox theologians. Mastricht was an exception. See Stephen R. Holmes, *God of Grace and God of Glory: An Account of the Theology of Jonathan Edwards* (Grand Rapids: Eerdmans, 2001), 62. Even though Edwards does not make explicit reference to Mastricht in his treatment of glory, he was well versed in the theologian. In *WJE* 16:217, Edwards claims, "But take Mastricht for divinity in general, doctrine, practice, and controversy; or as an universal system of divinity and it is much better than Turretin or any other book in the world, excepting the Bible, in my opinion."

41. Petrus van Mastricht, *Faith in the Triune God*, vol. 2 of *Theoretical-Practical Theology*, ed. Joel R. Beeke, trans. Todd M. Rester (Grand Rapids: Reformation Heritage, 2019), 472–75.

42. *WJE* 8:522.

extant, in a true and just exhibition, or external existence of it."[43] And this external expression corresponds to the inner life and processions of the Godhead: the eternal generation of the Son (God's idea or understanding or knowledge) and the spiration of the Spirit (as God's will, corresponding to love and joy). The communication of God's knowledge, love, and joy is "only a kind of second proceeding of the same persons, their going forth ad extra, as before they proceeded ad intra."[44]

The key difference between Edwards and Mastricht, in my view, is the emphasis Edwards places on God's emanation and communication of his excellencies of knowledge, love, and joy and the human's true participation in these. This is implied in Mastricht's talk of God allowing the creature to recognize something of what God recognizes in himself as well as the notion of humanity glorifying God by experiencing and "estimating" his internal excellency. There is "emanation" and "remanation" in Mastricht but not quite the same stress on the creature's participation being part and parcel of God's glory or self-glorification.[45] This particular emphasis, along with the unique Trinitarian stress, is a signature move in Edwards's particular doctrine of divine glory.

REVELATION ACCOMPLISHED AND APPLIED

Barth's discussion of glory comes at the end of his majestic treatment of the divine perfections in CD II/1 and has four stages: describing glory from Scripture and the tradition; elucidating his view of glory through a subtle interaction with Mastricht; describing beauty as the form glory takes; and discussing the creature's response to God's beauty. Our focus will be on only the second stage.[46]

---

43. WJE 8:527.

44. WJE 20:466.

45. On this basic point, I agree with Holmes. However, he also makes the unfair claim that Mastricht is insufficiently Trinitarian, thereby giving a vision of God's glory that is distant, otherworldly, and only able to be seen "across a gap." Holmes, God of Grace, 64. However, in Mastricht's polemical sections, for example, he makes plain his concern that the Socinians, Pelagians, Remonstrants, and Lutherans erode the glory of each divine Person in their teaching. See Mastricht, Faith in the Triune God, vol. 2, 475–79. Mastricht does not make the idiosyncratic Trinitarian moves Edwards does, but that does not make his account of glory less Trinitarian.

46. For a very helpful exposition of Barth's treatment of glory, see Robert B. Price, Letters of the Divine Word: The Perfections of God in Karl Barth's Church Dogmatics (London: T&T Clark, 2011), 170–83.

Barth's appropriation of Mastricht is summed up in four points that follow, but slightly modify, his predecessor's work. First, God's glory is his self-sufficiency, fullness, preeminence, and distinction from every other being. He is the source of light. Second, God's glory does not connote distance and relative independence from the creatures. He is not a light that illuminates nothing. His glory is not radiance in abstracto; it effectively illumines others in some way. Third, what reaches us when the light of God's glory shines is God himself. His shining of his light is for the purpose of relationship.[47] Fourth, God's glory is the accomplishment of revelation—revelation sent and received, "an illuminating and an illumination."[48] In an earlier section, Barth writes, "[Glory] refers to the legitimate, effective, and actual self-demonstration, self-expression and self-declaration of a being whose self-revelation is subject to no doubt, criticism or reservation. This being is glorious. It achieves recognition for itself in such a way that it need not and cannot be questioned."[49] God's glory is not some latent attribute, some resplendent potentiality that is only to be marveled at within the Godhead. Rather, God's glory is revelation accomplished and applied. God's glory is the successful eliciting of worship from his creatures. It is the participation of creatures in God's self-glorification, insofar as it is God who produces this response in his creatures: "All together and without exception they take part in the movement of God's self-glorification and the communication of His joy."[50] The glorification of God means the creature's participation in God's own joy that he imparts in the act of revelation.[51]

Barth's reworking of Mastricht is subtle and is bound up with Barth's concern to root our understanding of God in revelation. Thus, while God's glory is the infinite eminence or majesty of his perfections, it is the majesty of a God who chooses to be for and with humanity. While glory does refer to God's brilliance, it is not a brilliance that shines in an eternal abyss. Rather, it is brilliance directed at a world God has chosen. Like Mastricht, Barth draws attention to the fact that glory aims to be recognized. However, it is not the bland recognition of an attribute of God that is in view but rather a covenantal knowledge of God himself. In other words, God does not merely share knowledge; he gives

---

47. CD II/1, 647.
48. CD II/1, 647.
49. CD II/1, 642.
50. CD II/1, 647.
51. CD II/1, 648–49.

himself. Finally, like Mastricht, Barth stresses God's self-glorification both within himself and in his works, as well as the creature's response of glorification. Yet in Barth, God's self-glorification effectively produces the response of glorification, chiefly in the form of joy in God. It is clear that in Barth, the focus is on the effusive, self-communicative dimension of glory and not the attribute in the abstract.

Edwards's and Barth's accounts of glory are virtually identical. In both theologians (1) God's glory is the fullness of his perfections; (2) this fullness is decreed by God to be seen, known, and delighted in by creatures—it is inherently self-communicative; and (3) the creatures' glorification of God is their participation in God's own glory, his own self-glorification.[52] Their differences lie primarily in terms of the concepts used. In Barth, the language and conceptual world of revelation takes center stage. Yet this does not appear to be a difference in substance between him and Edwards. Indeed, when Edwards talks of emanation, communication, diffusion, and so forth, he is speaking of revelation in both cognitive and affective terms—ways consonant with Barth. Edwards, like Barth, speaks of God's glory as the actual and accomplished communication of God's self to his creatures. Another subtle difference appears to be in terms of emphasis. Barth stresses the self-communicative dimension at every turn, allowing it to control and define the term "glory." He is unwilling to think of glory apart from its self-communication. Though Edwards makes similar moves, it is not as prominent an emphasis. Nevertheless, given the similarities, we will have to look elsewhere for help to discern what underlies the potential difference in their accounts of God's end in creation. For this we turn to their respective doctrines of predestination.

PREDESTINATION IN CHRIST

We will begin our exploration of the relationship between election, Christ, and God's end in creation in reverse, first looking at Barth's famous Christocentric reworking of the doctrine of election before looking at Edwards's account. In due course, we will see that Barth's peculiar moves vis-à-vis this doctrine are the key to understanding the subtle difference between him and Edwards on our main issue.

---

52. More could have been said about how they both treat God's beauty as well.

The task of summarizing Barth's doctrine of election in a few words is daunting, but I will focus on those portions most immediately relevant to our present concern. The place to begin is in his opening thesis in *CD* II/2:

> The doctrine of election is the sum of the Gospel because of all words that can be said or heard it is the best: that God elects man; that God is for man too the One who loves in freedom. It is grounded in the knowledge of Jesus Christ because He is both the electing God and elected man in One. It is part of the doctrine of God because originally God's election of man is a predestination not merely of man but of Himself. Its function is to bear basic testimony to eternal, free and unchanging grace as the beginning of all the ways and works of God.[53]

Four themes in Barth's thesis shed light on the basic orientation of his doctrine. First, election is good news and not a mixed message. Second, the doctrine is grounded in the knowledge of Jesus Christ and not ultimately some mysterious unknowable reality like the *decretum absolutum*. Third, it is to be located specifically within the doctrine of God, not in the doctrine of salvation or the church. Finally, its function is ultimately to bear witness to the fact that sovereign love (not justice, or wisdom, or sheer will) is the foundation of everything God does.

The doctrine of election is founded on a knowledge of Jesus Christ (a theme we will return to later). In the face of Jesus Christ—the electing God and the elected man—we understand the true nature of election as grace. Jesus is the Word who, in concert with the Father and Spirit, eternally chose to be the Mediator. He is also chosen by God as Mediator. Thus, he is electing and elected. What this means is that "in Jesus Christ God in His free grace determines Himself for sinful man and sinful man for Himself. He therefore takes upon Himself the rejection of man with all its consequences, and elects man to participation in His own glory."[54] In place of an absolute decree that is powerful, mysterious, and unknowable, that somehow grounds God's election, we have the name "Jesus Christ."

Contrary to the (Reformed and Augustinian) tradition he seeks to correct, Barth is adamant that the doctrine of election is not a "mixed message of joy

---

53. *CD* II/2, 3.
54. *CD* II/2, 94.

and terror, salvation and damnation. ... It does not proclaim in the same breath both good and evil, both help and destruction, both life and death."[55] Rather, election is good news; it is God's yes to humanity in that (as his thesis proclaims) his sovereign love is directed not only inwardly but also outwardly toward humanity. Election is the sum of the gospel—the "gospel in a nutshell"—because it proclaims a God whose primal decision is to be a God with and for humanity in Jesus Christ. In other words, election is God's self-determination to be in covenant with humanity—this is the kind of God he is, and this will give shape to all his outward acts. By placing election within the doctrine of God, Barth's main aim is to show that the triune God is a God who determined himself to be a covenant God.[56] It is basic to who he is. The main function of the doctrine is to bear witness to God's love (not inscrutable justice) as the beginning of all God's works. His love is not an afterthought.

Now, included in and with the election of Jesus Christ is the election of the "mediate" and "mediating" community consisting of Israel and the church, whose function is to point the world to Jesus Christ.[57] Furthermore, it is as a member and through the ministry of the community that individuals are elected to reflect the glory of God as part of the community and carry out the work of proclamation.[58] A refusal to carry out this duty is a denial of one's election.[59]

A SPOUSE FOR THE SON

Many of Edwards's reflections on predestination, at least in his Miscellanies, focus on the question of the divine decrees. He offers at least three mutually informing answers to the question of what God's primary decree is. First, God's primary decree is to glorify his goodness, love, and happiness

---

55. *CD* II/2, 13. Barth acknowledges that the tradition (1) emphasized reprobation for good reason and (2) tried to expound the doctrine positively (for comfort, assurance, etc.). *CD* II/2, 13–16. See also *CD* II/2, 19–24, for Barth's commending of aspects of the tradition.

56. *CD* II/2, 76. He will outline the various placements of the doctrine among Lutheran and Reformed divines. *CD* II/2 , 77–90. Barth sees himself as unique in his placement. Richard Muller, however, shows that several sixteenth- and seventeenth-century theologians placed the doctrine of election under the doctrine of God. See Richard A. Muller, *Christ and the Decree: Christology and Predestination in Reformed Theology from Calvin to Perkins* (Grand Rapids: Baker Academic, 2008), 3–4.

57. *CD* II/2, 205–6.

58. *CD* II/2, 410–11.

59. *CD* II/2, 414–17.

and communicate these to certain creatures. In other words, the primary decree is the end for which God created the world (discussed earlier). Second, Edwards will also say that the end of creation is to provide a spouse, a body, for the Son. Third, he claims that the end of creation was that the Son specifically would communicate his fullness to a complete image of himself, that is, the church.[60] Thus, taken together, the primary decree is that the Son would glorify himself in the communicating of his happiness and holiness to a spouse, the church. This primary decree determines creation; it is what "gives being" to the creature.[61] Contained within these explanations of God's decrees, then, is a gesturing at, but not an explicit exposition of, his doctrine of predestination.

Edwards's view on predestination is in one sense traditionally Calvinistic, particularly in its insistence on God's good pleasure being the ultimate reason for the distinction between human beings. However, he toes the line between infralapsarian and supralapsarian views (a debate of which he is somewhat dismissive), offering a distinctive account that weaves in his more basic concern for God's end in creation. There are, for Edwards, two "elections" in the divine decrees, one preceding the decrees of creation and fall and one following. The first moment concerns the primary decree, namely, to communicate his fullness to a certain number of people in Christ. Edwards calls this the "first election."[62] The second moment comes after creation and fall and contains the twofold decrees of election and reprobation. This second election is sheer mercy and grace, but it presupposes a fallen humanity.[63] Election brings about the ultimate end of choosing a spouse for the bride from the so-called lump of perdition. Reprobation is an act of vindictive justice, contingent on the sin of humanity. It is not advancing any prior, more primal, decree. In other words, predestination to good is prior to creation and fall; the distinction between elect and reprobate is subsequent. Edwards

---

60. In Miscellany 104, Edwards, in his typically Trinitarian fashion, will argue that the begetting of the Son is the full communication of the happiness and goodness of the Father. Thus, it is technically the Son, who also has an inclination to communicate himself, who is the subject of this further diffusion of the Godhead (since there is no image of him within the Godhead). *WJE* 13:272.

61. *WJE* 18:317.

62. *WJE* 23:179.

63. *WJE* 18:317–18. We see this in his treatment of Romans 9 in his Blank Bible; see *WJE* 24:1022–24.

is emphatic that predestination (in terms of God's decreeing the good of the creature) is not parallel to the decree of reprobation.[64] Thus, he is able to hold that creation is an act of love, and damnation, an act of justice after the fact, since God's desire to make the creature happy precedes and gives being, while reprobation assumes the being and fall of the creature.

What does it mean, then, to be elect in Christ? Reflecting on Ephesians 1:4, Edwards provides four answers, describing the term from four angles. First, to be "in Christ Jesus" merely means that what God purposed, he purposed *for* Christ to be accomplished *by* Christ.[65] Second, the ultimate end of creation was to gain for the Son a spouse or mystical body. God's eternal purpose in Christ was for Christ to purchase and receive a spouse composed of individuals he chose. The election of these individuals to be part of the bride (or body) is what it further means to be chosen "in Christ" (i.e., chosen by Christ to belong to Christ through the work of Christ). Third, God's design was that the primary object of his self-communication be the one body of Christ: "Therefore, though many individual persons were chosen, yet they were chosen to receive God's infinite good and Christ's peculiar love in union, as one body, one spouse, all united in one head. Therefore they were all chosen to receive those divine communications no otherwise than in that head."[66] Yes, individuals are chosen, but their election is with a view to their being part of the body. They are chosen as individuals to help compose the body of Christ—to be united to Christ—which is the end of creation and all God's works.[67] Fourth, God chose Christ as the head of this one body.[68] Christ is *the* elect of God and the "head of election," meaning that all who are elected are elected only as members of his body.[69]

To be chosen in Christ, then, is to be determined by God for happiness and holiness through union with Christ as his body and spouse. It is to be chosen *for* Christ (to be his spouse) for reconciliation *by* Christ and conformity *to*

---

64. See, for example, Miscellanies 700 and 704.

65. "All things that God ever decreed he decreed for the sake of his beloved." *WJE* 23:178.

66. *WJE* 23:179.

67. *WJE* 23:179.

68. To nuance what was said earlier, it may be proper to say that Christ's office is the first decree related to predestination. *WJE* 23:180–81.

69. *WJE* 23:180. Edwards speaks of Christ as elect according to his divine nature, human nature, and by virtue of the union of natures as the Mediator. *WJE* 18:415.

Christ. Christ is the electing God and the elected man. In the end, Edwards's doctrine of predestination sits within his doctrines of God, creation, providence, salvation, and church—providing a robustly theological response to the primal question of God's end in creation.

CONVERGENCES AND DIVERGENCES ON PREDESTINATION

As Reformed theologians operating within similar theological confines, Edwards and Barth, not surprisingly, show significant overlaps on the matter of predestination. First, they both see Jesus Christ as in some way God's primary decree. Jesus (or the Son) is the reason for and means by which all God's works will be enacted. He is the electing God and elected man in both accounts. Second, and related, they are united in the conviction that God's primary decree is a positive one, one that is expressive of God's love. Therefore, neither allows the decree of reprobation to creep into the initial decree of God. Third, while both are concerned for the individuals that compose Christ's community, they are careful to show that individual election is mediated in some way by the community. Nevertheless, the devil is in the details.

While these convergences are real, they are mitigated by important differences. First, while Barth rejects the whole tradition of the absolute decree (subsuming it under Jesus Christ), Edwards retains belief in it. While Jesus Christ can be said to be the first decree, Edwards holds that we cannot fully answer the question of why some are chosen and others are not. Next, for Barth, the election of Jesus includes within it the election of all humanity. For Edwards, it is an election of particular individuals to compose a spouse for the Son. Individuals are chosen by the Son, and this shapes the being of the creation that will be. For Barth, election as God's overarching disposition to be for and with humanity gives a particular shape to the creation. In one, God loves the world for the sake of the elect; in the other, he loves the world because it is elect. It is possible that Barth would read Edwards's account as still presenting a mixed message, regardless of how vociferous Edwards may be in placing Christ at the beginning of God's decrees. Finally, the mediating communities take different forms in the theologians. In Edwards, the mediating community is the community chosen for salvation as Christ's body—i.e., the church. In Barth, the community is the duality of Israel and the church, and it has the earthly vocation to mediate the actualization of God's election in time. While more could be said, at this stage we should be able to see that these divergences are symptoms of a more fundamental issue that has not been addressed explicitly, namely, how we come to know *anything* about God's ways and works. This is our final query.

HOW WE COME TO KNOW
GOD'S END IN CREATION

One commentator on Barth rightly observes that his doctrine of creation is yet another attack on natural theology.[70] God's revelation in Jesus Christ is the way we understand creation and indeed formulate a *Christian* doctrine of creation. Of course, the substance of Christian teaching on creation derives from Scripture's witness. Yet as Kathryn Tanner observes, "One might avoid natural theology and base one's ideas on the Bible, and still not produce a distinctively Christian understanding of creation and providence."[71] Thus, for Barth, to understand creation (and all of God's ways and works), one must read the Bible through the lens of Jesus Christ as God's revelation, the center of Scripture, and he who unifies and gives meaning to Scripture. Jesus Christ is thus the hermeneutical key to Scripture, to the doctrine of creation, and, subsequently, to understanding its end.[72] If we begin with Jesus, we can more clearly see the divine intention as love. If Christ concretely reveals God's electing love, we are not free to speculate about, for instance, a decree that consigns some to acceptance and others to rejection. Revelation controls what we can say about God's decrees and, in fact, gives Christian content to our formulations. God is the One who loves in his freedom. We know this as we look in the face of Jesus. Therefore, whatever we say of God's glory must reflect this fundamental datum about God. Whatever we say about God's end must reflect this central and orienting truth as well.

In one of his early Miscellanies on the "end of creation," Edwards declares, "God is a communicative being."[73] God desires to communicate or reveal himself to our understandings and wills, imparting knowledge, holiness, and happiness—imparting himself. There are cognitive dimensions as well as

---

70. Kathryn Tanner, "Creation and Providence," in *The Cambridge Companion to Karl Barth*, ed. John Webster (Cambridge: Cambridge University Press, 2000), 111.

71. Tanner, "Creation and Providence," 112.

72. See, e.g., *CD* III/1, 23–28.

73. *WJE* 13:410.

affective dimensions of revelation, but our focus will be on the former. "Were it not for divine revelation," he writes, "I am persuaded that there is no one doctrine of that which we call natural religion [but] would, notwithstanding all philosophy and learning, forever be involved in darkness, doubts, endless disputes and dreadful confusion."[74] For Edwards, we know God and his ways chiefly from an exhaustive study of Scripture as God's special revelation, the results of which can be confirmed by nature and the use of reason.[75] He claims that had there been no special revelation, there would be unending disputes about the nature of God, the creation of the world, and the nature of that creation: "Ten thousand schemes there would be about it."[76] The main content of Scripture's revelation, particularly since the fall, is Jesus Christ, his work of redemption, his excellency, and his sufficiency.[77] Scripture's end is the same as God's end in everything he does, namely, to communicate his gloriousness. And this gloriousness is displayed in Christ and his work of calling a bride to himself.[78] Thus, the hermeneutical control for Edwards is in some sense the overarching message of Scripture regarding God's end, while for Barth it is more specifically the crucified and risen Jesus Christ, God's covenant love incarnate. These perspectives overlap greatly but feel different in the way they are executed.

CONCLUSION: GLORY SERVING LOVE?

Are Edwards and Barth saying different things or the same thing differently? The end of creation in both accounts is the glory of God, understood chiefly as the communication of himself to his creatures for their happiness in God. In both accounts, creation has a covenantal shape in that it is founded on God's decree to be with and for humanity in and through Jesus Christ. Finally, both accounts are rooted in a concern that revelation control our speech about God. Thus, God's self-disclosure in Jesus Christ is the main thing he wants to say to us about his ways and works. The differences, however, lie

---

74. *WJE* 13:421.

75. There is natural and special revelation in Edwards, but not a form of natural theology that begins from reason apart from prior special revelation. See Gary Finkbeiner, "Revelation," in *The Jonathan Edwards Encyclopedia*, ed. Harry S. Stout (Grand Rapids: Eerdmans, 2017), 498–99. See *WJE* 8:419–20, 463.

76. *WJE* 13:422.

77. *WJE* 14:250.

78. *WJE* 14:249.

in three main areas: (1) how we know the divine being and his ways; (2) who precisely is the object whose happiness is the end of creation; and (3) how they relate glory and love.

On the first point, it appears that Edwards asserts, on the basis of a rational argument, that God's being must overflow, or that the divine glory as such is disposed or inclined to overflow. Barth might simply retort: "How do you know that, even if it is true?" How do you even know what "glory" is? His own answer is that in the event of Jesus Christ, we can know for sure what God's disposition is because we have seen his disposition in action. We, furthermore, know what God's glory means and what God's ends are.

Second, in Barth, the primary function of God's election of Jesus and the doctrine of election itself is to bear witness to God's love for humanity in general. Creation in its basic shape as the context for covenant is rooted in this divine decision. In Edwards, creation exists chiefly to actualize a covenant between Christ and his chosen bride, *individuals* selected in his wisdom and love. Creation is made for covenant and is born of love, but it is a love mainly for the elect.

Last, would Edwards agree with Barth that love is an end in itself? Only if by "love" we mean God's love to his own glory resulting in an overflow to the creature for its own holiness and happiness in God. Moreover, it appears that Barth's notion that glory serves love, so to speak, makes love the ultimate end and glory a subordinate end—to use Edwards's language. Herein lies a subtle but real difference: Barth treats one as ultimate, another as subordinate, while Edwards sees them as mutually comprehended in each other. For Edwards, God's pursuits of his glory and our joy are one aim, not two. As he, in love, pursues our eternal happiness, God is pursuing his glory; as he pursues his glory, he pursues our joy. There is no ultimate or subordinate, nor chief versus inferior end. They are included in one another. This sense is found in Barth, to be sure, but his language of subordination mutes it. Perhaps we can say that in Edwards, God seeks to magnify his glory (or fullness) *in the expression of love* to creatures, while for Barth, God simply seeks to magnify the glory *of his love*.

7
—
AESTHETICS

Amy Plantinga Pauw

You, Lord, created heaven and earth.
They are beautiful because You are beauty. —*Augustine*

It is a pity that Karl Barth failed to discover Jonathan Edwards when he was searching for Protestant theologians who took beauty seriously. For both Reformation and Protestant Orthodox theologians, Barth complained, a theological emphasis on beauty "was always an alien element, not accepted with a very good conscience, and always looked on and treated with a certain mistrust."[1] Barth declared that he was compelled to go back to the pre-Reformation period to remedy this theological deficit. In fact, however, there was an eighteenth-century Reformed theologian in whose writings "beauty is more central and more pervasive than in any other text in the history of Christian theology."[2] If Barth had encountered Edwards, perhaps he would have overcome some of his own mistrust of beauty as a theological category and made it more than a "border-line" concept or "parenthesis" within his dogmatics.[3]

This essay attempts to make up for this missed opportunity for engagement by putting these two Reformed theologians in conversation about beauty. It is of necessity a truncated conversation because neither Edwards nor Barth paid much theological attention to representational art, though both appreciated the beauty of music. This means that this essay will ignore large areas

---

1. *CD* II/1, 651.
2. Edward Farley, *Faith and Beauty: A Theological Aesthetic* (Burlington, VT: Ashgate, 2001), 42.
3. *CD* II/1, 657, 666.

of contemporary reflection on aesthetics. Instead, it will align with Edwards and Barth's theocentric focus, exploring their convergences and divergences regarding the beauty of God and God's economic work and reflecting on their respective contributions to a contemporary Reformed aesthetic.

In different ways, Edwards and Barth both followed the lead of John Calvin in their theological reflections on beauty. For Calvin, the world of nature was a dazzling theater of God's glory,[4] and his writings are full of rapturous appreciations of the beauties of God's creation. This natural beauty had a deeply spiritual purpose: we are "formed to be spectators of the created world and given eyes that we might be led to its author by contemplating so beautiful a representation."[5] Calvin thus modeled what we might call an aesthetics of indirection. While he stopped short of declaring that God is beautiful, he affirmed that natural beauty can indeed be a path to God, and its primary route is via the emotions. The visible creation is "a mirror in which we can contemplate God who is otherwise invisible,"[6] and this contemplation makes us thirst and long for God. Drawing on the witness of the Psalms, Calvin found delight and yearning throughout the creaturely realm: "For the fledglings that sing, sing of God; the beasts clamor for God; the elements tremble before God; the mountains echo God, and the fountains and flowing waters wink at God, the grass and flowers laugh before God."[7] God's glory can be glimpsed in the radiant longing of all creaturely life, not only in designated religious places and practices. Theology cannot afford to ignore this beauty.

As Serene Jones notes, "Calvin understood the task of theology to be not just rational reflection but also aesthetic formation: it shapes our desires and imagination as much as convincing our minds."[8] While "the glory of God shines, indeed in all creatures on high and below," Calvin found its most

---

4. *Institutes of the Christian Religion*, ed. John T. McNeill, trans. Ford Lewis Battles (Philadelphia: Westminster, 1960), 1.14.20. Hereafter, *Institutes*.

5. John Calvin, Comment on Romans 1:19. Quoted in Belden C. Lane, "Spirituality as the Performance of Desire: Calvin on the World as a Theatre of God's Glory," *Spiritus: A Journal of Christian Spirituality* 1, no. 1 (2001): 1.

6. *Institutes* 1.5.1; also 3.10.2.

7. Preface to the French Bible translation by Robert Olivétan, in *Corpus Reformatorum*, vol. 37 (Braunschweig: C. A. Schwetschke, 1890), 795 (my trans.).

8. Serene Jones, "Glorious Creation, Beautiful Law," in *Feminist and Womanist Essays in Reformed Dogmatics*, ed. Amy Plantinga Pauw and Serene Jones (Louisville: Westminster John Knox, 2006), 24.

dramatic manifestation in the cross of Christ, where, "as in a splendid theatre, the incomparable goodness of God is set before the whole world."⁹ The
aesthetic formation wrought by the Holy Spirit shapes our desires and imagination so that we can see supreme beauty and goodness in the ugly suffering of the cross. Discerning the beauty of the cross properly draws forth our
adoration and praise for God.

For Calvin, the broken beauty of the crucified Christ was depicted better
in preaching than in "a thousand crosses of wood and stone."¹⁰ Calvin's theological aesthetics had little place for religious art. He was deeply suspicious
of human attempts to depict the glory of God or the beauty of the cross in
images or sculptures. Calvin harshly denounced what he regarded as the idolatry of Roman Catholic artistic practice and directed the eyes of faith away
from paintings, statues, and reliquaries. Even before Calvin arrived in Geneva,
the Reformed movement there removed all images of God and the saints from
worship spaces and went so far as to renumber the Ten Commandments to
emphasize the prohibition against making graven images of God. Preaching,
not devotional art, was the approved means of Christian aesthetic formation.

Using Calvin's aesthetics as a kind of Reformed baseline, we can see better
the distinctive contributions of Edwards and Barth. As we will see, they both
affirmed the incomparable beauty of Christ and extended that to include
the eternal beauty of the triune God. While Edwards carried forward and
developed Calvin's celebration of natural beauty, Barth carried forward and
developed Calvin's iconoclasm.

JONATHAN EDWARDS AND THE BEAUTY OF GOD

The spiritual danger of devotional art was not the pressing issue in Jonathan
Edwards's American colonial context that it was in Calvin's Geneva, but we
find in Edwards a similar lack of theological enthusiasm for artistic beauty.
For Edwards, as for Calvin, the beauty of human art pales in comparison to
the glimpses of divine glory available in God's creation. In Edwards's early
essay "Beauty of the World," he exults in "that wonderful suitableness of
green for the grass and plants, the blue of the sky, the white of the clouds,

9. Comment on John 13:31. *John Calvin, The Gospel according to John,* trans. T. H. L. Parker, Calvin's New Testament Commentaries (Grand Rapids: Eerdmans, 1961) 68.

10. *Institutes* 1.11.17.

the colors of flowers," noting that "this beauty is peculiar to natural things, it surpassing the art of man."[11] Like Calvin, Edwards affirms that the beauty of creation is not a self-contained good: it calls forth devotion to its Maker. He derides arguments that the beautiful harmoniousness of the world is an end in itself, finding it ridiculous to suppose "that the world was made to have all the parts of it nicely hanging together and sweetly harmonizing and corresponding ... , that when it was done it might be a nicely contrived world."[12] Instead, Edwards insists that the beauty and harmony of creation point beyond themselves to God and call forth our gratitude and praise.

For Edwards, "God's excellency, his wisdom, his purity and love" shine forth "in the sun, moon and stars; in the clouds, and blue sky; in the grass, flowers, trees; in the water, and all nature."[13] Here Edwards's theological aesthetics both echo Calvin and move decisively beyond him. The term *excellency* is for Edwards a synonym for beauty.[14] The beauty of the world not only testifies to God's wisdom and love; it is a reflection of God's own beauty. According to Edwards, God is "the foundation and fountain of all being and all beauty."[15] Unlike Calvin, Edwards shows no wariness about affirming divine beauty directly. Contrary to popular caricatures of him as a preacher obsessed with an angry God, Edwards in fact regarded beauty as God's most significant attribute. "God is God," he writes, "and distinguished from all other beings and exalted above 'em, chiefly by his divine beauty."[16] In Edwards's theology, beauty is a fundamental motif linking together the Trinity, God's work of creation and redemption, and the Christian life.

Modern western aesthetics was getting its start in Edwards's time, and terms like *excellency* and *beauty* were in common parlance in certain learned circles. Edwards's writings reveal his intellectual engagement with the ideas of moral philosophers like Francis Hutcheson and Lord Shaftesbury as well as the Cambridge Platonists John Smith and Henry More as he worked out his own theology of beauty. With them, Edwards echoed a powerful Western consensus on beauty stretching back as far as Pythagoras: pleasing

---

11. *WJE* 6:305.

12. *WJE* 13:189–90, no. tt.

13. *WJE* 16:793.

14. "Excellence, to put it in other words, is that which is beautiful and lovely." *WJE* 6:344.

15. *WJE* 8:551.

16. *WJE* 2:298.

proportion and harmony are the distinguishing marks of beauty.[17] Edwards also agreed with the moralists of his day that there is a profound connection between our sense of beauty and our moral sense: virtue is beautiful. But Edwards thought that only the converted heart is able to apprehend and embrace true goodness and beauty. What is distinctive about Edwards's aesthetics is the way in which he uses the language of beauty available to him to articulate the central themes of Calvinist theology.[18] Not content to confine aesthetics to considerations of natural human virtue and physical beauty, Edwards insists that aesthetic reflection begin and end with God and the work of redemption.

According to Edwards, God is "the fountain of all beauty" on account of the Trinity. Beauty is a matter of consent and harmony among different elements, and therefore, "one alone cannot be excellent."[19] God is beautiful because there is an eternally consenting "plurality" or "triplicity" within the Godhead.

> 'Tis peculiar to God that he has beauty within himself, consisting in being's consenting with his own being, or the love of himself in his own Holy Spirit; whereas the excellence of others is in loving others, in loving God, and in the communications of his Spirit.[20]

Like the seventeenth-century theologian Petrus van Mastricht, whose *Theoretico-practica Theologia* Edwards regarded as better than "any other book in the world, excepting the Bible,"[21] Edwards expresses the perfect beauty of the Trinity in social terms. Mastricht had insisted that "the perfection of the holy Trinity consists chiefly in the most perfect society and communion of the divine persons" and affirmed that the church is eventually adopted into "the eternal fellowship and society of this family."[22] Edwards likewise

---

17. Wladyslaw Tatarkiewicz, "The Great Theory of Beauty and its Decline," *Journal of Aesthetics and Art Criticism* 31 (Winter, 1972): 165–80.

18. Louis J. Mitchell makes this case well in *Jonathan Edwards on the Experience of Beauty* (Princeton: Princeton Theological Seminary, 2003).

19. *WJE* 13:284, no. 117.

20. *WJE* 6:365.

21. *WJE* 16:217.

22. Mastricht, *Theoretico-practica Theologia* (Utrecht, 1724), II.xxiv.28; II.xxiv.11 (my trans.). See *WJE* 13:524 (No. 482). As will become clear, Mastricht also provides a link between Edwards and Barth.

describes the Trinity as the "society of the three persons in the Godhead" and affirms that the saints will "be brought into the household of God, that [Christ] and his Father and they should be as it were one society, one family."[23] Beauty for Edwards is ultimately a matter of loving relations. Whereas classical theism faced the conundrum of how "an ultimate Simplicity give[s] rise to the proportioned complexity of beauty,"[24] Edwards freely affirms complexity within the Godhead itself. For him, the eternal loving consent within the Trinity renders God "the supreme harmony of all."[25] The work of redemption is the means by which the saints are made beautiful through their incorporation into this supreme divine harmony. Though Edwards frequently affirms the beauty and excellency of Jesus Christ, he identifies divine beauty especially with the Holy Spirit. The Spirit, whose work is to beautify all things, is fitted to *give* beauty because he *is* beauty: "Whose office can it be so properly to give all things their sweetness and beauty, as he who is himself the beauty and joy of the Creator?"[26]

The beauty of the triune God in Edwards's theology is a communicative, spreading beauty. "All the beauty to be found throughout the whole creation, is but the reflection of the diffused beams of that Being who hath an infinite fullness of brightness and glory."[27] The world exists because God's glorious beauty does not stay within the eternal perfection of the Godhead but emanates outward. There is "a disposition in the fullness of the divinity to flow out and diffuse itself."[28] All of God's economic work, beginning with creation, aims at an "increase, repetition, or multiplication" of divine beauty.[29] This overflow of divine beauty has natural manifestations in the material world and in the justice and order of human society. But it culminates for Edwards in the work of redemption and the everlasting life enjoyed by the angels and glorified saints in heaven, where loving union with God will be their all in all—all their beauty and all their blessedness.[30]

---

23. *WJE* 18:110, no. 571.
24. Farley, *Faith and Beauty*, 23.
25. *WJE* 13:329, no. 182.
26. *WJE* 21:123.
27. *WJE* 2:14–15.
28. *WJE* 8:435.
29. *WJE* 8:433.
30. *WJE* 20:193, no. 936.

THE BEAUTY OF HIERARCHY

Edwards stands firmly in the *analogia entis* tradition: God is the beautiful and beautifying source of all that exists, and all being bears some analogy to its Creator. Creaturely beauty and goodness are images and shadows of divine beauty and goodness. But all creatures are not created equal. Hierarchy is a fundamental principle within Edwards's aesthetics. Reality in Edwards's Neoplatonic scheme is ontologically ordered from least to greatest, with spiritual reality closer to God than material reality. Within this hierarchical framework, Edwards could sometimes posit a smooth continuity between humanity and God: "In the creation, there is an immediate communication between one degree of being and the next degree of being, but man being the top; so that the next immediate step from him is to God."[31] This is the kind of theologically dangerous *analogia entis* between God and human creatures that Barth would fulminate against. However, at his theological best, Edwards's use of the *analogia entis* tradition flows from "the deep religious intuition of the essential indigence of all creatures,"[32] not from a theological arrogance that finds in human excellence a bridge to God's being. Creation's analogical connection to God is rooted in its ontological dependence. What has been called panentheism in Edwards's thought is better understood as an elaboration of this essential creaturely dependence on God the Creator. Radical dependence on God, not absorption into God's reality, is what defines all creaturely existence, whether material or spiritual.

The beauty of the physical world is a matter of proportion and harmony within the object itself and in its relations with other objects. The beauty of creation derives from the fact "that God does purposely make and order one thing to be in an agreeableness and harmony with another."[33]

That sort of beauty which is called "natural," as of vines, plants, trees, etc., consists of a very complicated harmony; and all the natural motions and tendencies and figures of bodies in the universe are done according to proportion, and therein is their beauty.[34]

---

31. *WJE* 13:190, no. tt.
32. Miklos Veto, *The Thought of Jonathan Edwards*, trans. Philip Choinière-Shields (Eugene, OR: Wipf & Stock, 2018), 22.
33. *WJE* 11:53.
34. *WJE* 6:335.

Heaven will be a place of even greater physical beauty; Edwards speculates that "the abode of the saints after the resurrection will be so contrived by God, that there shall be external beauties and harmonies altogether of another kind from what we perceive here, and probably those beauties will appear chiefly on the bodies of the man Christ Jesus and of the saints."[35]

But physical beauty, whether earthly or heavenly, is for Edwards only "secondary": "the true, spiritual original beauty" is a matter of "being's consent to being, or the union of minds or spiritual beings in a mutual propensity and affection of heart."[36] "Primary beauty" for Edwards consists in loving consent among spiritual beings; "when we spake of excellence in bodies we were obliged to borrow the word 'consent' from spiritual things." God has made the "mutual consent and agreement of [material] things beautiful and grateful" to us because it is an image or shadow of this primary beauty of loving consent.[37]

In response to the materialist philosophies of his day, Edwards was drawn to metaphysical idealism, the conviction that only intelligent creatures have "proper being." Material reality is mind dependent: it realizes its full destiny in and through the saints' perception of it as an image of God's beauty. Yet it is important to place Edwards's idealism, which was neither fully developed nor consistently deployed, in the context of his larger theological commitments. According to Edwards, material things have no substantial reality of their own, but neither do they ultimately owe their existence to human knowing. Instead, material reality exists because of God's knowledge and agency: God "by his immediate influence gives being every moment and by his Spirit actuates the world."[38] Edwards's idealism of the divine understanding was a redefinition of material reality in terms of the perfect being and beauty of God. The reality of intelligent creatures was also redefined in Edwards's scheme. God alone is "Being itself," and everything else has its being only through participation in God's perfections. Since God is the sum and comprehension of all that is, "the *whole* system of created beings in comparison of the Creator" is "as the light dust of the balance."[39] Yet it must be acknowledged that Edwards's idealism significantly compromised his theological

35. *WJE* 13:329, no. 182.
36. *WJE* 8:564.
37. *WJE* 6:362.
38. *WJE* 13:279, no. 108.
39. *WJE* 8:424, my emphasis.

aesthetics. Material reality was accorded no intrinsic value in Edwards's scheme; its role was to provide an analogy and a conduit to spiritual reality.

In addition to the hierarchy between material and spiritual reality, there are also hierarchies *within* the spiritual world. In the earthly church, some saints are "more eminent in grace" than others, and these distinctions will be preserved in heaven, where spiritual rankings among the saints "will be for the beauty and the profit of the whole."[40] Indeed, Edwards insists that the heavenly "exaltation of some in glory above others, will be so far from diminishing anything of the perfect happiness and joy of the rest that are inferior, that they will be the happier for it."[41] The eschatological beauty of the "one holy and happy society" that Edwards envisions is predicated on a stable social hierarchy in which everyone knows their place.

Furthermore, hierarchy among the saints pales beside the spiritual hierarchy between the elect and the damned. The Spirit bestows on the elect a "sense of the heart," which Edwards understood in terms of an infusion of God's beauty. The result of this saving grace is both a new beauty within the elect, visible in their loving consent to God and each other, and their heightened receptivity to divine beauty. Edwards describes his experience of this new receptivity in his *Personal Narrative*. Walking in his father's pasture and looking up at the sky and clouds prompted for him "a sweet sense of the glorious majesty and grace of God." Even thunderstorms led him to "sweet contemplations" of God's greatness and glory.[42] The elect are able to perceive the beautiful continuity between God's creative and redemptive work. By contrast, the non-elect, who are not given this sense of the heart, are incapable of loving consent to God and are unable to perceive God's beauty in either natural or spiritual things. Like the devil, "they see God's awful greatness, yet they see nothing of his loveliness."[43] Their sin has rendered them incapable of the end for which intelligent beings were created: to know and love the beauty of God and to rejoice in God's glorious excellency.

Sinners threaten to mar the beauty of God's economy. To accommodate the failure of some creatures to serve their appointed end, Edwards had to

---

40. *WJE* 13:481–82, no. 430.

41. *WJE* 13:482, no. 431.

42. *WJE* 16:793.

43. *WJE* 8:327.

develop an adjunct aesthetics. Unredeemed sinners have disturbed the beautiful order of God's universe, and this order can be restored only by their everlasting punishment.[44] The Holy Spirit, elsewhere the very beauty and love of the deity, vanishes from Edwards's account of beauty at this point, and so does the identification of beauty with loving consent. Instead, he affirms the aesthetic fittingness of God's everlasting hatred and torment of sinners. Furthermore, Edwards insists that the saints' beautiful consent to God requires that they consent to this hatred and torment. He notes that in his own case, God's consigning some sinners "eternally to perish, and to be everlastingly tormented in hell … used to appear like a horrible doctrine to me." Only with Edwards's new sense of the heart did this doctrine become "exceeding pleasant, bright and sweet."[45] Just as the exaltation of some saints over others enhances the happiness and joy of them all, so the everlasting alienation and suffering of unredeemed sinners enhances the happiness and joy of the elect in heaven. Their sense of God's beauty is intensified by their view of God's pitiless hatred toward fellow human beings. This severing of the link between beauty and love creates unresolved problems in Edwards's theological aesthetics.

THE EXCELLENCY OF JESUS CHRIST

The hell torments of the damned are an undeniable dimension of Edwards's account of divine beauty, but they do not deserve a central place in interpretations of his aesthetics. Edwards does not posit the kind of cruel symmetry in God's double decree that Barth would later criticize, with "its opposing categories of 'elect' and 'reprobate.' "[46] Edwards's God is "a God that delights in mercy, and judgment is his strange work."[47] In fact, Edwards's insistence in a sermon on Ephesians 4 that "Love is the Great thing aimed at in the decree of Election"[48] anticipates Barth's radical recasting of the doctrine in *Church Dogmatics* II/2. Nowhere is this theological asymmetry between God's mercy and judgment clearer than in Edwards's reflections on the beauty of Christ.

---

44. See the similar argument in Anselm, *Cur Deus Homo* I.xiv-xv.
45. *WJE* 16:792.
46. *CD* II/2, 326.
47. *WJE* 14:221.
48. MS Sermon on Ephesians 4:15-16 (1743), no. 703. Transcript, Jonathan Edwards Center, Yale University.

Edwards let the vulnerability and historical vicissitudes of Christ's human life enter into his constructions of divine beauty, and this helped him counter the tendencies of the western consensus on beauty toward sentimentality or stasis. Christ's beauty is counterintuitive: Edwards notes that our natural inclination is to "despise a crucified Savior, one that suffered such disgrace, and humbled himself so low."[49] To see beauty in the shame of the cross, we need a converted sense of beauty. Ordinary human understandings of beauty must be overturned and expanded. For Edwards, the excellency of Christ subverts conventional oppositions between glory and shame, majesty and meekness. Just as Christ's weakness is stronger than human strength (1 Cor 1:25), so the ugliness of the cross is more beautiful than human beauty. In his reflections on Christ's beauty, Edwards reaffirms the foundational principle of his theological aesthetics: the connection between divine beauty and divine love—Christ's "loveliness shines in his love."[50] In love, Christ reaches out to sinners in their ugly deformity and clothes them with his beauty. Being "clothed with him who is so beautiful," sinners are accepted and loved by God and made beautiful through the grace of the Holy Spirit.[51] As we will see, Edwards's affirmation of the beauty of the incarnate Christ is the principal bridge between his theological aesthetics and those of Karl Barth.

KARL BARTH AND THE DANGERS
OF AN AESTHETIC THEOLOGY

Moving from Edwards to Barth, the first impression is one of contrast. Unlike Edwards, Barth made the deliberate decision not to let beauty become a central concept in his theology. While Edwards embraced the aesthetic categories current in his day and used them for his own theological purposes, Barth remained wary. By Barth's time, the notion of the disinterestedness of beauty—that the search for beauty transports us from the humdrum, self-interested world of human activity to an exalted world of aesthetic contemplation—had become the standard western view. Barth regarded the human pursuit of beauty on these terms as deceptive

---

49. *WJE* 20:118, no. 875.

50. *WJE* 18:494, no. 791.

51. *WJE* 13:454, no. 385.

and dangerous. "A dilettante contemplation and enjoyment" of beautiful things for their own sake[52] represents for Barth the kind of self-indulgent exaltation of human subjectivity that he found so objectionable in liberal Protestant theology. Furthermore, the aesthetics of National Socialism's blood and soil religion showed Barth how appeals to beauty were easily manipulated for idolatrous ends.[53] The great danger in the pursuit of beauty was that it may bring us too close to "the sphere of human oversight and control."[54] Barth's theological response was to marginalize the concept of beauty.

As a result, the terms *beauty* and *beautiful* (*die Schönheit, das Schöne, schön*) are peripheral to Barth's theological vocabulary. Indeed, there is often a sarcastic edge to Barth's use of these words: he regularly opposes human perceptions of beauty to the truth of divine revelation. When we fail to give Scripture precedence, we indulge in an "all too beautiful dream" of a pure and holy church.[55] Champions of open communion between Catholics and Protestants forget that "much that is beautiful in itself is a very long way from being true."[56] The witness of Christ reveals the stupidity of "every attitude in which we think we can authoritatively tell ourselves what is true and good and beautiful."[57] Barth does not follow Edwards in making beauty God's primary attribute and the pinnacle of the work of redemption. Nor does he follow Calvin in exalting the beauty of God's created world and its capacity to draw us to God. He judges the theological risks to be too great.

Barth's view of artistic beauty underwent something of an evolution. In his lectures on ethics at Münster and Bonn in the winter semesters of 1929 and 1930, Barth includes human artistic expression as part of the Christian ethics of gratitude: "the word and command of God demand art, since it is art that sets us under the word of the new heaven and the new earth."[58] The artist's work is "pure play," and its focus is eschatological: "redeemed reality in

52. *CD* I/2, 808.

53. See Frederic Spotts, *Hitler and the Power of Aesthetics* (New York: Overlook Press, 2003).

54. *CD* II/1, 651.

55. *CD* IV/4, 193.

56. Barth, *The Church and the Churches* (Grand Rapids: Eerdmans, 2005), 65.

57. *CD* IV/2, 413.

58. Barth, *Ethics*, ed. D. Braun (New York: Seabury, 1981), 510.

its sensed and anticipated perfections."[59] Aesthetic creativity is thus a human witness to the accomplishment of God's work of redemption: "a final word and last and boldest climax of human activity." Therefore, Barth proclaims, "in the proper sense, to be unaesthetic is to be immoral and disobedient."[60] His view of Christian art was expansive, not limited to explicitly religious subjects like "portrayals of Christ, oratorios, Christian novels, and the like."[61] For Barth, the music of Mozart remained the supreme example of this joyful aesthetic response.

By the time he was writing the fourth volume of CD, however, Barth's view of Christian artistic effort had soured, especially when it came to visual art. While he admired Matthias Grünewald's Isenheim altarpiece, with its unsentimental depiction of the crucified Christ, he disdained artistic depictions of the crucifixion that could "be admired at a safe distance from their theme" and metal crucifixes worn as "jewellery by ecclesiastical dignitaries and Christian ladies."[62] He concludes that

> no human art should try to represent—in their unity—the suffering God and triumphant man, the beauty of God which is the beauty of Jesus Christ. If at this point we have one urgent request to all Christian artists, however well intentioned, gifted or even possessed of genius, it is that they should give up this unholy undertaking—for the sake of God's beauty."[63]

Barth here reflects what William Dyrness has termed "both the genius and the limitation of Protestant aesthetics": there is a powerful sense of the beautiful, but little permission for the development of "cultural forms in which this aesthetic could come to expression."[64]

---

59. Barth, Ethics, 508. There are parallels here to Abraham Kuyper's insistence that the task of art is not to represent creaturely reality as it is but rather to anticipate the redeemed creation's "perfect coming luster." See Abraham Kuyper, "Calvinism in Art," in Lectures on Calvinism (Grand Rapids: Eerdmans, 1961), 155.

60. Barth, Ethics, 510.

61. Barth, Ethics, 37. Thus, Geoffrey Bromiley's dismissive assertion that "Barth has no liking for Christian art" needs considerable qualification. See An Introduction to the Theology of Karl Barth (Edinburgh: T&T Clark, 1979), 82.

62. CD IV/3, 443.

63. CD IV/1, 666.

64. William A. Dyrness, Reformed Theology and Visual Culture: The Protestant Imagination from Calvin to Edwards (Cambridge: Cambridge University Press, 2004), 286–87.

GOD'S GLORIOUS BEAUTY

Where Christian artists should fear to tread, however, Christian theologians need to enter. Theology is a "singularly beautiful and joyful science," and it would be "unpardonable, because ungrateful, to overlook or to fail to find it pleasing."[65] Even here, though, Barth is cautious. He rejects what he sees as Schleiermacher's tendencies toward an aesthetic form of theology that "surrenders to and loses itself" in the contemplation of its own beauty. When theology focuses on its own beautiful form, "this beauty becomes the beauty of an idol."[66] Instead, Barth insists with Anselm that "since there is a beauty of God there is also a *pulchritudo* of theology which cannot be ignored."[67] If devotional art is incapable of representing divine beauty, it is the task of Christian dogmatics not to shy away from this difficult and dangerous assignment.

An account of divine beauty is missing from the earlier *Göttingen Dogmatics*, but in *CD*, it appears within Barth's treatment of the perfections of God. The point of his dramatic recasting of divine attributes in *CD* II/1 is that the doctrine of God cannot be considered in abstraction from God's revelation to us and our response to it. Barth's treatment of the perfections is preceded by an exegesis of what it means to say that "God is." His memorable formulation is that "God is the One who loves in freedom."[68] This provides the framework for Barth's examination of divine attributes: they are the perfections of love and freedom. The perfections of divine loving are grace and holiness, mercy and righteousness, patience and wisdom. The perfections of divine freedom are unity and omnipresence, constancy and omnipotence, eternity and glory. Barth gives divine beauty a "subordinate and auxiliary" role in clarifying the meaning of God's glory.[69]

For his treatment of divine glory, Barth turns, as Edwards had, to Petrus van Mastricht's *Theoretico-practica Theologia*. God's glory is "the indwelling joy of his divine being which as such shines out from Him, which overflows in its richness, which in its superabundance is not satisfied with

65. *CD* I/2, 841–42.

66. *CD* I/2, 841–42.

67. Barth, *Evangelical Theology: An Introduction*, trans. Grover Foley (Grand Rapids: Eerdmans, 1963), 75.

68. *CD* II/1, 257–321.

69. *CD* II/1, 653.

itself but communicates itself."[70] Divine beauty for Barth has to do with the form and manner of God's glory, how God's perfect life is expressed and communicated to creatures. God's glory is not reducible to power; God does not deal with creatures simply by "ruling, mastering, and subduing with ... utterly superior force." Rather, God "enlightens and convinces and persuades" them[71] by drawing them into the joy of the divine life. God is beautiful because God "acts as the One who gives pleasure, creates desire and rewards with enjoyment."[72] Barth elaborates on three dimensions of God's beautiful form that elicit this creaturely joy and desire: the divine perfections in their multiplicity and unity, the triunity of God, and the incarnation of Jesus Christ.

Glory is not only the culminating perfection of God's freedom in Barth's scheme but also a microcosm of all the divine perfections, reflecting the union of divine freedom and love that characterizes all of God's engagement with creatures. In some ways, glory's role is parallel to that of beauty in Edwards's doctrine of God: it is a central divine perfection that calls forth creaturely response. As Barth declares, God's glory means that God is "beautiful in His love and freedom, beautiful in His essence as God and in all His works, beautiful, that is, in the form in which He is all this."[73]

ROADS NOT TAKEN

Despite these formal similarities between Barth and Edwards on God's glorious beauty, methodological differences reemerge. In Edwards's Neoplatonic scheme, creatures are infused with God's beauty. In their own creaturely ways, they increase, repeat, and multiply it. Barth uses the same language of shining, overflowing, and communicating to describe the emanation of God's glory, but when it comes to its reception by creatures, he substitutes *witness* for Edwards's concepts of *union* and *infusion*. This witness is not restricted to human creatures. While Barth's theological account of nature is thin, and he rarely accords intrinsic value to non-human creation, he affirms with the psalmist that witness to God's glorious beauty

---

70. *CD* II/1, 647.
71. *CD* II/1, 650.
72. *CD* II/1, 651.
73. *CD* II/1, 655.

sounds across the whole creation. In Barth's lovely image, humanity is "like a late-comer slipping shamefacedly into creation's choir in heaven and earth, which has never ceased its praise."[74] Yet in Barth's theology, creation echoes God's glory "in the same way as an echoing wall can serve only to repeat and broadcast the voice which the echo 'answers.' "[75] God's beauty bounces back to God in creaturely witness, but it does not indwell creation. Likewise, the Holy Spirit's work in human creatures is epistemic, not aesthetic: the Spirit does not beautify them but rather makes possible their perception and joyful acknowledgment of God's beauty.

Barth wants God to be "the basis and standard of everything that is beautiful and of all ideas of the beautiful."[76] He sees the *analogia entis* as an attempt to reverse this order of knowing by building a bridge from the human experience of beauty to God, and his rejection of it sometimes descends into caricature. In its place, Barth posits an *analogia relationis*, though his usage of this term is uneven. Sometimes, Barth uses it to posit an analogy between the immanent Trinity and God's economic relations. For example, the freedom exhibited by God in Trinitarian relations finds "a correspondence and similarity" in the Creator-creature relationship God freely establishes with us.[77] In other places, however, Barth's exposition of the *analogia relationis* draws very close to versions of the *analogia entis*. For example, in his tortuous argument for the analogy between "the relationship and fellowship" of the Father and Son and the fellow-humanity of men and women, Barth declares that "God created man in His own image, *in correspondence with His own being and essence*."[78] Here Barth seems to posit an analogy between the relational being and essence of God and the relational being and essence of humanity, albeit one that is known only through Christ. This approach is not so different from that of his Catholic contemporary von Balthasar, who embraced a view of the *analogia entis* that claimed the crucified Christ as the supreme revelation of God's beauty and left considerable room for developing a theological aesthetics. However, in

---

74. *CD* II/1, 648.

75. *CD* II/1, 670.

76. *CD* II/1, 656.

77. *CD* III/2, 220.

78. *CD* III/2, 324, my emphasis.

Barth, the connection between God's beauty and creaturely beauty is too tenuous to make possible a full-orbed theological aesthetic.

Not surprisingly, Christology is the strong suit of Barth's aesthetics. He joins Edwards in insisting that the incarnate Christ must challenge and shape any theological account of beauty. Edwards's declaration that the excellency of Jesus Christ holds together majesty and meekness finds an almost exact echo in Barth's claim that Christ's beauty is "the unity of God's majesty and condescendence."[79] As Barth declares,

> God's beauty embraces death as well as life, fear as well as joy, what we might call the ugly as well as what we might call the beautiful. It reveals itself and wills to be known on the road from the one to the other, in the turning from the self-humiliation of God for the benefit of man to the exaltation of man by God and to God.[80]

For both Edwards and Barth, God's beauty shines in the ugliness of the cross. Yet Barth goes further than Edwards in claiming the subversive and iconoclastic character of Christ's beauty, a claim that was especially important in his political context. As JinHyok Kim trenchantly puts it, "Not the German *Führer*'s heroic life, but one Jewish person's death on the cross under an ancient imperialistic regime is the revelatory form of beauty."[81] Since the revelation of divine beauty in Christ serves as the criterion for Christian theology, Barth concludes that "our creaturely conceptions of the beautiful, formed from what has been created, may rediscover or fail to rediscover themselves in the divine being."[82] We cannot assume a natural fit between our conceptions of the beautiful and the beauty of Christ.

Unfortunately, Barth rarely put this Christological criterion to use because he had little theological interest in "our creaturely conceptions of the beautiful." This is not to say that experiences of beauty were unimportant to him. In one of her surviving letters to Barth, Charlotte von Kirschbaum writes to him from the Bergli, the summer house of their friends Ruedi and Gerty Pestalozzi, where they spent summers together:

---

79. *CD* II/1, 665.

80. *CD* II/1, 665.

81. JinHyok Kim, *The Spirit of God and the Christian Life: Reconstructing Karl Barth's Pneumatology* (Minneapolis: Fortress, 2014), 204.

82. *CD* II/1, 656.

And it is *beautiful, beautiful,* beautiful, the forest and the lake, the grassy path, the little wall, all that you love and feel at home with. And it is so lovely that you want to come on Monday. Ruedi and Gerty were both so happy when I told them this. And it will be truly, truly lovely.[83]

The beauty of the natural world and of human relationships obviously meant a great deal to Barth, but his theological method had little room for experiences of beauty. His Christocentrism and fear of natural theology greatly constrained his theological aesthetics. Barth himself acknowledged the problem: the severity of his method deprived people of "many beautiful things."[84] In a letter to William Lachat, he credits his relationship with von Kirschbaum with introducing an element of "lived life" into his theology, which kept him from becoming the legalist he might have otherwise been.[85] Yet when it comes to his aesthetics, we might wish there had been a deeper integration between his lived life and his theology.

CONCLUSION

As P. T. Forsyth asserted at the turn of the twentieth century, faith severed from a sense of beauty risks becoming "harsh, strident, and unlovely, something to be stoutly asserted, blindly defended, and tenaciously held, rather than absolutely trusted, winsomely worshiped, nobly evidenced, and beautifully beloved." Faith without beauty leaves us with "a drought in our own souls."[86] By making beauty God's distinguishing attribute, and by his stunning integration of beauty into his theology of creation and redemption, Edwards counteracted Reformed tendencies to privilege intellectual assent and obedience as the primary markers of faith. In this regard, Edward's theology is a refreshing Reformed oasis.

Barth shows us that Reformed theology should respond to this aesthetic drought without altogether abandoning its reflexive suspicion toward the

---

83. Rolf-Joachim Erler, *Karl Barth-Charlotte von Kirschbaum Briefwechsel,* vol. 1, 1925–1935 (Zürich: Theologischer Verlag, 2008), 224, my translation. I have used both *beautiful* and *lovely* to translate von Kirschbaum's word *schön.*

84. *Barth-von Kirschbaum Briefwechsel,* 26.

85. *Barth-von Kirschbaum Briefwechsel,* xx, my translation.

86. P. T Forsyth, *Religion in Recent Art: Expository Lectures on Rossetti, Burne Jones, Watts, Holman Hunt and Wagner* (London: Hodder & Stoughton, 1901), 5–6.

beautiful. There is no way to disentangle our theologies of beauty completely from our social and cultural assumptions, and this means that the specter of idolatry is ever present. Barth was right: beauty is a dangerous theological category. Beauty's power can be seductive, reinforcing a religious or cultural status quo that has been deformed by sexist, racist, and commercial interests. A focus on beauty can be a form of intellectual escapism, turning us away from the gritty realities of the world, distracting us from responding to its suffering and injustice.

Yet the history of theology provides ample evidence that *all* theological categories and methods are dangerous and capable of misuse. As Barth noted, there is a brokenness to all theological efforts. Reformed iconoclasm must extend to the beautiful words of faith as well as to its images and celebrations of natural beauty. Words too can lie and distort; they provide no secure refuge from idolatry. A contemporary Reformed theology of beauty will acknowledge the importance of aesthetic formation. It will affirm that experiences of beauty can nourish and challenge faith. It will go beyond the anthropocentrism of both Barth and Edwards, recognizing the poverty and distortions of our creaturely self-understandings in formulating a theological aesthetics. In short, a Reformed aesthetics will make clear that Christian pursuit of beauty is inseparable from the truth about our creaturely identities and the love we are called to live out.

8
—

PHILOSOPHY

Kenneth Oakes

The following is a comparison of Jonathan Edwards and Karl Barth on philosophy and theology. This exercise may seem misguided given the differences between the two. Edwards was an eighteenth-century American preacher whose intellectual context was the Enlightenment, John Locke's empiricism and anthropology, Isaac Newton's natural philosophy, Puritan spiritual theology, the Cambridge Platonists, and the Continental metaphysicians, and whose spiritual context was broadly shaped by the First Great Awakening. Barth was an early twentieth-century Swiss-German theologian whose intellectual context was initially that of Friedrich Schleiermacher and Wilhelm Herrmann, then the Blumhardts, then the Reformers and continental Protestant Scholastics, and whose spiritual context was that of a European Christianity that was on the wane and unable to avoid the decadence of warmongering and fascism. Furthermore, Edwards's fascination with the natural world seems markedly different from Barth's interest in politics and social history, and while Edwards was at times concerned with scientific and philosophical movements and developments for the sake of responding to Christianity's cultured despisers, Barth deliberately devoted himself to the rehabilitation of Christian doctrine itself against what he took to be a feeble and reductionistic modern Protestantism. These incongruities appear to multiply when we remember that Barth's remarks on the Puritans were rarely favorable,[1] that he was generally suspicious of attempts to coor-

---

1. Barth could speak, for instance, of "the starchy Pharisaical confidence with which the pious Puritans of whom we just spoke assured themselves of their eternal salvation, their morality, and of course their private property." Barth, *The Theology of the Reformed Confessions*,

dinate theology with the latest developments in philosophy and the natural sciences, and that Edwards himself does not seem to receive a single mention in *Church Dogmatics*.[2]

There are, nonetheless, intriguing points of similarity between Edwards and Barth that would suggest that such a comparison is worth pursuing. Edwards's worries regarding the deistic elevation of reason over revelation and of natural theology over revealed theology parallel Barth's worries regarding the modernist tendency to reduce or refashion revelation before reason in the disciplines of history, psychology, or ethics. Furthermore, both Edwards and Barth were systematic theologians of a decidedly occasional sort; both spent a great deal of time and focus on preaching; and both were unmistakably Reformed theologians, with comparable sensibilities regarding the Scripture principle, election, the sovereignty of God, grace as full and free, the world as the theater of God's glory,[3] and the abiding presupposition that God's glorification includes the glorification of God's creatures.

It also seems worth the effort to compare Edwards and Barth on theology and philosophy given that their views on theology, philosophy, and metaphysics have occasionally served as points of contrast. The notable Edwards scholar Michael McClymond, for instance, has contrasted the two in these terms: "One thinks of Karl Barth's famous characterization of *analogia entis*, or the theological use of ontology, as 'the invention of the Antichrist!' His stridency derived from the assumption that metaphysics in practice becomes a tool wielded by sinner against God, to subjugate God to anthropocentric presuppositions. Metaphysics for Barth thus robs God of the glory. Yet this criticism does not stick to Edwards."[4] Such a sentiment is not fleeting, as McClymond has also observed that Edwards "showed none of the fear and distrust of philosophy that one senses in the writings of Luther, Pascal,

---

trans. Darrell L. Guder and Judith J. Guder (Louisville: Westminster John Knox, 2002), 135, 147. Puritan Sabbath prescriptions in particular seemed to amuse and annoy Barth; see CD III/4, 66.

2. The index of *CD* contains no references to Jonathan Edwards, nor does searching through *CD* using the online database of the Digital Karl Barth Library yield any references.

3. For a brief comparison of the two on this theme, see Stephen R. Holmes, *God of Grace & God of Glory: An Account of the Theology of Jonathan Edwards* (Edinburgh: T&T Clark, 2000), 64–66.

4. Michael J. McClymond, *Encounters with God: An Approach to the Theology of Jonathan Edwards* (Oxford: Oxford University Press, 1998), 35–36. For similar contrasts between Edwards and Barth, see Michael J. McClymond and Gerald R. McDermott, *The Theology of Jonathan Edwards* (Oxford: Oxford University Press, 2012), 102–6.

Kierkegaard, and Barth."[5] That Edwards's and Barth's theological contexts and projects vary in significant ways is undeniable, and thus it seems salutary to show the points of convergence and divergence in their understandings of philosophy and theology. In what follows, I consider Edwards on the theme of theology and philosophy, then cover Barth's views, and conclude with some remarks on their similarities and dissimilarities.

JONATHAN EDWARDS

A host of studies deal with Edwards on philosophy or on theology and philosophy. Work has been dedicated to the identification of his intellectual sources and inspirations,[6] with the common consensus being that the most significant are Isaac Newton, John Locke, and Francis Hutcheson, along with there being some uncertainty as to the relationship between Edwards's idealism or immaterialism and that of George Berkeley.[7] Additionally, it also seems as if Edwards had a rather selective knowledge of philosophers and philosophy, especially of the antique and medieval varieties, which makes the creativity, vim, and originality of Edwards's thought all the more impressive. Miklós Vető, for instance, has pointed out that Edwards thought Cicero among the greatest of philosophers, knew antique philosophers only through secondary literature, quoted Augustine from secondary sources, was relatively unfamiliar with medieval theology and philosophy but viewed it with some distaste, did not read Descartes or Thomas Hobbes, and references Leibniz only once.[8] There has been work been dedicated to the description and analysis of Edwards's philosophical theology and his understanding of divine simplicity,

---

5. McClymond, *Encounters with God*, 95.

6. In particular, see "The Development of Edwards' Philosophical Thought" in Jonathan Edwards, *Scientific and Philosophical Thought* [henceforth *WJE* 6], ed. Wallace B. Anderson (New Haven: Yale University Press, 1980), 52–136; Norman Fiering, *Jonathan Edwards's Moral Thought and Its British Context* (Chapel Hill: University of North Carolina Press, 1981); and Stephen Daniel, *The Philosophy of Jonathan Edwards: A Study in Divine Semiotics* (Bloomington: Indiana University Press, 1994).

7. For the extensive literature on this topic as well as arguments for the historical and conceptual dependence of Edwards upon Berkeley, see Scott Fennema, "George Berkeley and Jonathan Edwards on Idealism: Considering an Old Question in Light of New Evidence," *Intellectual History Review* (2017): 1–26.

8. Miklós Vető, "Edwards and Philosophy," in Gerald McDermott, *Understanding Jonathan Edwards: An Introduction to America's Theologian* (Oxford: Oxford University Press, 2009), 151–70; see specifically 153–54. See also Miklós Vető's *Le pensée de Jonathan Edwards* (Paris: Cerf, 1987).

the nature of virtue, free will, and his occasionalism.[9] There have also been attempts to situate Edwards's philosophy within the antinomies, concerns, and technicalities of the various philosophers of the Enlightenment.[10] In the face of this extensive and highly detailed literature on Edwards, what follows will be a far more modest and selective portrait of Edwards on natural philosophy, philosophy, and moral philosophy.

Edwards's deep interest in and curiosity about natural phenomena is readily apparent in his early forays into natural philosophy, such as his writings on spiders, on insects, on rainbows, on the sound of thunder, on blood circulation, on the compressibility of water, and on optics more generally. By his own later admission, his personal conversion brought about a heightened sense of God's presence and glory in creation: "God's excellency, his wisdom, his purity and love, seemed to appear in everything; in the sun, moon, and stars; in the clouds and blue sky; in the grass, flowers, trees; in the water and all nature; which used greatly to fix my mind."[11] Similarly, the study of natural phenomena could provide concrete examples of God's wisdom and providential care, as can be observed in the order and design of the atmosphere, the eye, the roundness of the earth, the distribution of comets, the place of the planets, and especially the temperature of liquid water on the earth.[12]

Other pieces within his natural philosophy—particularly "Of Being" (1722), "Of Atoms" (1722), and "The Mind" (1724)—have as one of their main aims the attempt to combat the deistic premises and implications of seventeenth-century mechanistic accounts of matter, motion, space, and causality. Edwards opposes these accounts by incorporating these phenomena within

---

9. See the influential yet controversial Sang Hyun Lee, *The Philosophical Theology of Jonathan Edwards* (Princeton: Princeton University Press, 1988); Stephen H. Daniel, "Edwards as Philosopher," in *The Cambridge Companion to Jonathan Edwards,* ed. Stephen J. Stein (Cambridge: Cambridge University Press, 2007), 162–80; and from an analytic perspective, Paul Helm and Oliver D. Crisp, *Jonathan Edwards: Philosophical Theologian* (Farnham, Surrey, UK: Ashgate, 2003).

10. Exemplary in this regard is Leon Chai, *Jonathan Edwards and the Limits of Enlightenment Philosophy* (Oxford: Oxford University Press, 1998). See also Avihu Zakai, *Jonathan Edwards' Philosophy of History: The Re-Enchantment of the World in the Age of the Enlightenment* (Princeton: Princeton University Press, 2003) and Josh Moody, *Jonathan Edwards and the Enlightenment: Knowing the Presence of God* (Lanham, MD: University Press of America, 2005).

11. Samuel Hopkins, *Life and Character of the Late Reverend Mr. Jonathan Edwards* (Boston, 1765), 27, as quoted in *WJE* 6:7.

12. See also "Wisdom in the Contrivance of the World" in *WJE* 6:307–10, as well as the later "Images of Diving Things in God's Works," in *Typological Writings,* ed. Wallace E. Anderson, Mason I. Lowance, Jr., and David Watters (New Haven: Yale University Press, 1993), 50–143.

a thoroughly theocentric physics and metaphysics that include and presuppose God's continuing activity within creation. Leaving aside his detailed arguments, in "Of Being" Edwards renders impossible a self-sufficient universe of senseless matter when he argues that the "universe would cease to be, of itself; and not only, as we speak, because the Almighty could not attend to uphold the world, but because God knew nothing of it,"[13] and we witness the inversion of the privileging of a crude account of matter when Edwards speaks of "the gross mistake of those who think material things the most substantial things, and spirits more like a shadow; whereas spirits only are properly substance."[14] In "Of Atoms" Edwards attempts to demonstrate that indivisibility and solidity both arise "from the immediate exercise of God's power"[15] and that it is reasonable to think "that the certain understood substance, which philosophers used to think subsisted by itself, and stood underneath and kept up solidity and all other properties"[16] is neither substance nor nothing, but is instead "the Deity acting in that particular manner in those parts of space where he thinks fit. So that, speaking most strictly, there is no proper substance but God himself."[17] In "The Mind" Edwards develops his characteristic themes of excellence, proportion, harmony, beauty, and the pleasure of the senses. These terms are once again given direct reference to God such that "so far as a thing consents to being in general, so far it consents to him. And the more perfect created spirits are, the nearer do they come to their creator in this regard."[18] Another name for this consent between spirits is "their mutual love one to another, and the sweet harmony between the various parts of the universe is only an image of mutual love."[19] God is infinitely active within and involved within creation to such an extent that "our perceptions, or ideas that we passively receive by our bodies, are communicated

---

13. *WJE* 6:204.

14. *WJE* 6:206.

15. *WJE* 6:215.

16. *WJE* 6:215.

17. *WJE* 6:215. Edwards later glosses this proposition and notes, "To bring in an observation somewhere in a proper place, that instead of Hobbes' notion that God is matter and that all substance is matter; that nothing that is matter can possibly be God, and that no matter is, in the most proper sense, matter (relating to the eleventh corollary of Prop. 2)". *WJE* 6, 235; from "Things to be Considered an[d] Written fully about," *WJE* 6, 219–95.

18. *WJE* 6:337.

19. *WJE* 6:337.

to us immediately by God while our minds are united with our bodies"[20]; that the substance "of all bodies is the infinitely exact and precise and perfectly stable idea in God's mind, together with this stable will that the same shall gradually be communicated to us"[21]; and that the connection between our ideas and organs depends on God as do our causal conceptual connections.[22]

While Edwards is enacting a series of stark physical and metaphysical inversions in these essays, he is careful to stress that his intent is not to deny our experience of the natural world or the exigencies of our reasoning: "We would not, therefore, be understood to deny that things are where they seem to be, for the principles we lay down, if they are narrowly looked into, do not infer that. Nor will it be found that they at all make void natural philosophy."[23] Instead, the guiding presupposition of Edwards's investigation is that "to find out the reasons of things in natural philosophy is only to find out the proportion of God's acting."[24] Understanding the "proportion of God's acting" does not entail deducing the character or attributes of God from created phenomena but instead forms a necessary element in any richly developed doctrine of God. For Edwards, God is "infinite beauty," "infinite love of himself," such that "the perfection of spirits may be resolved into that which is God's perfection, which is love."[25] God is eternally excellent in and of himself, and this excellence consists in the mutual love between the Father, Son, and Holy Spirit, "in infinitely loving and delighting in himself."[26] The mutual love between the Father and the Son is joined by the "personal Holy Spirit or the holiness of God, which is his general beauty, and this is God's infinite consent to being in general."[27] As intimated in this last remark, God's communication of himself, of his love, beauty, and holiness, to his creatures is appropriated to the Holy Spirit and is to be accounted as an aspect of the divine excellence. We would err, Edwards maintains, to think of God's self-love as exclusive or egoistic and should instead conceive of the mutual love

---

20. *WJE* 6:339.
21. *WJE* 6:344.
22. *WJE* 6:359.
23. *WJE* 6:353.
24. *WJE* 6:353.
25. *WJE* 6:363.
26. *WJE* 6:363.
27. *WJE* 6:364.

of the Father, Son, and Spirit in such as way "that this love includes in it, or rather is the same as, a love of everything, as they are all communications of himself. So that we are to conceive of divine excellence as the infinite general love."[28] We should remember that these comments on the infinite love of the triune God come in the course of expounding the ontological grounds for the perception of excellency in nature.

Edwards's four main works, *Freedom of the Will* (1754), *Original Sin* (1758), *The End for Which God Created the World* (1765), and *Nature of True Virtue* (1765), display some variability regarding the presence and use of philosophy and the relationship between theology and philosophy. On the one hand, the prominence of Locke's anthropology, particularly as developed in the "On Power" section of *An Essay Concerning Human Understanding* in *Freedom of the Will* has been noted.[29] Edwards's rejection of faculty psychology in favor of an emphasis on the integration of human capacities and capabilities seems indebted to Locke, and yet Edwards moves beyond Locke in being able to give a richer account of the unity of the human agent. On the other hand, engagement with philosophers is noticeably absent in *Original Sin*, which is primarily a response to John Taylor's criticism of the doctrine in his *Scripture-Doctrine of Original Sin* (1740) and secondarily a response to George Turnbull's arguments regarding humanity's natural ability for moral progression and enlightenment in his *The Principles of Moral Philosophy* (1740).

Among his four major works, it is in the two dissertations published together as *The End for Which God Created the World* and *Nature of True Virtue* that Edwards seems to grapple most with philosophy and philosophers. The philosophy to which Edwards is responding changes, but what remains remarkably consistent is how Edwards enfolds his response within his own positive theological project, which means that this engagement with philosophy takes place within a context replete with theological presuppositions, doctrines, and intuitions.

The End for Which God Created the World (1765) has been described as a response to deist and pantheist criticisms "that the God of orthodoxy is an egotistical being obsessed with applause" as offered by Matthew Tindal,

---

28. *WJE* 6:365.
29. See the Editor's Introduction in *WJE* 6:47–65.

Thomas Chubb, and John Toland.[30] If such is indeed the case, which is plausible to suppose, the way in which Edwards crafts his response is worth considering. The objection that God may be justly deemed selfish and egotistical for appointing himself the final and highest end of creation comes in the fourth section of the first chapter. Before considering this objection and others, Edwards has already presented a great deal of his own positive project and thus the foundation of his response. In the first section of chapter 1, Edwards argues that creation cannot be the result of God's seeking to enrich himself, for "it is evident, by both Scripture and reason, that God is infinitely happy, eternally, unchangeably, and independently glorious and happy"[31] and that as the best and highest being, God is thus properly the end of creation. Likewise, in the second section of chapter 1, Edwards argues that it is fitting that the God of infinite perfection, goodness, excellency, and beauty should wish to communicate such goodness *ad extra*, which in the case of God can only mean wishing to communicate himself, revealing in the process a divine disposition to effusiveness. Furthermore, in the third section of chapter 1, Edwards states that God's diffusion of his love, goodness, self-knowledge, excellency, virtue, holiness, and beatitude to his creatures is the diffusion of himself for the benefit of his creatures, such that "his respect to them finally coincides and becomes one and the same with respect to himself. The interest of the creature is, as it were, God own's interest."[32]

The objections to God ordaining himself the final and highest end of creation are outlined and answered in the fourth section of the chapter, and thus, notably, after his elaboration of the above points. As for the complaint that such an ordination demonstrates that God does everything "from a selfish spirit," Edwards first responds that it is fitting to treat things according to their value and worth, and so it is suitable for God, as "infinitely the most valuable Being," to "value himself infinitely more than his creatures."[33] Second, Edwards argues that it is impossible for God's self-interest to conflict with that of his creatures, for God is "the Supreme Being, the Author and Head of the whole system: on whom all absolutely depend; who is the

30. McClymond and McDermott, *The Theology of Jonathan Edwards*, 38.

31. Edwards, *Ethical Writings*, ed. Paul Ramsey (New Haven: Yale University Press, 1989) [henceforth *WJE* 8], 420.

32. *WJE* 8:443.

33. *WJE* 8:451.

fountain of being and good to the whole."³⁴ Third, it is God's accordance and agreement with his own nature that leads him to regard and bless his creatures: "It is a regard to himself that inclines him to seek the good of his creature. It is a regard to himself that disposes him to diffuse and communicate himself."³⁵

When considering the related objection that God's ordination of himself as the end of creation seems unworthy or ignoble, Edwards appeals to how "the late philosophers"³⁶ define virtue as universal benevolence and general affection. This definition of virtue means that to love virtue means to love universal benevolence and affection and that the virtue of loving virtue implies and depends on such benevolence and affection. He then argues that inasmuch as God is universal being, general benevolence implies and depends on love of God. For God to love virtue, then, can only mean that God loves himself and even loves himself when he loves the manifestation and exercise of virtue in his creatures. In this way, "it will be easy to suppose that it becomes him to make himself his supreme and last end in his works."³⁷ While the chain of reasoning may be a bit convoluted and depends on Edwards's definition of God as universal being, his intention should be clear: to argue from the definition and ideal of virtue offered by "the late philosophers" to show how it is fitting that God should love himself as the origin and fount of virtue and that his love for the virtues of creatures is included within this self-love.

In *Nature of True Virtue* (1765), Edwards seems to be engaging Francis Hutcheson and the British moralists, although there has been some disagreement as to the extent to which Hutcheson is the primarily target or interlocutor in this work.³⁸ What is clear, however, is the manner in which Edwards

34. WJE 8:452.
35. WJE 8:452. Edwards also covers the topic of God's ordination of himself as the final and highest end of creation in Miscellany 1182.
36. WJE 8:456.
37. WJE 8:456.
38. Edwards takes the term "moral sense" from Hutcheson, but "To claim more than that is to venture rashly into unknown territory and to wander along footpaths no one left. The important thing to keep in mind is that 'moral sense' encompassed a host of Edwards' opponents." WJE 8:695; from "Appendix II. Jonathan Edwards on Moral Sense, and the Sentimentalists," WJE 8:689–705. Compare these claims with the argument that "Hutcheson's moral sense theory informs Edwards' understanding of moral formation generally, and Hutcheson's influence is particularly evident in Edwards' account of the exercise of virtuous repentance, because approbation

responds to the moral philosophy of his time. First, Edwards develops his own constructive and positive account of true virtue. Succinctly put, "true virtue consists in love to Being in general,"[39] in benevolence, and in "consent, propensity and union of the heart to Being in general."[40] "True virtue" and the "truly beautiful" mean consent to universal Being, which is the same thing as saying "that true virtue must chiefly consist in love to God; the Being of beings, infinitely the greatest and best of being."[41] Defined and argued in this way, true virtue becomes inextricably related to and dependent on God, love, and beauty.

After these positive definitions and arguments, Edwards then turns to address "some writers on morality"[42] who minimize the significance of love of God in their moral philosophies. His overall argument is that when natural virtue and morality are detached from God, then they will become a matter of union and benevolence toward the particular and the private, which runs the risk of becoming contrary to general benevolence. Edwards also hypothesizes that this restricted account of benevolence and affection will end up denigrating Being itself, "which is infinitely superior in itself and infinitely more important."[43] He then expands the idea of love of Being in general to include the end for which God created the world: God's manifestation, exercise, and communication of his excellencies and glory within creation and the manifestation and exercise in turn of creaturely esteem for, love of, and delight in God. The "corollary" of this ruggedly theocentric and inclusive view of virtue and morality is that

> these *schemes* of religion or moral philosophy, which, however well in some respects they may treat of benevolence to *mankind*, and other virtues depending on it, yet have not a supreme regard to God, laid in the *foundation* and all other virtues handled in a *connection* with this,

---

of God's moral excellence is so central to its practice." Elizabeth Agnew Cochran, *Receptive Human Virtues: A New Reading of Jonathan Edwards's Ethics* (University Park: Pennsylvania State University Press, 2013), 123. For the latter position, see also A. Owen Aldridge, "Edwards and Hutcheson," *The Harvard Theological Review* 44, no. 1 (Jan. 1951): 35–53.

39. *WJE* 8:541.
40. *WJE* 8:540.
41. *WJE* 8:550.
42. *WJE* 8:552.
43. *WJE* 8:556.

and in a *subordination* to this, are no true schemes of philosophy, but are fundamentally and essentially defective.[44]

This final evaluation of moral philosophies that neglect to provide and presuppose a substantive account of love of God is startling; they are "no true schemes of philosophy" at all.

A different dynamic is operative when Edwards adopts and adapts Hutcheson's remarks on beauty from his *Inquiry into Beauty and Virtue* (1725).[45] In the third chapter of *True Virtue*, Edwards considers primary and secondary forms of beauty. As is to be expected, Edwards defines primary beauty as the consent to and agreement and union with being that occurs among spiritual or moral beings. Secondary beauty, by contrast, can also be found in inanimate things and again consists in consent and agreement but in this case "of different things in form, manner, quantity, and visible end or design."[46] Edwards notes that this secondary beauty is defined by Hutcheson as "uniformity in the midst of variety"[47] and that the greater the uniformity and the variety, the greater the beauty, and he generally seems to accept the descriptive power of Hutcheson's definition. As he continues, however, the theocentric framework of his aesthetics becomes more and more prominent. The reason that this secondary beauty exists at all is that "that there is in it some image of the true, spiritual original beauty, which has been spoken of; consisting in being's consent to being" and that "it pleases God to observe analogy in his works, as in manifest in fact in innumerable works."[48] Knowledge that this secondary beauty is a shadow, a resemblance, or an analogy to spiritual and moral beauty is not necessary for the general perception of the secondary beauty of music, geometry, or the natural world. In fact, perception of and delight in this secondary beauty does not depend on general benevolence or consent to being at all and can presumably be enjoyed by all, regardless of their spiritual or moral state. This inclusion of beauty within a wider theological context means that one can readily

---

44. *WJE* 8:560.

45. See also *WJE* 8:562–66.

46. *WJE* 8:561.

47. *WJE* 8:562. See also *An Inquiry into the Original of Our Ideas of Beauty and Virtue* (London, 1753), 17.

48. *WJE* 8:564.

172 REFORMED DOGMATICS IN DIALOGUE

acknowledge and appreciate the generosity and extravagance of beauty while also recontextualizing the beauty described by "some moralists": "a taste of this inferior beauty in things immaterial, is one thing that has been mistaken by some moralists, for a true virtuous principle, implanted naturally in the hearts of all mankind."[49]

A similar pattern of acknowledgement, appreciation, and recontextualization can be seen in how Edwards both praises natural morality wherever it may be found and points out how it is markedly dissimilar to Christian morality. In Sermon Ten of *Charity and Its Fruits* (1738), for instance, Edwards notes that "many heathens were very eminent for many moral virtues, and wrote excellently of them; as of justice, and of generosity, and of fortitude and others."[50] Yet he then goes on to say

> But they were far from a Christian poverty of spirit, and lowliness of mind; they sought their own glory, and gloried exceedingly in their virtue, and said nothing about such a walk as the gospel commands, a walking in self-emptiness, poverty of spirit, self-diffidence, self-renunciation. And they said little of meekness, and did not own love of enemies, and forgiveness to be a virtue.[51]

To move beyond "the mere moralist, or the heathen sage or philosopher" means that one must possess "special esteem for and delight in these virtues that do especially belong to the gospel."[52]

In sum, Norman Fiering's description of Edwards's relationship with the moral philosophers of his time seems to hold true of his relationship with the new natural philosophy and with philosophy more generally: "Moral philosophers had begun the process of converting into secular and naturalistic terms crucial parts of the Christian heritage. Edwards in a sense reversed the ongoing process by assimilating the moral philosophy of his time and

---

49. *WJE* 8:574. One could argue that a similar pattern also takes place in Edwards's handling of natural conscience in *True Virtue* inasmuch as he states that his own understanding of natural conscience is the same as the moral phenomenon that other philosophers have labeled "moral sense," but doing so is in effect denying or reclassifying what Shaftesbury and Hutcheson meant by "moral sense."

50. *WJE* 8:310–11.

51. *WJE* 8:311.

52. *WJE* 8:311.

converting it back into the language of religious thought and experience."[53] It also seems that Edwards's engagement with natural and moral philosophy was fairly eclectic and occasional in nature, inspired rather than hindered his originality, and was put to service within a decidedly theocentric physics, metaphysics, and anthropology. Additionally, one should note that Edwards's response to philosophers, especially as seen in the two late dissertations, primarily consists in the positive development and elaboration of Christian doctrine within which he then dispels a number of objections. Additionally, McClymond and McDermott observe, "Unlike for many theologians of the Reformation or Neo-Orthodoxy, philosophy provided Edwards with a means for affirming the transcendent greatness and glory of God."[54] The second half of this sentence seems incontrovertible and illuminating when it comes to Edwards's performance regarding philosophy and natural philosophy. The first half of the sentence, as we will shortly see, might not be as accurate.

KARL BARTH

Scholarship on Karl Barth's intellectual and philosophical sources seems rather undeveloped when compared with the secondary literature on Edwards.[55] Perhaps it is this paucity of works on this topic in Barth that has led to the ready dissemination of the impression that Barth is either anti-philosophical or anti-rational or that Barth's theology is a capitulation to modern, skeptical, even atheist philosophy. Many of these misimpressions regarding Barth on theology and philosophy can be dispelled by examining Barth's nineteenth-century inheritance as well as considering what he actually said regarding the relationship between theology and philosophy.

Barth's earliest writings, from around 1909–1914, place him squarely within the dominant presuppositions of modern theology, and many of these presuppositions would remain with him even after his "break with liberalism," which is often taken to have occurred in the summer of 1915. Modern

53. Norman Fiering, *Jonathan Edwards's Moral Thought and Its British Context* (Chapel Hill: University of North Carolina Press, 1981), 60–61.

54. McClymond and McDermott, *The Theology of Jonathan Edwards*, 102.

55. Some of this work has been attempted in Bruce McCormack, *Karl Barth's Critically Realistic Dialectical Theology: Its Genesis and Development* (Oxford: Clarendon, 1995); Johann Friedrich Lohmann, *Karl Barth und der Neukantianismus: die Rezeption des Neukantianismus im "Römerbrief" und ihre Bedeutung für die weitere Ausarbeitung der Theologie Karl Barths* (Berlin: de Gruyter, 2010), and Henri Delhougne, *Karl Barth et la rationalité: période de la dogmatique* (Paris: Cerf, 1978).

theology, which originated with Friedrich Schleiermacher and found adherents in Albrecht Ritschl and Wilhelm Herrmann, was Christocentric, ecclesial, concerned with religious experience, suspicious of metaphysics and natural theology, and intent on maintaining the independent and self-authenticating nature of faith and theology. The independence of faith and theology meant that neither of them could be subsumed within or explained by ethics, psychology, or history even as the modern theologians attempted to correlate positively faith and theology with modern intellectual culture. The result was a treaty or truce between a modern or cautiously revisionist Protestant theology and an ethically rigorous and critically inclined philosophy.

The early Barth clearly held to the convergence or congruence between modern Protestant theology and serious, critical philosophy. Perhaps the most famous example of this congruence can be found in the preface to the second edition of Barth's commentary on Romans:

> The relation between such a God and such a man, and the relation between such a man and such a God, is for me the theme of the Bible and the essence of philosophy. Philosophers name this the KRISIS of human perception—the Prime Cause; the Bible beholds at the same cross-roads—the figure of Jesus Christ.[56]

Scripture and critical philosophy overlap inasmuch as they view the human situation as one of crisis, and they diverge inasmuch as Scripture identifies this crisis with Jesus Christ, while philosophy identifies it as the irreducible insecurity of human existence and knowledge. The congruence thesis can also be seen in the 1924–26 *Göttingen Dogmatics*, a series of lectures in systematic theology that Barth held at the University of Göttingen. On the one hand, there is the sharp distinction between theology and philosophy, at least in the form of metaphysics: "If God were not the speaking subject who creates faith by his Word, then what could he be but the object of a scholarly metaphysics?"[57] On the other hand, theology should not be completely untethered from philosophy: "Not that we scorn participating in philosophical work, at least as vitally interested dilettantes. Not as though we could

---

56. Barth, *The Epistle to the Romans*, trans. Edwyn Hoskyns (Oxford: Oxford University Press, 1968), 10.

57. Barth, *The Göttingen Dogmatics: Instruction in the Christian Religion*, vol. 1, ed. Hannelotte Reiffen, trans. Geoffrey W. Bromiley (Grand Rapids: Eerdmans, 1991), 11.

promise no good from a dialogue of philosophy with theology."[58] Just as with
the second edition of his commentary on Romans, both revelation and critical philosophy presuppose a humanity in transit and in crisis. Barth notes
that "the contact that we make with philosophy at this point is welcome to
us as a secondary confirmation that even from a human standpoint we have
not been describing a phantom but the form that anyone might know. I think
that with or without this support from philosophy we may quietly assume
that as Christian preachers we are addressing real man."[59] While the work
of theology does not require or depend on it, critical philosophy provides a
"secondary confirmation" of the human predicament described by theology.
The terms of the congruence thesis can be readily seen when Barth clarifies
that "we must not get the wrong impression that the statement that God is
incomprehensible is merely the broken confession of the human spirit as it
becomes aware of the abyss of its own ignorance and despairs of itself, that
it is merely the sum of Kant's philosophy," and yet then adds, "Naturally it
is this *too*."[60]

As the late 1920s and 1930s went on, Barth increasingly endorsed a philosophical eclecticism within theological work and grew suspicious of this
treaty between modern Protestant theology and critical philosophy. In a
series of letters to Emil Brunner, for instance, Barth registers his worries
that Brunner was attaching his theology too heavily to Kant. He tells Brunner,
"Naturally with every theological statement I think under specific philosophical presuppositions, but I don't want to connect the *whole thing* to one; instead
I am looking for a theological platform from which I can interact with as
many philosophers as possible."[61] Similar worries were expressed to Rudolf
Bultmann, whom Barth judged to have merely exchanged Martin Heidegger's
critical philosophy for that of Kant.[62] Barth's alternative to this venerable
correlation of modern Protestantism and critical philosophy included the
reassertion of theology's independence as well as the recommendation of

58. Barth, *Göttingen Dogmatics*, 325.

59. Barth, *Göttingen Dogmatics*, 104.

60. Barth, *Göttingen Dogmatics*, 107.

61. Barth, *Karl Barth-Emil Brunner Briefwechsel 1916-1966*, ed. Eberhard Busch (Zürich:
Theologischer Verlag Zürich, 2000), 115.

62. See Barth, *Karl Barth-Rudolf Bultmann Letters: 1922-1966*, trans. Geoffrey W. Bromiley
and Bernd Jaspert (Edinburgh: T&T Clark), 58.

philosophical eclecticism. In the 1927 *Christliche Dogmatik*, for instance, Barth insists that "one can, with the same philosophical presuppositions, be a better or worse hearer of the Word."[63] This eclecticism also helps to prevent one from thinking that theology's primary task is correcting or struggling with philosophy rather than attending to its own business of following upon and explicating revelation: "The health of theology cannot be expected from its struggle with this or that philosophy or from the correcting of this or that philosophy."[64] In fact, one of the main reasons Barth revised his 1927 *Christliche Dogmatik* into 1932's *CD* I/1 was to remove any suggestion, or actually misimpression, that he was relying on any type of philosophical foundation or justification for his theology.[65]

The late 1920s show Barth putting forth a range of proposals regarding theology and philosophy. In *Ethics* (1928/29), Barth devotes a whole chapter to the relationship between theological and philosophical ethics. He considers the usual ways of relating theology and philosophy through apologetics, isolation, or subordinating philosophy to theology. He details how each of these three is problematic and how each may be modified to be constructive for both theology and philosophy, and he even notes that a discipline called "Christian philosophy" could potentially exist.[66] In *Protestant Theology in the Nineteenth Century*, Barth argues that Christianity became a problem for modern thought and philosophy and attempts to show how Kant, Hegel, and others ended up turning Christianity into an example or illustrations of their own philosophies in order to render theology innocuous.[67] In the 1929 lecture series "Fate and Idea in Theology," Barth discusses the relationship between theology and philosophy in response to the philosophical theology of the Jesuit Erich Przywara. Adopting a conceptual style from Przywara, Barth argues that all theology and philosophy take place between the two poles of realism and idealism, with the former emphasizing givenness and the latter, freedom. Both theology and philosophy must remain vigilant, restless, and open and must resist identifying their own projects and conclusions

---

63. Barth, *Die Christliche Dogmatik im Entwurf* (Zürich: Theologischer Verlag Zürich, 1971), 525.

64. Barth, *Die Christliche Dogmatik im Entwurf*, 525.

65. Cf. *CD* I/1, 26–27, 131.

66. Cf. Barth, *Ethics*, trans. Geoffrey W. Bromiley (Edinburgh: T&T Clark, 1981), 21–44.

67. Barth, *Protestant Theology in the Nineteenth Century: Its Background and History* (Valley Forge: Judson Press, 1976).

with the Word of God as such. When both theology and philosophy are cognizant of their respective limits, then "what can and will exist is not only a well-wishing neutrality, not only concord but—at least for the theology in whose name we speak here—a rich and instructive community of work."[68]

In *CD* I/2, Barth considers the use of philosophy, understood here as the explicit and implicit presuppositions guiding one's engagement with the world, when reading and interpreting Scripture. He understands that all human activity takes place within an essentially hermeneutical horizon and states that "we cannot basically contest the use of philosophy in scriptural exegesis. Where the question of legitimacy arises is in regard to the How of this use."[69] Barth offers five recommendations regarding the irreducible "how" of the presence and use of philosophy within Scriptural interpretation. First, there must be the fundamental awareness of the difference between my philosophy and "the philosophy of Scripture."[70] Second, I must remember that my philosophical presuppositions or commitments, while necessary for the interpretation of Scripture, must remain malleable and open to revision. It also means that "I cannot exclude the possibility that the same attempt can and must be ventured with the application of quite other philosophies than mine. Therefore I shall not radically deny to other philosophies than my own the character of useful hypotheses in the service of the same end."[71] Third, the criticism or correction of philosophy cannot be an end in itself when the task at hand is the interpretation of Scripture. Fourth, there is no absolute reason for preferring one philosophy to another within theological work. There may indeed be powerful and persuasive reasons and circumstances that lead one to adhere to a particular philosophy. Barth asks, nevertheless, "How can we bind ourselves to one philosophy as the only philosophy, and ascribe to it a universal necessity?"[72] Fifth, the final place of philosophy can only be that of theology: as subservient to Scripture. Here Barth enacts a leveling of both theology and philosophy before revelation: "It is not really a question of replacing philosophy by a dictatorial, and absolute and exclusive theology,

---

68. Barth, "Fate and Idea in Theology," in H.-M. Rumscheidt, *The Way of Theology in Karl Barth: Essays and Comments* (Pittsburgh: Pickwick), 25–61; here 54.

69. *CD* I/2, 729–30.

70. *CD* I/2, 730.

71. *CD* I/2, 731.

72. *CD* I/2, 733.

and again discrediting philosophy as an *ancilla theologiae*."[73] The overall aim of these remarks is not the denigration or discrediting of philosophy for the sake of theology's anxiety regarding its presumed superiority. Instead, the aim is to show how "philosophy—and fundamentally any philosophy—can be criticized in the service of the Word of God" and in this way "can then gain a legitimate critical power. It can be elucidated and then elucidate."[74]

One of the most surprising, novel, and interesting features of Barth's doctrine of creation in *CD* III is the appearance of long excursuses in which he deals directly with philosophers. Barth details and evaluates the views of Arthur Schopenhauer, René Descartes, and Gottfried Leibniz in *CD* III/1; Johann Gottlieb Fichte, Karl Jaspers, and Friedrich Nietzsche in *CD* III/2; Martin Heidegger and Jean-Paul Sartre in *CD* III/3; and Simone de Beauvoir in *CD* III/4. Barth acknowledges that many theological doctrines and claims have a noticeable "philosophical counterpart"[75] that deserves the keenest attention from theologians. The primary point of this attention to philosophy is so that theology can gain "an increasing elucidation and precision of its own attitude to its own theme"[76] and perhaps even "a certain confirmation of our results—a confirmation which we do not need and which will not cause us any particular excitement, but of which, in which of its occurrence, we shall not be ashamed."[77] While the goal of these engagements is the enrichment of theology's own themes and concerns, Barth is also open to this enrichment serving as an *ad hoc* apologetic. As the proponents of these philosophical counterparts "hear the uninterrupted witness to God the Creator," they may be "brought to realise that their restricted positing of the question is fundamentally superseded" and "will be invited at the very least to improve them, and finally to abandon them altogether."[78]

Barth occasionally returned to the theme of theology and philosophy later in his life. In the essay "Philosophy and Theology,"[79] a contribution to the *Festschrift* dedicated to his brother Heinrich, an academic philosopher in his own right,

---

73. *CD* I/2, 734.

74. *CD* I/2, 735.

75. *CD* III/1, 388.

76. *CD* III/1, 344.

77. *CD* III/2, 277.

78. *CD* III/1, 344.

79. Barth, "Philosophy and Theology," in Rumscheidt, *The Way of Theology in Karl Barth*, 79–95.

Barth advances several interrelated points: theology, properly understood, moves from above to below, while philosophy moves from below to above; theology then moves back from below to above, while philosophy moves from above to below; and while neither theology nor philosophy can exchange its respective movements for those of the other, both can indeed exchange friendly greetings and experience occasional overlaps while each performs its task of pursuing the one truth that is higher than both of them, which theology knows to be Jesus Christ. Additionally, Barth made clear in some late interviews that the issue at hand is not philosophy as such but how theologians use philosophy: "In fact, I am not opposed to philosophy. My position in regard to philosophical research is motivated by another concern. I refuse to presuppose a philosophical basis for Christianity; I do not accept philosophy as a basis of discussion in the domain of theology."[80] One should note that the earliest Barth, concerned as he was with the independence of faith and theology, would have agreed with such a statement, as would many of the modern theologians.

While admittedly brief, the above remarks should hopefully demonstrate that Barth's thoughts on theology and philosophy are varied and complex even while they consistently presuppose that theology is a substantive and comprehensive discipline in its own right that begins with revelation. Within this presupposition, Barth feels free to engage with philosophy for the sake of theology, to ignore the strictures or concerns of philosophy when necessary, and to admit that everyone always and already engages with texts, including Scripture, with certain philosophical presuppositions in place.

CONCLUSION

The differences between Edwards and Barth have been stated in the introduction to this chapter, and the above portraits are admittedly selective and roughly sketched, but there are two points worth mentioning by way of conclusion.

First, Barth was certainly more cautious and worried regarding certain uses of and recourse to philosophy than was Edwards. This caution and worry are perhaps also why Barth felt more pressure to thematize the relationship

---

80. Barth, "Interview von Henri-Charles Tauxe," in Barth, *Gespräche 1964–68*, ed. Eberhard Busch (Zürich: Theologischer Verlag Zürich, 1997), 572, as translated in Oakes, *Karl Barth on Theology and Philosophy*, 241–42.

between theology and philosophy as well as to outline the ways in which he thought this relationship could be pursued positively and productively for both disciplines. After what he saw as the myriad of anxious attempts to justify theology before philosophy or to correlate theology with philosophy in nineteenth-century Protestant thought and in theologians such as Brunner and Bultmann, Barth deliberately focused his efforts on the pursuit of extended descriptions of Christian doctrine itself, even to the point of including prolegomena within theology itself. While Edwards is also clear on the differences between theology and philosophy, he displays greater nonchalance regarding the adoption and adaptation of his current intellectual culture, and his forays into natural philosophy are much wider and deeper than anything Barth thought salutary or necessary to pursue.

Second, the most significant and interesting commonality between Edwards and Barth is the shared enfolding of their engagement with philosophy and philosophers within the elaboration of Christian doctrine. While the level of Barth's interactions with philosophy has often been underestimated, it still seems to be the case that Edwards's œuvre contains more frequent and direct appeal to and adaptation of the physics, metaphysics, and moral philosophy of his time. Nevertheless, works such as the two dissertations show Edwards discussing natural conscience, morality, and virtue; beauty and aesthetics; and complaints regarding the doctrine of God within the context of his development and description of Christian doctrine. The deep and worthy intuition present within this venture is that Christian doctrine itself can be intellectually, morally, aesthetically, and spiritually fulfilling and persuasive and that recourse to the specificities and particularities of Christian claims is not a hindrance to the discussion of subject matters shared with other disciplines. This basic confidence in the scope, substance, and competence of theology leads both Edwards and Barth to read, interact with, and contextualize philosophy and other disciplines in ways in which the disciplines and findings of physics, metaphysics, and philosophy do not need to be ignored, exorcised, or frantically subordinated. A theology already assured of its dignity, substance, principles, and ends need not deny a similar dignity and substance to other disciplines, and on this final point Edwards and Barth are in profound agreement.

9

HUMANITY

Kyle C. Strobel

It is not immediately obvious that a comparison between Edwards and Barth on anthropology would be a fruitful exercise. Beyond the differing historical and theological contexts of each thinker, it is concerning questions of anthropology in particular that Barth deviates from his Reformed Orthodox source material. Edwards is also a bit peculiar, functioning in a post-Lockean environment that altered, if nothing else, how Edwards himself received a traditional account of human personhood. But while these two thinkers constructed their theological anthropologies using different emphases, there is a narrow space in their discussions where an interesting overlap occurs. This overlap has to do with the implications for how a human being stands before another. To address this like-minded instinct, I want to narrate, briefly, Barth's development of the I-Thou relation with an eye to loving another, using that as a backdrop to think about Edwards's own development of similar themes.

Instead of providing a comparison between these two thinkers, therefore, the goal of this essay is to read Barth and Edwards on the narrow topic of the self-in-relation. I begin with Barth because I believe Barth develops some helpful language within which to understand some of what Edwards is doing in his own analysis. Considering Barth and Edwards in this order admittedly runs the risk of both oversimplification and anachronism, but I think it proves helpful for illumining an underappreciated strand of Edwards's thought. The overall goal will be to think along the contours of both thinkers on the nature of the self-in-relation, considering how their similar trajectories may provide space for constructive engagement. In doing so, it is important to note that I am excising these discussions from their overall thought in an attempt not to undermine broader theological impulses but to create the context for a more significant comparison. Any reduction, while unfortunate, is because of this overall goal. This is particularly true for Barth and his Christological reimagining of anthropology, which will not be addressed in this essay.[1]

BARTH ON THE "REAL MAN"

To begin with Barth, I want to consider "the primal phenomenon of man,"[2] tracing that formal feature of personhood into more theologically material matters. Barth addresses this primal phenomenon as a seeking after oneself by "always transcending" oneself, "going ever beyond the self which he is able to find."[3] Likewise, "[t]reading this path, he finds himself on the way which leads him to the limit where there will be no further image or object, but only himself."[4] Barth's worry, no less than Edwards's, will be that "natural man" (to use Edwards's phrase) will simply construct a deceptive mirror in which to gaze, deceiving oneself into thinking that true humanity is in our power to construct. In Barth's words, which will become important for our discussion of Edwards:

> It is not in vain that he [i.e., "man"] is in quest of himself. … His existence is in relationship, and therefore in a relationship to another being which transcends himself and his natural and ethical life. It is in that transcendent being that he seeks himself. Otherwise he does not seek himself but is ensnared by the delusion that he has found himself and possesses himself.[5]

But all of this is still done in a mode of self-examination that trades in the economy of autonomous self-understanding. Barth's worry is that in any attempt to analyze human personhood through natural, ethical, and existential angles, "real man" will never be encountered.[6] Of course, for Barth,

---

1. In light of the two thinkers' use of the term "man" for humankind (and other usages based on this), I have kept the masculine throughout unless I was able to adapt it without it being too cumbersome to change.

2. *CD* III/2 §44, 105.

3. *CD* III/2 §44, 106.

4. *CD* III/2 §44, 106.

5. *CD* III/2 §44, 107.

6. *CD* III/2 §44, 116.

"real man" will always be discovered only in "this history between God and man."[7] To think of "real man" as such is to never forget that this one stands in relation to God as creature to Creator.[8] Barth's Christological emphasis goes beyond seeing Christ as a mere exemplar of human existence but recognizes Christ as the one in whom humanity as such is known. In his reflection on Romans 5, Barth claims, "Here the new point is that the *special* anthropology of Jesus Christ—the one man for all men, all men in the one man—constitutes the secret of 'Adam' also, and so is the norm of *all* anthropology."[9] In following this line, Barth emphasizes, unsurprisingly, that there is no way to begin with "autonomous human self-understanding" to the free action of God, to then establish the reality of humanity. This can be established only by the "free initiative of God and His temporal and historical dealings with man."[10] Sharing Dostoevsky's instincts, Barth continues, "If it is to be attained, then the closed circle of man's self-understanding must be broken from without and made accessible to something outside itself."[11]

TOWARD A TRULY THEOLOGICAL ANTHROPOLOGY

It is possible for the creature to have the recognition and awareness of a transcendent other apart from revelation or faith, and it is furthermore, as Barth avers, possible to know *the actuality* of one's existence without these realities.[12] But in this sense, the notion of "God" remains undetermined,

---

7. *CD* III/2 §44, 116.

8. *CD* III/2 §44, 117. "Man exists only in his relation with God. And this relation is not peripheral but central, not incidental but essential to that which makes him a real man, himself. He is to the extent that not he himself but God is His sovereign Lord, and his own sovereignty flows from God." *CD* III/2, 117–18.

9. Barth, *Christ and Adam: Man and Humanity in Romans 5* (Eugene, OR: Wipf & Stock, 1956), 14.

10. *CD* III/2 §44, 119. Barth claims, "The relationship between Adam and us reveals not the primary but only the secondary anthropological truth and ordering principle. The primary anthropological truth and ordering principle, which only mirrors itself in that relationship, is made clear only through the relationship between Christ and us. ... Man's essential and original nature is to be found, therefore, not in Adam but in Christ." Barth, *Christ and Adam*, 17.

11. *CD* III/2 §44, 119. Barth continues, helpfully, "The instruction in question then consists in the recognition that the circle is open, in the acceptance of the instruction which comes to man from without, from God Himself. And the human self understood in this way is the reality concerning which man allows himself to be told from without, by God, that it is his own reality. ... In order to become knowledge of real man, human self-understanding must be reversed and refounded, being changed from an autonomous into a theonomous self-understanding." *CD* III.2 §44, 119.

12. E.g., *CD* III/2 §44, 120–21.

and therefore, the actuality and identity of the creature would remain so as well. To gain a truly *theological* idea of humanity requires something beyond what develops within the register of autonomous self-understanding; a theological notion of "real man" is one "grounded in the fact that one man among all others is the man Jesus."[13] A failure to ground theological anthropology concretely in Christ, for Barth, is a failure to address the "*reality* of man" rather than simply the "phenomena of man."[14] Furthermore, any account that fails to address humankind in relation to God, and in particular, "his participation in the history inaugurated between him and God, and the glory, lordship, purpose and service of God," fails to address the true meaning of human life.[15] This Christological orientation of theological anthropology means that human persons have a "true and absolute Counterpart," calling them to be "with this correspondence, reflection and representation of the uniqueness and transcendence of God, to be with the One who is unlike us. To be man is thus to be in this the true and absolute Counterpart."[16] Barth summarizes this by getting to his core instinct: "to be a man is to be with God."[17]

This instinct in Barth is grounded on his primary Christological impulse that governs his thought. As Mikkelsen notes, "The real man is ... a description of the human being seen in the light of God's determination of the human being. This determination is revealed in God's act toward the human being in the man Jesus Christ."[18] Christ is the true determining reality for humanity and not an account of human nature developed from within or from Adam. We are tempted, on a more superficial reading of the biblical narrative, to use Adam rather than Christ as the grounding reality of humanity. Barth

---

13. *CD* III/2 §44, 126.

14. *CD* III/2 §44, 127. Hans Vium Mikkelsen states, "To try to understand the human being apart from its relation to God is from a Barthian perspective to be evaluated as an abstract speculation. The human being can never cease to be in relation to God—and thereby to be determined by God—as God never ceases to be in relation to the human being (due to the will of God). Of course the human being can be viewed apart from the God-man relation, but it is then a description that is only able to take into account the phenomena of man and not the real man." Hans Vium Mikkelsen, *Reconciled Humanity: Karl Barth in Dialogue* (Grand Rapids: Eerdmans, 2010), 94.

15. *CD* III/2 §44, 127.

16. *CD* III/2 §44, 129.

17. *CD* III/2 §44, 129.

18. Mikkelsen, *Reconciled Humanity*, 96.

rejects this notion, claiming that "Adam is only the type, the likeness, the preliminary shadow of our relationship to Christ. The same human nature appears in both but the humanity of Adam is only real and genuine in so far as it reflects and corresponds to the humanity of Christ."[19] It is this move, characteristic of Barth's Christological reordering of the dogmatic material, that makes him so different from Edwards and his Reformed High Orthodox source material. With this in mind, however, it is important to narrow the scope of our inquiry in order to think alongside Barth and Edwards on the nature of the self-in-relation.

BARTH: I AND THOU[20]

In his development of the "real man," Barth provides four points on the being, and therefore the act, of man, which he claims characterizes the "being of man as history."[21] In the fourth heading, which serves to summarize the previous three, Barth describes the responsibility humankind has before God within the "character of the freedom which God imparts to it."[22] This is important because it serves to ground Barth's development of the I-Thou relation. Creaturely freedom can never be considered as such, for Barth, without first considering God's own freedom (and his gracious gift of freedom). Theological anthropology does not leave theology proper to construct an account of freedom apart from the gracious acts of God.[23] To consider the freedom we have as creatures, Barth argues, we must attend to the reality that our freedom is gift. In his words,

---

19. Barth, *Christ and Adam*, 22.

20. For this essay, I am not interested in considering the influence of Buber's work on Barth. Mikkelsen engages this, with an interesting contrast between Barth's engagement with Buber in *CD* versus the yet unpublished and untranslated lectures Barth gave on Buber in preparation for his work in *CD*, entitled "Des Menschen Menschlichkeit." See Mikkelsen, *Reconciled Humanity*, 98ff.

21. *CD* III/2 §44, 168–90.

22. *CD* III/2 §44, 185.

23. Barth has already, in *CD* III/1, employed the I-Thou relation between God and the creature as a unique feature of human existence compared with the creation. In the creation of man, Barth claims, exists "a real other, a true counter-part to God," and, furthermore, "Neither heaven nor earth, water nor land, nor living creatures from plants upward to land animals, are a 'Thou' whom God can confront as an 'I,' nor do they stand in an 'I-Thou' relationship to one another, nor can they enter into such a relationship. According to the first creation saga, however, man as such exists in this relationship from the very outset." *CD* III/1 §45, 182.

This is the unfathomable abyss into which we consciously or uncon-
sciously gaze whenever we say I, Thou, He or She, or use any personal
or possessive pronouns. Behind this I, Thou and He, as also behind
Mine, Thine and His, there always stands unexpressed but necessarily latent the human self and therefore the human freedom which we
cannot acquire for ourselves and which can and actually is given us
only by God, because He alone is originally free.[24]

But while Barth introduces the I and Thou here, he does not develop this
notion until he addresses "Man in his Determination as the Covenant-Partner
of God."[25] The proper sphere of the I-Thou relationality is first and foremost
the Trinity. "Entering into this relationship, He makes a copy of Himself.
Even in His inner divine being there is a relationship. ... He is in Himself the
One who loves eternally, the One who is eternally loved, and eternal love;
and in this triunity He is the original and source of every I and Thou, of the
I which is eternally from and to the Thou and therefore supremely I."[26] God
created humankind "in correspondence with His own being and Essence,"[27]
and he claims that man is the "repetition of this divine form of life; its copy
and reflection."[28] But it is in the humanity of Jesus, which is the "primary
text" of theological anthropology, that we discover that there can be no discussion of "man" theologically that is not man for others.[29]

   In contrast to this Christian judgment, Barth wonders, is not "man" at
bottom simply man for himself? This naturalistic "I am," Barth admits, can
still have real power and meaning behind it; this self-for-the-sake-of-self will
still find a place for others. No matter how narcissistic, even the naturalistic
self recognizes its need and desire for others. "The only trouble is that basically and properly it is without them or against them or only secondarily and
occasionally with them and for them."[30] This "I am" is simply projected outward at others. It was Nietzsche, for Barth, who was the one who embraced

---

24. *CD* III/2 §44, 186.
25. This is the title of §45.
26. *CD* III/2 §45, 16.
27. *CD* III/2 §45, 118.
28. *CD* III/2 §41, 183.
29. *CD* III/2 §45, 23, 26.
30. *CD* III/2 §45, 27.

without qualification this "I am"—this man without other men. But this is not the humanity discovered in Jesus. "The humanity of Jesus consists in His being for man."[31] In this context Barth addresses his use of "I."

> And the word "I" is meaningful in relation to the one with whom I speak about him. It has no reference to himself. If I speak to him and not about him, he is neither It, He nor She, but Thou. I then make the distinction and connexion in relation to him in the specific form of a demarcation in virtue of which my sphere is no longer my own but his, and he is like me. But there is more to it than this. For when I say "I" and therefore "Thou" to someone else, I empower and invite and summon him to say "Thou" to me in return.[32]

In this sense, Barth refuses to accept a notion of "I" that does not have the "Thou" internal to it. This does not undermine a formal depiction of the "I am"; Barth accepts that reality.[33] Barth rejects the notion, found frequently in the tradition, that "aptitudes" of a thinking and willing being somehow define one's humanity. In these things one can be human or inhuman.[34] So this formal reality is not enough to describe the true nature of humanity. More has to be said. This more is, for Barth, "I am as I am in relation."[35] There is a necessary "self-positing" to be an "I," just as there must be in the one before whom I stand as a "Thou." As such, "The work of the Thou cannot be indifferent to me, nor can I evade or master it. I cannot do this because as I do my own work, as I art myself and posit myself, I am necessarily claimed by and occupied with the being and positing of the Thou. My own being and positing takes place in and with the fact that I am claimed by that of the other and occupied with

---

31. *CD* III/2 §45, 40.

32. *CD* III/2 §45, 41–42. "Thus the word 'Thou,' although it is a very different word, is immanent to 'I.' It is not a word which is radically alien, but one which belongs to it. The word 'I' with which I think and declare my humanity implies as such humanity with and not without the fellow-man. I cannot say 'I,' even to myself, without also saying 'Thou,' without making that distinction and connexion in relation to another." *CD* III.2 §45, 42.

33. *CD* III/2 §45, 42. For instance, importantly, Barth notes, "An excess of zeal in conflict with the idealistic concept of humanity has sometimes led to the emptying out of the baby with the bath-water. Man has been constructed wholly in the light of the fellow-man, and the 'I am' has formally disappeared in the 'Thou art.' " *CD* III.2 §45, 44.

34. *CD* III/2 §45, 45–46.

35. *CD* III/2 §45, 43.

it."[36] The only retreat away from this reality, Barth argues, is a retreat into "inhumanity." Rather, true human being is being-in-encounter. "Being with means encounter. Hence being with the other means encounter with him."[37] But what is the nature of this *with*?

However one understands the nature of this withness, Barth avers, it must not mean that I become Thou, or Thou become I. But there is a togetherness that this withness entails that establishes rather than erodes the I and the Thou. The nature of this withness and togetherness is not static, Barth argues, "but dynamic and active. It is not an *esse* but an *existere*."[38] The I and the Thou stand in an active relation and therefore must "move out of themselves." To be with another truly entails that "one man looks the other in the eye," both to see the other as a Thou and to, likewise, be visible to them as a Thou to their I.[39] Key to standing eye to eye is an *openness* "to and on behalf of the other."[40] Barth uses the imagery of openness and closedness to the other to depict what it means to truly be with (to be open to) an other and to close oneself off from the other. This openness is what it entails to "move out of ourselves" and therefore "be known by them."[41] But to look another in the eye is only one aspect of the encounter Barth describes. He adds to this mutual speech and hearing, mutual assistance (to be at the disposal of the other), and that this mutual encounter be done with gladness.[42] Barth continues to describe the necessity of openness, but openness itself is insufficient; openness "alone is not guarantee that I reach thee and Thou me, that there is thus a real encounter."[43] I cannot be I without receiving the other and embracing the truth of who I am in the encounter I have with him. Barth glosses the Apostle Paul's development in 2 Corinthian 6–7 (without referencing this as

---

36. *CD* III/2 §45, 43.

37. *CD* III/2 §45, 44.

38. *CD* III/2 §45, 45.

39. *CD* III/2 §45, 46. "And it is a necessary part of the human meaning of the eye that man himself should be visible to the other: not an outward form, a something which might be like the rest of the cosmos; but man himself, the man who as such is particular and distinct within the cosmos." *CD* III/2 §45, 47.

40. *CD* III/2 §45, 47.

41. *CD* III/2 §45, 47.

42. *CD* III/2 §45, 46–60.

43. *CD* III/2 §45, 49.

a source): "The question may be raised whether I have any room for him."[44] Paul's pleading is similar but runs the other direction: "Make room in your hearts for us" (2 Cor 7:2).

EDWARDS, GOD, AND THE SELF IN GRACE

Like Barth, Edwards establishes his notion of the self-in-relation in his doctrine of God. In an early notebook entry, Edwards writes, "I cannot doubt but that God loves infinitely, properly speaking, and not only with that which some call self-love," before going on to claim, "We have shown that one alone cannot be excellent, inasmuch as, in such case, there can be no consent. Therefore, if God is excellent, there must be a plurality in God; otherwise, there can be no consent in him."[45] God's life, for Edwards, is a life of the consenting union of love between the Father and the Son, and this life is known in the economy as the Son and Spirit are received, catching the creature up into this life of love. This can be seen in Jesus' prayer to the Father in John 17:26, "I made known to them your name, and I will continue to make it known, that *the love with which you have loved me may be in them*, and I in them." In the economy, Jesus prays not that the Father would love his people but that the Father would *internalize* them in the love of the Father for the Son. For Edwards, this love is the Spirit, and this movement to internalize creatures into God's life is a movement to mirror the truth of what it means to be a self for others.

The inner-life of God is defined, for Edwards, by God's infinite blessedness. The first line of Edwards's "Discourse on the Trinity" states, "When we speak of God's happiness, the account that we are wont to give of it is that God is infinitely happy in the enjoyment of himself, in perfectly beholding and infinitely loving, and rejoicing in, his own essence and perfections."[46] The Father, Son, and Spirit are the one God whose inner-life is defined by standing in relations of personal knowledge and love. For Edwards, God's unity in knowing and loving creates the foundation for a threefold personhood in God by grounding personhood through perichoresis. The Father, Son, and Spirit are persons only insofar as they coinhere in one another in

---

44. *CD* III/2 §45, 54.
45. *WJE* 13:284.
46. *WJE* 21:113.

the single personal reality of Godself. The Father and Son, to borrow the Barthian idiom, stand eye to eye in the love of the Spirit, which is a relation reiterated in the economy to image the truth of the Father-Son relation *in se*. This emphasis on eye-to-eye, or, better, face-to-face, relationality in love serves to ground God's life as the archetypal beatific vision that glorified creatures come to partake in for eternity. In the economy, this relation is imaged through Jesus, who, we discover at his baptism, is the one seen by the Father in the belovedness of the Spirit. For Jesus to be truly the Son of God, Edwards avers, the Father must *look on him* as his own Son in the Fatherly love for the Son in the Holy Spirit.[47]

NATURAL AND SUPERNATURAL HUMANITY

The shape of Edwards's vision of the self-in-relation is determined by God's pure act in himself and is revealed in the economy in Jesus, who stands before the Father as Son. There is a kind of mirroring between our calls to love God and to love our neighbor as ourselves, with God's self-love being broken open to God's creaturely "neighbors" to internalize them within this love. Therefore, while it is still possible to talk about a formal dimension of the self that articulates what it means to be a human being generically, more must be said in light of God's self-revelation. Barth's distinction between being human and inhuman can be helpful here, although Edwards speaks instead about the natural and supernatural image of God on humanity. Natural man is one who, after the fall, is driven by self-love, natural appetites, and the passions, which, when "left to themselves," are called "the flesh" in Scripture.[48] When Edwards claims these natural features of the self "are left to themselves," he is claiming that they are not ordered by the supernatural in the soul. In Edwards's view, Adam and Eve had the Spirit of God infused in their souls and were therefore holy. This is the primal reality of human being, to have the love of God within the soul, upholding the person in love and ordering the natural by the supernatural. These are the "*superior* principles," Edwards avers, "that were spiritual, holy and divine, summarily comprehended in divine love; wherein consisted the spiritual image of God, and man's righteousness and

---

47. *WJE* 13:529.
48. *WJE* 3:381.

true holiness; which are called in Scripture the *divine nature*."[49] In this sense, the "natural" condition of Adam was a supernatural state.

In Edwards's view, the result of the fall was that the Spirit vacated the soul, leaving the natural to collapse in on itself. Now, self-love reigns where divine love used to. Edwards explains:

> Therefore immediately the superior divine principles wholly ceased; so light ceases in a room, when the candle is withdrawn: and thus man was left in a state of darkness, woeful corruption and ruin; nothing but flesh, without spirit. The inferior principles of self-love and natural appetite, which were given only to serve, being alone, and left to themselves, of course became reigning principles; having no superior principles to regulate or control them, they became absolute masters of the heart.[50]

It is important to note that the Spirit's supernatural presence in the soul is what allows the soul to function according to its created purpose. From another angle, the formal dimension of the self, a being with understanding and will, which Barth criticizes as inadequate for a view of humanity, is a construct that functions to highlight a person's end. This formal structure of the creature is to receive God in grace, to embrace their true end as creatures as those indwelt by the Spirit. To use contemporary language, we might say that the only way to be *truly human* (rather than *inhuman*), is to have the Spirit of God infused into the soul as a supernatural principle of life; to be truly human is to be indwelt by the Spirit. Humankind without the Spirit, therefore, cannot embrace the call of humanity. An unregenerate person can mirror the soul's teleology, but it will always be a broken and truncated sort of quest. An unregenerate person cannot accept the call of being and becoming *truly* human, to borrow terminology alien to Edwards's corpus.[51] But what is it

---

49. *WJE* 3:381. "Those may be called supernatural, because they are no part of human nature. They don't belong to the nature of man as man, nor do they naturally and necessarily flow from the faculties and properties of that nature. Man can be man without 'em. They did not flow from anything in the human nature, but from the Spirit of God dwelling in man, and exerting itself by man's faculties as a principle of action." *WJE* 24:1086.

50. *WJE* 3:382.

51. Edwards did not employ this kind of terminology, as noted, but instead used categories such as natural and supernatural to address this difference. I will continue to use the more modern notion of *true* humanity as a way to spell out implications of Edwards's position.

that this call entails? To answer this question, we have to consider Edwards's understanding of the self and the nature of self-love.

SELF- AND NEIGHBOR-LOVE

Self-love, for Edwards, is not synonymous with selfishness; self-love, at bottom, is willing what you will. To will, for Edwards is simply loving what you love, and therefore his account assumes the creature wills according to her loves.[52] In this sense, with Barth, the freedom of the Christian is tied up with the nature of the true self. But the notion of the "self" here is interesting. Edwards does not spend a lot of time meditating on the nature of the *self*.[53] The "I" of Edwards's anthropology is often lost behind the understanding and willing of that I. But there is something of an existential inclination embedded in Edwards's discussion. In a peculiar comment, he states,

> Man is as it were two, as some of the great wits of this age have observed: a sort of genius is with a man, that accompanies him and attends him wherever he goes; so that *a man has a conversation with himself*, that is, he has a conversation with his own idea. So that if his idea be excellent, he will take delight and happiness in conferring and communing with it; he takes complacency in himself, he applauds himself; and wicked men accuse themselves and fight with themselves as if they were two. And man is truly happy then, and only then, when these two agree, and they delight in themselves, and in their own idea and image, *as God delights in his*.[54]

It is important that Edwards is drawing parallels between human psychology and the divine life, something he consistently does in his anthropology. In particular, the notion that there is an I-I relationality within the human person that determines one's own happiness is fundamental for Edwards's understanding of the phenomena of human personhood. At bottom, in the formal reality of natural man, one must stand face to face with oneself, seeking to find happiness and love from within this self-relation. Like Barth,

---

52. *WJE* 8:575–76.

53. See my essay "Being Seen and Being Known: Jonathan Edwards's Theological Anthropology" in *The Global Edwards*, ed. Rhys Bezzant (Eugene, OR: Wipf & Stock, 2017), 158–78, for what I call there "The Forgotten 'I.'"

54. *WJE* 13:260, my emphasis.

Edwards recognizes that this natural man will seek to project his I selfishly *at* others, seeking to use them to find fulfilment. But this formal feature of humanity is necessary, for Edwards, to anticipate one's teleology, precisely because the creature must come to stand before God face to face in truth. Therefore, the call to self-denial, ubiquitous in Edwards's corpus, is not the same as the call to eradicate self-love. To do so would be to destroy one's humanity, and, as Edwards explicitly notes, "Christianity is not destructive of humanity."[55] Self-denial, in this sense, is to deny the project of the flesh, namely, a self-creation for the sake of the self.

As noted above, self-love, what we might call "mere" self-love, is not bad or necessarily selfish because self-love is simply willing what you will. Self-love is negative when it is an inordinate self-love. In contrast, the person who has their "self" displaced by the love of God and is therefore caught up into God's own self-loving places their happiness in God in a way that is not selfish. This "is not selfishness," Edwards claims, "because it is not a *confined* self-love, because his self-love flows out in such a channel as to take in others with himself. The self which he loves is, as it were, *enlarged* and *multiplied*, so that in those same acts wherein he loves himself he loves others."[56] (Just as in the economy, where God "enlarges" his self-love by sending the Son and the Spirit to usher the creature into his life by grace, so too the human person is called to this same movement of the self. Likewise, contrasting selfishness and love again, he states, "Selfishness is a principle which does, as it were, confine a man's heart to himself. Love enlarges it and extends it to others. A man's self is as it were extended and enlarged by love. Others so far as [they are] beloved do ... become parts of himself."[57] The movement of the person in love mirrors God, who overflows out of himself to offer himself in love. Unlike God, the creature does not focus on their own life as the greatest good. That would be an act of selfishness for a finite being. But creatures do offer themselves in grace, and this entails an overflowing of their own inner-life such that they are enlarged to take in the other. This, for Edwards, is describing *pure* love: "I have observed from time to time that in pure love to others (i.e., love not arising from self-love) there's a union of the heart with

---

55. *WJE* 8:254.
56. *WJE* 8:258, my emphasis.
57. *WJE* 8:263.

others; a kind of enlargement of the mind, whereby it so extends itself as to take others into a man's self: and therefore it implies a disposition to feel, to desire, and to act as though others were one with ourselves."[58]

INTERNALIZING FOR BEING WITH THE OTHER

There is a kind of I-Thou relationality at work in Edwards's thought, but it is established within the I-I relation.[59] This raises two important questions. First, where does Edwards get the idea that to love another one has to "enlarge?" Second, as we saw above, Barth worries that this kind of internalization will be an ownership over the other rather than a real *withness*. Is Edwards's view able to navigate this concern? Taking these in turn, it is clear that Edwards's description of the self that enlarges in love is based on his understanding of biblical anthropology. Even Edwards's word of choice, "enlarges," comes from the KJV translation of 2 Corinthians 6:11: "O ye Corinthians, our mouth is open unto you, our heart is enlarged." Verse 13 turns it into an imperative to the Corinthians to enlarge their heart to Paul as he has enlarged himself to them. Likewise, in 2 Corinthians 7:2–3, Paul calls them to *receive* them (Paul and his companions) because the Corinthians are "in our hearts," a claim made by Barth, as we saw, through his notion of being "open." Furthermore, Edwards recognizes that this is a theme in Scripture, where the call of those who know God is to love their neighbors *as themselves*. Edwards takes this call seriously, recognizing that Scripture claims that Jonathan loves David "*as his own soul*" (1 Sam 18:1—my emphasis) and that a husband should love his wife *as he loves himself*, since she is a *part of his own body* (Eph 5:28–30—my emphasis), and then he goes on to ground this in how God loves his people—who are members of himself. As love unites all things (Col 3:14), God unites the creature to his own life to internalize the creature in God—"Your life is hidden with Christ in God" (Col 3:3)—such that the person can be said to be a "partaker of the divine nature" (2 Pet 1:4). This union is a relational union, a union of hearts to become "members one of another" (Eph 4:25), as Paul states.

---

58. *WJE* 8:589.

59. It would be interesting to take Edwards's account of this I-I relation and hold it against Pannenberg's development of the exocentric self-transcendence of the ego, and how that relates to the other. See, for instance, Wolfhart Pannenberg, *Anthropology in Theological Perspective* (Philadelphia: Westminster, 1985), 85.

For Edwards, this material points forward to a vision of loving our neighbor that requires more than loving *at* them. To borrow the Barthian term, this requires a real *withness*, where true humanity is one in encounter, and where the I, to embrace its teleology, must stand before a Thou in a certain manner. Edwards still starts with an I-I relation, so this is not Barth's claim that to be an I requires that there is a Thou internal to it. Nonetheless, there is a broadly similar instinct at work here. But we still need to turn to the secondary question: Could this internalization be a rejection of real *withness*? Likewise, one might wonder, does one internalize God in their self-love, and is this not a reordering of soteriology around the self rather than around God? To protect himself from such worries, Edwards orders the believer's love to God in a particular manner, stating,

> [Believers] don't first see that God loves them, and then see that he is lovely; but they first see that God is lovely, and that Christ is excellent and glorious, and their hearts are first captivated with this view, and the exercises of their love are wont from time to time to begin here, and to arise primarily from these views; and then, consequently, they see God's love; and self-love has a hand in these affections consequently, and secondarily only.[60]

Loving God, as for Barth, is the creature's response to the gracious work of God. Edwards claims that true gratitude and thankfulness to God "arises from a foundation laid before, of love to God for what he is in himself; whereas a natural gratitude has no such antecedent foundation."[61] There is a kind of love of God that arises from self-love, but it is not a love founded on the work of God in Christ in his wisdom and love.[62] Along with Barth, Edwards worries that this approach to God would be undetermined by the reality of God in himself, the economy, and his self-identification as the God of not only grace and mercy but judgment and wrath.[63] Furthermore, in Edwards's words,

---

60. *WJE* 2:246.

61. *WJE* 2:247.

62. For an account of how wisdom and love orient Edwards's doctrine of the atonement, see Oliver D. Crisp and Kyle C. Strobel, *Jonathan Edwards: An Introduction to His Thought* (Grand Rapids: Eerdmans, 2018), 121–45.

63. *WJE* 2:244–45.

The grace of God may appear lovely two ways; either as *bonum utile*, a profitable good to me, that which greatly serves my interest, and so suits my self-love; or as *bonum formosum*, a beautiful good in itself, and part of the moral and spiritual excellency of the divine nature. In this latter respect, it is that the true saints have their hearts affected, and love captivated by the free grace of God in the first place.[64]

In this sense, God's love is the ground of believers' love to him, and, therefore, it is the only *true* ground for their enlarging in love for others (more below on what another *untrue* ground might be). Edwards gives a threefold pattern of this reality in that the creature who is for the other—who can enlarge their heart to internalize their neighbor in their own self-love—is one whose love is (1) the fruit of God's love, (2) the fruit of God's specific work of redemption in Christ, and (3) the fruit of God's love to *this one* specifically.[65] The saint's enlargement to the other is the fruit of God's love, known as God's love *pro me* and not only as God's love for creatures. Christians are not ones who, through their self-love, seek to use God to establish themselves but ones who, to use the words of Jesus, lose their lives for his sake in order to find them (Matt 16:25).

It is important to note that the saints' enlarging in love to receive another is not simply a byproduct of receiving God's love as such but is the fruit of loving God *above all else*. Loving God and loving neighbor, in this sense, are both ordered and intrinsically connected. These are ordered in that loving God has the love of neighbor intrinsic to it and connected in that they are founded on the same disposition of the soul. This stems from Edwards's grounding all virtue on loving God.[66] While unbelievers, for instance, could enlarge their hearts in love to another, this would only be what Edwards calls a "particular" beauty. In this sense, they would enlarge to their capacity and stand in relation to this "Thou" from within a "limited and, as it were, a private sphere."[67] Their enlargement would be from a natural self-love that has not been ordered by God's love, and their perceiving of the other person

---

64. *WJE* 2:262–63.
65. *WJE* 2:250.
66. See *WJE* 8:550ff.
67. *WJE* 8:540.

would not be of the truth because they would be seen apart from God and his glory. Put differently, in more modern parlance, to be a true I before a Thou is to know oneself, ultimately, as a Thou before God, the true I, and to stand before a Thou (i.e., my neighbor) is to see them not simply eye to eye but eye to eye in relation to God. Instead of viewing the other according to a "particular" beauty, Edwards calls for a true sight according to a "general beauty," "by which a thing appears beautiful when viewed most perfectly, comprehensively and universally, with regard to all its tendencies, and its connections with everything it stands related to."[68] The one who has love of God as her chief end can enlarge in love to receive another as a Thou in relation to God. To enlarge in love, so that I stand before a Thou truly, as I and Thou truly are, necessitates that this enlargement be grounded first on God's beauty in himself, his redemption, and his love *pro me*, but secondarily on how I see this Thou in relation to God and his ends. Standing eye to eye, as Barth desires, is, for Edwards, seeing the other in relation to who I am before God *and* who they are in God's order (the *pro me* is never truly isolated from the *pro nobis*). This is extremely close to how Barth understands Buber's view, as narrated by Mikkelsen:

> When the encounter between the I and the Thou takes place, this takes place through a medium: the encountering I. The encountering I is here the medium of the divine Thou, which means that it is the divine Thou that enables the individual human person to enter into an I-Thou relation. Thus the divine Thou is the precondition for the possible encounter between the human I and the encountering Thou. ... Without the gift of the Spirit it would not be possible for the human being to live in pure presence, which is what takes place in the actual encounter between the I and the Thou.[69]

What we see in Edwards's view is an attempt to understand the necessary features of personhood to make sense of Scripture's claim that we are to love our neighbors *as ourselves* through an "enlargement" of the heart to receive an other. This view does not feed into Barth's worry that an internalization

---

68. *WJE* 8:540.

69. Mikkelsen, *Reconciled Humanity*, 104–5. Edwards would not like the language of "medium" here, turning rather to images that connotes the ground and end of human personhood.

of the other might be an attempt of the flesh to make the other my own because of how Edwards understands the self before God as a Thou that grounds this self-opening. This notion of "enlargement" puts the other on even footing with myself; it is a refusal to see them as less than, or even other than, who I am.

A SHARED IMPULSE?

For further clarity, it is important to ask if Edwards's move to ground something like the I-Thou relation on a previous I-I relation would fall victim to two further worries Barth articulates. The first is Barth's concern that starting with the I in this manner, what he calls "my extended I," would be an attempt to find myself in the other.[70] But Edwards's view does the opposite. Edwards's view does not allow the I to find itself in anything other than God without being sinful. Enlargement is the response of the creature who has received God's grace and therefore comes to know others as a part of themselves and not the other way around. The second worry comes in his critique of Kierkegaard, when Barth asks, "What does it mean that, in interpreting the command 'Thou shalt love thy neighbour as thyself,' Kierkegaard could agree with St. Augustine and Scholasticism against Luther and Calvin that there must be a love of self that takes precedence over love of others?"[71] Barth worries that regardless of Kierkegaard's goals, he had fortified, rather than defeated, a man-centered Christianity.[72] The temptation for the human person (the "hypocrite" in Edwards's terms) is to try to ground one's identity in a kind of self-seeing, an I-I relation, to use the I as the starting point to transcend the I (which Barth worries Kierkegaard tried, but never fully achieved). But to be an I truly, in a theological sense, is to stand in more than an I-I relation but to discover God in his beauty in such a way that the I is displaced and re-grounded in God ("your life is hidden with Christ in God" [Col 3:3]). Edwards's view counters Barth's worries because the formal constitution of the human person is

---

70. *CD* III/2 §45, 65.

71. Barth, *Fragments Grave and Gay* (Eugene, OR: Wipf & Stock, 2011), 99. Furthermore, if space allowed, it would prove relevant to consider how Barth addresses what he calls "two misunderstandings" of his claims in *CD* III/2 §45, 64–66.

72. Barth, *Fragments Grave and Gay*, 100.

ultimately receptive. To be truly human, one must receive God's self-giving in grace in the "emanation" of himself into the world so that his glory could "remanate" back to him in the knowing and loving of the creature—what Edwards calls religious affection. This entails a reception of God—of what is alien to the creature—for a person to be *truly* human. For both Edwards and Barth, then, in differing ways, God is the center, a term both of them use to ground anthropology theocentrically.[73]

To narrow these two thinkers to a shared impulse would be, in one sense, difficult, but in another, rather easy. Both thinkers use the image of God as the center of humanity as a way to displace the self from trying to discover a center within themselves in a form of narcissistic self-creation. Both, interestingly, turn to images of "opening," Barth using that image specifically and Edwards using the term "enlargement," to articulate a view of the human person that needs to be open to God and others to be truly human. In Barth's words, "Man cannot remain in isolation. He must decide and open himself to see this Other, this alien, high and transcendent God who is his Creator; to see himself in relation to this God and this God to him; and to do so in order to go to the One without whom he would not and could not be, but who promises man to be his Saviour and Keeper."[74] This is Edwards's impulse as well. To receive God in his grace is the true calling of human personhood, epitomized by Christ, the man indwelt by the Spirit "without measure," and Adam, whose Spirit-infused person is the initial formal truth of human personhood. But Adam is not the decisive claim made upon humanity. Christ is the truly human one, in whom and by whom creatures are received by God as he enlarges himself in the Son to internalize creatures into the life of his Son so that they may grow up into him who is their head. Their differing Christologies aside (which is of course, a major qualification), Edwards and Barth seem to be navigating similar worries about human personhood that is attuned to questions of relationality but not governed by them. Rather, both thinkers share an impulse that anthropology, to use Webster's phrase, is a "derivative doctrine."[75] God in Christ is the mooring in which we discover the truth about what it means to be a self-in-relation.

---

73. See *WJE* 19:692 and *CD* II/1 §31, 238.

74. *CD* III/2 §44, 170.

75. John Webster, *Barth*, Outstanding Christian Thinkers (London: Continuum, 2000), 99.

CONCLUSION

For Edwards, starting with the Trinity and down into created realities, persons are porous. In the Trinity, personhood itself is grounded upon perichoresis, whereas in the creature, true personhood is personhood infused with the Spirit to be porous to others in love. In both realities, love is at the center of what it means to be a person, and therefore love of God and love of neighbor are not simply callings for the Christian but the proper orientation of true humanity. But love requires perception, such that being seen is central to human identity. Jesus could not be the Son, as noted above, without the Father seeing and knowing him as such, an act revealed in Jesus' baptism. This is simply an imaging of the Triune life, in which the Father gazes on the Son and the Son on the Father in the love of the Spirit as the archetypal beatific vision that governs the ectypal teleology of creaturely existence. To embrace one's humanity, therefore, requires that one come to see God in Christ for who he is in himself and to know that in Christ one shares in the Father's love of the Son (John 17:26). To be truly human requires that we know we are seen by the Father in his gaze of love and that we too can see him if we have seen his Son in the illumination of the Spirit. This is the precondition for truly enlarging in love to receive another, not as an end in itself but as a participation in God's glory and grace. This mirrors John Webster's claim about Barth's "reversal" in anthropology, grounding it in Christ rather than in Adam: "The reversal does not—despite much misinterpretation of Barth at this point—entail the repudiation of a robust sense of the human person as subject and agent, but rather the reintegration of anthropology into a teleological account of God and God's creatures in which to be human is to act out of gratitude for grace."[76] Edwards, *mutatis mutandis*, would agree entirely.

---

76. Webster, *Barth*, 95.

10

—

SIN

Marc Cortez and Daniel Houck

The doctrine of original sin is one of the more challenging topics in Christian theology. As Bavinck aptly summarizes, "The doctrine of original sin is one of the weightiest but also one of the most difficult subjects in the field of dogmatics."[1] The problem arises from the fact that the doctrine relies on a theological logic that some find objectionable. Many have no difficulty affirming the first three steps in that theological logic:

1. All humans are sinful (universality).

2. All humans are culpable for being in that sinful state (culpability).

3. As a result of the universal sinfulness and culpability of all humans, it is just for God to hold all humans accountable for their sinful condition (justice).

In other words, the logic at this point in the argument merely affirms that all humans are somehow culpable for being in a sinful state such that it is just for God to hold them accountable for being in that state. The challenge lies in finding some explanation for *why* all humans are culpable for their sinful condition in such a way that maintains both the universality of sin—thus preventing us from claiming that some humans do not really need salvation—and the justice of God—thus preventing us from claiming that God either is responsible for sin (in the sense of being culpable for it) or is being unjust when he holds people responsible for their sinful condition. The most

---

1. Herman Bavinck, *Sin and Salvation in Christ*, vol. 3 of *Reformed Dogmatics*, ed. John Bolt, trans. John Vriend (Grand Rapids: Baker Academic, 2006), 100.

famous difficulties arise with that last issue. If sin is a universal condition, it would seem that no individual has any control over whether they are in that condition. If they have no control over whether they are in that condition, how can it be just for God to hold them responsible for it?

As is well known, many theologians have answered this question by appealing to Adam, resulting in a fourth claim:

4. It is in virtue of some connection with Adam that all humans are in a state of sinful culpability (adamic connection).

For many, though, this proposition merely complicates the matter further, resulting in difficult questions about the precise nature of the relationship between Adam and the rest of humanity as well as the justice of somehow transferring the guilt of one person onto other persons. Consequently, theologians have offered innumerable ways of resolving the dilemmas created by original sin, but they largely fall into one of three categories: (a) denying one or more of the first three claims; (b) defending and/or reimagining the fourth claim; or (c) rejecting the fourth claim and developing some new way of conceiving how we might affirm universal sinfulness without grounding it in Adam.

Jonathan Edwards and Karl Barth make fascinating interlocutors for those seeking to navigate this difficult conversation. Despite their geographical, historical, and theological differences, Edwards and Barth each operated in theological contexts where the doctrine of original sin was receiving increased scrutiny and in which many theologians had opted for the first of our possible resolutions (i.e., reject one or more of the first three propositions). However, both explicitly critiqued this approach, maintaining the importance of all three propositions for any adequately orthodox understanding of the gospel. Yet each offered his own response to the fourth proposition. As we will see, Jonathan Edwards explored our second solution, seeking to defend original sin by reimaging the nature of our connection to Adam. Karl Barth, on the other hand, pursued the third solution, arguing for an entirely different way of understanding the universality of sin, one that does not rely on our connection with Adam.

In what follows, we will offer brief summaries of how each theologian approaches the issue of original sin, paying particular attention to how they ground their understanding of universal sinfulness. We will also identify several notable benefits of each approach, along with some key worries that would need to be addressed before utilizing that approach further. Given the brevity of this essay, those evaluative comments will need to be more illustrative than exhaustive. Yet we hope to present each of these theologians as excellent dialogue partners for thinking further about these complex issues.

JONATHAN EDWARDS'S REALISTIC FEDERALISM

Jonathan Edwards lived during a time when the doctrine of original sin was under considerable scrutiny. Several of his contemporaries had written works directly challenging the doctrine, sparking a theological controversy that produced a flurry of highly charged letters, pamphlets, and books. According to Clyde Holbrook, the debate reflected a broader shift in how Edwards's society was coming to view the human person:

> The controversy over human depravity in the eighteenth century was no mere intramural squabble among theologians. It was an important phase of a revolution that was occurring in Western man's estimate of his nature and potentialities. Literature, philosophy, economic and political theory, as well as theology, were to feel the decisive impact of this revolution. The notion of man as a fundamentally rational, benevolently inclined individual was emerging as the unquestionable postulate for the expansionist mood of Western culture.[2]

Consequently, when Edwards began working on his treatise *The Great Christian Doctrine of Original Sin Defended*, he was taking up one of the more contentious theological issues of his time, well aware of the difficulties he faced.[3]

Given that the title of Edwards's book specifically states his intention to *defend* the doctrine, it should come as no surprise that much of what he has to say about sin comes across as a notably traditional exposition of broadly Reformed commitments. Most importantly for our purposes, we

---

2. Clyde A. Holbrook, "Editor's Introduction," in *Original Sin, WJE* 3:1. See also John D. Hannah, "Doctrine of Original Sin in Postrevolutionary America," *Bibliotheca Sacra* 134 (1977): 238–56.

3. *Original Sin, WJE* 3. Although this is the first time Edwards addressed the doctrine of sin at length, Holbrook rightly notes Edwards's interest in the doctrine from the beginning. Holbrook, "Editor's Introduction," 17.

can move quickly through the first three of our hamartiological propositions since Edwards's commitment to the universality of sin, the culpability of all human persons, and the corresponding justice of divine judgment
are all well accepted. Indeed, Edwards devotes the first and longest part of
Original Sin to defending precisely these propositions.[4] When it comes to
the fourth proposition, however, matters become rather more complicated.
Like many theologians before him, Edwards affirms that the universality of
human sinfulness is grounded in the relationship between Adam and the
rest of humanity. However, although Edwards often sounds as though he
is merely affirming earlier accounts of adamic connection, he also offers
some interesting new twists, creative developments that mark his account
as interestingly different from what came before.

To begin, Edwards clearly affirms central elements of a federalist understanding of original sin, in which all humans immediately become guilty
of Adam's sin by virtue of the fact that God designated him to serve as the
representative head of humanity.[5] Edwards thus clearly affirms that Adam
is "the public head and representative of his posterity,"[6] and he expends
considerable effort demonstrating that Scripture supports the idea that God
includes all humanity in his judgment on Adam.[7] Edwards was well aware
that many have objected to this federalist account on the basis that there does
not seem to be any good account of what precisely grounds the connection
between Adam and the rest of humanity. Lacking such an explanation, God's
act of designating him to be the representative of all other humans seems
arbitrary, and imputing his sin to all other humans seems unjust.

Interestingly, though, Edwards does not dismiss this worry. He could have
just argued that it lies within the divine prerogative for God to appoint Adam
to this representative role, rejecting any suggestion that further explanation
is needed. However, although he recognizes that just "shutting our mouths,
and acknowledging the weakness and scantiness of our understandings"

---

4. WJE 3:107–349.

5. John Gerstner, The Rational Biblical Theology of Jonathan Edwards, 3 vols. (Powhatan, VA:
Berea, 1992), 2:323; Michael J. McClymond and Gerald R. McDermott, The Theology of Jonathan
Edwards (New York: Oxford University Press, 2012), 351.

6. WJE 3:247; cf. 348.

7. WJE 3:252–57.

is one possible way of responding to this problem,[8] he seems to share the concern that the federalist approach would be weakened if it could not say anything about the underlying ontology that might support Adam's representative function. Here Edwards shares the intuition of more *realist* explanations of original sin, in which the transmission of sin is grounded in some real (i.e., ontological) connection between Adam and the rest of humanity, usually by virtue of the fact that all other humans have descended from Adam and have thus received from him their common human nature.[9] However, despite sharing the intuition that some real explanation is needed, or would at least be desirable, Edwards offers an explanation that differs considerably from most other realist accounts.[10]

Given the limitations of space, a brief sketch of Edwards's proposal will have to suffice.[11] The core of his approach lies in his explanation of how *any* object has an identity that perdures through time.

> Some things, being most simply considered, are entirely distinct, and very diverse; which yet are so united by the established law of the Creator, in some respects and with regard to some purposes and effects, that by virtue of that establishment it is with them as if they were one. Thus a tree, grown great, and an hundred years old, is one plant with the little sprout, that first came out of the ground, from whence it grew, and has been continued in constant succession; though it's now so exceeding diverse, many thousand times bigger, and of a very different form, and perhaps not one atom the very same:

---

8. *WJE* 3:247, 395.

9. For a good summary of the differences between federalism and realism, see Thomas H. McCall, *Against God and Nature: The Doctrine of Sin* (Wheaton, IL: Crossway, 2019), 161–70.

10. As Oliver Crisp points out, it is entirely possible that Edwards intends his "explanation" as a "just-so story," which means an account that *may* be true and which offers a coherent way of thinking about the situation but which one may not necessarily be endorsing as offering the true fact of the matter. Oliver D. Crisp, *Jonathan Edwards among the Theologians* (Grand Rapids: Eerdmans, 2015), 120.

11. For more detailed discussions, see esp. Samuel Storms, *Tragedy in Eden: Original Sin in the Theology of Jonathan Edwards* (Langham, MD: University Press of America, 1986); Oliver D. Crisp, *Jonathan Edwards and the Metaphysics of Sin* (New York: Routledge, 2005); Joseph Gilbert Prud'homme and James Hoitsma Schelberg, "Disposition, Potentiality, and Beauty in the Theology of Jonathan Edwards: A Defense of His Great Christian Doctrine of Original Sin," *American Theological Inquiry* 5, no. 1 (2012): 25–53; Andrew C. Russell, "Polemical Solidarity: John Wesley and Jonathan Edwards Confront John Taylor on Original Sin," *Wesleyan Theological Journal* 47, no. 12 (2012): 72–88.

yet God, according to an established law of nature, has in a constant succession communicated to it many of the same qualities, and most important properties, as if it were one. It has been his pleasure, to constitute an union in these respects, and for these purposes, naturally leading us to look upon all as one.[12]

Edwards clearly maintains that we should view the sapling and the mature tree as comprising a single entity (the sapling-tree). Given that the material comprising the tree has completely changed over time, however, it's not obvious *why* we should think that the mature tree is the same as the sapling that was planted years ago. Most would appeal here to some kind of causal continuity, arguing that the mature tree is numerically identical with the sapling as long as it stands in the right kind of causal relation with the sapling. We can thus view the sapling and the mature tree as involving discrete life stages of the same entity as long as the latter life stage is rightly caused by the prior. However, although Edwards refers to "an established law of nature" in this quote, he immediately associates that with divine action rather than with any causal powers of the sapling-tree. This is an expression of Edwards's occasionalism, which maintains that God alone is the one who establishes the existence of any created thing at each moment in time.[13] Consequently, although Edwards here affirms that there is a real identity between the sapling and the tree such that we can and should view the sapling-tree as a real entity, its identity (i.e., its "realness") is grounded in divine action (i.e., the divine act of establishing the identity between each of the life stages of the tree) and not in any causal powers or properties that we might think of as intrinsic to the tree itself.[14] In other words, the fact that the sapling-tree comprises a single, real entity is entirely grounded in the divine determination to constitute it as such.

---

12. *WJE* 3:398–99.

13. For good discussions of Edwards's occasionalism, see Oliver D. Crisp, "How 'Occasional' Was Edwards's Occasionalism?" in *Jonathan Edwards: Philosophical Theologian*, ed. Paul Helm and Oliver D. Crisp (Farnham, Surrey, UK: Ashgate, 2004), 61–77; Stephen H. Daniel, "Edwards' Occasionalism," in *Jonathan Edwards as Contemporary*, ed. Don Schweitzer (New York: Peter Lang, 2010), 1–14.

14. See Michael C. Rea, "The Metaphysics of Original Sin," in *Persons: Human and Divine*, ed. Peter Van Inwagen and Dean Zimmerman (New York: Oxford University Press, 2007), 319–56. For an interesting change of perspective on this issue, see Crisp, *Jonathan Edwards among the Theologians*, 118–20.

It might seem at this point that we have strayed rather far from the matter at hand, yet Edwards uses precisely this same framework to explain other kinds of creaturely continuity through time. Indeed, for Edwards the identity of all created things is grounded in divine action. "Thus it appears, if we consider matters strictly, there is no such thing as any identity or oneness in created objects, existing at different times, but what depends on *God's sovereign constitution*."[15] Edwards goes on to maintain that this provides a framework for thinking about the unity of humanity as well.

> And I am persuaded, no solid reason can be given, why God, who constitutes all other created union or oneness, according to his pleasure, and for what purposes, communications, and effects he pleases, may not establish a constitution whereby the natural posterity of Adam, proceeding from him, much as the buds and branches from the stock or root of a tree, should be treated as one with him, for the derivation, either of righteousness and communion in rewards, or of the loss of righteousness and consequent corruption and guilt.[16]

In other words, once Edwards has concluded that God can establish the identity of things that are materially, causally, and temporally disconnected from one another (e.g., the sapling and the tree), it becomes quite reasonable to think that God can do so with humanity as well. In that case, Adam and I can simply be viewed as distinct life stages of a single entity: humanity. But if Adam and I are both parts of a single, real entity, it follows that we share in at least some of the same moral qualities. Just as I can be held responsible for the actions committed during some prior stage of my life, so humans now can be viewed as guilty of Adam's sin insofar as they comprise a single entity by virtue of the divine action that makes it so.

Edwards thus provides an account that affirms our connection with Adam, albeit a connection that has now been reimagined through the lens of his occasionalism. In the context of contemporary conversations about original sin, this account comes with several notable benefits. Many today would agree with Edwards's interlocutors that original sin is *unjust* in that it involves God holding humans accountable for actions in which they had

---

15. *WJE* 3:404.

16. *WJE* 3:404, 405.

no direct involvement. Others have argued that such an account is *incoherent* given that one person cannot actually be guilty of actions committed by others. I might be able to experience the consequences of those actions, but I should not be viewed as personally guilty of them.[17] And here it is important to note that the traditional forms of both federalism and realism struggle to address these concerns. Since both affirm that Adam and other humans are distinct entities, thus seeking to provide different accounts of how these discrete individuals might be related, they are liable to the injustice and incoherence worries. But Edwards's account operates with a subtly different logic, maintaining that we should view Adam-humanity as *a single entity*. Consequently, we no longer need to explain how it could be just or coherent to hold *different* entities liable for the same action.

However, the injustice and incoherence worries threaten to return once we note the apparent arbitrariness of this arrangement. Since Edwards grounds the connections between the various life stages of a creaturely entity in divine action and not in any intrinsic creaturely powers, it appears to be merely arbitrary that God connects two or more life stages in such a way as to make them comprise a single entity. Edwards himself makes this concern acute when he declares that his view entails that all creaturely entities depend "on an *arbitrary* divine constitution."[18] If the connection truly is as arbitrary as this suggests, it would raise the question of whether it simply reintroduces the worries it was designed to address. However, we need to be careful in how we interpret the language of arbitrariness here, particularly any attempt to interpret arbitrariness as involving randomness or a complete lack of explanation. Edwards makes it clear that what he means by arbitrary here is simply that the Adam-humanity connection is established by the divine will rather than any supposed natural powers intrinsic to humanity. In other words, the Adam-humanity connection is established *volitionally* rather than *naturally*, and Edwards's compatibilistic account of free will would strongly resist any kind of random arbitrariness in our understanding

---

17. This worry could hold even if one maintained the importance of certain kinds of corporate identities. For example, one might claim that a modern American participates in the corporate responsibility that all Americans have for their complicity in and corresponding benefit from slavery and still maintain that such a person is not guilty in the same way as a particular nineteenth-century slaver.

18. *WJE* 3:403, my emphasis.

of the divine volitions. Instead, it is entirely possible to suppose that Edwards envisions a situation in which God establishes the continuity of each life stage of any particular entity, including the Adam-humanity entity, in such a way that each life stage is fully consistent with that which came before. In other words, even if there is no direct causal link between each life stage, it may well be that God only establishes "fitting" links—i.e., those that are somehow in accord with the prior life stage. If so, that would still allow God to serve as the sole causal ground of the transtemporal identity of each entity, but he would do so in ways that avoid the arbitrariness worry.

It thus seems that Edwards offers a coherent account of original sin that draws on aspects of both federalism and realism, uniting them in a creative synthesis that has resources for responding to a number of important contemporary concerns. However, doing so comes with a cost. As far as I can tell, there is no way to reap the benefits of this approach to original sin without affirming Edwards's occasionalistic ontology, along with the corresponding worries about whether this entails some form of panentheism.

KARL BARTH AND THE UNIVERSAL ACT OF UNBELIEF

Karl Barth offers a rather different entrée into contemporary discussions about original sin.[19] Unlike Edwards, who explored a different way of conceiving the Adam-humanity relationship, Barth offers the opportunity to explore the option of reconceiving how to affirm universal sinfulness without grounding that claim in our relation to Adam, at least not as that relation has traditionally been understood. As we will see, however, his approach raises questions of its own.

Karl Barth's mature view of the doctrines of the fall and original sin is found in *The Fall of Man*.[20] In critical conversation with Kant, Barth interprets the doctrine of original sin as the universal act of unbelief in Jesus Christ. It is important to put Barth's account in its immediate context, which requires beginning with a brief discussion of the knowledge (§60.1) and nature (§60.2) of sin.

---

19. Portions of this discussion of Barth are found in Daniel W. Houck, *Aquinas, Original Sin, and the Challenge of Evolution* (Cambridge: Cambridge University Press, 2020).

20. *CD* IV/1 §60.3.

Barth argues that Christian theologians have often made the egregious mistake of assuming that the knowledge of sin precedes the knowledge of Jesus Christ. What mistake did he have in mind? What exactly does it mean for the knowledge of sin to "precede" the knowledge of Jesus Christ?

> [I]n the *locus de peccato* which precedes the doctrine of reconciliation the agreement of older and more recent theology consists concretely in the view that by the knowledge of God, which makes possible and actual the knowledge of sin, we mean the knowledge of God in His basic relationship with man—as distinct from His presence, action and revelation in Jesus Christ.[21]

Here Barth is criticizing the view that human beings are able to understand sin (i.e., disobedience to God) without knowledge of Jesus Christ. It is reflected in the order of systematic theologies that treat hamartiology before Christology, as well as sermons that preach damnation before salvation. For Barth, sin is the "negative presupposition" of reconciliation: as such, sin can be known *only* in light of Christ.[22] "Within the sphere of the self-knowledge not enlightened and instructed by the Word of God there is no place for anything worthy of the name of a 'knowledge of sin.' "[23]

This should come as no surprise to readers familiar with Barth's broader theological project. He vigorously and consistently rejected "natural theology," the attempt to ground the knowledge of God in anything apart from Jesus Christ. (Recall his famous claim that the "analogy of being"—which he thought was the basis of natural theology—was the "invention of the Antichrist."[24]) This epistemology of sin follows directly from the rejection of natural theology. Since sin is disobedience to God, the one who knows sin must know God. Since God cannot be known except through Jesus Christ, neither can sin.

After making that fundamental point, Barth offers a genealogy of hamartiology within Protestantism from Calvin to liberalism.[25] Calvin held that

---

21. *CD* IV/1, 5.

22. *CD* IV/1, 2.

23. *CD* IV/1, 3.

24. *CD* I/1, xiii. For a contextualization of this claim and treatment of Barth's account of the "analogy of faith," see Bruce L. McCormack, "Karl Barth's Version of an 'Analogy of Being': A Dialectical No and Yes to Roman Catholicism," in *The Analogy of Being: Invention of the Antichrist or the Wisdom of God?*, ed. Thomas Joseph White (Grand Rapids: Eerdmans, 2011), 88–144.

25. *CD* IV/1, 9–41.

postlapsarian humanity retains a *divinitatis sensum*, a sense of God, including a sense of his law. Insofar as God's law is imprinted on the hearts of
human beings who do not know Christ, it is called the "natural law." For
Barth, the natural law was a disastrous idea. It functioned like a cancerous
tumor in Protestantism's theology of grace. Barely detectable in Calvin's own
thought, the tumor metastasized in Protestant liberalism. Liberalism denied
that humanity stands under the judgment of a wrathful God and reduced
"sin" to underdeveloped God-consciousness. In turn, it reduced Jesus to a
moral exemplar, an exemplar that reason can provide for itself.[26] By Barth's
lights, the inner logic of the "natural law" leads to the denial of Jesus Christ.
Once we "begin to toy with the *lex naturae*," we are on our way to content-
ment with "the hope and peace which we can have and know without the
resurrection of Jesus Christ."[27]

What would a hamartiology that *followed* Christology consist in? In the
first place, the concept of "sin" must be understood with reference to Jesus
Christ. Though there are different words that can rightly be used to describe
our sin against Christ (disobedience, transgression, pride, etc.), Barth argues
that sin's paradigmatic form is *unbelief* in Jesus Christ.[28] We all, like the
Pharisees, pridefully refuse to believe in him. But what of those who have
never heard the gospel? It seems that, in an important sense, there *are* no
such people: divine law commands belief in Jesus Christ, and this "law of
faith" is objectively present to everyone. Even "among the nations," sin is
fundamentally unbelief in Jesus Christ, action that does not "correspond"
to Jesus Christ.[29] Yet unbelief is not the sheer absence of belief: the human
being culpably "contradicts" and "opposes" Christ.[30] God created us with the
capability of obedience, but we disobeyed.[31]

---

26. *CD* IV/1, 16.

27. *CD* IV/1, 17.

28. *CD* IV/1, 42.

29. "This Law [*scil.*, the law of faith] as now proclaimed is the truth which was objectively
present to all nations from the creation of the world, standing before them in nature and history
and speaking of the One from whom it came." *CD* IV/1, 37.

30. *CD* IV/1, 61.

31. "That for which God has made man capable and which He might expect of him is not
forthcoming." *CD* IV/1, 126. Though he says it would be anachronistic to call Barth's view of
human freedom "compatibilist" in a philosophical sense, Jesse Couenhoven has argued that Barth
operated with a "compatibilist conception" of human freedom. "Karl Barth's Conception(s) of
Human and Divine Freedom(s)," in *Commanding Grace: Studies in Karl Barth's Ethics*, ed. Daniel
L. Migliore (Grand Rapids: Eerdmans, 2010), 239–55. However, the drift of §60.3 seems to

Which brings us to Barth's view of the fall and original sin. Human nature has not been corrupted by Adam, as though sin were our fate. No, the human being is the "one who poisons himself in his pride."[32] Yet Barth does not simply follow Pelagius. It is *not* the case that because nature is incorrupt, some of us are saved by obeying God while (most) of us disobey and need forgiveness. Our nature was not corrupted by Adam, but we *are* evil. Barth approvingly cites Kant in this connection:

> [I]n relation to the transgression and therefore the corruption of man there is no time in which man is not a transgressor and therefore guiltless before God. To use the phrase of Kant, he lives by an "evil principle," with a "bias towards evil," in the power of a "radical evil" which shows itself virulent and active in his life, with which in some incomprehensible but actual way he accepts solidarity, with which he is not identical, but to which he commits himself and is committed. ... He was always on that way and at that goal. ... Because he himself as the subject of these activities is not a good tree, he cannot bring forth good fruit. Because his pride is radical and in principle, it is also total and universal and all-embracing, determining all his thoughts and words and works, his whole inner and hidden life, and his visible external movements and relationships. He is not just partly but altogether "flesh."[33]

We have not fallen from a state of original righteousness in time. We are *always* acting from an all-encompassing pride. Barth cites Kant in the course of making these claims. Why? What role does Kant's view play in Barth's account?

Kant's account of radical evil has been the subject of scholarly debate since he first published it.[34] One common reading is the following. Every

---

contain a decidedly *incompatibilist* strain. Adam—who represents each one of us (on which more shortly)—was made good and apparently capable of faithful obedience. Barth sharply criticized Schleiermacher's compatibilism, suggesting that it opens the door for human beings to make excuses for their sins. "Will he [the human being who believes his sins are determined] not finally be able to reassure and console himself with the thought that secretly and at bottom his evil is a good, or the transition to it, that his sinning is imposed and posited and ordained by God[?]"*CD* IV/1, 32. It may well be, though, that the compatibilist/incompatibilist labels do not adequately account for Barth's view of free will, and since Couenhoven does not discuss this section, his analysis may be accurate as far as it goes.

32. *CD* IV/1, 135.

33. *CD* IV/1, 136–37.

34. See the first book of his *Religion within the Boundaries of Mere Reason*. For a recent treatment, see Stephen R. Palmquist, *Comprehensive Commentary on Kant's Religion within the Bounds*

human being who reaches the age of reason fails to adopt obedience to the moral law as a sufficient incentive for her action. Yet every human being, upon reaching the age of reason, *could* have done so. Evil is universal (among those who have reached the age of reason) *and* freely chosen. Barth may have read Kant along these lines. Certainly, culpable unbelief is universal, and as we are about to see, Barth denies that unbelief is inherited. In any case, Barth's own view of radical evil is different from Kant's in a crucial respect: for Kant, evil consists in the violation of a self-given moral law, whereas for Barth, it consists in the prideful refusal to believe in Jesus Christ. In light of this, we might say that Barth "Christologizes" Kant's account of radical evil, at least in the sense that he keeps the core of the concept while insisting that it can only properly be understood with reference to Jesus Christ.[35]

Barth then proposes that *Erbsünde*—the standard German term for *peccatum originale*—should be replaced with *Ursünde*.[36] *Erbsünde* should be abandoned because "there can be no doubt that the idea of a hereditary sin which has come to man by propagation is an extremely unfortunate and mistaken one."[37] *Ursünde*, by contrast, should be used to refer to

the voluntary and responsible life of every man—in a connexion with Adam that we have yet to show—which by virtue of the judicial sentence passed on it in and with his reconciliation with God is the sin of every man, the corruption which he brings on himself so that as

---

of Bare Reason (West Sussex: Wiley-Blackwell, 2016).

35. For a treatment of Christocentricity in Barth, see Marc Cortez, "What Does It Mean to Call Karl Barth a 'Christocentric Theologian'?" *Scottish Journal of Theology* 60, no. 2 (2007): 1–17.

36. The English translation of *Erbsünde* is "hereditary sin." The English translation of *Ursünde* is "original sin."

37. CD IV/1, 141. Barth argues as follows: "What I do as the one who receives an inheritance is something that I cannot refuse to do, since I am not asked concerning my willingness to accept it. It is only in a very loose sense that it can be regarded as my own act. It is my fate which I may acknowledge but for which I cannot acknowledge or regard myself responsible. And yet it is supposed to be my determination for evil, the corrupt disposition and inclination of my heart, the radical and total *curvitas* and *iniquitas* of my life, and I myself am supposed to be an evil tree merely because I am an heir of Adam. It is not surprising that when an effort is made to take the word 'heir' seriously, as has occasionally happened, the term 'sin' is necessarily dissolved. Conversely, when the term 'sin' is taken seriously, the term 'heir' is necessarily explained in a way which makes it quite unrecognisable, being openly or surreptitiously dissolved and replaced by other and more serious concepts. 'Hereditary sin' has a hopelessly naturalistic, deterministic and even fatalistic ring. ... It is perhaps better to abandon altogether the idea of hereditary sin and to speak only of original sin [*Ursünde*] (the strict translation of *peccatum originale*)." CD IV/1, 142.

the one who does so—and again in that connexion—he is necessarily and inevitably corrupt.[38]

The *Ursünde* (original sin) of the human being is the voluntary sin of every human being. This sin is depicted in Genesis 3, the story of Adam's fall and Everyman. The Bible gives "the general title of Adam" to all human beings.[39] History "constantly re-enacts the little scene in the garden of Eden. There never was a golden age. There is no point in looking back to one. The first man was immediately the first sinner."[40] The biblical authors assume that Adam was the historical parent of the human race, but this is incidental to the story's theological import.[41] The story is not history but *saga*: "historical narration at the point where events are no longer susceptible as such of historical proof."[42] Our Adamic identity is our own fault. "No one has to be Adam. We are so freely and on our own responsibility."[43] As he puts it elsewhere, "Our understanding of the enslaved will of sinful man has nothing whatever to do with determinism."[44] We are like Adam because we *act* as he did; "the successors of Adam are ... those who are represented in his person and *deed*."[45]

We have thus seen that Barth clearly affirms the universal sinfulness of humanity along with the corresponding claim that all humans are culpable for this sinful situation such that God's judgment on humanity is just.[46] When it comes to the fourth claim, however, the situation has changed notably from Edwards's position. Rather than seeking to defend the claim that our universal sinfulness is grounded in a particular relation to Adam, Barth draws on a Christologized account of Kant's concept of radical evil. For Kant, evil is radical because every human being freely subordinates the moral law to

---

38. *CD* IV/1, 141.

39. *CD* IV/1, 149.

40. *CD* IV/1, 149.

41. "Who is Adam? The great unknown who is the first parent of the race? There can be no doubt that this is how the biblical tradition intended that he should be seen and understood. But it is interested in him as such only for what he did." *CD* IV/1, 150.

42. *CD* IV/1, 149.

43. *CD* IV/1, 151.

44. *CD* IV/2 §65.3, 117.

45. *CD* IV/1, 152 (emphasis added).

46. A full account of judgment in Barth's theology would, of course, have to discuss Barth's doctrine of election with its emphasis on Jesus as both "Rejector and Rejected." *CD* II/2, 325.

self-love; for Barth, sin is radical because every human being—as represented by the saga of the fall in Genesis 3—refuses to believe in Christ. With Kant, Barth denies that Adam's descendants inherited his sin or corrupted nature. Such an account comes with at least two potential advantages. First, it should be clear that such an account is not susceptible to many of the concerns addressed against more traditional views of original sin, which we encountered in the dialogue with Edwards. Since universal sinfulness is grounded in universal unbelief, and since this is something in which all humans freely participate rather than receiving through some putative connection with Adam, it seems that worries about injustice and arbitrariness fall by the wayside. Second, those who want to reject an Augustinian view of original sin while simultaneously avoiding any Pelagian emphasis on self-salvation will appreciate Barth's affirmation of universal sinfulness and his corresponding insistence that no one obeys the law unto salvation.

However, some additional concerns remain. First, it is not clear how Barth's approach would relate to the situation of infants and other persons with limited capacity to participate in the kind of unbelief Barth has in mind. One need not endorse the totality of Augustine's account of original sin to agree with him that the gospel is for all human beings, from "wailing infants" to "old grey heads."[47] But if sin is reduced to the act of unbelief, then it seems that such persons are not in sin, not yet in need of Jesus Christ. Given the universal scope of election in his theology, Barth would obviously reject any suggestion that such persons do not need Christ. However, it is not clear precisely how Barth would explain their involvement in universal sinfulness.

That leads to a second, related worry: Does Barth provide an adequate explanation of the universality of culpable unbelief among adults? Given the universality of sinfulness, Barth cannot mean that unbelief requires an explicit proclamation of the gospel; otherwise, he would not be able to account for the culpability of those who never hear such a message. And Barth elsewhere makes it clear that Jesus himself constitutes God's address to all human persons.[48] However, can Barth account for the universality of this unbelief without turning this into the very kind of predetermined condition he seeks to avoid? For instance, Barth at times seems to speak as

---

47. Augustine, *Nature and Grace*, trans. Roland Teske (Hyde Park, NY: New City Press, 1997), 60.
48. *CD* III/2, 147–50.

though universal culpability is grounded in the objective promulgation of the law of faith.[49] If this is what Barth has in mind, it is hard to see how a merely objective presence of the law of faith is sufficient. If Sally, who is deaf, is working in her cubicle, and her boss shouts from the common room, "Meet in the conference room in five," is she culpable if she misses the meeting? It seems obvious that she is not—unless she was informed of the meeting via a method of communication intelligible to *her* (such as sign language). Something more than the merely objective presence of the announcement is needed. If Barth were to respond by suggesting that the objective reality of the announcement is adequate irrespective of subjective response, he would seem to be not only undermining his own emphasis on unbelief as a choice but also describing a situation of objective, universal sinfulness that would be remarkably similar to the traditional view of original sin that he sought to replace.

CONCLUSION

Given the prominent role that original sin has historically played in western theologies as well as the number of important objections that have been raised against original sin in modern theology, now would seem to be a good time to explore alternate approaches to understanding original sin. Jonathan Edwards and Karl Barth offer just such an opportunity for insightful dialogue. Each operated in theological contexts where important questions were being raised about the doctrine of original sin, and each offered interestingly new ways of navigating those difficult conversations while still retaining their fundamental commitment to universal sinfulness, culpability, and the justice of God's judgment.

Despite these important similarities, though, their discussions of original sin differ in at least two fundamental ways. First, they offer two very different perspectives on the appropriate starting point for talking about original sin. Edwards exemplifies a far more traditional approach, focusing his attention on the fall and our corporate solidarity with Adam as the necessary basis for affirming original sin. Although Edwards certainly understood the importance of Christology for thinking adequately about the human condition, his is a decidedly adamic approach to the discussion. Barth, on the other hand,

---

49. *CD* IV/1, 37.

in a move that will surprise no one, maintains that the only adequate way to think about original sin is to start with Jesus Christ. Although Barth does not dismiss adamic reflections entirely, he consistently maintains that only Christology can rightly orient our understanding of sin.

The second difference likely arises to some degree from the first. Edwards and Barth not only disagree regarding the person around whom this discussion rightly revolves, but they also disagree on how best to explain universal sinfulness. For Edwards, the adamic connection remains primary, and much of his account focuses on addressing the biblical, theological, and conceptual difficulties that arise from affirming the adamic ground of universal sinfulness. With his radically different starting point, Barth instead orients his account of universal sinfulness around belief or unbelief specifically as it relates to the divine address that all humanity has received in and through Jesus Christ. Each arrives at a similar conclusion—universal sinfulness and culpability—but each does so in notably different ways.

We have also seen through the course of this discussion that both of these accounts face some important challenges of their own. And since we intended the critical portions of each conversation to be more illustrative than exhaustive, other concerns almost certainly remain. Nonetheless, each of these theologians remains a valuable dialogue partner on these issues, pointing in new directions and offering creative insights that are well worth reflecting on today.

11
—

ATONEMENT

Adam J. Johnson

Edwards and Barth offer us accounts of the doctrine of the atonement that are simply monumental in scope, by which I mean two things. First, their views are exceptionally rich and diverse, calling for sustained exploration and contemplation.[1] It might be said of both theologians that "instead of

---

1. In this chapter, we will focus on one particularly important strand of thought, but it bears noting that both Edwards and Barth offer remarkably diverse understandings of the atonement. Edwards, for instance, argues at length for Christ's defeat of Satan (Misc. 298, 324, 344, 402, 554, 618, 619, 798, 915, 1159; WJE 9:123; "The Sacrifice of Christ Acceptable," WJE 14:579–80; "The Free and Voluntary Suffering and Death of Christ," WJE 19:496, 501; "Christ's Sacrifice," WJE 10:600). Among these, Miscellany 402 is notable for Edwards's argument that Jesus purchases the Holy Spirit over against the evil spirit (cf. 1159), as is Miscellany 619, which weaves together a defeat of Satan with governmental themes. Barth argues along the same lines, as we see in Barth, *The Humanity of God*, trans. Thomas Wieser and John N. Thomas (Richmond, VA: Westminster John Knox, 1960), 60; Barth, *Dogmatics in Outline*, trans. G. T. Thompson (New York: Harper, 1959), 115; and CD IV/1, 230, 74. As we will see at length in this chapter, both Edwards (Misc. 1005, 1035; "Christ's Sacrifice an Inducement to His Ministers," WJE 25:660) and Barth (*Dogmatics in Outline*, 119) have developed accounts of satisfaction (developed in the direction of penal satisfaction or penal substitution). As is the case with most theologians in the church, both offer exemplarist themes (Edwards: Misc. 781; see also Oliver D. Crisp and Kyle C. Strobel, *Jonathan Edwards: An Introduction to His Thought* [Grand Rapids: Eerdmans, 2018], 139–41; Barth: CD IV/1, 88), without reducing the atoning work of Christ to exemplarism per se. Beyond these three themes developed and popularized by Gustaf Aulen, it is worth noting that both Edwards (Misc. S, 1/4) and Barth (CD IV/1, 6) utilize the logic of recapitulation for which Irenaeus and the church fathers are justly famous, and both Edwards (Misc. bb, 179; Michael J. McClymond and Gerald R. McDermott, *The Theology of Jonathan Edwards* [New York: Oxford, 2012], 410ff. Kyle C. Strobel, "Jonathan Edwards's Reformed Doctrine of Theosis," *Harvard Theological Review* 109, no. 3 [2016], 371–99) and Barth (CD IV/1, 112, 16; Bruce L. McCormack, "Participation in God, Yes; Deification, No: Two Modern Protestant Responses to an Ancient Question," in *Orthodox and Modern: Studies in the Theology of Karl Barth* [Grand Rapids: Baker Academic, 2008, 347–74]) develop their thinking along lines that might roughly be called theosis or divinization. Though neither theologian develops this line of thought at great length, both Edwards (Misc. 113, 619, 779, 833, 1217; WJE 9:123) and Barth (*Dogmatics in Outline*, 106; CD II/1, 380) work on the outskirts of a governmental theory of the atonement, and both Edwards (Misc. 319, 779) and Barth (CD IV/1, 172, 75, 216, 59, 61) make similar points relating to the view made famous by J. M. Campbell.

pitting one aspect of the biblical data against others, [they] construct ... an account that shows how Christ has fulfilled, satisfied, honored, and earned all things necessary for human salvation in a way that could never have been anticipated."[2] Second, both theologians anchor their respective views by means of a set of thoroughly worked-out theological commitments, yielding a great depth and richness of thought. In this chapter, I will explore one main feature of their understandings, one in which they share a great deal in common: their shared heritage and development of Anselm's theory of satisfaction, in which they argue that the doctrine of satisfaction should ultimately be understood not *negatively* as satisfaction *for* sin but *positively* as satisfaction *of* God.

A COMMON HERITAGE IN ANSELM

To properly understand the commonality of Edwards and Barth, we will take our bearings from Anselm's *Cur Deus Homo*.[3] In this devotional exercise, Anselm posits that "to sin is nothing other than not to give God what is owed to him" and that "the will of a rational creature ought to be subject to the will of God," and "this is the sole honor, the complete honor, which we owe to God and which God demands from us. For only such a will, when it can act, performs actions which are pleasing to God."[4] Having sinned, and so dishonored God, either the honor we have taken "should be repaid, or

---

A good deal of care is required when it comes to thinking about Edwards and a governmental theory of the atonement, particularly because of the way that historicism changed the theological landscape in the nineteenth century, bringing with it a propensity to compartmentalize the views of theologians into different competing "theories of the atonement." Edwards, for instance, does not write of "theories of the atonement," but Park, writing a century later, uses the concept as a given for organizing his summary of the former. Edwards Amasa Park, *The Atonement, Discourses and Treatises* (Boston: Congregational Board of Publication, 1859). My intuition is that while there can be governmental accounts of Christ's work that are meant to be opposed to other views of the atonement and sufficient as such, in many cases, Grotius included, governmental accounts are meant to be held alongside a range of other commitments regarding the meaning and significance of the death and resurrection of Jesus. This essay does not explore Edwards's relationship to governmental accounts. For more, see S. Mark Hamilton, "Re-Thinking Atonement in Jonathan Edwards and New England Theology," *Perichoresis* 15, no. 1 (2017),85–99; S. Mark Hamilton, "Jonathan Edwards, Anselmic Satisfaction and God's Moral Government," *International Journal of Systematic Theology* 17, no. 1 (2015), 46–67.

2. Crisp and Strobel, *Jonathan Edwards*, 132.

3. All Anselm citations are from Anselm, "Why God Became Man," in *The Major Works*, ed. Brian Davies and G. R. Evans (New York: Oxford University Press, 1998), 260–536.

4. Anselm I.11.

punishment should follow."[5] These insights form the basis for Anselm's thinking, upon which he develops an account of satisfaction as that which the God-man offers God as repayment, in place of punishment, to restore the honor of God.[6]

Both Barth and Edwards develop a qualified appropriation of Anselm's thought. Barth, for instance, writes that the Bible "attest[s] Him as the Lord, to whom man owes everything, to whom he owes himself with everything that he is and has, to whom he owes it to give the glory which belongs to Him in the sphere of our humanity, the glory which He can receive if we do the best we can in His service."[7] Speaking of Good Friday, Barth writes, "As a fulfilment of the righteousness of God it necessarily meant that in the conflict between God's faithfulness and man's unfaithfulness, the faithfulness of God Himself was maintained, and therefore His honour was not violated. It was only in this way that it could also be exercised as His faithfulness to man, for how could man be really helped by a God who actually surrendered His own honour?"[8] These insights could have come straight from the pages of *Cur Deus Homo*—honor shapes the thinking, the debt we owe is our very selves, and the challenge is to satisfy God's righteousness within this context.

---

5. Anselm I.13.

6. Medieval feudalism need not be the only background for satisfaction, which plays a rich role in biblical thinking, often associated with the joy and fullness of eating and feasting (שָׂבַע), such as in Ruth 2:14; Psalm 22:26; and Isaiah 66:11, and then spills over into a more relational sense of the word: Psalm 63:5; 90:14; 107:9, Isaiah 53:11; and Jeremiah 31:14. Scripture also knows of a negative mode of satisfaction (נָחַם), when God satisfies his fury or wrath: Ezekiel 5:13; 16:42. Such notions far exceed any mere concept of "enough" or "adequate" such as we find in ἱκανός, as in Luke 22:38 or 2 Corinthians 2:16. It is particularly helpful to read Anselm's *Prayers and Meditations* in order to grasp more of the biblical foundation of his emphasis on honor, such as one sees in his "Meditation 1: A Meditation to Stir up Fear." Anselm, *The Prayers and Meditations of Saint Anselm with the Proslogion*, trans. Benedicta Ward (New York: Penguin, 1973), 221–24.

7. CD II/1, 217–18. Barth, to be sure, had an uneasy relationship with Anselm's soteriology. For instance, he challenges the notion that "He has suffered this punishment of ours" as being "a main concept as in some of the older presentations of the doctrine of the atonement (especially those which follow Anselm of Canterbury), either in the sense that by His suffering our punishment we are spared from suffering it ourselves, or that in so doing He 'satisfied' or offered satisfaction to the wrath of God." CD IV/1, 253. In this case, Barth must be speaking of those who came after Anselm chronologically, rather than those who followed his views, as Anselm clearly thought nothing of the sort. Elsewhere, Barth is clearer on his divergence with Anselm, which has more to do with freedom and necessity in God than anything strictly pertaining to the question of punishment. See CD IV/1, 486.

8. CD II/1, 400.

Along the same lines, Edwards argues that "there are two things that [are] intended by [Christ's purchasing of redemption], viz. his satisfaction and merit," which are precisely the categories developed by Anselm: satisfaction of God's honor, which atones for the sin of humankind, and the merit that Christ receives for this good work and that he subsequently shares with his people.[9]

Edwards and Barth diverge from Anselm by reframing the doctrine of satisfaction around the divine attribute of justice or righteousness rather than honor[10] and by rejecting Anselm's dichotomy that satisfaction must be made *either* by satisfactory repayment *or* by punishment. Edwards and Barth, following the post-Anselmians[11] and the Reformers, argue that satisfaction was a repayment that included punishment.[12] Along these lines, we see Edwards arguing:

> Christ, that gave himself in sacrifice, is so united to them he died for, that it may well be accepted as their sacrifice. It may well be accepted of God as if we had offered that price, and justice in Christ's suffering may well be satisfied for our sins. ... Therefore God looks upon him as our head, and the head being united to the members, the sufferings of the head may be looked upon as the suffering of the members.[13]

But this is not all, of course, for Christ's "was a meritorious sacrifice. That is, the sufferings of Christ did not only satisfy justice for our sins, but merited Christ's favor."[14] Barth argues similarly, writing that "this truth is the man who satisfies the Law by suffering the punishment of its transgression

---

9. Edwards, *A History of the Work of Redemption*, ed. John F. Wilson, WJE 9 (New Haven: Yale, 1989), 304.

10. Anselm clearly develops the role of justice and mercy in relation to Christ's satisfaction (cf. Anselm, "Why God Became Man," II.20, 354)—my point is merely that honor, more than any other attribute, shapes the structures of his account.

11. J. Patout Burns, "The Concept of Satisfaction in Medieval Redemption Theory," *Theological Studies* 36 (June 1975): 294; Andrew Rosato, "The Interpretation of Anselm's Teaching on Christ's Satisfaction for Sin in the Franciscan Tradition from Alexander of Hales to Duns Scotus," *Franciscan Studies* 71 (2013), 411–44.

12. Michael J. Plato, "Atonement," in *The Jonathan Edwards Encyclopedia*, ed. Harry S. Stout (Grand Rapids: Eerdmans, 2017), 51–52.

13. *WJE* 14:453–54.

14. *WJE* 14:453–54; see also Miscellany 449; *WJE* 9:117, 304; McClymond and McDermott, *The Theology of Jonathan Edwards*, 251.

and who at the same time keeps and fulfils it by doing what it commands"[15] and that "in the giving up of His Son to death, God has done that which is 'satisfactory' or sufficient in the victorious fighting of sin to make this victory radical and total," in the judging of the Judge, within which our sin was judged and done away with.[16] Satisfaction for both Edwards and Barth, as with many in the Reformed tradition, is a concept indebted to Anselm, but one thoroughly reworked around the satisfaction of justice, with punishment playing an integral role in the concept.

SATISFACTION OF GOD

But to argue that Edwards and Barth share common ground by departing from Anselm in this way is little more than to argue that Edwards and Barth were both Reformed theologians.[17] Their most provocative development lies in a subtler shift in thinking to do with the doctrine of satisfaction—one that harkens back to a subtle yet problematic shift within Anselm's thought. As we saw earlier, Anselm posits that "to sin is nothing other than not to give God what is owed to him."[18] What, then, is owed to the Creator? Whatever "is his." What then can satisfy God? That those things which are God's a) remain so and b) function according to God's plan and purposes. Rational creatures must use their reason in submission to God, obeying God's will and law. The heavenly city should be fully populated; creation itself should abound. To dishonor God is to disturb, "as far as [possible], the order and beauty of the universe," of God's creation.[19] So far, so good—but when Anselm turns to the doctrine of satisfaction proper, we see a shift: satisfaction shifts from "the order and beauty of the universe" to the question of satisfaction for sin, for God "demands recompense in proportion to the magnitude of sin."[20]

---

15. *CD* II/1, 153.

16. *CD* IV/1, 254-55.

17. H. Dermot McDonald, "Models of the Atonement in Reformed Theology," in *Major Themes in the Reformed Tradition* (Grand Rapids: Eerdmans, 1992), 117-31; Leanne Van Dyk, "Toward a New Typology of Reformed Doctrines of Atonement," in *Toward the Future of Reformed Theology: Tasks, Topics, Traditions*, ed. David Willis-Watkins, Michael Welker, and Matthias Gockel (Grand Rapids: Eerdmans, 1999), 225-38; Robert S. Franks, *A History of the Doctrine of the Work of Christ in Its Ecclesiastical Development*, vol. 1 (London: Hodder and Stoughton, 1871), 353-444.

18. Anselm, I.11.

19. Anselm, I.15. See also David S. Hogg, *Anselm of Canterbury: The Beauty of Theology* (Burlington, VT: Ashgate, 2004).

20. Anselm, I.21.

The shift is profound: from the positive emphasis on God's creation, satisfaction takes on a negative emphasis. The two are not necessarily at odds, but they signal two directions, two emphases, that must be carefully coordinated lest we introduce imbalance into our meditation on human redemption. Compounding this problem is the way that Anselm narrows his reflection down to a concern with the honor of God, which the Reformed tradition then largely replaced with an emphasis on the justice/righteousness of God. Where the impetus of satisfaction lay in the order and beauty of the universe that it received from its Creator, the material reflection on satisfaction was much narrower in scope, focusing on the problem of sin and constraining itself to a consideration of the honor (Anselm) or justice/righteousness (Reformed tradition) of God.

It would seem that Edwards and Barth follow this way of understanding satisfaction. Edwards writes that Christ "was willing to take their sins to himself and have them put on his account, and to bear the punishment himself,"[21] and "were it not that the sins of men are already fully punished in the sufferings of Christ, all, both angels and men, might justly hate all sinners for their sins."[22] Christ suffered the wrath of God, having a keen sense of "the dreadfulness of the punishment of sin, or the dreadfulness of God's wrath inflicted upon it. Thus Christ was tormented not only in the fire of God's wrath, but in the fire of our sins"[23]—a work he accomplished for them by standing for them, by substituting in their stead, as "his love and pity fixed their calamity in his mind, as if he had really been they, and fixed their calamity in his mind, as though it really was his."[24] In this way, God's "justice and vengeance is ... executed and ... satisfied"[25]—for God's justice is at the heart of God: "God was obliged by his justice to punish the offense, for it is not agreeable to infinite and exact justice for God, who governs the world, to let sins that are committed in it go unpunished."[26]

---

21. Miscellany B, *WJE* 13:165

22. Miscellany 781, *WJE* 18:450

23. Miscellany 1005, *WJE* 20:330

24. Miscellany 1005, *WJE* 20:332

25. Miscellany 1062, *WJE* 20:433

26. "Christ's Sacrifice," *WJE* 10:601, see also 598. "At its heart," note McClymond and McDermott, "is the notion of infinite divine justice which 'must be satisfied.' " McClymond and McDermott, *The Theology of Jonathan Edwards*, 250.

Barth argues much the same way. In an extended passage, Barth explores how Jesus is the Judge, judged in our place.[27] "He is the One whose concern is for order and peace, who must uphold the right and prevent the wrong,"[28] and as this one, he took our place as our Judge.[29] But he did so as one who takes our place as sinners:[30] he "accepts responsibility," gives Himself ... to the fellowship of those who are guilty ... [and] makes their evil case His own."[31] And because he does this, "it ceases to be our sin" and becomes his: "His the sin ... His the accusation, the judgement and the curse."[32] And as this one, as the great sinner, Jesus "suffered and was crucified and died," fulfilling in himself judgment upon sin,[33] "completing our work ... by treading the way of sinners to its bitter end in death, in destruction, in the limitless anguish of separation from God, by delivering up sinful man and sin in His own person to the non-being which is properly theirs."[34] But as this man, as the one who was justly judged in our place, he is established as the man of righteousness: the great positive act of God establishing the risen Lord as the just and righteous man for us.[35]

Anchoring this account, which is so judicial in nature, is the substitutionary/representational work of Christ. The lynchpin of satisfaction is the notion that the God-man is able to enter the human situation, taking human nature on himself, so that in Jesus Christ, God is able to offer satisfaction to God. Edwards tells us that the Son "took them into an union with himself; so that they may be called members of him, may be called his body ... [so that] if the head suffers, the members and body may go free."[36] Put somewhat differently, "Christ took upon him our nature, that he might as it were appropriate human nature in general to himself, that he might become the head of those that had the human nature, that he might represent the whole, that he might

---

27. *CD* IV/1, 211–73.
28. *CD* IV/1, 217.
29. *CD* IV/1, 231.
30. *CD* IV/1, 235.
31. *CD* IV/1, 236.
32. *CD* IV/1, 236–37.
33. *CD* IV/1, 244.
34. *CD* IV/1, 253. See also *CD* II/1, 396–67, expressed in terms of the history of Israel.
35. *CD* IV/1, 256–67.
36. Miscellany B, *WJE* 13:165; see also *WJE* 13:284.

be as they, to be for them, to appear in their stead and to answer for them."[37] Barth offers much the same account.[38] "Man's reconciliation with God takes place through God's putting Himself in man's place and man's being put in God's place, as a sheer act of grace."[39] The emphasis, once more, is on the act of God: God is the one who brings about the exchange, who puts himself in our place, and on that basis is able to bear our sin and death, offering himself satisfaction. For Barth, as for Edwards, for God to be able to satisfy God without annihilating us[40] means taking our place in Jesus Christ, that in him God might satisfy God for us.

But note: there are two possible emphases within the material we have covered in both Edwards and Barth. On the one hand, we can develop the problem of sin and ask: *how does the death and resurrection of Jesus satisfy for sin?* And the material we have covered offers a cogent answer to this question. But though this way of approaching the material is warranted, there is a second way of approaching the material that is strikingly different, though not incompatible with the first: *how does the death and resurrection of Jesus satisfy God?* For as we will see, satisfying *for* sin and satisfying *God* are fundamentally different concerns, though the latter surely encompasses the former. The shift from satisfaction *for* sin to satisfaction *of* God is no mere semantic matter—it takes an arsenal of theological resources to offer a sufficiently robust and expansive account of satisfaction, which is precisely what we find in both Edwards and Barth, as we will see, considering each in turn.

EDWARDS'S EXPANSIVE ACCOUNT
OF SATISFACTION

Throughout his writings, Edwards tends to adopt the traditional distinction between satisfaction and merit that we find in Anselm, the former making recompense for sin and the latter being the positive benefits of Christ.[41] But that is not all Edwards has to say on the matter, as he admits, here and there,

---

37. Miscellany 385, *WJE* 13:453; see also *WJE* 13:463-4.

38. For a fuller account of Barth's theology on this matter, see Adam Johnson, "Barth on the Atonement," in *Companion to Karl Barth*, ed. George Hunsinger and Keith L. Johnson (Chichester: Wiley Blackwell, 2020), 147-58.

39. Barth, *Dogmatics in Outline*, 115.

40. *CD* II/1, 399.

41. Cf. *WJE* 19:117; *WJE* 19:513.

of a positive role of satisfaction. For instance, in Miscellany 846, he notes that "Christ's sufferings don't satisfy by any excellency in them, but by a fulfillment. To satisfy by fulfillment and to satisfy by worthiness, or excellency, are different things." In other words, the sufferings of Christ are not in and of themselves a good thing, but they play a role in fulfilling God's response to human sin and guilt. But, and this is most important for our purposes, there is another kind of satisfaction—one rooted not in fulfillment (in the sense of "doing enough") but rather in worthiness. In this latter view, satisfaction has more to do with "making full," or rejoicing in the excellence and abundance of a thing—a matter of excess and joy rather than standards and quotas in which the goal is to break even or neutralize.

We find something along these lines in Edwards's distinction between the limited and the more expansive senses of the work of redemption. The former pertains to "the purchase of salvation," while the latter explores "all that God works or accomplishes tending to this end, not only the purchasing of redemption but also all God's works that were properly preparatory to the purchase, or as applying the purchase and accomplishing the success of it."[42] Viewed together, Edwards refers to these as comprising "the one great work" of Redemption.[43] Later in this same work, Edwards softens this distinction, noting that some divines refer to the whole work as merit, and others as satisfaction: "And so the word satisfaction is sometimes used, not only for his propitiation but for his meritorious obedience." And the reason for this soft distinction is that "satisfaction and merit don't differ so much really as relatively. They both consist in paying a valuable price, a price of infinite value."[44] This soft distinction is further ratified by the fact that while satisfaction and merit are distinct, "not only a being redeemed from sin, but a being redeemed to God, is attributed in Scripture to the blood of Christ (Rev 5:9)."[45]

This loosely affirmed distinction is precisely what we see in Edwards's statement that Jesus "thought of their [our] being brought up from their depth of woe, and being advanced to glory by his pain and disgrace with great

---

42. *WJE* 9:117.
43. *WJE* 9:121.
44. *WJE* 9:304.
45. *WJE* 19:513.

satisfaction. The thought of it was most sweet to him."[46] Jesus is satisfied with *both* our elevation from the depths *and* our advance to glory.

The soft distinction between satisfaction and merit is but one of the many ways Edwards offers an expansive understanding of satisfaction. A second approach revolves around his doctrine of the Trinity. Though Edwards does not mention satisfaction in this particular context, in Miscellany 327a, he explores the work of Christ as an extension of the love shared between the Father and the Son, such that the manifestation and repetition of God's own life with us is a key goal of the incarnation. Miscellany 402 extends this line of thought to the role of the Holy Spirit: "The sum of all that Christ purchased is the Holy Ghost. ... The great thing purchased by Jesus Christ for us is communion with God, which is only in having the Spirit." The roots of satisfaction lie in God manifesting and revealing himself within his creation, sharing or repeating God's own life with us. Satisfaction, we might say, has an intrinsically Trinitarian basis and shape within Edwards's theology.[47]

While Edwards takes some steps toward exploring the Trinitarian shape of satisfaction, he does far more by way of the doctrine of divine attributes. Recall that Anselm focused on satisfying God's honor, while the Reformers took that in the direction of God's justice or righteousness. While Edwards continues this emphasis, we find time and time again that he extends satisfaction to other aspects of God's character. For instance, Edwards refers to the delight Christ had in glorifying his holiness, justice, grace, and wisdom, in glorifying "the glorious excellency of God in general ... of showing forth his perfections to the views of men and angels."[48] Speaking of satisfaction in Miscellany 306, he notes that God did not have to punish sin, though "it would not be a prudent, decent and beautiful thing for a being of infinite glory and majesty, and the sovereign of the world, to let an infinite evil go unpunished. And as God's nature inclines him [to] order all things beautifully, properly and decently, so it was necessary that sin be punished." The key to understanding this insight, which Edwards labels under the category of

---

46. *WJE* 19:505.

47. McClymond and McDermott, *Theology of Jonathan Edwards*, 244: "Edwards's Christology seems to have developed ... [in part from his] concern to defend Christian orthodoxy against attacks from deists and other anti-Trinitarians."

48. *WJE* 19:504.

"Satisfaction," is the fact that satisfaction is here broadly understood as the joy God has in manifesting and extending his character into his creation (which includes but is not limited to a negative mode). The doctrine of satisfaction, in this case, is the soft necessity of his free joy, the necessity of his natural inclination, we might say. Elsewhere, Edwards extends this reflection to the majesty, holiness, authority, sovereignty, justice, mercy, condescension, love, grace, power, prudence, goodness, and glory of God.[49]

For Edwards, the twin engines driving this expansive account of the full range of the divine attributes within his account of satisfaction are the divine glory on the one hand and the divine wisdom on the other.[50] "Redemption," for Edwards, "is ordered by the concepts of emanation and remanation, grounded in God's act of creation and oriented toward God's act of glorification."[51] And concerning the divine wisdom, Edwards writes that "here the divine wisdom shines in reconciling righteousness and grace together, and accomplishing our salvation in the way and method of an eternal redemption."[52] This harmonizing, "bringing together" work of wisdom extends far beyond these two attributes, however, and plays a shaping influence throughout the Miscellanies.[53] Elsewhere, Edwards speaks of this as the "contrivance" of God's wisdom: the way God found, in his eternal wisdom, to accomplish or satisfy his diverse ends with regard to creation[54]—a point that brings us to Edwards's *The End for Which God Created the World*, and, as he puts in in Miscellany 702, his expansive vision

---

49. Miscellanies 327a, 337, 553, *WJE* 13 and *WJE* 18.

50. Barth would probably choose to reframe this in terms of God's love and freedom. *CD* II/1, 257–321.

51. Kyle C. Strobel, *Jonathan Edwards's Theology: A Reinterpretation* (London: Bloomsbury T&T Clark, 2013), 16.

52. Miscellany 1226, *WJE* 23:157–159.

53. Kyle C. Strobel and I explored this together in Adam J. Johnson and Kyle C. Strobel, "Atoning Wisdom: The Wisdom of God in the Way of Salvation," in *Locating Atonement*, ed. Oliver D. Crisp and Fred Sanders (Grand Rapids: Zondervan, 2015), 89–100. See also Adam J. Johnson, *The Reconciling Wisdom of God: Reframing the Doctrine of the Atonement* (Bellingham: Lexham, 2016), 129–32.

54. The flip side of this vision is that just as satisfaction is about more than justice, so is sin: "As sin is an opposition to God's nature, so it implies a contrariety to all his perfections, for the nature of God and his perfections are not different," (*WJE* 25:664). Satisfaction, in its richest and fullest form, is a matter of satisfying God, for God is the key agent, God is the one who is sinned against, and for this reason merely overcoming sin is insufficient, as is narrowing sin to a rebellion against one of God's attributes. To offer satisfaction to God includes, but far transcends, satisfying for sin against the honor or justice of God. To offer satisfaction is to satisfy God.

of redemption as "the great end and drift of all God's works and dispensations from the beginning, and even the end of the work of creation itself; yea, the whole creation."[55]

BARTH'S EXPANSIVE ACCOUNT
OF SATISFACTION

With Barth, we find a similar set of commitments driving his expansive account of satisfaction, the most important being what we might call the distinction between the immanent and economic satisfaction of God.

> He is no less the One who loves if He loves no object different from Himself. In the fact that He determines to love such another, His love overflows. But it is not exhausted in it nor confined or conditioned by it. On the contrary, this overflowing is conditioned by the fact that although it could satisfy itself, it has no satisfaction in this self-satisfaction, but as love for another it can and will be more than that which could satisfy itself.[56]

Or, again:

> God stands in need of nothing else. He has full satisfaction in Himself. Nothing else can even remotely satisfy Him. Yet He satisfies Himself by showing and manifesting and communicating Himself as the One who He is. He is completely Himself and complete in Himself. But He comes forth and has an outer as well as an inner side. He is not only immanent in Himself but He moves over to others. He is what He is in irresistible truth and power and act even for that which is not God, which is something else, which exists only through Him. He can and will not only exist but co-exist. This is the δόξα τοῦ θεοῦ, the *gloria Dei*, and all God's works from the greatest down to the least, each in its own way, are works of this divine glory, witnesses of the overflowing perfection of His Godhead.[57]

---

55. *WJE* 18:284.

56. *CD* II/1, 280–81.

57. *CD* II/1, 666–67. For those concerned that these quotes predate Barth's developed account of election, cf. *CD* II/2, 121, 167–68; *CD* III/1, 68–69; *CD* IV/2, 777; see also *CD* I/1, 140, to demonstrate the continuity of this line of thought across *CD*.

Passages like these have a complex history of interpretation among Barth scholars, but for our purposes it suffices to attend to the way Barth utilizes the concept of satisfaction. The starting point is the internal, or immanent, life of God, apart from creation. "He could have remained satisfied with Himself and with the impassible glory and blessedness of His own inner life."[58] "God could satisfy His love in Himself. For He is already an object to Himself and He is an object truly worthy of His love."[59] "He could have remained satisfied with the fulness of His own being. If He had willed and decided in this way, He would not have suffered any lack."[60] The reason we can and should talk about the doctrine of satisfaction with regard to the work of Christ is that this doctrine has a place within the eternal life of God. God is satisfied by, fulfilled, and completed in his own divine life as Father, Son, and Holy Spirit. Put negatively, there is no need or lack in God motivating him to seek satisfaction outside his own eternal life. The doctrine of satisfaction, simply put, is an extension of the life of God into the sphere of our sinful dilemma.

But the good news is that God in Christ extends, or overflows, his own proper satisfaction into our circumstances, such that he satisfies himself not merely for himself but for us. "This overflowing is conditioned by the fact that ... as love for another it can and will be more than that which could satisfy itself."[61] In other words, God brings his own eternal life of satisfaction into his creation through the incarnation of Jesus Christ, such that from within our life and nature, that pattern, that relationship can continue in a new mode: God satisfying God from within the life of Jesus. In this way God's eternal satisfaction becomes the means, the driving force, of satisfaction between God and humankind: since we as fallen humans cannot offer God satisfaction, God brings his own satisfaction into our realm that he might satisfy himself as man.

This distinction draws on an exceptionally rich vein of theological reflection having to do with Barth's doctrine of election. It is vital to Barth that we anchor our reflection on the work of Christ on God's covenant:

---

58. *CD* II/2, 166–67.

59. *CD* I/1, 140.

60. *CD* III/1, 169.

61. *CD* II/1, 280–81.

> To satisfy His righteousness they would have to perish genuinely and finally, to fall from His hand. But then God would not be the God who has sworn to be faithful to them. Or He for His part would not have kept His oath and covenant with them.[62]

The context of satisfaction is not merely the eternal satisfaction of the triune God but the constraints put on the overflowing of this satisfaction into the creaturely realm by the covenants and oaths of God. God, as the electing God, determined in Christ to have a certain way and goal of relating to creation and will not deviate from this. Satisfaction is not merely a matter of fulfilling the righteousness of God in the face of human sin; for that, the mere judgement and destruction of sinful humankind would do. No, satisfaction is a matter of fulfilling the righteousness and whole character of God within God's election to be the God of his people in Jesus Christ, to be God for them. Only the fulfillment of the covenant offers God the economic extension of the immanent satisfaction that he seeks as the electing God.

This commitment to be the God of his people in Jesus Christ, and only as such to satisfy himself, brings about a tension in Barth's thought, which he resolves through the image of the two hands of God (which bears some parallel to the strict and loose definitions of satisfaction in Edwards's thought). "God does not turn toward [sinful humankind] without uttering in inexorable sharpness a 'No' to his transgression," for God's righteousness and justice must in fact be satisfied. And for this reason, "theology has no choice but to put this 'No' into words within the framework of its theme." But that is not all we must say, for it must be "the 'No' which Jesus Christ takes upon Himself for us men, in order that it may no longer affect us and that we may no longer place ourselves under it."[63] The negative, destructive work necessary to God's opposition to sin is fully present in Barth's thought, but present only as a lesser, particular work within a larger and more comprehensive and re-creative work. Barth distinguishes these two works as those of the left (negative) and right (positive) hands of God:

> We have to say at once that on both sides God acts righteously, because He acts in consequence of His right, of His faithfulness to Himself, and

---

62. *CD* IV/1, 553.

63. Barth, *The Humanity of God*, 60.

in execution of His right over and to man. On the left hand He acts righteously in His wrath which consumes the sinner, and on the right hand He acts righteously in the limitation, or more exactly in the interpretation of His wrath, in His holding fast to the man who even as a sinner that He can only chide is still His man. And God is righteous in this distinction as such: for satisfaction would not be done to His right if He could only chide on the left hand or only pardon on the right, if He accepted the identification of man with wrong, and was content simply to banish from the world both wrong and the wrongdoer, or if in spite of the wrong which man has done and his identification with it He allowed him to live at the price of not destroying the wrong which man has committed, of recognising *de facto* its right to exist. The righteousness of God would not be God's righteousness and therefore it would not be true righteousness if it did not proceed on both sides, i.e., if its fulfilment did not involve this division which cuts right across the whole of man's existence.[64]

Barth here seeks to affirm God's satisfaction of his own righteousness by simultaneously affirming two things. First, he affirms God's satisfaction of God's righteous response to sin in its left-handed, negative mode of operation: judgment and destruction of sin and the sinner. But this would only be a one-sided satisfaction, unworthy of the God of the gospel who elected himself as the God of his people, as the God who will raise up a people in the way of righteousness. And for this reason, his second and ultimately determinative move is to affirm God's satisfaction of God's righteousness toward humankind in its right-handed, positive mode of operation: transforming and fulfilling humankind's existence in the way of God's own proper life-giving righteousness.[65]

But like Edwards, Barth finds that this broader vision of satisfaction simply cannot be constrained to the satisfaction of God's righteousness and justice (or honor, for that matter). The emphasis on the satisfaction *of God* is simply too expansive to allow for such narrow constraints. Barth's emphasis here, as with Edwards's, is on the satisfaction God has in his self-communication to the creature:

---

64. *CD* IV/1, 541; see also 553–54.
65. Cf. *CD* IV/1, 46–47, 93–95.

> God's glory is the indwelling joy of His divine being which as such
> shines out from Him, which overflows in its richness, which in its
> super-abundance is not satisfied with itself but communicates itself.
> All God's works must be understood also and decisively from this point
> of view. All together and without exception they take part in the move-
> ment of God's self-glorification and the communication of His joy. They
> are the coming into being of light outside Him on the basis of the light
> inside Him, which is Himself. They are expressions of infinite exulta-
> tion in the depth of His divine being. It is from this point of view that
> all His creatures are to be viewed both first and last.[66]

The overwhelming concern here is the shining forth of the divine glory and
indwelling joy of God in all his works, as God enacts his divine being among
us for our salvation. God's super-abundance is not satisfied with itself but
communicates itself; more precisely, it satisfies itself *by* communicating itself.
And for this reason, Barth, like Edwards, weaves in a host of divine attributes
into his account of satisfaction.

For instance, Barth writes of honor and faithfulness: "On the other hand,
the faithfulness of God Himself could not and must not exclude and suspend
His faithfulness to man, nor must His honour be safeguarded by the visitation
upon man of that which he has properly deserved: eternal death and destruction. In the death of Jesus Christ God remained true both to Himself and to
man."[67] He says much the same of divine glory[68] and wisdom: "It is to be noted
that the wisdom of God characterises His whole activity as reliable and liberating, as something in which we can have confidence, just because His wisdom
consists in and finally evinces itself as His firmness and self-consistency, the
satisfaction of His *decentia*."[69] Throughout *Church Dogmatics*, Barth weaves in
similar considerations about a host of divine attributes, most notably in the
latter half of *CD* II/1, where Barth's reflections on each of the divine attributes
move toward a consideration of their enactment in the life and work of Jesus.[70]

---

66. *CD* II/1, 647–48.

67. *CD* II/1, 400.

68. *CD* II/1, 647.

69. *CD* II/1, 427.

70. Cf. Robert B. Price, "Letters of the Divine Word: The Perfections of God in Karl Barth's
Church Dogmatics" (PhD diss., University of Aberdeen, 2007). In the fine print section following his exposition of the judge judged in our place, Barth develops a more biblical or exegetical

CONCLUSION

Edwards and Barth follow the Reformed tradition, modifying Anselm's account of satisfaction to emphasize the satisfaction of God's righteousness by means of both punishment and merit. But while the continuity is evident, Edwards and Barth share a great deal of common ground in the way they develop this account in a more expansive direction, considering the ways that Christ's death and resurrection not merely offer satisfaction for sin but rather satisfy God himself (which includes, necessarily, the narrower concern of satisfying God with regard to sin). This move, bolstered by a range of distinctions, doctrinal interconnections, and images, is vital for several reasons.

First, such a move pushes reflection on the doctrine of the atonement away from the problem of sin and to the problem of God. As odd as it may seem, sin is not the primary problem facing the atonement. The problem is fundamentally that of how God will continue to be God in relation to a sinful creation. The problem, to be precise, is God's problem.[71] How will God be who he is, how will he be the God of Abraham, Isaac, and Jacob, the God of Israel who is faithful to his covenants with his people, in view of their sin? How will God continue to be the righteous, wise, good, merciful, patient, omnipotent God that he is in the face of human sin? To break God up into parts, making him merely righteous or merely merciful, or to forget the history of his oaths and covenants such that Israel does not inform our thinking—solutions such as these domesticate the doctrine of satisfaction, making it manageable in scope, while distorting the Christian witness.

The real problem is far more complex than that: How can God, in Christ, fully and perfectly satisfy God for us and for salvation? How does Christ satisfy the covenants and purposes of God for his creation, his creatures? How does Christ satisfy the whole character of God? Such reflection demands far more of us than a casual glance at the doctrine of satisfaction might seem to imply, requiring that we reach back into the doctrines of the Trinity and the divine attributes and attend more carefully to the history of God with his people.

---

foundation for a similar diversity, noting that the judicial theme is but one way the Scriptures explore the work of Christ. Barth does not connect this to the doctrine of the divine attributes in this section. Cf. Adam J. Johnson, *God's Being in Reconciliation: The Theological Basis of the Unity and Diversity of the Atonement in the Theology of Karl Barth* (New York: T&T Clark, 2012), 92–132.

71. Cf. Athanasius, *On the Incarnation*, trans. John Behr (Yonkers, NY: St Vladimir's Seminary Press, 2011), 59–73.

Edwards and Barth's greatest contribution to the doctrine of the atonement, in my esteem, is the way they move us in precisely this direction, helping us dwell not merely on Christ's satisfaction for sin but on God's satisfaction of God in face of human sin, through the work of Jesus Christ, for us and for our salvation.

While we do not have space to explore this here, one of the most important implications of this line of thought is the way it demands a rich account of the resurrection within Christ's work of satisfaction. God "is not God of the dead, but of the living" (Mark 12:27), and if Christ is not raised, we are still in our sins (1 Cor 15:17). Anselm did the church a great disservice here, completely forgoing a consideration of Christ's resurrection within *Cur Deus Homo*, but both Edwards and Barth restore what was lacking in Anselm with robust accounts of the resurrection as the completion of satisfaction. For if satisfaction is truly the satisfaction *of the living God*, then nothing short of the completion of his creative project will suffice, bound to his character as it is by act and covenant—and for this, nothing short of the completion and goodness of the resurrection will do.

12

—

MORAL THEOLOGY

Kirk J. Nolan

Traditionally, moral theology is considered one of two major branches of systematic theology, the other being dogmatic theology. While the aim of dogmatic theology is a deeper knowledge of God, the aim of moral theology is a better understanding of appropriate human action considering that knowledge. D. Stephen Long helpfully compares the term "moral theology" with another, "Christian ethics." Christian ethics, a child of the Enlightenment as much as it is of the Christian tradition, typically seeks broader relevance in the public square and relies more heavily on the social sciences. Compared with moral theologians, Christian ethicists tend to place ethics closer to the center and theology more at the periphery of their investigations.[1] Given this set of distinctions, the label "moral theology" is most apt for the kind of moral inquiry Jonathan Edwards and Karl Barth pursue. When the term "ethics" appears in their writing or is applied to their work, the reader should translate that term into "moral theology." For example, in the Foreword to the first volume of his massive *Church Dogmatics*, Barth writes, "Ethics so-called I regard as the doctrine of God's command and do not consider it right to treat it otherwise than as an integral part of dogmatics, or to produce a dogmatics which does not include it."[2] As Barth notes, while these two branches may be logically separated from each other for the purposes of investigation, in practice they logically entail

---

1. Duane Stephen Long, "Moral Theology," in *Oxford Handbook of Systematic Theology*, ed. John Webster, Kathryn Tanner, and Iain Torrance (New York: Oxford University Press, 2007), 456–57. See also Charles Curran, *The Development of Moral Theology: Five Strands* (Washington, DC: Georgetown University Press, 2013), 12ff.

2. *CD* I/1, xiv.

each other: an ethics without theology is blind, and a theology without ethics is empty. As we will see, Jonathan Edwards would concur.

EDWARDS'S COVENANTAL
MORAL VIRTUE ETHICS

Jonathan Edwards's moral theology was shaped by two sometimes competing influences: Puritan tradition and Enlightenment thought. Regarding the Puritan tradition, Edwards's father and maternal grandfather were both Puritan pastors. Edwards was deeply touched by the revivals his father led and in which he participated from childhood.[3] These revivals emphasized the need for a religious experience that impacted one's emotions as well as one's intellect. The New England Puritan practice of religion was all encompassing, a reflection of the desire to purify one's faith from any outside influences that led seventeenth century English Puritans to make the arduous journey to North America. Without a heartfelt faith, its stringent demands became deeply burdensome, but with such a faith, these demands became the works by which faith was genuinely expressed. Consequently, Puritan pastors looked for signs that God's grace was at work in their congregants' life. Congregants should be able to narrate their religious experiences and show tangible signs of transformation. Edwards's moral theology focuses on such religious experience. The Christian life is the work of the Holy Spirit in concert with the believer, who is empowered by the Spirit to perform works of love.

Jonathan Edwards's moral theology was also deeply impacted by the ministry of his grandfather, Solomon Stoddard, particularly in terms of the social location from which Edwards developed that theology. When Edwards was in his mid-twenties, he took over the role of head pastor of the church in Northampton, Massachusetts from Stoddard. Stoddard's leadership stretched from 1669 until his death in 1729, a period of sixty years. He wielded immense political and religious authority over Northampton, and Western Massachusetts, during that time. Thus, when Edwards became head pastor, he was stepping into a position of power and influence. That power

---

3. George Marsden, *Jonathan Edwards: A Life* (New Haven: Yale University Press, 2003). Marsden notes that for Edwards, one's status before God was an essential question throughout his life, for his thought and his ministry. See 25ff.

emanated as much from his biological connection to Stoddard as it did from the office Edwards now held. Edwards could count on revered family members like his uncles Colonel John Stoddard and Reverend William Williams, to back him up in times of controversy, as well as having the patronage of several important families who had developed alliances with Stoddard during his tenure.

The effects of Edwards's social standing on his moral theology were varied. The stringent expectations that Edwards placed on himself he also expected of his parishioners. In 1742, during yet another religious revival in Northampton, Edwards created an extensive covenant, setting strict guidelines for moral behavior. His congregants, swept up in the awakening, signed the contract. For years, the covenant was a source of contention and was one reason among many for his dismissal in 1750. Edwards, convinced by his reading of the Bible, and particularly the Old Testament, was not willing to compromise his principles. His congregants, however, resisted his authoritarian tendencies and eventually drove him out.

On the other hand, Edwards could be remarkably attuned to those who were often left at the margins of society. In A Faithful Narrative, his account of the 1734–35 revivals, Edwards highlights the experiences of Abigail Hutchinson, a young woman, and Phebe Bartlet, a four-year-old girl, as models of true conversion.[4] After Edwards's dismissal from the church in 1750, he chose to work as a missionary to the Mahican Indians, fulfilling an interest that he had maintained for decades. Throughout his life, Edwards cultivated habits of simplicity, humility, and austerity. The effects of these habits were pervasive, down to Edwards's choice of a plain rather than ornate literary style and the tendency to fill reused paper with his tiny handwriting.[5]

The influence of Enlightenment thinkers on Edwards was profound as well, though Edwards did not always agree with what he read. Edwards shared with many Enlightenment figures, such as Isaac Newton, a fascination with nature at a time when most scientific inquiry emphasized minute observation rather than experimentation under controlled conditions.[6] For Edwards, the physical world demonstrated evidence of its metaphysical

---

4. Jonathan Edwards, *The Great Awakening*, WJE 4. See 191ff.

5. Marsden, *Jonathan Edwards*, 59–60.

6. Marsden, *Jonathan Edwards*, 63–64.

origins. "Of Insects," one of Edwards earliest writings, carefully describes his observations of spiders. After five pages of such observations, Edwards notes the following corollary: "We hence see the exuberant goodness of the Creator, who hath not only provided for all the necessities, but also for the pleasure and recreation of all sorts of creatures, and even the insects and those that are most despicable."[7] Edwards's inclination to enjoy nature, and the habits of mind fostered by thinkers like Newton, resulted in a moral theology that emphasized beauty as a motivating force to transform one's intellectual orientation toward godly ends. While Trinitarian in form, it consistently placed God's role as creator, and God's acts of continuous creation, in the foreground.

In the political and social spheres, Edwards grappled with John Locke's arguments for more tolerance and openness in religion that centered on the reliability of human reason but eventually settled on a Calvinistic reading of God's sovereignty that emphasized human frailty. Somewhat ironically, Edwards's opposition to Lockean ideas depended on rational argument and empirical observation. Whereas John Locke, in *Reasonableness of Christianity*, challenged the justice of condemning millions of lives to eternal damnation for the sin of Adam, Edwards pushed back by observing that human sinfulness is endemic to "all countries, climates, nations, and ages."[8] How else could such a universal condition befall all humankind, if not by way of a common ancestor? Edwards thus attributed human sinfulness to the fall. Prior to the sin of Adam, human beings were imbued with supernatural principles that enabled them to apprehend the love of God, thus making moral perfection possible. These supernatural principles depended on an intimate relationship with God, which was shattered by Adam's first disobedience. As a consequence, humans no longer directly apprehend the love of God, and therefore, all inevitably sin.[9]

Edwards's virtue ethics are a clear example of the way in which Puritan and Enlightenment influences combine in his thought. As Edwards writes in *The Nature of True Virtue*, virtue depends on a benevolent disposition, in

---

7. See *WJE* 6:147ff.

8. *WJE* 3:124. See also William J. Danaher Jr., *The Trinitarian Ethics of Jonathan Edwards* (Louisville: Westminster John Knox, 2004), 172–86. Edwards's target is actually John Taylor, not Locke, but Taylor's *The Scripture-Doctrine of Original Sin* is dependent upon Locke's work.

9. *WJE* 3:382–83.

which one is inclined to love and care for others. If this disposition encompasses only a limited group of people, such as one's extended family and friends, it is false. But if this disposition is grounded in being in general, rather than accidental features of particular beings, then true virtue results. If one has true virtue, then, one's love extends to all living things. God, the source of all life, is thus in the best position to exhibit it. Humans, though, in reflecting on the source of all life, may share in this virtue as well.[10]

The arguments Edwards makes in this treatise do not explicitly depend on divine revelation.[11] He is engaging in a disagreement with the moral sense theory of Scottish philosopher Frances Hutcheson by using terms native to that theory. Hutcheson, in answer to deist concerns over grounding morality in divine revelation, proposed the idea that all human claims to justice are in fact grounded in a common moral sense. When disagreements arise regarding how certain goods should be distributed, all but one (or perhaps all) of the positions taken must be the result of faulty reasoning. Once these faults have been worked out, all parties should be moved by this moral sense to agree, at least in principle, on the best course of action.[12]

In contrast to Edwards's *The Nature of True Virtue*, *Religious Affections* uses explicitly Trinitarian vocabulary to extend his understanding of virtue. Here, true virtue is the result of a permanent indwelling of the Holy Spirit, who empowers the believer to see God's love more clearly and thus to be inspired to respond through similar acts of love. The Spirit creates in Christians a spiritual sense that is distinct from, but nonetheless conceptually related to, Hutcheson's concept of the common moral sense. Like Hutcheson's concept, the spiritual sense relates to a capacity that enables its bearers to discern how to think and act well. But unlike Hutcheson's concept, this capacity is

---

10. WJE 8:552–53.

11. However, *The Nature of True Virtue* is not a stand-alone volume. It is the second work in Edwards's *Two Dissertations*. The first, *Concerning the End for which God Created the World*, is a thoroughly scriptural argument for a Trinitarian moral theology.

12. See Alasdair MacIntyre, *Whose Justice? Which Rationality?* (Notre Dame: University of Notre Dame Press, 1988), 260–80; Stephen A. Wilson, *Virtue Reformed: Rereading Jonathan Edwards's Ethics* (Boston: Brill, 2005), 97; William A. Danaher, "Beauty, Benevolence, and Virtue in Jonathan Edwards's *The Nature of True Virtue*," *Journal of Religion* 87, no. 3 (2007): 386–410; and Ki Joo Choi, "The Role of Perception in Jonathan Edwards's Moral Thought: *The Nature of True Virtue* Reconsidered," *Journal of Religious Ethics* 38, no. 2 (2010): 269–96. For the influence of Hutcheson's concept on Edwards's concept of a spiritual sense common to all Christians, see Elizabeth Cochran, *Receptive Human Virtues* (University Park: Penn State University Press, 2011), chap. 5.

always dependent on God's intervention. True virtue is associated with the triune God alone. To the extent that human beings acquire such virtue at all, they do so in tandem with God, such that God's activity is primary and theirs is secondary (though nonetheless active).[13] Christians, through the work of the Holy Spirit, are uniquely positioned to experience true virtue, but for those outside the faith, it is elusive. So-called pagan virtue is real but partial in Edwards's schema. Like Hutcheson, Edwards believed that all human beings have a common moral sense, but Edwards was careful to distinguish this from true virtue. Our common moral sense may see the beauty of the moral life and aspire to participate in it, but such beauty is still secondary and provisional next to God's primal beauty. Acts of justice that stem from common moral sense retain an element of self-concern that true virtue, guided by our spiritual sense, avoids.[14]

Thus, Edwards's virtue ethics is best described as Christian, and, more specifically, covenantal in nature. To get a sense of how such an ethic worked itself out in practice, consider Edwards's position on baptism, which he elucidated during what is typically referred to as "the communion controversy" of 1748–50. Even during Solomon Stoddard's tenure as pastor of the church at Northampton, Puritan rigor over what constituted conversion created pastoral concerns around access to the sacraments of baptism and communion. Since there was so much emphasis placed on conversion, and since the sacraments were intended as a means of grace for those already thus converted, the key question then became how one determines whether somebody is converted.[15] Puritan New Englanders developed a tradition of baptizing only the children of full members. If these baptized children showed no later signs of conversion, should their children be allowed to be baptized? A synod of clergy declared in 1662 that they could.

Similar controversies surrounded communion. Once baptized, was it necessary to show evidence of conversion to participate in communion? Solomon Stoddard argued for a relaxed position, allowing anyone to the table who articulated belief in Christ so long as their conduct was free from scandal.

---

13. Thus, the title of Cochran's monograph on Edwards's ethics, *Receptive Human Virtues*. See 60ff.

14. See Ramsey's analysis in *WJE* 8:43ff.

15. Marsden, *Jonathan Edwards*, 29ff.

Jonathan Edwards later rejected his grandfather's position, a decision that contributed to his undoing.

When the controversy came to a head, Edwards asked the leaders of his congregation for permission to explain himself to the congregation. They denied the request but permitted him to present his case to a broader audience. Edwards's response, *An Humble Inquiry*, was written in the spring of 1749. At the heart of Edwards's position was the idea of covenanting, drawn from the Old Testament. Eighteenth-century Puritans could no longer fully maintain a separate society predicated on the idea that they were the new Israel, God's chosen people set apart by the new covenant. Enlightenment ideas and religious diversity were realities they had to face that their seventeenth-century forebears did not. One solution, taken by the New Lights (some of whom became Baptists), was separation from the established church, which had a stronghold on town politics. Another was moderation, such as Stoddard's halfway covenant. Stoddard's stance enabled the close connection between church and state to function but undermined the strictness of church discipline. Edwards argued for a different solution. All people, including those who led questionable lives and those who had not publicly professed their faith, were welcome to worship, but only members in complete standing, those who had shown moral reform and publicly and genuinely professed their Christian faith, were welcome to participate in the sacraments of baptism and the Lord's Supper.[16]

Yet Edwards, unlike the Baptists, still affirmed infant baptism. Because the overall legitimacy of infant baptism was not in question, he did not seek to defend it in this treatise.[17] Rather, the question was which infants could be baptized. Again, the heart of the matter was the covenant. When adult believers were baptized, they took a public oath like that of the Abrahamic and Mosaic covenants.[18] When infants were baptized, their parents also took an oath. But if the parents themselves could not obey the covenant, what good was such an oath?

At the end of *An Humble Inquiry*, Edwards considers an objection to his position on infant baptism. The objection argued that if full profession of

---

16. Marsden, *Jonathan Edwards*, 350.

17. WJE 12:175–76.

18. WJE 12:202.

faith is required of adults so that their children could be baptized, then a great many children would go unbaptized. Without "the external badge of Christianity," they would remain outside the covenant community.[19] Over the years, so many people would stand in need of God's grace as to bring disgrace to whole families, and unbaptized individuals would not be taught the fear of the Lord. Edwards's rebuttal ridicules the concern for outward appearance behind this objection. Was not the spiritual health of both the parent and the child even more urgent than its outward appearance, Edwards exclaims, concluding, "Let parents pity their poor children, because they are without baptism; and pity themselves, who are in danger of everlasting misery, while they have no interest in the covenant of grace, and so have no right to covenant favors or honors, for themselves nor [their] children."[20] Therefore, Edwards used the sacraments to enforce covenantal loyalty. In his reading, the new covenant that Christ established required a visible community of believers who were bound to a moral code like that found in the Old Testament. While the Holy Spirit empowered these believers to lives of moral virtue, and thus free from the condemnation of Jewish law, they were nonetheless constrained by communal and covenantal commitments. They were part of the household of God, under the constraints of its paterfamilias, in this case the head pastor of Northampton. The implications for Edwards's moral theology are profound and will be explored further. But first it will be helpful to sketch Karl Barth's distinctive theology and the implications that follow from it. Once that sketch is made, the contrast between these two thinkers will become clearer in terms of both their fundamental convictions and the consequences of those convictions.

KARL BARTH'S ESCHATOLOGICAL ETHICS OF DIVINE COMMAND

Ethicists who engage Karl Barth's work often turn to paragraphs 36–39 of *CD*, in which Barth works out the ethical implications of his doctrine of election. Even though these paragraphs deserve scrutiny, the theology that precedes them and underpins them ought not to be left behind. In addition, Barth's later ethical reflections on the Christian life, and particularly his views on

---

19. *WJE* 12:315.

20. *WJE* 12:316.

baptism, found in a fragmentary volume at the end of his doctrine of reconciliation, need to be considered to gain a fuller understanding of his moral theology. With all this material in view, the tilt of Barth's ethics shifts from a backward glance at God's election in Jesus Christ to a forward glance in the direction of the consummation of that election in the eschaton.

Two snapshots of Barth's theological development up to paragraphs 36–39 stand out as particularly significant: Barth's radical critique of religion found in his second commentary on Romans (hereafter R2) and his doctrine of election found in *CD* II/ 2, paragraphs 32–35. In R2, Barth takes on early twentieth-century German liberalism and pietism. Against German liberalism, he shifts the focus of investigation from the individual and the individual's experience of God to God as the primary actor in the encounter between God and us. Here Barth is challenging the legacy of Schleiermacher, for whom the personal encounter with God, experienced as a feeling of absolute dependence, became the *sine qua non* of the Christian life. Scheiermacher's theology thus placed emphasis on the subjective experience of God rather than on God's objective reality. The effect, Barth observes, was to domesticate God: "any claim to direct relationship with Him depresses Him to the level of time and things and men, and deprives Him of His true meaning."[21] R2 acts as a bulldozer, leveling all claims to Christian uniqueness, demolishing any effort to corner the God market. The task of the Christian community was not relevancy but humility: "But the activity of the community is related to the Gospel only insofar as it is no more than a crater formed by the explosion of a shell and seeks to be no more than a void in which the Gospel reveals itself."[22]

Barth's critique of religion had a larger purpose: to turn the church's attention toward God and away from itself. Central to that purpose was a renewed emphasis on Scripture as the word of God and a new doctrine of revelation. Barth's commentary challenges a way of reading the Bible that relativizes its impact by extracting the gospel message from the cultural thought forms in which it was expressed. Barth's response to Rudolph Bultmann's critique in the preface to the third edition of *Romans* is illuminating:

---

21. Barth, *The Epistle to the Romans* (Oxford: Oxford University Press, 1968), 113.

22. Barth, *Romans*, 36. According to Eberhard Busch, Barth's criticism of the church owes a debt to Hans Overbeck, whose posthumous book *Christianity and Culture* was published in 1919 and devoured by Barth between the first and second editions of his commentary. See Eberhard Busch, *Karl Barth and the Pietists: The Young Karl Barth's Critique of Pietism and Its Response*, trans. Daniel W. Bloesch (Downers Grove, IL: InterVarsity Press, 2004), 73ff.

Bultmann writes: "Other spirits make themselves heard, as well as the Spirit of Christ." I do not wish to engage in a controversy with Bultmann as to which of us is more radical. But I must go farther than he does and say that there are in the Epistle no words at all which are not words of those "other spirits" which he calls Jewish or Popular Christian or Hellenistic or whatever else they may be. Is it really legitimate to extract a certain number of passages and claim that there the veritable Spirit of Christ has spoken?[23]

German historical criticism in the nineteenth century pioneered a way of investigating the biblical text that treated it like any other historical text and thus questioned its historicity in the process. Bultmann was certainly not uncritical about this method, particularly when it claimed scientific objectivity.[24] However, he was not ready to throw the baby out with the bathwater. He insisted that Paul's ways of thinking, due to his historical context, limited his ability to convey the Spirit of Christ. Thus, historical criticism matters because it throws light on these limitations. Barth rejected that way of reading the text not because he wished to return to an uncritical reading of the biblical text as direct revelation from God but rather because he understood the impossibility of separating the two, and because separating the two out was unnecessary:

> He [Bultmann] asks me to think and write WITH Paul, to follow him into the vast unfamiliarity of his Jewish, Popular-Christian, Hellenistic conceptions; and then suddenly, when the whole becomes too hopelessly bizarre, I am to turn round and write "critically" ABOUT him and against him—as though, when all is strange, this or that is to be regarded as especially outrageous.[25]

David Congdon's recent book *The Mission of Demythologizing* defends Bultmann's stance. Congdon argues that Barth is also guilty of a selective reading of the Bible.[26] As Bultmann himself notes in a response to Barth, why did

23. Barth, *Romans*, 16–17.

24. Rudolf Bultmann, "Wissenschaft und Existenz" in *Glauben und Verstehen: Gesammelte Aufsätze* (Tübingen: Mohr Siebeck, 1933), 3:107–21.

25. Barth, *Romans*, 18.

26. David Congdon, *The Mission of Demythologizing: Rudolph Bultmann's Dialectical Theology* (Minneapolis: Fortress, 2015), 723–37.

he write a commentary on Romans and not the Pastorals? It must be because he recognizes there the Spirit of Christ is more clearly communicated.[27]

Barth's doctrine of revelation in his commentary is still a work in progress. Later he will highlight the unique role that Jesus Christ plays in disclosing who God is. In Barth's mature doctrine, Christ is the primary revelation of God, whereas Scripture stands as a secondary witness. God's disclosure of Godself is always partial and incomplete not because of any imperfection in the mode of revelation but because of our limited human capacity to experience God directly.

R2 is also critical of German pietism. Like his criticism of German liberalism, Barth's criticism of pietism is not that of an ignorant outsider. When he was a young boy, his family sang pietist hymns, and as a young man, he heard his father lecture favorably on the pietists. Wilhelm Herrmann, arguably the most influential teacher Barth ever had, was deeply influenced by pietism, though Herrmann's influence on Barth was not in a pietistic direction.[28] In the formative years leading up to R2, Barth was inspired by the pietist Christoph Blumhardt, whom he met in 1915 through a mutual friend, Eduard Thurneysen. Eberhard Busch attests that as a result of this meeting, "he [Barth] learned to understand God afresh as the radical renewer of the world who is at the same time himself completely and utterly new."[29] What was emerging in Barth's thought was a new appreciation for God's initiative and a way forward in the face of the horrors of World War I that involved patiently waiting on God but also openly and boldly defying convention, whether political, religious, or otherwise.

Given this background, what was it about pietism that Barth found so objectionable? Busch distinguishes Barth's criticism of pietism found in the first edition of his commentary on Romans from R2.[30] In the first edition, it is the individualism of the pietists that bothers Barth, who argues instead that the Bible is concerned with the salvation and sanctification of the church as

---

27. See *Karl Barth-Rudolph Bultmann Letters, 1922–1966*, ed. Bernd Jaspert, trans. and ed. Geoffrey W. Bromiley (New York: Continuum, 1982), 6.

28. Busch, *Karl Barth and the Pietists*, 10–12.

29. Eberhard Busch, *Karl Barth: His Life from Letters and Autobiographical Texts*, trans. John Bowden (Minneapolis: Fortress, 1990), 85.

30. Bruce McCormack carefully traces the shifts in Barth's theology during this time in *Karl Barth's Critically Realistic Dialectical Theology* (Oxford: Oxford University Press, 1995). These shifts are helpfully outlined in the introduction to the book, 21ff.

a whole rather than that of particular individuals. In addition, Barth takes the pietists to task for their forced display of faith, which revealed an insecurity over its basis. If, as Barth argues, faith was the result of God's initiative, then the pietists should not have to worry so much about proving their faith was effective.[31]

In the first edition, Barth had proposed a process of sanctification that happened organically. However, this growth process could not be mechanized by human beings. Church programs for spiritual growth were doomed to failure because of a fundamental misunderstanding about the process itself. While not Barth's direct target, the methodism associated with the Wesleys in England and then the United States certainly fell under such criticism. But in R2, Barth abandons this notion of organic growth. Instead, he emphasizes God's radical otherness, which extends to God's revelation to us and to the transformation we must undergo before we can stand in the presence of God. Because of this radical distinction between God and us, it was impossible for Barth to maintain that Christians could grow closer to God through a gradual process of improvement. Such quantitative progress meant nothing in the face of the qualitative distinction between creature and Creator. Thus, whereas in the first edition Barth attacks the heightened individualism he found in pietism, in R2 his critique is leveled at all religion, again as an attempt to domesticate God.[32]

Barth's first expansive treatment of moral theology in CD takes up the second half of CD II/2. Here he defines ethics as a task not just of dogmatics in general but of the doctrine of God in particular. By rooting his doctrine of God in election, and election in the life, death, and resurrection of Jesus Christ, Barth draws humankind into the doctrine of God: for God is now defined in terms of God's determination to be a God for us. But who is this "us," and how do we as humans respond? These "who" and "how" questions are ethical questions. In responding to the "who" question, Barth finds that humans are responsive and responsible creatures, capable of making ethical decisions. In answering the "how" question, Barth finds that humans are fully human when recognizing and responding to the claims that God

---

31. Busch, Karl Barth and the Pietists, 57–62. Busch notes that Barth's attack on German pietism doesn't apply to Swabian pietists, who, like Barth in the first edition, emphasize the concept of the kingdom of God over the emphasis on the individual.

32. Busch, Karl Barth and the Pietists, 84.

has made on them because of their election. Such a system of ethics, wholly dependent on divine revelation, appears to many outside of Christianity, as well as within it, as too sectarian. Barth claims the alternate is even worse, a system of ethics rooted in human capacities that is blind to the power of sin:

> For man is not content simply to be the answer to this question by the grace of God. He wants to be like God. He wants to know of himself (as God does) what is good and evil. He therefore wants to give this answer himself and of himself. So, then, as a result and in prolongation of the fall, we have "ethics," or, rather, the multifarious ethical systems, the attempted human answers to the ethical question. ... The grace of God protests against all man-made ethics as such. But it protests positively. It does not only say No to man. It also says Yes. But it does so by completing its own answer to the ethical problem in active refutation, conquest and destruction of all human answers to it.[33]

Barth's rejection of anthropocentric ethics echoes his denunciation of anthropocentric religion in R2, except that here in *CD* II/2, his Christology is more robust. Whereas R2 raises questions about character in the Christian life, due to its emphasis on God's spontaneous and radical disruption of our existence, *CD* II/2 restores the underpinnings necessary for this enduring character. These underpinnings come not from human initiative but rather from God's electing decision to be a God for us in Jesus Christ. The driving actor shifts from the Holy Spirit in R2 to the Son of God in *CD* II/2. In R2, Barth describes the Christian life as a series of encounters with the Holy Spirit in which faithfulness does not dwell within us but is evoked through our response to the Holy Spirit's intervention. The problem with this way of thinking, from a human point of view, is that it limits moral decision making to ad hoc obedience. In contrast, Barth's doctrine of election in the first half of *CD* II/2 describes God's advocacy on our behalf differently. As witnessed to in Scripture through the life, death, and resurrection of Jesus Christ, this advocacy is traced back to God's determination, logically prior to creation, to be God for us.

The Christian life thus has an enduring basis rooted in God's eternal commitment to advocacy. Grace's manifestation in our lives, through faith, is still

---

33. *CD* II/2, 517.

largely eschatological. We get glimpses here and there of what it looks like, but there is no enduring, or gradual, increase in grace in our lives.[34] Grace is not something in us but a relationship with Christ.[35] God remains free to act when and where God sees fit. Nonetheless, Christian action is truly human action. Barth is clear that there is no synergy, no secret power of the Holy Spirit that boosts our decision making in discerning the commands of God and enacting them. The relationship between God and us mirrors that found in Christ. In other words, the relationship between Christ's divine and human natures, laid out at the ecumenical Council of Chalcedon, provides the framework for Barth's understanding of how human beings respond to God's commands. In Christ, the relationship is asymmetric; the Word of God incarnate dictates the terms of hypostatic union, but the humanity of Christ is real. And just as the relationship between divinity and humanity perdures through time in Christ, the relationship that God establishes with humankind also has a continuous, as well as a disruptive, influence. The eschatological impact of this relationship can only be hinted at in this life, but it is felt nonetheless.[36]

While Barth's doctrine of election provides key contours for Barth's moral theology, his doctrine of reconciliation, covered extensively in CD IV, provides a fuller picture. The ethical sections at the end of this volume are incomplete. Barth felt that only his treatment of baptism was ready for publication, and he died before it was published. This work has still not received the attention it deserves, perhaps because it was written so late in Barth's career.[37]

---

34. For an extended discussion of what this looks like within the Christian community, see Barth's treatment of church witness in CD IV/3.2 §72.4, 830–901.

35. See Adam Neder, *Participation in Christ* (Louisville: Westminster John Knox, 2009).

36. See George Hunsinger's explanation of how the Chalcedon Definition impacts Barth's thinking in *How to Read Karl Barth* (New York: Oxford University Press, 1991), 185–224. For an explanation of how this pattern may support a virtue ethic inspired by Barth's theology, see my book, *Reformed Virtue After Barth* (Louisville: Westminster John Knox, 2014), 83–90. Paul Nimmo has challenged Hunsinger's use of the Chalcedonian Definition, observing that Barth never employs the term "Chalcedonian" when explicating the relationship between divine action and human action; see Nimmo, "Karl Barth and the Concursus Dei—a Chalcedonianism too far?," *International Journal of Systematic Theology* 9, no. 1 (January 2007): 58–72.

37. Notable exceptions include Eberhard Jüngel, "Karl Barths Lehre von der Taufe: Ein Hinweis auf ihre Probleme," in *Barth-Studien* (Zürich: Benziger, 1982), 246–90; John Webster, *Barth's Ethics of Reconciliation* (Cambridge: Cambridge University Press, 1995); and W. Travis McMaken, *The Sign of the Gospel* (Minneapolis: Fortress, 2013). Jüngel's essay traces the development of Barth's views on baptism from 1943 on, making clear that Barth's final views were consonant with earlier theological commitments. Webster's book is particularly helpful for understanding the ethical implications of Barth's stance on baptism. McMaken's monograph

However, Barth's position on baptism is consistent with his mature theology; it is also not a new position but reflects a shift begun years before. CD IV/4 addresses key questions raised by Barth's doctrines of election and reconciliation: What does it mean for the church that its role is primarily that of witness, that the work of reconciliation between God and us was completed in Jesus Christ, and that the salvation of humankind rests solely on that work and not on anything the church has to contribute? Is Christian ethics really inconsequential, at least in light of Barth's *ordo salutis*? And what about the role of the Holy Spirit? Is the Spirit relegated to the role of witness as well, for the same reasons?[38]

Although Barth recognizes the validity of infant baptism in CD IV/4, he argues against its practice for profoundly ethical reasons. Baptism marks the beginning of the Christian life. Granted, God's electing grace manifested in Jesus Christ precedes all things, yet a genuine and free human response to God's grace is also necessary. Barth writes,

> Baptism is the first step of the way of a human life which is shaped and stamped by looking to Jesus Christ. It is the first step which the baptized person who has come to see Jesus Christ takes along with the community. It is also the first step which the community, which is already on that way, takes along with the one baptized. In baptism a human life comes into the life of the community.[39]

Here Barth is emphasizing the proper relationship between the individual baptized and the church community that supports the baptism. That community cannot stand in for the individual, as parents and sponsors do in infant

---

provides a thorough review of the literature on the subject to date. Most recently, McMaken has coined the term "paradoxical identity" to characterize the relationship between divine and human action in Barth's theology of baptism. This term refers primarily to the identity of Jesus Christ, who is at the same time fully God and fully human. The history of the church and its witness through the Holy Spirit shares the same paradoxical pattern as that of the history of Jesus Christ. See McMaken, "Definitive, Defective or Deft? Reassessing Barth's Doctrine of Baptism in Church Dogmatics IV/4," *International Journal of Systematic Theology* 17, no. 1 (January 2015): 89–114.

38. See Stanley Hauerwas's criticism of Barth's ecclesiology, *With the Grain of the Universe: The Church's Witness and Natural Theology* (Grand Rapids: Baker Academic, 2013), 193. Hauerwas is criticizing a comment that Barth makes in CD IV/3.2, 826, in which Barth states that the world would "not necessarily be lost" without the church. Hauerwas argues that it would. For a critical examination of Barth's pneumatology, see Robert Jenson, "You Wonder Where the Spirit Went," *Pro Ecclesia* 2, no. 3 (1993): 296–304.

39. CD IV/4, 149.

baptism. Instead, individuals must make the first step themselves. But they do not take that first step alone; without communal support, such a step is impossible. One cannot baptize oneself.

Barth compares his position on infant baptism with that of the Genevan Reformer John Calvin. Calvin emphasizes continuities between the Abrahamic and Mosaic covenants of the Old Testament and the new covenant that Jesus proclaims at the Lord's Supper. While the mode of dispensing that covenant is different (circumcision in the Old Testament, baptism in the New), the material basis of that covenant is the same.[40] Based on the unity of this covenant, Calvin argues that the sacrament of infant baptism serves the same function as circumcision for the nation of Israel. Both represent regeneration, signs of God's favor, forgiveness of sins, and eternal life.[41] And if circumcision takes place on the eighth day after birth, a precedent has been set for Christian baptism of newborn infants.

Barth's objection is two-fold. First, Calvin does not take seriously enough the different makeup of the Israelite community, which is biologically related, from that of the Christian community, which is not. Quoting John 1:12–13 to describe the Christian community, Barth writes, "Those who join it are 'born, not of blood, nor of the will of the flesh, nor of the will of man, but of God.'"[42] Second, and more fundamental to his theology, Barth objects to using covenant as the overarching framework within which to understand baptism. Instead, baptismal practice is rooted in God's election of Jesus Christ. Calvin's argument is historical: God establishes a covenant with Abraham that serves not only as the basis for God's relations with Israel but also as the covenant with all the nations. The Old Testament explores in depth God's relations with Israel; the New Testament covers both the completion of God's covenant with Israel and the extension of that covenant to all the nations. Sacraments such as baptism thus indicate the sign of God's covenantal grace rooted in the Abrahamic covenant. In Barth's schema, the basis for baptism is found logically prior to God's decision to create, in God's decision to be a God for us, demonstrated in the incarnate Jesus Christ. Barth reads the Old Testament with this doctrine of election in mind, whereas Calvin reads the covenantal

---

40. John Calvin, *Institutes of the Christian Religion*, ed. John T. McNeill, trans. Ford Lewis Battles, Library of Christian Classics 20 (Philadelphia: Westminster, 1960), 2.10.2.

41. Calvin, *Institutes*, 4.16.4.

42. *CD* IV/4, 178.

promises of the New Testament in light of the Old Testament Abrahamic covenant. For Barth, the Abrahamic covenant is merely the consequence of a commitment that God made earlier. His claim is not that the incarnation of Jesus Christ somehow took place prior to creation but that God's decision to become incarnate was made logically prior to creation.[43]

At first glance, then, Barth's doctrine of election would seem to point backward to God's original decision to be for us. Yet on further review, there is an eschatological thrust to Barth's ethics. The Christian witness that is the church's defining ethical task has an important forward dimension to it. For embedded in Barth's rejection of the practice of infant baptism is the question of our ultimate identity. The church is not a biological entity. Instead, we are the adopted children of God. Our confession of faith is our recognition of our already adopted status. But we need individually to claim it as such; until we do, we live under the false pretense that our true nature will not one day be fully determined by grace.

CONCLUSION

Given the respective theological commitments of Edwards and Barth, what are the possibilities for human action? What moral responsibilities are entailed? For Edwards, the ethical life consists in virtue. To a limited extent, all human beings participate in this virtue insofar as they love others. True virtue depends on a spiritual sense that God freely bestows on some, but not all. Those who are chosen participate in a covenant of grace, which though rooted in God's freely given grace, nevertheless requires high moral standards. In determining full membership, and thus access to the sacraments, the church is tasked with discerning true piety in its members. Edwards writes in *Humble Inquiry*, "I say 'in the eye of the church's Christian judgment,' because 'tis properly a visibility to the eye of the public charity, and not of a private judgment, that gives a person a right to be received as a visible saint by the public."[44] Such a judgment was based on a public and heart-felt profession of faith in the triune God, as well as enough evidence of Christian piety in one's everyday life as to make genuine faith probable.

---

43. More precisely, Barth's position is a Christologically modified supralapsarian one. See chapter three of McMaken, *The Sign of the Gospel*.

44. *WJE* 12:178–79. See also Oliver Crisp, "Jonathan Edwards and the Closing of the Table: Must the Eucharist be Open to All?," *Ecclesiology* 5, no. 1 (2009): 48–68.

Edwards was so convinced of this responsibility of the church, which ultimately fell on his shoulders, that he was willing to give up his leadership
position at Northampton to defend it.

In what does such piety consist? Love of neighbor is a prerequisite, particularly toward those who are poor. Such love involves an inward feeling of
pity that leads to concrete actions taken to relieve their suffering.[45] These
acts should be not sporadic but the result of a settled disposition; and they
should be not solitary but communal. Edwards even goes so far as to say
that the measure of Christian piety in a community can be ascertained by
the number of its poor.[46] While such acts are necessary for determining
true piety, they are not sufficient. True Christian piety must be animated by
saving grace; moral sincerity alone cannot comprise true godliness.[47] Even
though true virtue is possible only in the saints, Edwards does allow for some
semblance of pagan or civic virtue. God has bestowed in all humankind a
moral sense. When a person acts immorally, this sense makes him aware
of an inconsistency between his true self and his actions. This moral sense
is limited by self-interest, but it may nonetheless expand to a wide circle of
friends, family, work relations, and one's immediate community.[48]

Barth, like Edwards, recognizes God's covenantal relationship with us,
but unlike Edwards, he stresses God's unconditional claim on us rather than
the covenantal requirements that claim imposes on us. Barth's objections
to pietism, expressed throughout his career, reflect his concern that God's
grace is obscured when attention is focused on its effects in a person's life
rather than on its source. Regarding sanctification, Barth embraced Luther's
dictum, *simul iustus et peccator*. That is, he affirmed with Luther that one
remained totally in sin while at the same time completely justified by God. Yet
our justification is not merely forensic if we understand it eschatologically.
God's determination to be for us is unconditional and eternal; in contrast,
our determination to sin is conditional and time sensitive. In the eschaton,

---

45. *WJE* 2:355.

46. See Gerald R. McDermott, "Poverty, Patriotism, and National Covenant," *Journal of
Religious Ethics* 31, no. 2 (2003): 235. McDermott is referencing a sermon Edwards preached in
1743 on Malachi 3:10–11.

47. *WJE* 12:185, 230.

48. For further explanation, see Nolan, *Reformed Virtue After Barth*, 29–30.

all that will remain is who we are as claimed by God; that claim on us challenges and encourages us to live into a life of faith today.[49]

Barth's emphasis on God's command would seem to limit the scope of human participation in God's plan of redemption, thus crippling Barth's ethics. However, as Barth's mature stance on baptism attests, human freedom is essential to his theology. On the one hand, God the Holy Spirit cannot be coerced by a human act (baptism by water); on the other hand, God's act of baptism by the Spirit is properly correlated with a human response (baptism by water). One way to think of this relationship between God and us is as a dance in which God is both the choreographer and our lead partner. In the life to come, we will have learned the music and the dance by heart. But for the time being, all we know are two things: God has chosen irrevocably to be our partner despite our having two left feet, and God is leading us even now into our next responsive move. Interestingly, Barth's characterization of God as the electing God leaves open the possibility that God elects all human beings to participate in this dance.[50] While God would never coerce those waiting on the fringes of the dance floor to participate, God hopes that one day they will respond to the invitation to join the dance.[51]

---

49. See Bruce McCormack, "What's at Stake?" in *Justification: What's at Stake in the Current Debates*, ed. Mark Husbands and Daniel J. Treier (Downers Grove, IL: InterVarsity, 2004), 81–117, especially 109.

50. See Nolan, *Reformed Virtue After Barth*, 34.

51. I am grateful to W. Travis McMaken for his comments on an earlier draft of this chapter.

13

—

CHURCH

Matt Jenson

The twentieth century has been called "the century of the church."[1] Yet despite, or perhaps because of, the minute and expansive attention paid to ecclesial matters, too often ecclesiology has been unmoored and set adrift from its dogmatic location in the triune economy. The church has been naturalized, treated as a mere thing among things, a society that can be investigated exhaustively with the tools of social science, psychology, management, critical theory, and cultural analysis. The church is a human institution, made up of human agents. Perhaps it, too, like other corporations (at least, legally speaking, in the United States) is a "person," though this, too, is a natural phenomenon.

There is more to be said, to be sure. Throughout the twentieth century and in this new century now twenty years old, Christians have reminded us that the church finds its source and end in the triune God, the God who calls, redeems, and perfects his people, the God and the Lamb around whom the church gathers and worships in the power of the Spirit. Figures as disparate as Henri de Lubac, Jürgen Moltmann, and, more recently, John Webster make this point, as have Vatican II, the century-long charismatic renewal movement, and the missionary movement, with its laser-like focus on the fellowship of all who have entered into a saving relationship with Jesus Christ.

Still, this triune focus can easily blur, or shift into the background, present only atmospherically, like the setting of a picture in the iPhone's "portrait"

---

1. Much of this article appeared previously in Matt Jenson, "'Where the Spirit of the Lord is, there is freedom': Barth on Ecclesial Agency," *Pro Ecclesia* 24, no. 4 (2015): 517-37. Used by kind permission of *Pro Ecclesia*.

mode. The *real* subject, we might think, is the church. Nor does denomina-
tional or ideological alignment matter much here: church planters, activists,
intentional communitarians, and mega-ministers can all become so busy
with the church that they neglect the one thing needful: adoring acknowledgment of her Lord. Barth and Edwards both offer a stiff tonic to such eccle-
siologically torpid souls, appealing to the triune God as Lord in and over the
church. In what follows, I will consider chiefly how Barth construes the relation between divine and human action in answering the question, "Who is
the subject of ecclesial action?" It will be left to Edwards to correct Barth on
a pneumatological point of some significance.

THE PRIORITY OF DIVINE ACTION

No one could accuse Barth of neglecting the work of the triune God in ecclesiology—or any doctrine, for that matter. True to the genius of Reformed
theology, he begins with divine action, preferring to take up the challenge of
how to account for meaningful human action rather than first emphasizing
human action and anxiously trying to fit God in here and there. The church
is God's creation, and her life and worship take their bearings from him as
he reveals himself in Christ. In the upbuilding of the Christian community,
"it is God Himself who is primarily at work: not merely in the totality but
in all the details; not merely in the inauguration but in the completion; not
merely in the background but in the foreground."[2]

> Karl Barth's dogmatics is a theology of the Second Article of the
> Creed, which can be faithfully stated only with the help of the First
> Commandment. The major points within Barth's theology—not all of
> them but certainly the essential ones—rise out of this partnership of
> the First Commandment with the Second Article.[3]

Gerhard Sauter's programmatic comment obtains in ecclesiology, too, in
which Jesus is the present and living Lord by whose Spirit the church is
empowered to witness in the world. The church in itself can do no such thing.
Blessed are the churches who are poor in spirit, Barth might say, for they see

---

2. *CD* IV/2, 632, 633.

3. Gerhard Sauter, *Eschatological Rationality: Theological Issues in Focus* (Grand Rapids: Baker,
1996), 131.

things as they are; and so, they pray. Because the church lives only as it is united to Christ and empowered by the Spirit, "[t]he community is constituted as it prays."[4] Here we might amend Sauter's comment in Barth's own words, articulating the first commandment also with reference to the *third* article. "Utter the words, '*Veni creator spiritus!*', which is for now, according to Romans 8, more hopeful than triumphant, as if one already had it. Once you have heard this sigh, you have been introduced to 'my theology.' "[5] "In the longing, in the crying for the Creator Spirit, which will once again blow across even this field, full of dry bones, we will meet up with the Fathers, whose legacy we have not yet earned fully enough to own."[6]

This much—that the church lives, moves and has its being in the triune God—should be relatively uncontroversial. It is far more difficult to describe faithfully how divine and human action are coordinated in the life of the church. Next, I will consider the shape of freedom in the life of the church, closely following Barth's patterns of speech to provide a nuanced account of ecclesial agency, along the way addressing and, where possible, clarifying questions regarding the adequacy of Barth's ecclesiology.

THE BODY OF CHRIST

We have to qualify any judgments about Barth's ecclesiology for two reasons. First, in the fragment of the ethics of reconciliation that he drafted to conclude volume IV of *Church Dogmatics*, he rejected infant baptism outright and strongly distinguished baptism in the Spirit from water baptism. This move surprised many, and it leaves the trajectory of his ecclesiology open to question. Second, and more significant, is the absence of Volume V of the *Dogmatics*, the doctrine of redemption, in which Barth would have taken up the question of eschatology directly and privileged the role of the Spirit.

With that said, Barth wrote an extensive account of the work of Christ by the power of the Spirit in the church as part of the subjective aspect of reconciliation. In each of the parts of *CD* IV, he appeals to the Pauline image of the church as the body of Christ. In some ways, it is surprising that the man who proclaimed the "infinite qualitative distinction" between

---

4. *CD* IV/2, 705.

5. Barth, *The Word of God and Theology*, trans. Amy Marga (New York: T&T Clark, 2011), 128.

6. Barth, *The Word of God and Theology*, 237.

God and humanity in his commentary on Romans would in maturity make so much of an organic image. Admittedly, it is a major New Testament image, but hardly the only one at Barth's disposal; and if anything, Barth's deployment of "body of Christ" eclipses the other images of the church in the New Testament.[7]

"Body of Christ" emphasizes at once the identification of Christ with the church and his agency within the church. It allows Barth to articulate the ever-present "whence" of the church. "As the *unus Christus, solus* yet also *totus*, He is the basis and secret of its existence."[8] Christ is *one*; he and he alone is this one; yet he is not alone but with his people. Barth does not shrink from the implications of this for the church, writing that "the being of the community is a predicate or dimension of the being of Jesus Christ Himself. ... For He does not exist without it. He alone is who and what He is. But He is not alone as who and what He is. He is it for Himself, yet not only for Himself, but also with His own."[9]

While the body belongs to Christ, however, Christ does not belong to the body—or if he does, only dialectically so. Christ has covenanted to be ever with his body, but he is not thereby dependent on it.[10] "Jesus Christ is the community." However,

> the statement cannot be reversed. It is a christological statement, and only as such an ecclesiological. The community is not Jesus Christ. ... There can be no thought of the being of Jesus Christ enclosed in that of His community, or exhausted by it, as though it were a kind of predicate of this being. The truth is the very opposite. The being of the community is exhausted and enclosed in His.[11]

Christ is Lord, the head of the church (Eph 5:23), its cornerstone (1 Pet 2:6) and the risen one who walks among the churches addressing them (Rev 1:12–13).

---

7. See Paul S. Minear, *Images of the Church in the New Testament* (Louisville: Westminster John Knox, 2005). Minear identifies the people of God, the new creation, the fellowship in faith, and the body of Christ as major New Testament images.

8. *CD* IV/3.2, 758.

9. *CD* IV/3.2, 754.

10. *CD* IV/2, 655.

11. *CD* IV/2, 655.

What does this mean for ecclesial agency? If the church's being is tied so closely to Christ's, with him as head of his body, can the church really be said properly to act? On the one hand, "He is the primary and proper Subject acting in and with the community."[12] "Primary" might allow for "secondary," though "proper" seems to shove any other subjectivity to the margin as alien to the church's true subjectivity in Christ. On the other hand, "even if only in faith and not in sight, to say 'Christ' is to say 'Christ and His own'—Christ in and with His fullness, which is His community. As His community (His body), this cannot be merely a passive object or spectator of its upbuilding."[13] The church, we might say, is a construction crew in its own building. Barth's comment is borne out in long sections discussing the church in action, praying, serving, and witnessing to its Lord.

The one thing the church does *not* do, however, is replace its Lord or act *in loco Christus*.[14] Barth's vigilance surpasses even that of Luther, who excoriated a popish temptation to act as the vicar of an absent Christ rather than the servant of a present Christ.[15] The body of Christ language, for Barth, secures the presence and lordship of Christ as head over his body as much as it identifies Christ with his own.[16] It evokes a differentiated, ordered unity in which "the church cannot be said to incarnate Christ or continue him because Christ is always the active agent of his own presence."[17] The church may not and need not "incarnate" Christ; it is already a present form of the risen Lord who was conceived by the Holy Spirit and born of the virgin Mary. Thus "it is not Christ, nor a second Christ, nor a kind of extension of the one Christ. The supreme and final thing to be said of it …

---

12. *CD* IV/3.2, 791.

13. *CD* IV/2, 634.

14. Barth notes the importance of ordering the church so that "there is place for His rule." *CD* IV/1, 723.

15. Martin Luther, "An Open Letter to Leo X," in *The Freedom of a Christian*, in *Martin Luther's Basic Theological Writings*, ed. Timothy F. Lull, 2nd ed (Minneapolis: Augsburg Fortress, 2005), 392.

16. "Yahweh lives and will live in solidarity, but not in identity, with Israel. The same holds true for Jesus Christ, the word and deed of God, with regard to His community. … The head does not become the body and the body does not become the head." Barth, *The Humanity of God*, trans. John Newton Thomas and Thomas Wieser (Louisville: Westminster John Knox, 1960), 74-75.

17. Christopher R. J. Holmes, "The Church and the Presence of Christ: Defending Actualist Ecclesiology," *Pro Ecclesia* 21, no. 3 (2012): 272.

is quite simply that it is His body, His earthly-historical form of existence."[18] The church is not a sacrament that makes Christ present but the form in which he presents himself as Lord of all.

Ian McFarland criticizes Barth for "a one-sided development of this image, in which 'body' is viewed primarily in opposition to 'head' rather than being interpreted as an integrated whole composed of head and members."[19] This reflects Barth's jealousy for divine freedom, his concern to speak of the church in such a way that God always remains subject and never object. If, as Robert Jenson supposes, one's body is one's availability for another, Barth constantly reminds his readers that Christ is present as Lord even in his body.[20] He is available only as he actively *makes* himself available. McFarland suggests that "while bodies always mark the objective presence of the one embodied (the third-person dimension), they do not become means by which such an entity is known in the second person apart from some deliberate act of self-disclosure on her or his part."[21] We can know and love Christ in his body, which is the church, only if he continues to make himself known and offer himself in love.

McFarland concludes that "the ecclesiological figure of the body suggests a relation to Christ and community that is basically Chalcedonian in form."[22] But two qualifications are necessary. First, Christ and the church do *not* constitute one person.[23] Second, the nature of sin involves the church in an antagonistic relation with God—one of at least attempted "division" and "separation"—wherein ecclesial agency challenges divine agency.[24] Call this the body in revolt. In any case, despite any flaws in Barth's treatment of the body of Christ, he agrees with McFarland's conclusion. The *totus Christus*, head and members, are united by the Spirit. "He is the One who constitutes

18. *CD* IV/3.2, 729.

19. Ian A. McFarland, "The Body of Christ: Rethinking a Classic Ecclesiological Model," *International Journal of Systematic Theology* 7, no. 3 (July 2005): 231.

20. Robert W. Jenson, *The Triune God*, vol. 1 of *Systematic Theology* (New York: Oxford University Press, 1997), 205. Applying this to the question at hand, Jenson writes that "the entity rightly called the body of Christ is whatever object it is that is Christ's availability to us as subjects; by the promise of Christ, this object is the bread and cup and the gathering of the church around them. *There* is where creatures can locate him, to respond to his word to them."

21. McFarland, "The Body of Christ," 243.

22. McFarland, "The Body of Christ," 244.

23. A point McFarland acknowledges and Fred Sanders underscored for me in conversation.

24. Ironically, then, by invoking Chalcedonian logic, McFarland steers into the swamp where he locates Barth, in which the "real" church is something other than the sinful church.

and guarantees the unity of the *totus Christus*."[25] Notice how closely this unity parallels the language of Chalcedon, as Barth describes the Spirit's work "to bring and to hold them together, not to identify, intermingle nor confound them, not to change the one into the other nor to merge the one into the other, but to co-ordinate them, to make them parallel, to bring them into harmony and therefore to bind them into a true unity."[26]

We turn now to consider the Spirit in relation to the church.

THE SPIRIT OF FREEDOM

The first thing to know about the Spirit is that he is God. He is not the spirit of the *Volk*, nor is he a part—even the best part—of humanity. "He makes man free, but He Himself remains free in relation to him: the Spirit of the Lord."[27] Here Barth marks out the territory of his pneumatology. In brief, the Holy Spirit is the Spirit of God and no other spirit. The Spirit is and ever remains free as God is free. The Spirit liberates humanity as the one who loves in freedom. And throughout, the Spirit is to be understood in closest proximity to Christ the Lord.

Too often, we presuppose the Spirit, pretending he is at our disposal.[28] That is, we assume that God's ways are our ways. We conscript the Holy One for our projects and invoke his name for our agendas, thereby taking it in vain. Recall Sauter's point about the critical role the first commandment plays in Barth's theology, something that can be detected in his dismay over the defection of his liberal theology teachers, in his fiery Romans commentary, in his suspicion of pietism and Roman Catholicism, and in his protests against Nazism in the Barmen Declaration. In one way or another, each of these sought to domesticate the Holy Spirit.

> In such a situation, theology forgets that the wind of the Spirit blows where it wills. The presence and action of the Spirit are the grace of God who is always free, always superior, always giving himself undeservedly and without reservation. But theology now supposes it can deal with the Spirit as though it had hired him or even attained

---

25. *CD* IV/3.2, 760.

26. *CD* IV/3.2, 761.

27. *CD* IV/1, 646.

28. Barth, *Evangelical Theology: An Introduction*, trans. Grover Foley (Grand Rapids: Eerdmans, 1963), 57–58.

possession of him. It imagines that he is a power of nature that can be discovered, harnessed, and put to use like water, fire, electricity, or atomic energy. ... The Spirit is thought to be one whom it knows and over whom it disposes. But a presupposed spirit is certainly not the Holy Spirit.[29]

Because we cannot presuppose the Holy Spirit, because the Holy Spirit is not *our* spirit, the church must "never neglect at any stage or at any turn of the way" to pray, "*Veni, Creator Spiritus!*"[30] To invoke divine action is to invoke divine freedom as the shape of that action and human freedom as its goal.[31] The God of the covenant exercises his freedom in love; and so his freedom is never wanton or capricious but always a freedom for others.[32]

> Where the Spirit of the Lord is, there is freedom. If we wish to para-phrase the mystery of the Holy Spirit it is best to choose this concept. To receive the Spirit, to have the Spirit, to live in the Spirit means being set free and being permitted to live in freedom.[33]

Still, Barth will not let us forget that in the church, we "do not 'have' this freedom; it is again and again given to us by God."[34] Neither the Spirit nor the freedom he brings can be presupposed. And so prayer remains the church's posture throughout its life, during which

> Christians live spiritually as and to the extent that they live *ec*-centrically. What are they in and of themselves but poor, weak, and foolish sinners who have fallen victim to death? They can only look beyond themselves, clinging to God himself, and to God only in Jesus

---

29. Barth, *Evangelical Theology: An Introduction*, 57–58.

30. *CD* IV/3.2, 832.

31. John Webster refers to "the combination of a very powerful doctrine of God's perfection and freedom with an emphasis upon the calling of humankind to action in creaturely time (success in interpreting Barth's theology as a whole depends in part on attending to the variations which he offers on this theme)." Webster, *Barth's Earlier Theology* (New York: T&T Clark, 2005), 35.

32. This is true within the triune life, as Father and Son are free for one another in the power of the Spirit, and it is true in the Trinity's moving outward to creation. Note the dialectical pairing of freedom and love, central to Barth's treatment of the divine perfections in his doctrine of God (see *CD* II/1).

33. Barth, *Dogmatics in Outline*, trans. G. T. Thomson (London: SCM, 1949), 138.

34. Barth, *Dogmatics in Outline*, 139.

Christ, and this only as they are freed to do so, and continually freed to do so, by the Holy Spirit.[35]

The Spirit is God in us, awakening and sustaining faithfulness in response to God's faithfulness to us in Christ.[36] "If this twofold disclosure takes place, the opening up of the fact and the opening up of the human subject to receive it, it does so in the event of the speaking of the Holy Spirit—the Spirit who is God Himself—to the human spirit. ... He is the *doctor veritatis*."[37] The eloquent Spirit "acts and works in the concrete form of the power and truth of their word"—that is, the word of the apostles in Scripture—and just so leads and guides his people into the truth.[38] Keeping in mind the tightly knit relation between revelation and reconciliation in Barth's theology,[39] we find him acknowledging the Spirit as the one who "creates the Christian community."[40]

The Spirit is God as he takes responsibility for humanity's response from the side of humanity.[41] "He is God intervening and acting for man, addressing Himself to him, in such a way that He says Yes to Himself and this makes possible and necessary man's human Yes to Him."[42] In making possible and necessary our "Yes" to God in Christ, the Spirit establishes fellowship between Christ and his church.[43] The Spirit moves the church to remember the crucified and risen One in her midst; he also spurs her on to the day of Jesus' coming, being himself her momentum. He is "the *forward* which majestically awakens, enlightens, leads, pushes, and impels, which God has spoken in the resurrection of Jesus from the dead."[44] The

---

35. Barth, *The Christian Life: Church Dogmatics* IV/4, *Lecture Fragments*, trans. Geoffrey Bromiley (Grand Rapids: Eerdmans, 1981), 94.

36. *CD* IV/2, 126.

37. *CD* IV/2, 126.

38. *CD* IV/1, 718. "Scripture upholds the community." *CD* IV/2, 674. "As the One whom it attests verifies its witness, it is He who primarily and properly upholds the Church. He verifies Scripture simply by the fact that He is its content; that as it is read and heard He Himself is present to speak and act as the living Lord of the Church." *CD* IV/2, 675.

39. George Hunsinger, "The Mediator of Communion: Karl Barth's Doctrine of the Holy Spirit," in *The Cambridge Companion to Karl Barth*, ed. John Webster (Cambridge: Cambridge University Press, 2000), 194n17.

40. *CD* IV/2, 126.

41. *CD* IV/1, 645.

42. *CD* IV/1, 646.

43. *CD* IV/2, 323.

44. Barth, *The Christian Life*, 256.

Spirit provokes the people of God toward that final day, praying with the Bride, "*Maranatha. Come, Lord Jesus!*"

THE SPIRIT OF THE LORD

The Holy Spirit is none other than the Spirit of the Lord Jesus Christ.[45] Even if "the New Testament does not describe the Holy Spirit as consistently as we might at first sight expect as the Spirit of Jesus Christ,"[46] it is nevertheless true that "the only content of the Holy Spirit is Jesus."[47] The Spirit attests Christ, and "He actually spends Himself in His attestation." That is precisely what makes him holy, and *this* Spirit rather than another—"the fact that He does not bear witness to Himself."[48] Again, so closely does Barth identify Christ and the Spirit that he will also call the Spirit "the power in which Jesus Christ attests Himself, attests Himself effectively, creating in man response and obedience."[49] But his task is "more than a mere indication of Jesus. ... Where the man Jesus attests Himself in the power of the Spirit of God, He makes Himself present."[50]

Barth identifies the perennial pneumatological problem:

> The Holy Spirit, the Spirit of Christ, is, so to speak, the Christ heard, accepted, obeyed by us. ... The Holy Spirit is not an increase of what we were given in Christ, but he is the gift itself, actual and living.
>
> Here we are perhaps confronted with the most important mistake, and possibly the only one that is made in every age, with respect to the Holy Spirit. Time and again there are those who always fall into the error of inevitably considering the Holy Spirit as something new and peculiar beside the sole truth of faith and the life of faith. ... But

---

45. *CD* IV/2, 332, 654. Barth is aware of a fourfold sense of the Spirit as the Spirit of Jesus Christ in the New Testament: "As the Spirit who is first the Spirit of the man Jesus Himself; who proceeds from Him and only from Him; who witnesses to Him and only to Him; and in whom we know ourselves in this man and may therefore be with Him." Or, more briefly: "The Spirit of this man—His own Spirit, who proceeds from Him and attests Him and unites other men with Him—is the Spirit of God the Son." *CD* IV/2, 347.

46. *CD* IV/2, 332.

47. *CD* IV/2, 654.

48. *CD* IV/2, 347.

49. *CD* IV/1, 647, 748.

50. *CD* IV/2, 654.

the Holy Spirit distinguishes himself from any other spirit by his absolute identity with the person and work of Christ. [51]

To consider the Holy Spirit as something new would be to consider it outside the realm of Christ. But as God has revealed himself perfectly in Christ, that would be to leave the realm of theology for the realm of anthropology.[52]

One final comment about the way in which Barth unites the work of Son and Spirit in the economy of salvation is in order. George Hunsinger notes that one can speak either of the Spirit making Christ present or of Christ making himself present through the Spirit. While Barth uses the second form in CD IV, "that should not be taken to imply that he holds a merely non-agential view of the Spirit." Instead, Barth's Christocentric doctrine of reconciliation renders that the appropriate form. The other, "more agential form (which recurs throughout the dogmatics)" might have appeared again in the doctrine of redemption.[53] That may have been so. Still, there is a certain stiffness of form in Barth's constant description of divine action in the church in terms of Jesus' acting by the Spirit, when often more naturally biblical patterns of speech would turn to the Spirit as agent—certainly doing things "in Christ," "through Christ," "for the sake of Christ." Barth strains the language in an effort to ensure that the Spirit's work remains tethered to Christ's. That in itself is a laudable aim, but in CD IV, Barth's relentless recourse to Christ's subjectivity becomes something of a linguistic tic that limits Barth in his treatment of the breadth of the Spirit's work in freeing the church for worship and witness—even if Ben Rhodes is right to suggest that "Barth believes this is a necessary critical claim that does not entail impersonality, inequality, or subordination."[54]

---

51. Barth, *The Faith of the Church: A Commentary on The Apostles' Creed according to Calvin's Catechism*, trans. Gabriel Vahanian (New York: Living Age Books, 1958), 128–29.

52. Barth, *The Theology of Schleiermacher*, trans. Geoffrey W. Bromiley (Grand Rapids: Eerdmans, 1982), 279. This migration of pneumatology from theology to a godless anthropology is just what Barth suspected Schleiermacher to have accomplished.

53. Hunsinger, "The Mediator of Communion," 192–93n5. Hunsinger cites W. Krusche's deployment of this distinction in his *Das Wirken des Heiligen Geistes nach Calvin* (Goettingen: Vandenhoeck & Ruprecht, 1957), 146–51.

54. Ben Rhodes, "The Spirit of Fellowship: Karl Barth's Pneumatology and Doctrine of Sanctification" (PhD diss., University of Aberdeen, 2012), 219.

Furthermore, Barth is convinced that salvation history has been completed in the death and resurrection in Christ in such a way as to raise the question of whether there is anything left for the Spirit to do.[55] It is not that Barth has nothing to say about this time between the advents. The "time of the community" is a time in which to shout a grateful "Yes!" to the Word of God in Christ.

> God will not allow His last Word to be fully spoken or the consummation determined and accomplished and proclaimed by Him to take place in its final form until He has first heard a human response to it, a human Yes; until His grace has found its correspondence in a voice of human thanks from the depths of the world reconciled with Himself; until here and now, before the dawning of His eternal Sabbath, He has received praise from the heart of His human creation.[56]

There are two difficulties here. First, Barth has already argued beautifully that the one, decisive human "Yes" has already been spoken in the history of Jesus Christ, his way into the far country and his homecoming. Grace *has* found its correspondence in gratitude—the gratitude of Jesus Christ. Barth might insist on the fittingness of a wider human response, and rightly so; but it is difficult to discern the reason for it. Barth seems perplexed about the time of the church: "God is still at work as its Lord. Strangely enough, for what more can God will and work when everything has already been accomplished?"[57] Barth neglects a key aspect of the time of the church as a time to repent and believe the gospel. The time of the church is the time of divine patience.[58] It is not a time for him but one for us, and one under the threat of judgment; or, differently put, it is a time for the Spirit in particular, in which the Spirit leads people to repentance. "The Lord is not slow to fulfill his promise as some count slowness, but is patient toward you, not wishing

---

55. Joseph Mangina comes away "with the uneasy feeling that Barth has left precious little for the Holy Spirit to accomplish. The Spirit illuminates with the powerful, self-involving knowledge of Jesus Christ; but does its activity *take up time and space* in the created order?" "Bearing the Marks of Jesus: The Church in the Economy of Salvation in Barth and Hauerwas," *Scottish Journal of Theology* 52, no. 3 (1999): 300.

56. *CD* IV/1, 737.

57. *CD* IV/1, 736, though see the more salutary comments at 737–79.

58. This neglect is strange, given the prominence of patience among God's perfections. *CD* II/1, 406–39.

that any should perish, but that all should reach repentance" (2 Pet 3:9). The delay of the *parousia* is God's mercy.

Here is where the specter of universalism comes in. It is as if Barth could not imagine that any *should* perish, so convinced was he of the finality and sufficiency of the judgment Christ the Judge suffered in our place. And really, how could this *not* lead to universalism? By nearly conflating the agency of Christ and the Spirit, Barth impairs the biblical imagination, which requires one to conceive simultaneously of the sufficiency of Jesus' death and resurrection in our place as an expression of the Father's will that "all should reach repentance" and the very real threat of perishing.[59] The Spirit of Christ is the one in and by whom those who were formerly "not my people" turn back to God and become "my people" (Rom 9:25). If his work can never be divorced from the work of the Son—and indeed if it is best described with reference to the Son as an "application" of his death and resurrection or a "uniting" of the church and "conforming" it to Christ—he nevertheless has discrete work to do in the time of the church.[60]

IS THERE ANYTHING LEFT FOR
THE CHURCH TO DO?

The all-sufficiency of Christ raises questions about the nature and necessity of the Spirit's work; it raises similar questions about the work of the church. The charge of "Christomonism," while off the mark, arises from a concern that Jesus plays his role in such a way as to crowd out all other actors. It would be a holy blunder, and far from unthinkable, were Barth to be so enraptured by the free, self-giving love of God in Christ that he were unable to make much of anything else. Would we even blame him if he did?

Actually, I believe we would, or at least we should. In his meditation on Jesus Christ, Barth came to see with radical consistency that in Jesus we see the face of God *and* the face of humanity. At the end of his career, he pointed out that because evangelical theology is "concerned with Immanuel, God with us," it must concern itself with humanity, "that creature destined by

---

59. See Hans Urs von Balthasar, *Dare We Hope "That All Men Be Saved"? With a Short Discourse on Hell*, trans. David Kipp and Lothar Krauth (San Francisco: Ignatius Press, 1988).

60. "The way beyond Barth at this point, it seems to me, lies in the direction of a 'concrete pneumatology' that is able to recognize the Spirit as a salvific economy in its own right." Mangina, "Bearing the Marks of Jesus," 301.

God to be a conqueror." It must consider "the free love of God that evokes the response of free love, his grace (*charis*) that calls for gratitude (*eucharistia*)."[61]

A certain kind of Christomonism might eclipse the grateful response of the very humanity whose cause God took up in Christ. More precisely, it might construe the faithful response of the one, true human, Jesus, in such a way that further human response is simply redundant.[62] The question, then, is whether Barth manages to follow through with his theoanthropology in his consideration of the church. I believe he does, though I will qualify that in my closing comments. Barth is clear that "where the Holy Ghost is at work the step to visibility is unavoidable."[63] He warns against the danger of an "ecclesiological Docetism" that suggests that the visible church is not *really* the church.[64] Barth speaks of the church's "very special visibility"[65] while recognizing that the marks of the church "must be perceived by faith and described dialectically."[66]

Insofar as the church is visible, it has a history. "The Church is, of course, a human, earthly-historical construct, whose history involves from the very first, and always will involve, human action. But it is *this* human construct, the Christian Church, because and as God is at work in it by His Holy Spirit."[67] The church is a theater of human action, and (it would be inaccurate to say "but") this human action is possible in that God acts. His action animates, though not in such a way that ours is less ours. So "God is at work" *and* "there is a human work which He occasions and fashions. Except in this history whose subject is God—but the God who acts for and to and with specific men—it is not the true Church."[68] Notice the precision of the language. God is the subject of the church's history, but the God who is this subject is *our* God, the one who "acts

---

61. Barth, *Evangelical Theology*, 12.

62. As Kevin Vanhoozer writes, in a comment on revelation that could apply equally to ecclesiology, "While a christological concentration is entirely appropriate in light of the canonical witness (Lk. 24:27), however, a christological *reduction* is not." *Remythologizing Theology: Divine Action, Passion, and Authorship* (Cambridge: Cambridge University Press, 2010), 418.

63. *CD* IV/1, 658.

64. *CD* IV/1, 653. Also see Barth, *Dogmatics in Outline*, 142.

65. Cited in John Webster, *Holiness* (London: SCM Press, 2003), 71. In this, Barth "sought to affirm that the Church has such visible form by virtue of the presence and action of Christ through the Spirit. 'Visibility' is therefore a spiritual event."

66. Kimlyn J. Bender, *Karl Barth's Christological Ecclesiology* (Burlington, VT: Ashgate, 2005), 185.

67. *CD* IV/2, 616.

68. *CD* IV/2, 616.

for and to and with" his people. As long as divine action includes an "acting with," Barth cannot be accused of eliminating human agency.[69]

His is not an occasionalist ecclesiology (another common critique), then, for two reasons.[70] First, while the church has its being only insofar as God acts by his Spirit, even in that action the Spirit frees the church to act with and for God. So the church's act is fully human precisely because and as it is empowered by the Spirit. In other words, this is not *mere* divine action, which disparaging comments about occasionalism suppose. In fact, Barth has little time for a church that would hide its laziness behind an appeal to divine action.[71] When God encounters man, man "is not run down and overpowered, but set on his own feet. He is not put under tutelage, but addressed and treated as an adult."[72]

Second, because this is not mere divine action, it is not punctiliar. Again, the church has a history; it can be identified through time. "The Church *is* when it takes place, and it takes place in the form of a sequence and nexus of definite human activities."[73]

> Therefore it not only has a history, but—like man—it exists only as a definite history takes place, that is to say, only as it is gathered and lets itself be gathered and gathers itself by the living Jesus Christ through the Holy Spirit. To describe its being we must abandon the usual distinctions between being and act, status and dynamic, essence and existence. Its act is its being, its status its dynamic, its essence its existence.[74]

Note again the way divine action circumscribes human action, as the receptive church is freed for activity by Christ through the Spirit. It *is* gathered,

---

69. Barth describes ecclesial agency "in terms of correspondent witness rather than direct cooperation or mediation." Bender, *Barth's Christological Ecclesiology*, 278.

70. For another argument that actualism need not entail occasionalism in ecclesiology but can yield a theologically appropriate concreteness, see Christopher R. J. Holmes, "The Church and the Presence of Christ: Defending Actualist Ecclesiology," *Pro Ecclesia* 21, no. 3 (2012): 268–80.

71. "Let us leave it all to the Holy Ghost, cry some impetuously. They are right enough, but the fact that we leave it to the Holy Ghost does not mean that we leave it to the rash and wilful, but that we ask ourselves unitedly and conscientiously, and in the light of Holy Scripture, what obedience means in this matter." CD IV/2, 710.

72. *CD* IV/4, 22–23.

73. *CD* IV/1, 652.

74. *CD* IV/1, 650.

lets itself be gathered, and gathers *itself*. Here Barth's frequent recourse to an actualist ontology, in which being and act are one, extends into ecclesiology.[75] It is only in the act of gathering that the church is the church. I suspect that, at least in ecclesiology, actualism serves to protect the freedom of the Spirit, who can never be presupposed but, like the wind, blows where it will. For Barth, writes Joseph Mangina, the Christian life has "more to do with surprises than with certainties, more to do with the drama of a life lived in history than with a neat calculus worked out in advance."[76] It may be that Barth's relative reticence regarding the church's concreteness is meant to serve the surprising Spirit and honor his freedom.[77]

THE MINISTRY OF WITNESS: ON THE RELATION BETWEEN THE CHURCH AND THE WORLD

God chose the church in Christ before the foundation of the world, "that we should be holy and blameless before him" (Eph 1:4). Barth grounds ecclesiology in the doctrine of election, insisting that "the community is not made the body of Christ ... by the Spirit of Pentecost" but "in Jesus Christ, in His election from all eternity."[78] Election in Scripture is oriented to mission from the start, with Abraham promised blessing and called to bless others. For all

---

75. See Bruce McCormack, "Grace and Being: The Role of God's Gracious Election in Karl Barth's Theological Ontology," in Webster, *The Cambridge Companion to Karl Barth*, 92–110. McCormack suggests "covenantal ontology" is even more apt. We do well, though, to keep in mind Barth's remark that the free theologian "is a philosopher 'as though he were not,' and he has his ontology 'as though he had it not.'" *The Humanity of God*, 93.

76. Joseph L. Mangina, *Karl Barth: Theologian of Christian Witness* (Louisville: Westminster John Knox, 2004), 148.

77. This is the argument of Theodora Hawksley, "The Freedom of the Spirit: The Pneumatological Point of Barth's Ecclesiological Minimalism," *Scottish Journal of Theology* 64, no. 2 (2011): 180–94. Perhaps a different theological form might capture more of the church's concreteness without trespassing on divine freedom. Nicholas Healy suggests that a narrative ecclesiology would reflect the church's historical character better than Barth's theoretical account. See his Nicholas M. Healy, "The Logic of Karl Barth's Ecclesiology: Analysis, Assessment and Proposed Modifications," *Modern Theology* 10 (1994): 266. Given the massive word count in the *Dogmatics* and Barth's dialectical method, one can easily find contradictory statements on many points of theology. But rather than assume incoherence, might this not be a way in which to capture the being-in-act of the church, by seeking a form that displays multiple moments at once? In referring to the "cubist picture" that results from seeking to synthesize Barth's ecclesiological claims, Hawksley recalls a movement that sought to do just that (186). See, most iconically, Marcel Duchamp's *Nude Descending a Staircase, No. 2* (1912).

78. CD IV/1, 667. It is not the eucharist but election that makes the church (to borrow de Lubac's phrase). In turn, it is not the sacraments but election that grounds assurance of salvation. Steve Holmes points out that the use Calvin gives predestination, "replacing sacramental

his debts to Calvin, Barth faults the Reformer for neglecting the connection of election to service in ecclesiology.[79] Election is vocation, and thus the corresponding "sanctification of man as the work of the Holy Spirit has to be described as the giving and receiving of direction."[80] "Called out of the world, the community is genuinely called into it."[81] Given life in Christ, the community is called to witness to the living Christ in its midst. "It is in this, in its whence [the Word of God] and whither [the world], that it has its specific basis of existence."[82] Like John the Baptist, the church "can exist only as it points beyond itself."[83]

How does the church point beyond itself? What is the proper form of its witness to Christ in the world, and what is the specific content of that witness?

> The origin, theme and content of its witness is the divine decision which has been taken in Jesus Christ in favour of all men and for their deliverance from sure and certain destruction, namely, the decision that they are free and not slaves, that they may love and are not compelled to hate, that they shall live and not die, that all this is given to them, that it is true and ready for them without any co-operation on their part and against all their deserts. This decision and its revelation are that which inwardly holds the world together, whether it realises it or not.[84]

Election is vocation, but the vocation is itself a calling to witness to election, to the divine decision in which the triune God elects himself to be with and for humanity in Jesus Christ. This is true, whether the world realizes it or not. The world does not realize it, of course; this is what makes the world the world. What makes the church the church is that it does realize, acknowledge, and rejoice in the divine decision.

---

theology as the grounds for Christian hope, is certainly original." Holmes, *God of Grace and God of Glory: An Account of the Theology of Jonathan Edwards* (Grand Rapids: Eerdmans, 2001), 255.

79. Barth, *The Faith of the Church*, 137.
80. *CD* IV/2, 523.
81. *CD* IV/3.2, 764.
82. *CD* IV/3.2, 830.
83. *CD* IV/2, 623.
84. *CD* IV/3.2, 749.

This is the way the world is; it is a world in which humanity has been freed for God and one another in Christ. The church knows this as the Spirit brings it into communion with Christ, and "as the body of Christ it has to understand itself as a promise of the emergence of the unity in which not only Christians but all men are already comprehended in Jesus Christ."[85] The people of God were never meant to be a closed society; even their separation for the sake of holiness is oriented to the ingathering of the nations. Barth's ecclesiology of witness allows him to focus on Christ as the forefront of God's action in the world without sanctioning the kind of ecclesial pride and sloth that presumes upon God's favor and forsakes its vocation to mission. It allows for a dynamic ecclesiology, one in which the church moves in a clear direction. "The goal in the direction of which the true Church proceeds and moves is the revelation of the sanctification of all humanity and human life as it has already taken place *de iure* in Jesus Christ."[86] This leads the church to "solidarity with the world," though Barth is quick to clarify: "Not their conformity to it! The community cannot be conformed to the world."[87] But while the body of Christ can never take on another's form (which would amount to apostasy), it may never withdraw from the world to a safe distance.[88] "It stands or falls with this relation," and Barth can even say that while "the world would not necessarily be lost if there were no Church," "the Church would be lost if it had no counterpart in the world."[89]

Materially, the church witnesses to the humiliation and exaltation of all of humanity to fellowship with God in the covenant fulfilled in Christ. It is that company of people who know this as the meaning of history and know that history, at least insofar as it is an open question about humanity's trajectory, has been included and concluded in him. Turning to the formal character of the church's witness, Barth describes it as "an address of radiant content and cheerful manner."[90] It is the church's "grateful response to

---

85. *CD* IV/1, 665. The *communio sanctorum* is "a provisional representation of the new humanity in the midst of the old." *CD* IV/2, 642.

86. *CD* IV/2, 620.

87. *CD* IV/3.2, 773.

88. For a compelling account of the temptation to ecclesial distance in a divided church, see R. R. Reno, *In the Ruins of the Church: Sustaining Faith in an Age of Diminished Christianity* (Grand Rapids: Brazos, 2002).

89. *CD* IV/3.2, 826.

90. *CD* IV/3.2, 802.

the fact that first and supremely Jesus Christ has confessed it, does confess it, and will continually do so. It is its own free action, yet not an arbitrary but an obedient action."[91] The Spirit of the Lord frees the church for its own proper action in obedient witness to Christ.

More expansively, witness is "declaration, exposition and address, or the proclamation, explication and application of the Gospel as the Word of God entrusted to it."[92] This requires the church to be "listening to the voice of the Good Shepherd, which means in practice its constant listening to the prophets and apostles called by Him."[93] Having heard the word of God, the church witnesses to the word in the world.[94] In explicating the gospel, the church makes it "perceptible, perspicuous and intelligible to the world."[95] The puzzling question is how Barth can say that the church makes the gospel intelligible to the world and yet also that "what they say can and should in any case only precede the Word of God as a herald making an opening and creating respect for it."[96] Barth takes pains to separate, not merely distinguish, the word of God and the word of man. It is difficult to resist the conclusion that divine speech remains aloof from human speech and only ever settles on it unpredictably. Perhaps this is the shape of disruptive grace in the church's witness; I suspect that it is rather an unfitting anxiety on Barth's part left over from the domestication of the Spirit in liberal Protestantism.[97]

Will the witnessing church meet with success? Consider that this is a *ministry* of witness—that is, a work of service. Christ's body must follow his lead and play the servant. "It is in the humility of the flesh that Christ appeared, and what is true of the head is true also of the body."[98] Like its Lord, who "found no room in the inn and still cannot find any," the church "can only lodge and camp here and there as the pilgrim people of God." It has no home on earth, and it is only a servant. "Service is not just one of the determinations

91. *CD* IV/3.2, 790. "To confess Him is its business." *CD* IV/3.2, 787.
92. *CD* IV/3.2, 843.
93. *CD* IV/3.2, 832.
94. Note that ecclesial witness to the Word is ruled by the biblical witness to the Word.
95. *CD* IV/3.2, 850.
96. *CD* IV/3.2, 739.
97. "Disruptive grace" is George Hunsinger's luminous term in his *Disruptive Grace: Studies in the Theology of Karl Barth* (Grand Rapids: Eerdmans, 2000), 16–17.
98. Barth, *The Faith of the Church*, 148.

of the being of the community. It is its being in all its functions."[99] In any case, "the self-witness of God neither depends on nor lives by their witness, but ... their witness depends on and lives by the self-witness of God."[100] After all, God can speak for himself. He is his own best advocate, himself the truth, Jesus Christ the "primary and true Witness."[101] While Jesus sees fit to witness to himself in and through the church, he need not. He is "King over all men and all things, and as such He is not idle even *extra muros ecclesiae*."[102] Were God's people to refuse to praise him, the rocks would cry out (Luke 19:40). Were his people to refuse to witness to him, perhaps the rocks would proclaim the kingdom. Or perhaps Jesus would witness to himself directly in the world. Perhaps; though God is yet the one who *loves* in freedom, the one whose freedom frees his people for witness. While he need not employ them in announcing the good news, he has covenanted to be *Emmanuel*, God with us, and no other God. And so he graciously gives the church a "participation in His mission, in His prophetic work."[103]

DOWN PAYMENT OR PROMISSORY NOTE? A QUESTION ON BARTH'S PNEUMATOLOGY

Aware that his disciples are insufficient of themselves to witness to him in the world, Jesus promises that his Father is better than any earthly father and "will ... give the Holy Spirit to those who ask him" (Luke 11:13). But in what sense is the Spirit received on Barth's account? He writes, "The community exists in this fruitful expectation [of the Holy Spirit] which can never cease and never be unrealised."[104] Barth acknowledges the church's reception of the Spirit here, though he does so through a carefully constructed double negative. Unraveling the grammar reveals that the church's expectation of the Spirit is continuously fulfilled in his presence. Yet we find him elsewhere suspicious of a theology (and, we can imagine, a church) that "supposes it can deal with the Spirit as though it had hired him or even attained possession [*Besitz gebracht hätte*] of him." This is the problem of "a presupposed spirit"

---

99. *CD* IV/2, 692.
100. *CD* IV/3.2, 738.
101. *CD* IV/3.2, 836.
102. *CD* IV/2, 724.
103. *CD* IV/2, 792.
104. *CD* IV/1, 151.

who is "certainly not the Holy Spirit."[105] Pietism fails precisely here, and its pretension to possession of divine grace unsurprisingly entails a triumphant failure of self-criticism.[106]

Jonathan Edwards knew the dangers of presupposing the Spirit, too; despite a revivalism that would have made Barth cringe, Edwards describes revival as an entirely unpresupposed "surprising work of God." He shares Barth's concern to magnify the freedom of God and, like Barth, insists that we have no other gods before the Lord who is the Spirit. "Spirit" does not signal a broader category than "Christ" for Edwards, as it does for many contemporary theologies keen to uncover common ground among religions. To speak of the Spirit is to name God's work with and in his creation. Thus, a Spirit-oriented theology would not for that be less Trinitarian; nor would it shunt Christology offstage in an effort to bring the Spirit into the limelight. While the Spirit has his "own" work in the economy of salvation, his chief task is to communicate the gifts and graces Jesus has purchased in his life, death, and resurrection. Edwards shuttles back and forth between a description of the gifts and graces of God and the Spirit who bears but also is those gifts and graces.

Edwards is an experimental theologian, one whose empirical mind hankers after phenomena to sort and analyze. But he is far from a psychologist of religion—or, if he is that, he is so only in the interests of a doctrine of the Holy Spirit that accounts properly for his work in the conversion of sinners. For all his psychological acuity, Edwards's aim in *Religious Affections* is an identification of the saving work of the Spirit, not religious experience *per se*. He is after (to borrow the title of another of Edwards's works) the distinguishing marks of the Spirit, those pious evidences that God himself is at work in the regeneration of those chosen in Christ before the foundation of the world.

---

105. Barth, *Evangelical Theology*, 58. While Barth will occasionally speak of a believer or the church possessing the Spirit (*CD* II/2, 349; IV/2, 326), his more forceful, frequent, and characteristic move is to deny the possibility and condemn the presumption of possessing the Spirit. *CD* IV/1, 646; IV/1, 719; IV/2, 655. The problem, in Barth's mind, is that possession implies control and reverses the order of lordship between the Spirit and the church. But "neither the Christian community nor the individual Christian can subjugate or possess [*besitzen*] or control Him." *CD* IV/1, 646. In a less careful moment, Barth refers to "the event of their reception [*Empfangens*] and possession [*Besitzens*] of the Holy Spirit," but later in the same volume, he insists, "It [that is, the church] does not 'possess' ['*hat*'] Him. It cannot create or control Him. He is promised to it. It can only receive [*empfangen*] Him and then be obedient to Him." *CD* IV/2, 655.

106. See Eberhard Busch, *Karl Barth and the Pietists: The Young Karl Barth's Critique of Pietism and Its Response*, trans. Daniel W. Bloesch (Downers Grove, IL: IVP Academic, 2004).

But how to characterize that work? In his sermons on "Charity and Its Fruits," Edwards makes two key distinctions within the "gifts and operations of the Spirit." They may be common or saving, and they may be ordinary or extraordinary.[107] Extraordinary gifts (like the more miraculous apostolic gifts) are "great privileges," but they do not inhere in a person. "They are something adventitious ... precious jewels, which a man carries about him. But true grace in the heart is, as it were, the preciousness of the heart ... by which the very soul itself becomes a precious jewel." The ordinary, saving grace, which is the Spirit, is far better.[108]

Though the extraordinary gifts draw a crowd, their glory fades. Saving grace abides, however, because the Spirit makes himself at home in the believer.

> The Spirit of God is given to the true saints to dwell in them, as his proper lasting abode; and to influence their hearts, as a principle of new nature, or as a divine supernatural spring of life and action. The Scriptures represent the Holy Spirit, not only as moving, and occasionally influencing the saints, but as dwelling in them as his temple. ... And he is represented as being there so united to the faculties of the soul, that he becomes there a principle or spring of new nature and life.[109]

The Spirit is not an occasional visitor, not the unexpected God who "rushed upon" Saul (1 Sam 10:10). When he comes, he stays, finding and making of the saints "his proper lasting abode." At home with the saints, he becomes within them a fountain of life from which all faithful action flows. It is the very fixity of all this that marks the new covenant for Edwards. Here is a fitting answer to the calamity of the fall, when death entered in after Adam and Eve turned from God and "the Holy Spirit, that divine inhabitant, forsook the house."[110]

At creation, God had implanted two kinds of principles in humanity: an inferior, natural kind oriented to self-love and made up of "natural appetites and passions," and a superior, spiritual kind, oriented to the love of God,

---

107. *WJE* 8:152–53.
108. *WJE* 8:157–58.
109. *WJE* 8:200.
110. *WJE* 3:382.

"wherein consisted the spiritual image of God, and man's righteousness and true holiness." The former "are like fire in an house; which, we say, is a good servant, but a bad master; very useful while kept in its place, but if left to take possession of the whole house, soon brings all to destruction."[111] As in Ezekiel's vision, in which the glory of the LORD departs from the temple and Israel languishes in exile, a sinful humanity suffers the absence of the Spirit and banishment from Eden. In Jesus, however, the Holy Spirit returns to the temple; and in conversion, those who are united to Christ receive his Spirit and become the dwelling place of God.[112]

For Edwards, the abiding presence of the Spirit in his people as in a temple allows him to speak more naturally and confidently than Barth of the Spirit's ordinary role in ecclesial action, *precisely as* the Spirit is a new principle of human action in believers in the church.

> So the saints are said to live by Christ living in them (Gal. 2:20). Christ by his Spirit not only is in them, but lives in them; and so that they live by his life; so is his Spirit united to them, as a principle of life in them; they don't only drink living water, but this living water becomes a well or fountain of water, in the soul, springing up into spiritual and ever-lasting life (John 4:14), and thus becomes a principle of life in them.[113]

If Edwards tends to construe this primarily in terms of the Spirit's indwelling the individual believer and fails to exploit the image of the church as the temple to its fullest potential, his account of the Spirit's permanent presence within the elect lays the foundation for seeing the Spirit-indwelt community as the subject of ecclesial action. Edwards is far more comfortable than Barth with the biblical claim that the Spirit abides with, in, and among the people of God. This does not represent a threat to Edwards but is cause for meditation and praise.

---

111. *WJE* 3:381–83.

112. See G. K. Beale, *The Temple and the Church's Mission: A Biblical Theology of the Dwelling Place of God* (Downers Grove, IL: IVP Academic, 2004), and Nicholas Perrin, *Jesus the Temple* (Grand Rapids: Baker Academic, 2010). Note that, like Paul, Edwards can speak of individual believers (e.g., *WJEO* 8:200; 21:196) or the corporate church as the temple of the Holy Spirit (e.g., *WJEO* 15:246, 25:401). He can even, awkwardly, describe believers together as many "temples of the Holy Ghost" (e.g., *WJEO* 21:181, 195).

113. *WJE* 8:200. Edwards locates the indwelling Spirit who becomes a vital principle in the believer and the Pauline description of believers (both individually and corporately) as the temple of the Spirit in close proximity to one another conceptually (e.g., *WJEO* 14:384).

Christ is become theirs [i.e., the regenerate's], and therefore his fullness is theirs, his Spirit is theirs, the Spirit of Christ is their purchased
and promised possession.[114]

For Barth, the Spirit is the promise of future possession, whereas for Edwards,
the Spirit is in addition the present possession of the promised Spirit.[115] Both
Barth and Edwards insist that the Spirit remains Lord, but Barth's nervous-
ness about human tendencies to manipulate the Spirit, to reduce him to a
possession by appropriating his gifts for their own ends (thereby violating
the first commandment), leads him to emphasize the outstanding character
of the promise.[116] The Spirit as ἀρραβὼν (see 2 Cor 1:22; 5:5; Eph 1:14) seems
to operate in Barth more as a promissory note than as a down payment on
our inheritance.[117]

But this is unnecessary. Barth's worries to the contrary, to "have" the
Spirit need not imply that we have him at our disposal. Where Barth sees in

114. WJE 8:354.

115. Given how negatively Barth characterizes "possession," one might wonder whether
even *future* possession of the Spirit in the *eschaton* would be countenanced by Barth. But given
that his complaint is of possession's tendency to devolve into control, perhaps we can say that
possession in the *eschaton* will be purified entirely of its manipulative sense. Where there is no
sin, perhaps even Barth would speak, with the tradition, of our possessing the Spirit.

116. Both Barth and Edwards would agree with David Kelsey's remark that "God is free to
be intimately related, and as intimately relating God is always free of the control of the term of
the relation." Kelsey, *Eccentric Existence: A Theological Anthropology* (Louisville, KY: Westminster
John Knox, 2009), 1:457. But Barth insists further that "possession" suggests "control" in a way
that Edwards resists. It is strange that one who so emphasized the dawning of the end in Christ
and the presence of Christ in the church would shrink back from this element of an inaugurated
eschatology. Jonathan Norgate comes to a similar conclusion: "While Barth's theological agenda
limits an overrealized eschatological ecclesiology, we suggest that with his questionable reading
of 1 Corinthians 3:16, 17 and 2 Corinthians 6:16, with their simple indicatives ('you are [God's
temple]'), he has also threatened the spiritual character of the church as it awaits the consummation: perhaps for Barth there is not enough *now* and too much *not yet*?" Norgate, "Temple in
the Theology of Karl Barth," in *Heaven on Earth: The Temple in Biblical Theology*, ed. T. Desmond
Alexander and Simon Gathercole (Carlisle: Paternoster, 2004), 231–43.

117. On Paul's use of *arrabōn*, see A. J. Kerr, "APPABΩN," *Journal of Theological Studies* 39, no.
1 (April 1988): 92–97, and James D. G. Dunn, *Christology*, vol. 1 of *The Christ and the Spirit* (Grand
Rapids: Eerdmans, 1998), 163. As is sometimes the case, Barth's exegesis is more careful on this
point than his more thematic work. When explicitly considering the biblical passages where
arrabōn is used, he recognizes that the Spirit constitutes a first installment of the promise (e.g.,
CD III/2, 494; IV/1, 330), though he characteristically wonders what this can amount to "when
measured by the fulness promised to Christians in and with this beginning." CD IV/4, 77. Note:
His citations suggest Barth intends *arrabōn* when he writes *aparchē* at CD III/2, 494. In either
case, whether he means "first installment" or "first fruits," the point holds.

"possession" the seeds of manipulation, it has more commonly functioned in the tradition to name what is necessary for our proper enjoyment of God. We must "have" him if we are to really and fully delight in him. Bonaventure brings possession and enjoyment into close proximity:

> Again, the one who enjoys God possesses [habet] God. Hence, it follows that together with that grace which, by its God-conforming nature, leads to the enjoyment of God, there is also bestowed the uncreated gift, the Holy Spirit. Whoever possesses it possesses God's own self.
>
> Now no one possesses God without being possessed by God in a special way. And no one possesses and is possessed by God without loving God and being loved by God in a particular and incomparable manner, as in the case of a bride and groom where each loves and is loved by the other. And no one is loved in this way without being adopted as a child entitled to an eternal inheritance. Therefore, the "grace which makes pleasing" [gratia gratum faciens] makes the soul the temple of God, the bride of Christ, and the daughter of the eternal Father. And since this cannot occur except through a supremely gracious condescension on the part of God, it could not be caused by some naturally implanted habit, but only be a free gift divinely infused. This is most evident if we consider what it truly means to be God's temple and God's child, and to be joined to God as in wedlock by the bond of love and grace.[118]

---

118. Bonaventure, *Breviloquium*, trans. Dominic V. Monti, O.F.M. (Saint Bonaventure, NY: Franciscan Institute, 2005), 5.1.4–5. Similarly, Thomas writes that "we are said to possess [habere] only what we can freely use or enjoy: and to have the power of enjoying the divine person can only be according to sanctifying grace [gratiam gratum facientem]. And yet the Holy Ghost is possessed by man, and dwells within him, in the very gift of sanctifying grace. Hence the Holy Ghost Himself is given and sent." *Summa Theologica*, trans. Fathers of the English Dominican Province (Allen: Christian Classics, 1981), I.43.3. Importantly, we find the same thing frequently in Calvin, albeit with a Christological accent. Calvin speaks of our possessing Christ and God in him by the Spirit through faith, and he, too, links possession to enjoyment. "The Spirit alone causes us to possess [possideamus] Christ completely and have him dwelling in us." *Institutes of the Christian Religion*, ed. John T. McNeill, trans. Ford Lewis Battles (Louisville: Westminster John Knox, 1960), 4.17.12. "Faith is called *the only work of God*, because by means of it we possess [possidentes] Christ, and thus become the sons of God, so that he governs us by his Spirit." *Commentary on the Gospel According to John*, trans. William Pringle, Calvin's Commentaries, vol. 17 (n.d.; repr., Grand Rapids: Baker, 2009), on John 6:29. "For those who possess [possident] Christ have God truly present, and enjoy Him wholly." *Commentaries on the Epistles of Paul the Apostle to the Philippians, Colossians, and Thessalonians*, trans. John Pringle, Calvin's Commentaries, vol.

If the idiom is far from Barth's, the point remains: possession can be seen as the grace-initiated way in which God gives himself to his people and fits them to receive him, to become his temple, his children, and his bride. We possess God in order to enjoy him, and in order to enjoy him as God, we must continue to honor him as the holy one in our midst. To speak of the Spirit dwelling in the church, then, even dwelling in the church as its possession, is not to compromise his lordship or reverse the order of authority, for "the LORD is in his holy temple; let all the earth keep silence before him" (Hab 2:20).

Edwards's daring language suggests none of the theological hand-wringing that characterizes Barth's discussions of piety. For him, we can—indeed must—say that the Spirit "belongs" to believers. That is precisely what distinguishes them from the unregenerate. The Spirit is a new divine principle within them, has somehow become native to them. Furthermore, this gift, unlike the original presence of the Spirit, is inalienable; the saints will persevere. Where Barth wants to protect the Spirit's lordship by refusing to speak of our possessing the Spirit, Edwards wants to magnify his saving grace, signaling the depth of his work. What could be more complete than for "his Spirit" to be "theirs"? Possession might be likened to marriage, in which there is potential for abuse and manipulation, but where the accent falls on mutual self-giving. Having become one flesh, writes Luther, the soul and Christ share all things in common.[119] The Spirit of Jesus brings with him wedding gifts, too, a luxurious concatenation of graces in conversion.[120] Edwards describes such mutuality in terms of belonging and possession: "All shall have propriety one in another. Love seeks to have the beloved its own, and divine love rejoices in saying, 'My beloved is mine, and I am his,' as Cant. 2:16."[121] This is a "special propriety," such that each is the other's in a way unparalleled in creation. For the church's part, "though other things are hers, yet nothing is hers in that manner that her spiritual bridegroom is hers: as great and glorious as he is, yet he, with all his dignity and glory is hers; all is wholly given to her, to be fully possessed and enjoyed by her, to

---

21 (n.d.; repr.: Grand Rapids: Baker, 2009), on Colossians 2:9. Barth's rejection of "possession" language is idiosyncratic rather than a genuinely Reformed protest.

119. *Luther's Works*, American Edition, 55 vols., ed. J. Pelikan and H. Lehmann (St. Louis and Philadelphia: Concordia and Fortress, 1955), 31:351.

120. See *WJE* 8:327–34.

121. *WJE* 8:380.

the utmost degree that she is capable of."[122] The church, after all, is not only Christ's body; she is also his bride.

CONCLUSION

While he generally avoids an occasionalism in which churchly speaking and doing is merely the occasion for divine action and not theologically meaningful in itself, Barth vacillates between a dissolving of ecclesial agency into Christ's agency and a separation of ecclesial agency from Christ's agency. This suggests that Barth failed to integrate consistently his lifelong commitment to divine transcendence and his growing sense of proper, if relative, creaturely autonomy. Edwards offers a pneumatological corrective on this point. He upholds Barth's insistence that the Spirit who is the LORD must not and cannot be manipulated, while adding that believers really have received the first installment of the eschatological Spirit, who lives in them as a new vital principle, animating and enabling ecclesial action that is as divine as it is human and is faithfully human precisely because divine.

Barth's clarion call to attend to and obey the Lord who stands over even as he fellowships with his people demands a hearing.[123] The anxiety of influence Barth felt under the shadow of neo-Protestantism led him to attenuate the mediation of the Spirit in the church, however. After Barth, we cannot neglect the presence of the risen Christ in the church. But Barth's anxieties need not be ours, and we can rejoice more confidently than he in the present possession of the liberating Spirit who frees the church for faithfulness and who is the Bridegroom's most precious wedding gift to his bride. After all, if it is true, as Edwards writes, that God created the world so that "the eternal God might obtain a spouse," he would hardly fail to give that spouse the best of all wedding gifts, his very self, which is just what he does in giving his Spirit.[124]

---

122. *WJEO* 25:179–80.

123. On the importance of this polemic, see Rhodes, "The Spirit of Fellowship," 221–22.

124. *WJE* 25:187, quoted in Rhys S. Bezzant, *Jonathan Edwards and the Church* (Oxford: Oxford University Press, 2014), ix.

LAST THINGS

Nathan Hitchcock

Too often, Reformed dogmatics suffers from drab eschatology. Confessions and systematic presentations nearly always address the biblical themes of the last things, the parousia, the resurrection of the dead, the final judgment, eternal life. Yet such endeavors can come across as something of a postscript. The end-time landscape is flattened out by assurances of providence, preterist categorizations, and amillennial hermeneutics. It is lured far afield by the glittering distraction that is the intermediate state. Is it any wonder that Revelation was the only major book of the Bible for which John Calvin failed to produce a commentary?

Jonathan Edwards and Karl Barth stand out as noteworthy exceptions to the trend. Each makes creative appropriations of the biblical testimony and the Christian tradition. Further, the shape of each man's work has an eschatological impress. The end is, as it were, written into the very DNA of their theological structures. In this essay I explain how Edwards and Barth fundamentally disagree on the historicization of divine revelation and thereby promote very different descriptions of the penultimate age. Edwards offers a postmillennialism consistent with God's actualized glory in the church and world, while Barth positions God's revelatory moment vis-à-vis history as such and so refrains from commenting on the last days unless they are re-expressed as Christological statements. Even so, in the case of the final state, both modify the Augustinian doctrine of heaven in which glorification hangs on the idea of translation to the eternal abode in which the totality of God's glory is manifested.

EDWARDS'S PENULTIMATE

Coming to the doctrines of the end time, the final days before the parousia, Jonathan Edwards had plenty to say. He did not necessarily say it publicly (his reluctance to preach speculative eschatology is evident), yet his entire career exhibits a fascination with the concluding events of human history. Behind the scenes, Edward populated his "Scripture" notebook with exegetical remarks. He pollinated his "Blank Bible" with typological references and opined about the consummation of history in his Miscellanies. More formally, Edwards's *Notes on the Apocalypse* (1723) offers a running commentary on the book of Revelation, and one finds considerable treatment of eschatological themes in *An Humble Attempt to Promote Union in Prayer* (1748).

The productions we have of Edwards, however, pale in comparison to a magnum opus he was planning. In October 1757, Edwards wrote to the trustees of The College of New Jersey, his imminent employers, disclosing, among other things, his intentions to write *The History of Redemption*. It would be a theological history, a narrative of creaturely events, first to last, sacred and mundane, subsumed in the eschatological purposes of God. It would be a God's-eye view of the totality, for it would introduce "all parts of divinity in that order which is most scriptural and most natural: which is a method which appears to me the most beautiful and entertaining, wherein every divine doctrine, will appear to greatest advantage in the brightest light, in the most striking manner, showing the admirable contexture and harmony of the whole."[1] Five months later after the announcement Edwards was dead, leaving the project unattempted. What present day readers know as *A History of the Work of Redemption* is actually a heavily edited version of thirty lecture-sermons preached in Northampton in 1739.

Edwards's vision of the last days is organized around the doctrine of the millennium. The cryptic thousand-year reign of the saints described in Revelation 20:1–6 figures prominently in his writings. Edwards is decidedly postmillennial in his framework, placing the return of Christ after a lengthy period of peace on earth. That peace, brought about by various means given to the saints, would be a time of relative rest from the spasms of evil, a "sabbatism of the world."[2]

---

1. *WJE* 16:728.
2. *WJE* 5:410.

Three dimensions of Edwards's doctrine of the millennium are worth reciting here: the headway of the gospel, the victory of the church, and the advancement of human culture. As for the first, Edwards anticipated a great proclamation of the gospel and coming in of the elect in the last days. Old Testament prophecies supplied sure evidences. For example, with the oracle in Zechariah 8 that "many people and strong nations shall come to seek the Lord of Hosts in Jerusalem," Edwards avoids the preterist interpretation altogether. Rather, the prophecy concerns "that *last* and greatest enlargement and most glorious advancement of the church of God on earth; in the benefits of which especially, the Jewish nation were to have a share, and a very eminent and distinguishing share."[3] Edwards makes much of the incoming of the Jews, though the blessings of the evangel would be shared worldwide among the gentiles too. In the coming millennium, "the heathen nations shall be enlightened with the glorious gospel ... and many shall go forth and carry the gospel unto them."[4] The recent revivals in New England were harbingers of the millennium in this respect, pointing to a significant (though limited) role for America in the last days.[5] The Holy Spirit would soon be at work among all the races, facilitating the work of missions to the ends of the earth.

Closely related, the millennium will also be a time characterized by the church victorious, a temporary overcoming of the antichrist at the end of the ages. As Edwards saw it, the power of the antichrist had cropped up in Islam and various paganisms, though most pervasively through Roman Catholicism. Just as Babylon had birthed various heathenisms, the Roman church had become "the mother of the apostasy of the Christian church,"[6] "the spiritual Babylon, or the idolatrous empire of Rome."[7] Like the beast and the false prophet, Rome set forth pompous claims and claimed sundry

---

3. *WJE* 5:313.

4. *WJE* 9:471.

5. E.g., Edwards believes the outpouring of the Spirit in the latter days will originate in America. *WJE* 4:353-58; see also his Blank Bible, 1 Kgs 18:44, *WJE* 24:385. His modest optimism about America in the plan of redemption drew some criticism from followers of Joseph Mede. Compared with other futurist voices in the colonies at the time, however, Edwards comes across as restrained. Cf. Stephen J. Stein, "Editor's Introduction," in *The Cambridge Companion to Jonathan Edwards*, ed. Stephen J. Stein (Cambridge: Cambridge University Press, 2007), 21.

6. *WJE* 5:136.

7. *WJE* 15:255.

miracles. Popery had triumphed through centuries of western history, but its waning influence in recent years indicated that the millennium was at hand. The thousand years of peace would be a rest from the corruption of the churches. In that age, "men shall see plainly the very foundation and inward frame, of the wonderful doctrines of Christianity; and truth shall shine forth bright, pure and unmixed."[8] The religious wars and heretic pyres would be extinguished. In their place, "religion shall in every respect be uppermost in the world."[9] As external conflict wanes, new order will commence. The churches will exercise "excellent order in the church discipline and government," by which "all the world [shall then be] as one church, one orderly, regular, beautiful society, one body, all the members in beautiful proportion."[10]

A third feature of the millennium is worldwide prosperity. Human flourishing, as the outward consequence of spiritual renewal, will be evident across the globe. The spiritual blessing of the eon will have "a natural tendency to it: to health … ease, quietness, pleasantness, wealth, great increase of children."[11] Divine and human learning will be dispersed throughout the world, far beyond Britain. In a rather prescient prediction for the mid-eighteenth century, Edwards writes, "It may be hoped that then many of the Negroes and Indians will be divines, and that excellent books will be published in Africa, in Ethiopia, in Turkey."[12] Indeed, the millennium will be a time "when the most barbarous nations shall become as bright and polite as England."[13] Advances in the sciences will abound; antiquities of every nation will be brought to light. Every metric of human flourishing will excel, according to Edwards. In contrast to the muted colonialist wars of the early modern age, nations will be knit together in the millennium. Even navigation, so much a technology for greed and competition in the present age, will be "improved for holy uses."[14] An atmosphere of peace shall descend on the

---

8. *WJE* 5:106.

9. *WJE* 9:481.

10. *WJE* 9:484. By induction, one might argue that Edwards anticipates that the churches of the millennium would be presbyterian in structure, with shared governance. *WJE* 16:355.

11. *WJE* 9:484.

12. *WJE* 9:480.

13. *WJE* 13:212.

14. *WJE* 9:484.

world. Governments, while varied in structure, shall follow the Puritan civil reform in being free of the tyranny of absolute, despotic powers: "Kings shall rather be as the judges were before Saul ... and as the kings of England now are in civil matters."[15] Liberty abounds in the penultimate period.

Edwards was not persuaded that the millennium had yet begun. Despite encouraging signs of the times, especially in revivalistic America, the time was not yet inaugurated. The use of various "means" (extraordinary prayer key among them) would be required for the saints to see the dawning of that day. It was near, however, nearer than other postmillennialists were predicting.[16] Edwards hedges his bets as to the exact duration of the coming golden age, claiming simply that it would be a lengthy period of time. It would also necessarily be limited, he said, lest the earth be overrun with inhabitants or the saints lose perspective on their status as foreigners on earth.[17]

None of Edwards's chiliastic interpretations is especially remarkable for the time. His millennial vision springs from dialogue with a range of contemporaries and fits naturally enough within the writing corpus of Puritanism.[18] In contrast to the rest of the reformed tradition, Puritans in England and America alike were happy to conjecture about the last events. In keeping with a covenantal theology colored by radical Reformation apocalypticism on one hand and Anglican state-church cooperation on the other, Puritans made regular forays into premillennial or postmillennial thought.[19] Edwards felt what many others felt in the seventeenth and eighteenth centuries, namely, that the end times were about to emerge from the fiery furnace of the western church's reformation.

---

15. *WJE* 2:136.

16. He deviated from Moses Lowman, his main interlocutor in eschatology, claiming that the millennium would start well nearer than the year 2000. Cf. *WJE* 5:394ff.

17. *WJE* 20:50–52; *WJE* 23:156.

18. See Stein's thorough documentation of Edwards's religious sources in Stein, "Author's Introduction," *WJE* 5:54–74. One also finds discernable links to evangelicals like John Erskine and John Willison, who were busy popularizing similar millennial visions in Scotland, and Lutheran pietism, which had been sprouting its own apocalyptic hypotheses, in large part from the pen of J.A. Bengel. James A. De Jong, *As the Waters Cover the Sea: Millennial Expectations in the Rise of Anglo-American Missions 1640–1810* (Kampen: J.H. Kok, 1970), 119–21. Taking a different tack, Perry Miller attends to Edwards's possible interaction with early modern apocalyptic physicists. Perry Miller, *Errand into the Wilderness* (Cambridge: Belknap, 1956), 233–35.

19. Though one does well to concede at the outset that it is virtually impossible make neat categorization of Puritan eschatology. Cf. Crawford Gribben, *The Puritan Millennium: Literature and Theology, 1550–1682* (Eugene, OR: Wipf & Stock, 2008), 28ff.

What is it, then, that makes Jonathan Edwards "the greatest artist of the apocalypse" in America?[20] Historically speaking, it has to do with his implementation of progressive concepts for a conservative agenda. Dogmatically speaking—and more important here—it is the *totality* of his vision. Edwards sees continuity between the whole of history, indeed, a confluence of God's history with humanity's, played out in the common narrative of salvation. For Edwards, there is a whole. He claims he can see it. He attempts to exposit it. Successful or not, he always keeps an eye fixed on the whole, never letting the final days of earth be unhitched from the coming day. That is what makes him stand out from the other eschatologists. Everything is eschatological for Edwards. His conjectures about the millennium were part and parcel of the providential arc of history, all of which was being drawn into the final telos of heavenly joy. Everything coheres.

Returning to his would-be literary crescendo, *A History of the Work of Redemption*, Edwards pitched it as "a body of divinity in an entire new method, being thrown into the form of a history."[21] It would be *divinity*, which is to say a heavenly narrative, though formatted as a *history*. Divinity is the narration of God, and history is the narration of humanity—but the two are to be read and told together. As the manifestation of God's works, history offers the skeleton on which to hang divinity's doctrines and disputations. Or is it the other way around? Are divinity's revelatory data the skeleton, and the Spirit's saving will in earthly vicissitudes the muscle and skin? From the altitude of *A History*, the exact schema does not matter, for Edwards dares to tell the double narrative with one voice.[22] By doing so Edwards attempts something comparable only to Augustine's *City of God*.[23]

---

20. Miller, *Errand into the Wilderness*, 233.

21. *WJE* 16:727.

22. This agnostic posture *pace* Wilson, who insists *A History* is fundamentally a piece of divinity, a "grand theological disquisition." John F. Wilson, "History," in *The Princeton Companion to Jonathan Edwards*, ed. Sang Hyun Lee (Princeton,: Princeton University Press, 2005), 214.

23. Here Wilson is spot on, acknowledging the similarity of the two projects while pointing out that Edwards departed from Augustine "in looking to the future for the external reference point (specifically, to the creation's return to the Godhead through the millennium) rather than to the past." "History," 221. Avihu Zakai calls Edwards "America's Augustine," even in the matter of eschatology, though he notes the divergence on issues of prophecy, the millennium, and the possibility of human progress in history. *Jonathan Edwards' Philosophy of History: The Reenchantment of the World in the Age of Enlightenment* (Princeton: Princeton University Press, 2003), 160ff.

To restate his thoughts on the penultimate, Edwards believed a time of rest and victory was imminent for the church. Recent spiritual events in New England and abroad indicated it, as did a reading of historical movements in conjunction with typological readings of the Old Testament. Through various means, the saints were about to usher in the glories of the millennium and on that basis could pray and act with hope.

I have so far claimed that Edwards's views of divine providence in history permitted him, like other Puritans, to speculate on the last days. His vision exceeded his contemporaries, however, in the scope he sought to bring to the task. Divinity and humanity could be laid out diachronically. In Edwards one finds revelation, in the profoundest sense for an orthodox theologian, utterly historicized.

BARTH'S PENULTIMATE

One finds in Karl Barth a very different approach to penultimacy. His intense resistance to the historicization of revelation all but extinguishes specific interpretations of the last days. Thus, it is something of a fool's errand to go looking for Barth's doctrine of the end *time*. He rarely commented on futuristic prophetic texts, and what was to be his grand exposition of redemption, volume V of *Church Dogmatics*, was never penned. Even so, it is instructive to look to a group of early writings set in the apocalyptic key, notably the two versions of *Der Römerbrief* (1919, 1922), *Das Wort Gottes und die Theologie* (1924), and *Die Auferstehung der Toten* (1924), which together offer a powerful critique of over-realized eschatology. Furthermore, one can cobble together plenty of Barthian material about what might be called eschatological ethics. In this section I will address both his critique and the Advent ethic substituted for the doctrine of the last things on earth.

So far as the critique is concerned, the tone of Barth's early theological writings is decidedly resistant to over-realized eschatology.[24] Even before his abandonment of the liberal Christian enterprise (at the start of the Great War in 1914), Barth held to a Christian socialism that understood God's action as a disruption of any easy sense of national progress or religious triumph.

---

24. The preferred idiom for theological biographers of Barth is epistemology, not eschatology. Such narration makes sense when evaluating Barth's larger critique, which in the late twenties moves to the Thomistic *analogia entis* and then natural theology. Even then, however, eschatology, sibling to epistemology, is never out of view entirely.

Around the same time, he became familiar with the eschatological preaching of Christoph Blumhardt and began to use neo-Kantian categories. The first edition of *Der Römerbrief* attacks religious individualism, targeting in particular pietistic versions of Christianity. Barth claims that God's revelatory presence is a genuine transcendence, a power beyond history. Speaking in language that would have been familiar to his parishioners, factory workers in Safenwil, Switzerland, Barth argues that Spirit's power is the weft to the world's warp, a "beyond" that has to "interlock" for the world to become whole.[25]

Around 1919, Barth grew uneasy with the belief that God's history was in any way organically intertwined with the earth's. His lectures and writings of the time took a severe turn.[26] This world in its present state is not the kingdom of heaven, says Barth. God's self-disclosure highlights the disjuncture between the heavenly kingdom and the earthly, and "if we do not want to be left behind and outside of the truth of Christ and the power of his resurrection, we will have no choice but to enter *fully into* the shock and contradiction."[27] What God reveals in the event of revelation is his God-ness, necessarily revealing that human history, either external or internal, is not God. To assume otherwise is idolatry. In the rewriting of the Romans commentary, Barth plays with the German verb *aufheben* ("to sublate"; substantially comparable to the English homophone "to raze/to raise"). Revelation "dissolves" and "establishes" the world in God, according to the Barthian refrain. The religious intuition of God is real, but only as it is intuited *in God.* God's "no" therefore comes with a greater "yes." Revelation throws us into existential contradictions, "but in God [they are] as negations which have been negated, as positions which have been dissolved, they are at peace, reconciled, redeemed, and resolved; in Him they are one."[28] Through all these writings, Jesus' resurrection figures prominently as the archetypal and echoing event of revelation. In *Resurrection of the Dead*, written at the same time

---

25. Barth, Sermon, 20 April 1919, in *Karl Barth Gesamtausgabe* I, Predigten 1919 (Zürich: Theologischer Verlag Zürich, 1971–), 155.

26. For the radicalizing of Barth's dialectic, see Nathan Hitchcock, *Karl Barth and the Resurrection of the Flesh: The Loss of the Body in Participatory Eschatology* (Eugene, OR: Pickwick, 2013), 35–62.

27. Barth, *The Word of God and Theology*, trans. Amy Marga (London: T&T Clark, 2011), 63.

28. Barth, *The Epistle to the Romans*, trans. Edwyn C. Hoskyns (London: Oxford University Press, 1933), 329.

as the second Romans commentary, Barth makes the novel claim that "the resurrection of the dead" is the axiomatic center of 1 Corinthians, a dialectic that informs all the issues broached in the epistle, not just the matter of the coming bodily salvation. The ideas of 1 Corinthians "could be better described as *the methodology of the apostle's preaching*, rather than eschatology, because it is really concerned not with this and that special thing, but with the meaning and nerve of its whole."[29]

If Barth's description of the eschatological feels strange, it is because he has moved "doctrines of the end" into the pneumatic moment of revelation. Put plainly, resurrection is revelation, revelation is resurrection.[30] The importance of this move should not be missed. Eschatologizing the religious-existential moment has the effect of breaking up any romantic unity of God with the soul, shattering any identification of the Spirit with world-process. Each instance of divine immanence is a cataclysmic run-in with the totally other God, a fresh apocalypse. Scholars have struggled to categorize Barth's method, calling it a "theology of crisis" or "consistent eschatology."[31] To be sure, it does not much resemble any pre-twentieth-century descriptions of penultimacy, orthodox or heterodox.[32]

Barth's approach makes it exceedingly difficult, indeed, wholly improper, to pursue futurist readings of Scripture. How does Barth (who stands as one the most active expositors of the modern age) interpret texts of foretelling? A couple of examples will suffice. What of Romans 8:11, the promise that the Spirit "will also give life to your mortal body"? Barth says the event is un-narratable: "Therefore the Gospel of the Resurrection of our body ... cannot refer to any past or present or future, but only to the all-embracing *Futurum resurrectionis: He shall quicken*."[33] Concerning the vision in Revelation 12:6 of the woman fleeing to the wilderness for 1,260 days, Barth uses it as

---

29. Barth, *The Resurrection of the Dead*, trans. H.J. Stenning (New York: Fleming H. Revell, 1933).

30. Cf. Hitchcock, *Karl Barth and the Resurrection of the Flesh*, 72–73.

31. By any name, it conveys itself as a severe application of the Reformed *finitum non capax infiniti* within religious epistemology or, perhaps better, an apocalyptic form of the Lutheran *theologia crucis*.

32. It did, however, bear striking resemblance to certain German theologians translating Christianity into existential parlance. For Barth's proximity to Paul Tillich, Friedrich Gogarten, Rudolf Bultmann, and others, see Stephen R. Haynes, "Between the Times: German Theology and the Weimar *Zeitgeist*," *Soundings* 74, no. 1/2 (Spr/Sum 1991): 9–44.

33. Barth, *The Epistle to the Romans*, 289.

a supplemental text regarding the claim that the saints may need to evade persecution for a time but that "the Christian church cannot evade [affliction] by ceasing to be a witness or to be active as such."[34] Both examples highlight the total orientation Barth has to witness (first the Spirit's, then the church's). Witness, not historical prediction, is "the theme and content and also the divinely motivating and impelling power of prophecy, which in the language of Revelation and according to the context means the origin and force of the human witness of the seer and his brethren, Christians."[35]

If one must use the well-worn millennial classification system, Barth is amillennial. But not all amillennialisms are alike, since each system emphasizes different "zones" of fulfillment, earthly (the second temple period, primitive Christianity, the expansion of the Christian mission, etc.) and/or heavenly (the spiritual reign of the church on earth, the spiritual reign of the dead saints with Christ in heaven, etc.). For Barth, the "zone" of fulfillment is simple: Christ and Christ alone.[36] *This* person, *this* God-man, is the only touchpoint. He is the Omega. Formally speaking, He and He alone is eschatology realized.[37] Thus, Barth's eschatological hermeneutic in tandem with his Christology defies the use of predictive instruments.

His resistance to futuristic interpretation should not suggest that Barth is uninterested in penultimacy. On the contrary, Barth's perspective actually intensifies the urgency of the Christian life. Jesus continually exercises his prophetic ministry, making the objective salvation he won through his completed life manifest itself in human lives. By the Spirit, the Christ impels others to live by faith. In faith, believers are "constantly chasing" the

---

34. *CD* IV/3, 626.

35. *CD* IV/3, 614.

36. Space does not permit me to rehearse Barth's turn to a thoroughgoing Christocentric theology in the 1930s. For that, see especially Bruce L. McCormack, *Karl Barth's Critically Realistic Dialectical Theology: Its Genesis and Development 1909-1936*, (Oxford: Clarendon, 1995) 451–63; in Barth's own words, Barth, "The Humanity of God," in *The Humanity of God* (Louisville: Westminster John Knox, 1960), 37–65.

37. "[O]ne could say that it is only Christ who participates in eschatological fullness." John C. McDowell, *Hope in Barth's Eschatology* (Farnham, Surrey, UK: Ashgate, 2000), 169. Bolstering the finality of Christ, Barth closes the work of reconciliation between the conception and cross of Jesus. The resurrection, in which Jesus crosses over to reach us after His saving death, does not add anything to Jesus' saving work but is the "noetic" flowing from the divine "ontic." This raises a battery of scriptural and theological problems with which Barth deals at length in *CD* IV. For a summary, see R. Dale Dawson, *The Resurrection in Karl Barth* (Farnham, Surrey, UK: Ashgate, 2007), 6–8, 122–23, 214ff.

perfection presented to them in Christ, waiting and hastening in "one long Advent season."[38] They, whether Israel before Pentecost or the church after Pentecost, participate in the eschaton by serving as witnesses to Jesus Christ's history. In prayer they keep intoning, "Thy kingdom come." In the last days, they repent and forgive, stand against antichrist powers, and extend mercy to the poor. Christians demonstrate a human correspondence to Christ in the Spirit, echoing the grace of God through their feeble but real ministry.[39] Without postulations or predictions, they press into the future, knowing that (to use one of Barth's favorite phrases) "Jesus is Victor."

Barth comes at the end times in a totally different programmatic way than Edwards, then. He maintains that revelation cannot be historicized in any substantial way since the true encounter with the divine future is a pneumatic moment, a "resurrective" event that defies temporalization. Therefore, prophecies in Scripture call out for kerygmatic, not futuristic, interpretation. Barth's Christology underwrites the pneumatic dialectic. Revelation comes to us as apocalypse and crisis because the true Future has been actualized singly and wholly in the person of Jesus Christ. He alone is (to use Edwards's nomenclature) "a body of divinity thrown into history." Even so, Christians are called to embrace an Advent ethos in which the future, which is already in Christ, breaks into their lives, anticipating the great Day.

EDWARDS'S AND BARTH'S ULTIMATE

For all their differences with penultimacy, Edwards and Barth hold similar understandings of the final state. They offer sibling descriptions of the true end. In a word, each one teaches that the final state involves *a translation into the eternal habitation in which a person has full perception of God's glory*. In their own creative ways, Edwards and Barth reproduce an Augustinian doctrine of glorification informed by robust participatory soteriology.

A first shared teaching on ultimacy concerns *translation into the eternal habitation*. Both theologians contend that the final state means a collection of the saints (and with them, all redeemed creation), communicated into a heavenly

---

38. *CD* IV/4, 40.

39. That is, Christians are determined as free beings in action, given the telic direction of "participating in, witnessing to, and glorifying the divine work." Paul T. Nimmo, *Being in Action: The Theological Shape of Barth's Ethical Vision* (London, T&T Clark, 2007), 185).

abode suited for them. That which is holy on earth will be transported into an eternal home (Edwards) or eternalized in God's simultaneity (Barth).

Edwards understands heaven as the destination for Christian pilgrims on earth. God's home becomes the saints' home. Whether by death or resurrection, individually or corporately, the saints are moved from earth to the heavenly house.[40] Edwards conceives of heaven in dimensional terms. The heavenly abode is, to use a favored expression, a "glorious *place*." To be clear, Edwards permits no confusion between earth and heaven. He teaches that life in heaven means leaving the earth permanently: the saints will fly heavenward and "never shall set foot on [earth] again."[41] Their home in the heavens will be what the Bible calls the new earth, albeit new "materially as well as in form," situated at "some glorious place in the universe prepared for this end by God, removed at an immense distance from the solar system."[42] Indeed, in a cynical moment, he opines that the present earth will, at the fiery conflagration, be designated the new hell.[43]

His disdain for the physical notwithstanding, Edwards teaches that there is a certain collection of earthly things in the eternal habitation. The saints are extracted, of course, and with them the fellowship of the church. Relationships, even specific friendships, are preserved and perfected in the reconstitution of a godly society.[44] Bodies too are raised, changed to be "uncapable of ... all that deformity that their bodies had before," and unified with their respective souls.[45] Continuity of the earthly body obviously perturbed Edwards, who early in his career echoed the medieval scholastics' explanation of the resurrection of the dead as the soul's "inclination" to the body, the celestial soul completing its happiness by uniting the body to itself.[46] Over

---

40. For Edwards's account of heaven, see, e.g., "True Saints, When Absent from the Body, Are Present with the Lord," *WJE* 25:236; *WJE* 20:151; *WJE* 20:471.

41. *WJE* 9:498; see also *WJE* 18:503.

42. *WJE* 5:141. In one instance, Edwards leverages the implications of Copernican cosmology to explain biblical language about the saints' terrestrial future: being on "earth" is perspectival. *WJE* 13:294. On the last day, a new home is required for glorified humanity, for "the very material frame of the old heavens and old earth are destroyed." *WJE* 9:509.

43. *WJE* 13:376.

44. See, for example, the sermons in *WJEO* 50.

45. *WJE* 9:497-98.

46. Likewise, with the scholastics, Edwards refuses to admit that the soul is incomplete without the body, for the "hope" of the restoration of that to which the soul is inclined "completely satisfies this inclination during the separation." *WJE* 13:178-79.

the years Edwards seems to have entertained the possibility of physical components in heaven, if only to have beautiful objects to augment the beatific
vision.[47] Thus, the eternal home of the saints will have a material component
among its celestial, otherworldly contours.

If Edwards operates within a dialectic of spatiality, Barth describes the
eschatological gathering through a dialectic of temporality. Heaven is the
eternalization of humans' delimited earthly histories. The concept requires
a little unpacking.[48] What Barth means is that each person has a history: an
existence in time that is the totality of themselves, a brief, creaturely period
in which they enact everything. It is a timeframe marked off by conception
on one side and death on the other. There is no natural immortality, then,
but God is able to offer to human lives a "Beyond." The entirety of a person's
history can and may and will be summed up and translated into the divine
mode. By participation in Christ, humans are resurrected, receiving "the
'eternalizing' [die «Verewigung»] of this ending life."[49] Since God exceeds all
time, risen humans can escape their finitude and enjoy his pure duration.
They can rise above the vicissitudes of earthly time and dwell within the
divine omnitemporality. Accordingly, at this day of days, "all the dead will
live through [God] as that which they have been through Him and in relation to Him in their time."[50]

Despite the full transposition of the person's life-act into eternity, Barth
does not admit any surrender of earthly predicates. God's eternity *embraces*
time.[51] By extension, participation in the divine simultaneity means the

---

47. In heaven there will be "external beauties and harmonies"—except they will be "altogether of another kind" and "will appear chiefly on the bodies of the man Jesus Christ and the
saints." *WJE* 13:328. Michael J. McClymond and Gerald R. McDermott interpret Edwards's connections between the revived earthly churches and the eschaton as a softening disdain for the
material. *The Theology of Jonathan Edwards* (New York: Oxford University Press, 2012), 300ff. Such
a generous reading is not necessarily warranted, though one may detect in Edwards a persistent
concern for the revival of the body (politic) congruent with the revival of souls: the embodiment
of saints "is so obvious within Edwards' interpretation of reality, that he hardly notes the matter,"
so long as one understands the future embodiment of the saints to be "exactly coordinate to
the transformation of their souls." Robert W. Jenson, *America's Theologian: A Recommendation
of Jonathan Edwards* (New York: Oxford University Press, 1988), 181.

48. For the following, see Hitchcock, *The Resurrection of the Flesh in Karl Barth*, 74ff.

49. *CD* III/2, 624 = *KD* III/2, 760.

50. *CD* II/2, 283.

51. Barth plays with articulations of God's pantemporality. See his discussion of "contingent contemporaneity" in *CD* I/1, 145–49, 205ff., later expressed via the Augustinian-Boethian
tradition of simultaneity in *CD* II/1, 608ff.

full preservation of one's corporeal, historical existence. Everything (at least everything worth keeping) will be recapitulated into the heavenly mode. The body, the selfsame body, is gathered, for redemption involves the totality of what a human was. In this roundabout way, Barth dares to affirm the resurrection of the flesh.[52]

Controlling for the factor of spatiality/temporality, Edwards and Barth are saying the same thing about the eschaton. In the end, humans live in God's domain, the eternal habitation that is capable of containing earthly-historical components. Edwards and Barth also ground their concept in an actualized Christology. Edwards insists on the sufficiency of Christ's life and death, a purchase of redemption completed at the cross that has no further work from Jesus.[53] The resurrection period, facilitated by the application of redemption by the Holy Spirit, moves from the finished work of the Son of God in humiliation. Barth says the same thing even more adamantly (and ontologically), seeing Jesus' resurrection as adding nothing to his conception-to-cross existence. Rather than a new narrative, the risen life of Jesus is the revealing of His delimited history. He is the historical Jesus expressed "in the mode of God," unveiling "the perfection of this limited temporally restricted life."[54] In this way, Easter is the pattern for the general resurrection.

Even more prominent in Edwards's and Barth's eschatologies is *the full perception of God's glory*. Each theologian hopes for the vision of God. The saints will see God with a clear eye, enjoying him as the source of all. They will also see all things in the divine radiance, able to contemplate the fullness of God's works.

Beginning with Edwards, he describes heaven in rich noetic terms. The destination of the saints is the place where God's presence is manifested, a place purposed for "the beholding of God's own excellency."[55] On earth, the saints see only glimmers and refractions of God's glory, but in the life to come, the full revelation of God is before them. In heaven, a place with immediacy to the divine, "all the faculties of the soul shall be completely satisfied."[56] Knowledge of God is key. The saints will perform actions of service

---

52. E.g., *CD* IV/1, 653.

53. *WJE* 9:295; though see his hedging of the concept in *WJE* 9:117.

54. *CD* III/2, 448, 571.

55. *WJE* 14:147.

56. *WJE* 10:324.

and worship to God in heaven,[57] but heaven will be blissful chiefly on account of the psychic, meditative activities. That is precisely why Edwards devoted much of his career to purifying the affections of his listeners, preparing them to enjoy the deity. The earthly sojourn is a long practice in enjoyment of God, just as "the happiness of heaven consists in the enjoyment of God's love."[58]

As an important adjunct to the beatific vision, the saints will perceive God's glory in his redemptive work in the earth. At the great judgment, "things shall be turned upside do[w]n in a very visible & publick & every way a more Remarkable manner."[59] Edwards believes that heaven, at least after the parousia, will disclose the secret workings of providence. Only at the end of the age will the whole of redemptive history be unveiled, offering itself up for contemplation. At that time, the happiness of the saints will be made complete insofar as "the happiness of the saints in heaven consists much in beholding the displays of God's mercy toward his church on earth."[60]

Barth's approach is very much alike. At the last day, humanity will see God manifested. Upon death or at the parousia, humans will face their Beyond. Jesus Christ will no longer be concealed but revealed. What has been accomplished by God in Christ will become evident:

> The *visio Dei, visio immediata, intuitiva, facialis, visio essentiae divinae,* the unbroken awareness of God in the totality of His personality and aseity. That's the thing which even now the angels do not see, and what the prophets have not yet seen. But the redeemed, enlightened by the *lumen gloriae*, shall see and comprehend it.[61]

The saints will obtain a final, direct, universal, and undialectical awareness of Christ. The divine proximity inaugurated at Easter is carried on through the season of Pentecost and consummated at the end of human life.[62] In all three ways, "resurrection" is the manifestation of God in Christ. Yet only at the end of time may an individual behold the fullness of the divine glory.

---

57. *WJE* 25:242.

58. *WJE* 10:475.

59. Edwards, Sermon 966, *WJEO* 68.

60. *WJE* 20:395; see also *WJE* 18:427–34 and *WJE* 20:515.

61. Barth, *Unterricht in der christlichen Religion* III, in *Gesamtausgabe* II (Zürich: Theologischer Verlag Zürich, 1971-), 485–86. See also *CD* II/1, 630.

62. For Barth's fully developed concept of the three-fold parousia, see *CD* IV/3, 292–96.

For Barth there is a final eschatological correspondence: the manifesta-tion of God is the manifestation of the human being. Specifically, the resur-rection is the revelation of *human* lives in the divine life of Jesus Christ. At the end, the truth of redeemed humanity streams forth: "It is this life, but the reverse side which God sees although it is as yet hidden from us—this life in its relation to what He has done for the whole world, and therefore for us too, in Jesus Christ."[63] At Jesus' appearing there is a disclosure of human dignity. Everything that is good and right, everything that is in Christ, is made known. In this way, whether speaking of Jesus Christ or another individual, the res-urrection will be "the declaration and pledge of his total life-exaltation."[64]

What one cannot miss in Edwards's and Barth's understandings of the eschaton is the decidedly Augustinian perspective. The translation of things into a heavenly collection resonates with Augustine's account of the after-life, and the emphasis on the *visio Dei* is the centerpiece of his eschatologi-cal structure. Edwards, of course, has modified the system to accommodate some of the pietistic, ecclesiastical concerns of the Puritans, and Barth has reconfigured Christian doctrine in his signature modern, postliberal fashion. Yet both are Reformed in the end, building from the Augustinian foundation. One should not be surprised by this, given the long-standing Reformed tra-dition. One is a little surprised, however, to detect the deificationist trajec-tory of the eastern church in Edwards and Barth as they link glorification so closely to participation in the divine nature.[65]

Space does not permit an analysis of problems in the eschatologies of these two theological giants. Suffice it to say that serious questions arise with their accounts of body-soul dualism (Edwards especially), the histori-cal return of Christ (Barth especially), an anemic depiction of the new earth (Edwards especially), and a nagging insinuation of universalism (Barth espe-cially). Both writers privilege the noetic at the risk of the ontic while trying

---

63. Letter to Werner Rüegg, 6 July 1961, in Barth, *Letters, 1961–1968*, ed. Jürgen Fangmeier et al., trans. Geoffrey W. Bromiley (Grand Rapids: Eerdmans, 1980), 9.

64. *CD* IV/2, 317.

65. Recent scholarship has veered toward the eastern question for both theologians. For reflections on Edwards, see Jenson, *Jonathan Edwards*, 177ff.; Kyle C. Strobel, *Jonathan Edwards's Theology: A Reinterpretation* (London: Bloomsbury T&T Clark, 2012). For Barth, see Adam Neder, *Participation in Christ: An Entry into Karl Barth's Church Dogmatics* (Louisville: Westminster John Knox, 2009), 86–92; Hitchcock, *Karl Barth and the Resurrection of the Flesh*, 188–90.

to address potential problems by leaning into participationist soteriology—
again a provocative parallel with eastern theology.

IN THE END, COHERENCE

This essay outlined the respective eschatologies of two of the church's great
theologians, showing how they are divergent about the penultimate state.
Edwards teaches a historicized concept of revelation in which the revival of
the elect brings about the millennium on earth, where Barth's neo-Kantian,
Christocentric doctrine of revelation underwrites an eschatological ethic
that defies predictive instruments. Yet each man hangs his eschatological
structure on *revelation*. And it was shown in some detail that their accounts
of the final state are quite comparable. Edwards and Barth make creative
modifications to the Augustinian doctrine of heaven, teaching a translation
of the earthly things into an eternal dwelling in which the saints behold the
glory of God, that is, God's own glory *and* the glory refracted in the redeemed,
gathered creation.

In the final analysis, one may say that the theme of *coherence* figures prominently in these theologians. Each one hopes for the moment in which all
things in heaven and earth are presented as a whole. In the present age, such
coherence is experienced in part, through either the temporarily revived soul
(Edwards) or the dialectical encounter with the word of God (Barth). In the
end, however, they anticipate a display of the unity of all things.

For Edwards, coherence is deeply theocentric. In *The End for Which God
Created the World*, he writes that the divine plan includes both "emanation
and remanation": "The beams of glory come from God, and are something
of God, and are refunded back again to their original. So that the whole is
of God, and *in* God, and *to* God; and God is the beginning, middle and end in
this affair."[66] Therefore, the ultimate knowledge of God far exceeds any bare
ratiocinative knowing: to be perfected is to see the unity, to feel it, to revel
in it. The saints' knowledge is a participative, panoptic vision of the totality
of God's redemptive history. To be with God in the end, to behold all things

---

66. Edwards, *Concerning the End for Which God Created the World*, WJE 8:531. One may detect a
Neoplatonic architectonic here, or it may be better to say more succinctly and simply, "The key
to Edwards' thought is that everything is related because everything is related to God." George
Marsden, *Jonathan Edwards: A Life* (New Haven: Yale University Press, 2003), 460.

made beautiful in his beauty—that is the beatific.[67] Put in the auditory mode, the eschaton is music.[68]

Barth's eschatology is shot through with the same harmonious aesthetic. Everything in heaven and earth will cohere in Christ Jesus, for the final day is the "one indivisible, divine, sovereign act which comprehends at once both the living and the dead."[69] In contrast to the present age of veiledness and contradiction, the age to come will disclose the fullness of God and the *totus Christus*. The eschaton will be beautiful because all things will be properly incorporated into him who was and is and ever will be. In eternity, "we shall then see the final and unequivocal form of [Christ's] own glory which even now shines forth from His resurrection into time and history, all times and all histories."[70]

Earlier, I contended that Edwards and Barth are exceptional among Reformed theologians when it comes to eschatology. Where Calvinistic doctrines of the end time can feel rather bland, these two make rather colorful interpretations of the eschatological content of holy Scripture. I repeat that claim here, except to offer the important caveat that their eschatological aesthetic (if one may call it that) is very much in keeping with the Reformed tradition. They desire to behold the providential order. They ache for the beauty of the whole. They have seen the promised land at a distance and long to be gathered to it.

---

67. Edwards's doctrine of heaven is consistent with his philosophical conception of general beauty: "a general beauty is that by which a thing appears beautiful when viewed most perfectly, comprehensively and universally, with regard to all its tendencies, and its connections with every thing to which it stands related." *WJE* 8:540. Puritans were those looking for "the ultimate signifier in literature, politics, and the psychology of the self." Gribben, *Millennium* (Eugene, OR: Wipf & Stock, 2008), 234.

68. Accordingly, Edwards's sentiment on the importance of singing, which is "[t]he best, most beautiful, and most perfect way that we have of expressing a sweet concord of mind to each other." *WJE* 13:331. See also Jenson, *America's Theologian*, 19–20, 182.

69. Barth, *Epistle to the Philippians*, trans. James W. Leitch (Richmond: John Knox, 1962), 117.

70. *CD* IV/3, 103.

CITATIONS
—

Works of Jonathan Edwards

Jonathan Edwards, *Freedom of the Will,* ed. Paul Ramsey The Works of Jonathan
    Edwards vol. 1 (New Haven: Yale University Press, 1957).
Jonathan Edwards, *Religious Affections,* ed. John E. Smith The Works of Jonathan
    Edwards vol. 2 (New Haven: Yale University Press, 1959).
Jonathan Edwards, *Original Sin,* ed. Clyde A. Holbrook The Works of Jonathan
    Edwards vol. 3 (New Haven, Yale University Press, 1970).
Jonathan Edwards, *The Great Awakening,* ed. C. C. Goen The Works of Jonathan
    Edwards vol. 4 (New Haven: Yale University Press, 1972).
Jonathan Edwards, *Apocalyptic Writings,* ed. Stephen J. Stein The Works of Jonathan
    Edwards vol. 5 (New Haven: 1977).
Jonathan Edwards, *Scientific and Philosophical Writings,* ed. Wallace E. Anderson
    The Works of Jonathan Edwards, vol. 6 (New Haven: Yale University Press,
    1980).
Jonathan Edwards, *The Life of David Brainerd,* ed. Norman Pettit The Works of
    Jonathan Edwards, vol. 7 (New Haven: Yale University Press, 1984).
Jonathan Edwards, *Ethical Writings,* ed. Paul Ramsey The Works of Jonathan
    Edwards, vol. 8 (New Haven: Yale University Press, 1989).
Jonathan Edwards, *A History of the Work of Redemption,* ed. John F. Wilson The
    Works of Jonathan Edwards, vol. 9 (New Haven: Yale University Press,
    1989).
Jonathan Edwards, *Sermons and Discourses, 1720-1723,* ed. Wilson H. Kimnach The
    Works of Jonathan Edwards, vol. 10 (New Haven: Yale University Press,
    1992).
Jonathan Edwards, *Typological Writings,* ed. Wallace E. Anderson and David Watters
    The Works of Jonathan Edwards, vol. 11 (New Haven: 1993).
Jonathan Edwards, *Ecclesiastical Writings,* ed. David D. Hall The Works of Jonathan
    Edwards, vol. 12 (New Haven: Yale University Press, 1994).
Jonathan Edwards, The "Miscellanies": A-500, ed. Thomas A. Schafer The Works of
    Jonathan Edwards, vol. 13 (New Haven: Yale University Press, 1994).
Jonathan Edwards, *Sermons and Discourses, 1723-1729,* ed. Kenneth P. Minkema The
    Works of Jonathan Edwards vol. 14 (New Haven: Yale University Press,
    1997).
Jonathan Edwards, *Notes on Scripture,* ed. Stephen J. Stein The Works of Jonathan
    Edwards, vol. 15 (New Haven: Yale University Press, 1998).

Jonathan Edwards, *Letters and Personal Writings,* ed. George S. Claghorn The Works of Jonathan Edwards vol. 16 (New Haven: Yale University Press, 1998).

Jonathan Edwards, *Sermons and Discourses, 1730-1733,* ed. Mark Valeri The Works of Jonathan Edwards vol. 17 (New Haven: Yale University Press, 1999).

Jonathan Edwards, *The "Miscellanies": Entry Nos. 501-832,* ed. Ava Chamberlain The Works of Jonathan Edwards, vol. 18 (New Haven: Yale University Press, 2000).

Jonathan Edwards, *Sermons and Discourses, 1734-1738,* ed. M. X. Lesser The Works of Jonathan Edwards, vol. 19 (New Haven: Yale University Press, 2001).

Jonathan Edwards, *"The "Miscellanies": Entry Nos. 833-1152,* ed. Amy Plantinga Pauw The Works of Jonathan Edwards, vol. 20 (New Haven, Yale University Press, 2002).

Jonathan Edwards, *Writings on the Trinity, Grace, and Faith,* ed. Sang Hyun Lee The Works of Jonathan Edwards, vol. 21 (New Haven: Yale University Press, 2003).

Jonathan Edwards, *Sermons and Discourses, 1739-1742,* eds. Harry Stout and Nathan Hatch The Works of Jonathan Edwards, vol. 22 (New Haven: Yale University Press, 2003).

Jonathan Edwards, *The "Miscellenies": Entry Nos. 1153-1360,* ed. Douglas A. Sweeney The Works of Jonathan Edwards, vol. 23 (New Haven: Yale University Press, 2004).

Jonathan Edwards, *The Blank Bible,* ed. Stephen Stein The Works of Jonathan Edwards, vol. 24 (New Haven: Yale University Press, 2006).

Jonathan Edwards, *Sermons and Discourses, 1743-1758,* ed. Wilson H. Kimnach The Works of Jonathan Edwards, vol. 25 (New Haven: Yale University Press, 2006).

Jonathan Edwards, *Catalogues of Books,* ed. Peter J. Thuesen The Works of Jonathan Edwards, vol. 26 (New Haven: Yale University Press, 2008).

SUBJECT INDEX

—

A

Adam
  and humanity, 183-85, 183n9, 183n10
      190-1, 199-200
  and sin, 81, 202, 204-9, 212-17, 240, 278
Aesthetic(s)
  and Calvin, 142-3
  of Christ, 150-51, 157-58
  and creation, 146-50
  danger's of, 151-53
  of God, 143-46, 154-55
  of hierarchy, 147-50
  and redemption, 153
  and the Trinity, 144-46
  See also beauty
angel(s)
  and Christ, 123, 224, 228
  and man, 146, 299, 72-73
antichrist, 162, 210, 287, 295
apostasy, 274, 287
apostle(s), 41, 44, 265, 275, 293
Apostles' Creed, 267n51
Arminian(ism) 48, 50
aseity, 22, 24-25, 299
atonement
  and Anselm, 220-23
  and God, 226-36
  and satisfaction 223-34
attributes of God
beauty, 144, 152-54, 158, 166
  and glory, 128, 130-31, 229
  and God's self-revelation, 17-22, 119
  honor, 222n10
  justice, 222
  righteousness, 222, 228

simplicity, 92-93, 98
wisdom, 229

B

baptism
  and the Holy Spirit, 81, 255
  of Jesus, 190, 200
  as sacrament, 242-45, 250-55, 259
beauty. *See* aesthetic(s)
being of God, 11, 14, 19, 55, 97
blessing
  and end times, 287-88
  and election, 47-64
  of Gentiles, 287
  of God himself, 12
  of Scripture, 33
body
  for Christ, 49-50, 134-36, 225, 260-64
      274-75, 283
  as the church, 49-50, 134-36, 225,
      259-64, 272, 274-5, 283, 288
  human, 75, 78n9, 110n125, 194, 293, 296
      297n47, 298-300

C

Calvinism, 85, 134, 145, 240, 302. *See also*
      election
Catholicism, 143, 152, 210n24, 263, 287
Christ
  beauty of, 151-53, 157-58
  body of, 49, 135, 259-62, 272-74, 259-63.
      See also church
  and the church, 49, 135, 259-62, 272-74,
      133-36, 258-83

NAME INDEX

—

A

Ables, Travis E., 90
Anatolios, Khaled, 114n152
Anselm of Canterbury, 105n100, 150n44, 154, 220-28, 235-36
Aquinas, Thomas, 57n29, 92n17, 93, 101n72, 113, 209n19, 291n24
Augustine, 18n49, 89-97, 92n17, 93-96, 97, 105, 107-8, 111n132, 113-14, 141, 163, 198, 215, 290, 295, 297n51, 300-301

B

Balthasar, Hans Urs von, 156, 269n59
Bartlet, Phebe, 239
Bavinck, Herman, 93n26, 201
Bender, Kimlyn, 270n66
Berkeley, George, 163
Bonaventure, 103n88, 281
Bromiley, Geoffrey, 63n48, 153n61, 174n57, 175n62, 176n66, 247n27, 265n35, 267n52, 300n63
Brouwer, H. Reeling, 19n52, 48n2
Brunner, Emil, 83, 175, 180
Buber, Martin, 185n20, 197
Bultmann, Rudolf, 84n61, 175, 180, 245-47, 293n32
Burgess, Andrew, 112n40
Busch, Eberhard, 46n50, 57n29, 175n61, 179n80, 245n22, 247-48, 277n106

C

Caldwell, Robert W., 78n41, 86n67, 95n41, 96n45

Calvin, John, 28-29, 39, 113, 125n34, 133n56, 142-45, 153n64, 198, 210-11, 252, 267n51, 272n78, 273, 281n118, 285
Canlis, Julie, 113n149
Chalamet, Christophe, 84
Clement of Alexandria, 29n4
Cochran, Elizabeth Agnew, 71n11, 170n38, 241n12, 242n13
Congdon, David, 246
Cortez, Marc, 110n125, 201, 213n35
Crisp, Oliver, 14, 62n46, 65n51, 93n24, 103n85, 104n96, 120n9, 164n9, 195n62, 205n10, 205n11, 206n13, 206n14, 219n1, 220, 229n53, 253n44

D

Danaher, William J. Jr, 240n8, 241n12
Daniel, Stephen H., 163n6, 164n9, 206n13
Davidson, Ivor, 65n52, 65n53
Descartes, Rene, 163, 178

E

Edwards, Sarah, 111n133
Emery, Gilles, 93

F

Farley, Edward, 141, 146
Fichte, Johann Gottlieb, 99n60, 178
Fiering, Norman, 163n6, 172-73
Finkbeiner, Gary, 138n75
Forsyth, P. T., 158

SCRIPTURE INDEX

—

Old Testament

New Testament

LEXHAM PRESS

STUDIES IN HISTORICAL & SYSTEMATIC THEOLOGY

Studies in Historical and Systematic Theology is a peer-reviewed series of contemporary monographs exploring key figures, themes, and issues in historical and systematic theology from an evangelical perspective.

———

Learn more at LexhamPress.com/SHST

Printed in the United States
by Baker & Taylor Publisher Services